History of Economic Management in North Korea

This book seeks to understand how the economic construction of the Democratic People's Republic of Korea (DPRK) evolved, shaped by the formulation and execution of various economic management systems spanning the years 1949 to 2023, in response to numerous challenges faced by the country.

Split into four chapters, Park charts the developmental phases of the DPRK economy under Kim Il Sung, Kim Jong Il, and current leader Kim Jung Un. He carefully cross-examines sources from within the DPRK, including the *Complete Works of Kim Il Sung, Selected Works of Kim Jong Il*, the *Rodong Shinmun*, and the *Chosun Central Yearbook*. Where related literature relies on testimonies and interviews of defectors, this book offers a novel and comprehensive analysis of sources taken from North Korea, furnishing readers with new insights into the DPRK's economic management and construction policies.

With its novel approach, this book will be of interest to researchers and advanced undergraduates of Korean history, Korean studies, and economic history.

Phillip H. Park is a professor of Political Science and Diplomacy at Kyungnam University in the Republic of Korea. He is the author of four books written in Korean and four in English. Seven of his works delve into the intricacies of the DPRK, while one offers a profound analysis of the history of neutral states and its relevance to the Republic of Korea. Phillip has also written numerous articles on Northeast Asia and the DPRK, in both Korean and English.

Perspectives in Economic and Social History

Series Editors: Andrew August and Jari Eloranta

For more information about this series, please visit: www.routledge.com/Perspectives-in-Economic-and-Social-History/book-series/PESH

History of Economic Management in North Korea

From Planned Economy to Socialist Enterprise System

Phillip H. Park

LONDON AND NEW YORK

First published 2025
by Routledge
4 Park Square, Milton Park, Abingdon, Oxon OX14 4RN

and by Routledge
605 Third Avenue, New York, NY 10158

Routledge is an imprint of the Taylor & Francis Group, an informa business

British Library Cataloguing-in-Publication Data
A catalogue record for this book is available from the British Library

ISBN: 978-1-032-77056-7 (hbk)
ISBN: 978-1-032-77193-9 (pbk)
ISBN: 978-1-003-48173-7 (ebk)

DOI: 10.4324/9781003481737

Typeset in Galliard
by SPi Technologies India Pvt Ltd (Straive)

Contents

Tables

Acknowledgments

Writing, whether original or through translation, is fundamentally a creative act. During the translation of my own book, I came to internalize this truth. Initially, my approach was mechanical–word-for-word substitution. Yet the essence of translation lies not in replication, but in reimagining the work anew. True translation demands the spirit of authorship.

Though the original manuscript of this book took two years to compose, this translated version spanned over two and half. This was not due to error correction, but rather due to the conscious decision to craft a new experience based on the original foundation. While the phenomenon of "lost in translation" is an inevitability born from the inherent differences between languages, I am confident this work transcends the limitations of mere translation. It is fundamentally a re-creation, informed by my own perspective and insights. Thus, I might even argue that it surpasses its Korean counterpart in refinement and depth.

The genesis of this book was a decade in the making, meticulously analyzing a century's worth of embellished, even deified accounts chronicling the DPRK's supreme leaders. Indeed, the Korean edition would not have been possible without Dr. Jae-Kyu Park, president of Kyungnam University. His unwavering support and the exceptional research environment he fostered were instrumental to my exploration of DPRK studies.

With this project's completion, I wish to express my deepest gratitude for my parents, Heung Jong and Hwa Sung. From my father, I inherited the gift of unwavering consistency. His decades-long adherence to a precise routine—from his waking hours to his water intake—has been a testament to discipline. My mother, on the other hand, is a relentless seeker of novelty. Her refusal to repeat a single recipe resonates with my own approach to this endeavor. It was through her bold decision that we moved to America, ensuring that my sibling and I would escape the uniformity of Korea's educational system. The uniqueness of my research on DPRK economic development—drawing solely from the country's internal materials—likely stems from her influence.

Finally, my heartfelt appreciation goes to my wife, Ji Hye. Acts of creation bring inherent challenges, amplified by the sheer volume and enigmatic nature of the DPRK source material. It was her presence that made the pain bearable.

An interior designer by trade, she transformed my workspace into a haven of inspiration. More importantly, she listened with genuine interest to my research findings, her unwavering smile offering the silent reassurance that my pursuit held value. This support fueled my relentless exploration. While this book bears my name alone, Ji Hye's steadfast companionship throughout makes her its unspoken co-author.

Note on Transliteration

Except for the commonly accepted usage in English of Korean names such as Kim Il Sung, Kim Jong Il, and Kim Jong Un, the McCune-Reischauer transliteration is used for Korean.

Prologue

The Democratic People's Republic of Korea (DPRK) stands as a unique testament in the world, operating under a socialist system meticulously guided and controlled by the State, devoid of any semblance of private ownership of production materials or land.[1] Regrettably, for many, the DPRK's economy has become a subject of ridicule, stretching the bounds of common sense. They cynically question its existence, pondering the dire conditions endured by those trapped within such an absurd economic framework. Even scholars who dedicate themselves to studying the intricacies of the DPRK's economy often regard it as a "bastard child," an ill-conceived creation born in the wrong hands. They perceive it as an inherently flawed system, doomed to descend into an irreversible decline.

This prevailing perception of the DPRK's economy gained traction following the fall of the Berlin Wall and the subsequent collapse of the socialist economic bloc in Eastern Europe. Among experts of North Korea studies, it is taken for granted that the DPRK, much like the former socialist countries of the Soviet Union and Eastern Europe, is destined to crumble, and many anticipate its imminent demise.

Even U.S. intelligence agencies, entrusted with monitoring the trends within the DPRK, predicted its internal collapse within a few years, drawing parallels to the fate of Romania. Based on this understanding, the United States approached its commitments under the 1994 Geneva Agreement with caution. Essentially, the belief that the DPRK's eventual collapse was inevitable led the United States to postpone promises such as normalizing diplomatic relations and transforming the armistice agreement into a lasting peace accord. In return for these concessions, the United States sought to freeze the DPRK's graphite-moderated nuclear reactors and associated facilities capable of producing plutonium.[2]

Even within the Republic of Korea, theories surrounding the imminent collapse of the DPRK have intermittently surfaced since the passing of Kim Il Sung in 1994, becoming an integral aspect of DPRK studies. Undoubtedly, the economy stands out as the foremost factor contributing to the inevitable decline of the DPRK. According to a leaked confidential report from a U.S.

DOI: 10.4324/9781003481737-1

intelligence agency via WikiLeaks, Yŏngu Ch'ŏn, then-Vice Minister of Foreign Affairs, purportedly revealed in a February 2010 meeting with then-U.S. Ambassador Catherine Stevens that the DPRK had already witnessed an economic collapse. Ch'ŏn further asserted that the nation was poised for a political collapse within two to three years following the passing of Kim Jong Il.[3]

The prevailing sentiment suggests a bleak future for the DPRK's economy, and such projections have been deeply ingrained in the collective consciousness. Nevertheless, it is incumbent upon us to approach this subject with measured discernment, remaining open to the possibility of unforeseen outcomes. Only through comprehensive understanding and rigorous analysis can we hope to unravel the enigma that is the DPRK's economy and chart a more nuanced path toward its future.

In the year 2023, over a decade has elapsed since the passing of Kim Jong Il, and intriguingly, the DPRK not only evaded collapse but has demonstrated resilience by augmenting its nuclear and long-range missile capabilities. This defiance not only challenges anticipated projections of decline but also positions the DPRK in a stance of assertiveness against the global hegemonic power, the United States, both militarily and economically.

On one front, the DPRK stands firm against U.S. military pressures, while on the economic front, it withstands the relentless economic sanctions imposed since 2016. These sanctions, implemented with unprecedented severity, make them arguably the most stringent ever imposed on any country in history.[4] Despite such challenges, the DPRK persists, presenting a complex and resilient narrative that defies conventional expectations.

Let us delve into the impact of key sanction measures, particularly U.S. Executive Order 13810 (EO 13810) and U.N. Security Council Sanctions 2397 (SCS 2397), to grasp the severity of their implications on the country. Following the DPRK's sixth nuclear test on September 3, 2017, the United States promptly issued EO 13810. This executive order not only prohibits the DPRK from engaging in financial transactions with U.S. financial institutions but also freezes the assets in the United States for all individuals and companies involved in business dealings with the DPRK. Uniquely designed as a Secondary Boycott, it aims to obstruct China from conducting business with the DPRK.[5]

On September 11, 2017, the U.N. Security Council unanimously adopted its strongest sanctions yet against the DPRK. Resolution 2397, spearheaded by U.S. Ambassador Nikki Haley, aimed for a two-pronged attack: crippling the DPRK's nuclear program and inflicting significant economic damage.[6] While presented as a measure to curb the DPRK's nuclear ambitions, Resolution 2397 went far beyond. It included a series of crippling economic sanctions designed to strangle the DPRK's ability to fund its nuclear program.

These measures included slashing DPRK exports by over 90% compared to pre-sanction levels, severely restricting essential supplies like machinery, transport equipment, and metals crucial for the DPRK's industrial development. The resolution further limited oil imports by capping refined oil exports to the

DPRK at a meager 500,000 barrels per year. To further choke off trade, additional bans were imposed on DPRK imports, encompassing everything from food and agricultural products to machinery, electronics, and other essential goods. Finally, the resolution mandated the repatriation of overseas DPRK workers within 24 months, further squeezing the regime's access to hard currency. These measures collectively underscore the comprehensive and far-reaching nature of the sanctions, aiming not only to curtail the DPRK's nuclear pursuits but also to significantly impact its economic landscape.[7]

As acknowledged by the editors of the Washington-based think tank, the Council on Foreign Relations, the U.S.-led sanctions imposed to penalize the DPRK have, to date, proven ineffective in compelling Pyongyang to pursue denuclearization.[8] This suggests that the intended objective of these sanctions, primarily designed to undermine the DPRK's economy, has not been realized. In essence, the DPRK's economic status remains robust despite the comprehensive sanctions, including the implementation of "secondary boycotts" specifically directed at China.

Many scholars specializing in North Korea studies point to China as the "lifeline" supporting the DPRK.[9] However, even China, fearful of secondary boycotts, has complied with stringent U.S. sanctions imposed in 2017.[10] Moreover, since the outset of 2020, the DPRK has sealed its borders entirely to prevent the spread of COVID-19.[11] These circumstances suggest that the DPRK's economy may possess a resilience and self-reliance that challenges prevailing conventional and mainstream views.

The subsequent analysis scrutinizes the incongruity between the conventional and the mainstream perspectives and common sense. According to the Korea Institute for Defense Analysis (KIDA), the DPRK launched 71 missiles in 2022, with the collective cost of all ballistic missiles reaching US$530 million (68.9 billion wŏn). KIDA estimates that this sum surpasses the US$417 million required annually to feed the DPRK's population.

In the September 2022 International Food Security Assessment, the United States Department of Agriculture (USDA) disclosed that 68.6% of the DPRK's population, equivalent to 17.8 million people, faced food insecurity. Put differently, according to the USDA, the country grappled with a severe food shortfall of 1.21 million metric tons of staple grains. If the DPRK were to procure this volume of rice and corn at a 50:50 ratio, based on crop futures prices at the Chicago Board of Trade on December 2, 2022, the cost would amount to US$417 million—a sum over US$100 million less than the expenditure on missiles in the same year.[12]

Nevertheless, examining the extensive construction projects in the DPRK initiated since 2010, especially accelerating after 2020 amid border closures, challenges the prevalent view that the country prioritizes weapon development over the welfare of its citizens. Many of these projects involve creating new towns for scientists, engineers, and flood victims, as well as constructing recreation facilities and hospitals. To grasp the magnitude of these endeavors, let's explore the Songshin, Songhwa, and Hwasŏng districts in P'yŏngyang.

At its Eighth Congress in January 2021, the Workers' Party of Korea (WPK) announced a plan to construct 10,000 homes annually in P'yŏngyang through 2025, totaling 50,000. By April 2022, a housing project yielding 10,000 flats in the Songsin and Songhwa Districts was completed within a year. Encompassing over 160 blocks of skyscrapers, high-rise apartments, public buildings, and service amenities, this project spans more than 1 million square meters in an area of 56 hectares.[13] The latest Hwasŏng housing district, also finished in just one year in April 2023, accommodates 10,000 flats and spans more than 150 hectares of service areas.[14] Completed amid border closures, these projects strongly imply that the DPRK financed them entirely from its internal resources.[15]

Regardless of their location, individuals universally prioritize addressing sustenance before housing concerns—a principle rooted in common sense. In the inhabited DPRK, the significant construction and renovation of new housing serve as a positive indication that the food problem has been addressed to some extent. Regrettably, conventional and mainstream views often overlook this common sense, fixating solely on the DPRK's military buildup program. These perspectives are often based on outdated information from the DPRK's Arduous March era and the assumption that the nation's socialist economy is bound to fail and can never recover from the mid-1990s crisis.

This skewed focus leads to conclusions that are detached from the reality of the DPRK economy. Consequently, it is crucial to consider the 2022 missile development program, estimated to be worth over US$500 million, not as the DPRK solely concentrating on military capabilities at the expense of civilian needs. Rather, it should be seen as a demonstration of the DPRK's economic capacity to fulfill both civilian and military requirements.

The DPRK's economy stands as a curious anomaly, a socialist system enduring in a world dominated by market forces. This tenacious survival sparks an urgent question: how has it managed to weather the storms of the past 70 years? To unravel this mystery, we must delve into the very essence of the DPRK's economic system, its goals, historical roots, and remarkable adaptability.

Over the past seven decades, the DPRK has navigated a turbulent sea of environmental and political challenges. Yet, its socialist economic system has not only persevered but also evolved, constantly adjusting to survive while staying true to its core principles. This raises a critical question: how has the DPRK's socialist economic management system managed to evolve, not just endure?

The primary aim of this book is to offer answers to the aforementioned questions. We'll dissect the system's foundational elements, its historical trajectory, and its ongoing transformations. Through meticulous analysis, we'll explore how the DPRK has navigated economic storms, implemented reforms, and maintained its unique socialist identity.

Numerous endeavors have been undertaken to tackle these inquiries, often relying on information acquired from defectors from the DPRK through testimonies and interviews.[16] However, such sources present several challenges.

Foremost among these challenges is the potential outdated nature of defectors' accounts. As the DPRK rapidly evolves, experiences recounted by defectors from years past may no longer provide an accurate reflection of the present reality. Additionally, defectors might have a vested interest in amplifying the negative aspects of the DPRK, seeking sympathy or support from their new environments.

Another limitation lies in the reliance on personal experiences within defectors' accounts, which may not represent the broader population. Defectors often hail from specific regions, such as those distant from major cities or sharing borders with China. Consequently, their experiences may not be representative of the lives led by ordinary individuals in the DPRK.

Lastly, defectors' accounts are susceptible to distortion when filtered through the lens of the media. Media outlets have a penchant for sensationalizing or even fabricating stories shared by defectors, embellishing them to captivate their audiences.[17]

In this scholarly inquiry, we aim to illuminate the evolution of economic construction and the management system by drawing upon materials sourced from the DPRK. There are compelling grounds for favoring the use of DPRK materials over testimonies and interviews with defectors. Notably, materials from the DPRK possess a higher likelihood of accuracy. As we elucidated earlier, defectors may harbor biases or possess incomplete and unreliable information regarding their homeland. In contrast, the comprehensive nature of DPRK materials, when scrutinized diligently and impartially, allows for the extraction of data that genuinely mirrors the realities of the DPRK. Consequently, these materials are less prone to bias and more attuned to current circumstances.

Furthermore, a chronological examination of these materials can yield insights into the country's economic system that are not readily attainable from defectors alone. Defectors may solely provide information grounded in their own personal experiences, often lacking a comprehensive view of the country's economic landscape. However, albeit with going the extra mile than usual research,[18] as the nation maintains a socialist planned economy, holds the potential to furnish insights into the country's economic system that elude defectors' accounts.

Through a diligent and scholarly approach, our pursuit is to illuminate the intricate dynamics of economic management and construction within the DPRK. Under the unique political system known as the "Yuilchidoch'eje (Monolithic Guidance Regime)," all crucial information pertaining to the DPRK is gathered and relayed to the supreme leader through the Party organization. It is through the meticulous management and analysis of this information that a supreme leader prioritizes State affairs. In our quest for answers to the aforementioned questions, we turn to the actions, words, and writings of former supreme leaders Kim Il Sung and Kim Jong Il, and the current supreme leader Kim Jong Un. In particular, we will delve into the profound impact of the supreme leaders' field guidance, significant discourses, and speeches, subjecting them to thorough analysis.

To delve into the words and actions of the late leaders of the DPRK, Kim Il Sung and Kim Jong Il, we refer to the *Kimilsŏngjŏnjip* (*Complete Works of Kim Il Sung* (*CWK*)) and the *Kimjŏngilsŏnjip* (*Selected Works of Kim Jong Il* (*SWK*)). The *CWK*, encompassing volumes 1 through 100, provides comprehensive coverage of his expressions and actions from October 1926 to his passing in July 1994. Meanwhile, the Enlarged Edition of the *SWK*, comprising volumes 1 through 25, presents a curated collection of discourses, speeches, and conclusions delivered by Kim Jong Il from 1952 until his passing in December 2011. Furthermore, the *Kimjŏngiljŏnjip* (*Complete Works of Kim Jong Il*), which consolidates all of Kim Jong Il's discourses, speeches, and conclusions chronologically, has been published across volumes 1 through 54; however, it is essential to note that these complete works span only the period from July 1952 to March 1999. Consequently, for the purposes of this study, the *CWK* and *SWK* will be employed as primary sources.

It is worth noting, however, that the term *Works* (*CWK* and *SWK*) may be misleading, as neither Kim Il Sung nor Kim Jong Il authored any written works. These *Works* can be likened to the *Chosŏnshillok* (The Annals of the Chosun Dynasty). However, one crucial distinction exists. The historiographers of the *Chosŏnshillok* faithfully recorded every utterance and act of the Kings of Chosun with impartiality; they even included their criticisms.

In contrast, the recorders of the *Works* imbued them with a divine undertone, presenting them in a beautified manner resembling religious texts. As such, most students of North Korea studies cast suspicious eyes on these primary sources from the DPRK. They believe that these sources may have been manipulated or fabricated by the DPRK regime to amplify their efforts and achievements or to portray their actions in a more favorable light. However, it is crucial to recognize that once these primary sources are committed to writing and published, any subsequent editing or fabrication would be counterproductive, as they are subject to cross-verification by other sources.

In light of this, this study has not solely relied on *Works* as my primary source but have also incorporated materials from the *Chosŏnjungangnyŏn'gam* (*Chosun Central Yearbook* (*CCY*))[19] and *Rodong Sinmun* (the DPRK's official daily newspaper). This choice is substantiated by the fact that the activities of the supreme leaders are initially reported in *Rodong Sinmun*, and the comprehensive annual records of these activities are compiled and published in the following year's edition of *CCY*. Subsequently, the full version of the leader's words and actions is published in the *Works*. Thus, any accounts of the leaders' words and deeds found within the *Works* can be cross-verified by referencing *Rodong Sinmun* and the *CCY*, ensuring their authenticity. As one can discern, the *Works* hold immense value and are indispensable not only for research on

DPRK's economic construction but also for a comprehensive understanding of the nation as a whole.

As a matter of fact, the *Works* extend beyond being mere DPRK propaganda or a documentation of the country's intended actions. They serve as comprehensive compilations, chronicling the supreme leaders' on-the-spot guidance, speeches delivered during plenary sessions of the Party's central committee, and their interactions with economic and administrative officials. Within these *Works*, diligent readers, who thoroughly go through the entire series and cross-reference with other sources like *Rodong Sinmun* and *CCY*, can uncover not only indirect insights but also explicit information that illuminates the reality and challenges faced by the DPRK's economy.

Furthermore, the DPRK's distinctive model of political governance, characterized by the Monolithic Guidance Regime, necessitates the supreme leader's active involvement in policy decision-making, monitoring the implementation of procedures, and addressing existing issues on the ground. In practice, this entails that most of the nation's problems are reported to the leader by Party and State institutions, and the leader offers guidance and solutions, if not resolutions, to these challenges.

Additionally, the Monolithic Guidance Regime mandates direct engagement and communication between the leader and workers and individuals in various fields. The leader's visits to factories and farms, often in remote locations, serve not only as symbolic gestures but also as opportunities to address issues directly with the people. These interactions, along with the leader's assessments of previously issued directives and the suggestion of new solutions, are meticulously documented in the *Works*.

While embracing the concept of the Monolithic Guidance Regime may present challenges for many critics of the DPRK, it's essential to recognize that these accounts stem from the analysis of materials originating within the DPRK itself. Essentially, if the events documented in the *Works* are accurate—verified through cross-referencing with sources like *Rodong Sinmun* and *CCY* to ensure consistency, such as supreme leaders visiting nationally significant factories or remote cooperative farms and engaging with people to address on-the-ground issues—then these actions did indeed occur as part of the leaders' duties within the Monolithic Guidance Regime, a system they established. Therefore, the activities of these supreme leaders, as depicted in the *Works*, cannot be easily dismissed as mere "propaganda" intended to exalt and portray the leaders as great and benevolent figures. Instead, they serve as a portrayal of the leaders fulfilling their mandated roles within the regime they have established.

While perusing the *Works*, one may be initially struck by the hyperbolic and deified descriptions of the leader's guidance in resolving specific factory issues. However, these collections also furnish contextual information concerning the reasons for the leader's visits to particular factories, farms, or locations at specific times. In instances where a factory holds national significance, these accounts provide insights into the state of the national economy during that specific period. A meticulous and diligent chronological analysis of the *Works* facilitates a clearer understanding of the DPRK's economic reality.

For any researcher seeking to unravel the intricacies of the DPRK's economic evolution, primary sources originating within the country itself are not merely valuable; they are absolutely indispensable. The content encapsulated in the *Works* of DPRK leaders, complemented by official publications such as the *CCY*, *Rodong Sinmun*, and *Kŭlloja* (Workers' Party of Korea (WPK) Bulletin),[20] along with two pivotal economic journals,[21] *Kimilsŏngdaehak'akpo: ch'ŏrhak, kyŏngjehak* (*Kim Il Sung University's Academic Bulletin* (*KUAB*)) and *Kyŏngjeyŏn'gu* (*Economic Research* (*ER*)), transcends mere propaganda or government pronouncements. In essence, a thorough exploration of the contents within these journals, bulletins, and yearbooks provides a more nuanced understanding of the economic landscape in the DPRK, unraveling valuable insights that significantly contribute to our comprehensive analysis.

These sources are not simply mouthpieces for State messaging or glossy showcases of aspirations. They are, instead, invaluable repositories of concrete, on-the-ground events that have shaped the DPRK's economic reality. Certainly, if the DPRK had initially chosen to manipulate the words and actions of the supreme leaders for the purpose of glorification, the credibility of everything within the *Works* would understandably be called into question. However, skepticism arises when considering that the most widely read texts in the DPRK are precisely those authored by the supreme leaders. Individuals, especially students and scholars, are mandated to delve into these *Works* and incorporate quotations from them at the outset of their writings published in *Kŭlloja*, *KUAB*, and *ER*.

In the hypothetical scenario where these *Works* were filled with falsehoods and fabrications, readers could easily identify them, given the meticulous dating of every recorded event within the *Works*. Moreover, if the *Works* were mere fabrications, how then can one explain the fact that writers for *Kŭlloja*, *KUAB*, and *ER* derive meaningful insights from these alleged fabrications to formulate specific policies and address real-world economic issues? Despite their somewhat intrusive writing style, lacking the comfort of casual reading, a compelling argument exists for the authenticity of these *Works*. Their value lies in being records of actual events that have unfolded in the real world, leaving little room for doubt about their genuineness.

The real challenge does not lie in determining whether the words and deeds of the DPRK's supreme leaders, as recorded in the *Works* and other texts, are genuinely authentic. Instead, it lies in the meticulous and intricate task of extracting pertinent information from this vast and complex corpus. Navigating the extensive *Works*; meticulously combing through the pages of the *CCY*, *Rodong Sinmun*, and *Kŭlloja*; and painstakingly sifting through the nuanced analyses in economic journals are indeed comparable to unearthing a "needle in a haystack."

This book stands as a testament to this very challenge, a decade-long odyssey of research and analysis dedicated to unlocking the secrets hidden within the DPRK's official materials. By meticulously traversing this intricate landscape, it unveils the nuanced realities of the DPRK's economic journey, offering a deeper understanding that would be impossible to achieve solely through external observations or secondary sources.

This study exclusively relies on primary sources from the DPRK. One might argue that triangulation is essential for a more holistic perspective on the book's specific research question, as it can enhance credibility and validity. For instance, when considering the DPRK's economic situation and performance, some may assert the need for triangulation with studies based on defectors' accounts and external statistics, such as those provided by the Bank of Korea.

However, as mentioned earlier, studies relying on defectors' accounts often fail to accurately portray the country due to inherent limitations and distortions. Triangulation with external statistics, like those by the Bank of Korea, is deemed meaningless, as the Bank's estimation of the DPRK's GDP is not verifiable; the Bank does not disclose its methodology or the specific information it uses for this estimation. Additionally, given that, apart from the Republic of Korea, no other country publishes or provides statistics or information on DPRK economic construction, triangulation with external statistics, other than primary sources from the DPRK, is not feasible.

Therefore, sole reliance on DPRK primary sources, while unconventional, is the most feasible and reliable approach in this study. By meticulously and diligently analyzing these internal materials, we can gain a nuanced understanding of the DPRK's economic landscape and uncover valuable insights that contribute significantly to our comprehensive analysis. This in-depth exploration of DPRK sources itself constitutes a form of rigorous research, offering valuable insights that would be impossible to achieve solely through external data, which is often flawed or unavailable.

This book delves into the economic trajectory of the DPRK across distinct historical epochs. Chapter 1 meticulously deconstructs the era of Kim Il Sung (1949–1994), dissecting the distinctive "Taean System" that served as the cornerstone of their socialist economy. Chapter 2 unpacks the tumultuous "Arduous March" crisis (1995–2011) under Kim Jong Il, intricately analyzing the strategies employed to navigate this period of adversity. Chapter 3 delves into the "Socialist Enterprise Responsibility Management System" instituted under Kim Jong Un (2012–present), a pivotal component of their contemporary economic governance. Lastly, Chapter 4 synthesizes the preceding chapters, presenting a comprehensive portrayal of the DPRK's economic metamorphosis while contemplating its future trajectories.

As we approach the book's conclusion, we engage in a thoughtful discussion on the future prospects awaiting the DPRK's economic construction and management system, enriching our final reflections with depth and substance. With each chapter meticulously crafted, this book aims to deliver an unparalleled analysis of the DPRK's economic evolution, empowering readers to gain a firm understanding of the intricate dynamics underlying its economic management and construction.

Notes

1 Cuba can be characterized as a socialist economic system, given that the State predominantly owns the means of production. Nonetheless, a noteworthy shift has occurred since 2011, as Cuba has progressively introduced economic reforms. These measures involve diminishing the State's stake in the economy, fostering self-employment, permitting private ownership of select real estate, and facilitating the sale of produce by private farmers to hotels and other entities. Consequently, classifying Cuba within the same category as the DPRK poses challenges, as the latter strictly prohibits private ownership of the means of production or real estate.

2 Hukŏn Pak, "Helshingk'ich'oejonghyŏbyaksŏwahanbandojŏkyongŭimunje: In'gwŏnjonjunggaenyŏmŭlchungshimŭro" (The Helsinki Final Agreement and the Problem of Its Application to the Korean Peninsula: Focusing on the Concept of Respect for Human Rights), *Yŏksabip'yŏng* (*Critical Review of History*) (2010), vol. 90, no. 2, Spring, p. 497.

3 "The DPRK, Ch'ŏn said, had already collapsed economically and would collapse politically two to three years after the death of Kim Jong-il." https://wikileaks.org/plusd/cables/10SEOUL272_a.html.

4 For example, Nikki Haley, who served as the U.S. Ambassador to the United Nations and played a pivotal role in the initiation of U.N. Security Council Sanctions 2397, deemed it as the "strongest possible" sanctions imposed on the country (Carol Morello, Michelle Ye Hee Lee and Emily Rauhala, "U.N. agrees to toughest-ever sanctions against North Korea," *Washington Post* (September 11, 2017, 7:46 p.m. EDT). https://www.washingtonpost.com/world/in-the-push-for-oil-embargo-on-north-korea-china-is-reluctant-to-sign-off/2017/09/11/3a5b56fe-96e5-11e7-a527-3573bd073e02_story.html.

5 Woo-Jun Min and Sukhee Han, "Economic sanctions against North Korea: The pivotal role of US–China cooperation," *International Area Studies Review* (2020), vol. 23, no. 2, pp. 180–183.

6 Carol Morello, Michelle Ye Hee Lee and Emily Rauhala, "U.N. agrees to toughest-ever sanctions against North Korea," *Washington Post* (September 11, 2017, 7:46 p.m. EDT).

7 Rodrigo Campos and Hyonhee Shin, "U.N. Security Council imposes new sanctions on North Korea over missile test," *Reuters* (December 22, 2017, 12:30 p.m. GMT). https://www.reuters.com/article/us-northkorea-missiles-idUSKBN1EG0HV.

8 CFR.org Editors, "What to Know About Sanctions on North Korea," *Council on Foreign Relations* (July 27, 2022, 3:00 PM EST). https://www.cfr.org/backgrounder/north-korea-sanctions-un-nuclear-weapons.

9 Some of the representative reports are as follows: Patricia Kim, "How to Persuade China to Squeeze North Korea's Lifeline," *Foreign Policy* (February 27, 2017). https://foreignpolicy.com/2017/02/27/how-to-persuade-china-to-squeeze-north-koreas-lifeline/; Daniel Wertz, "China-North Korea Relations," *The National Committee on North Korea*. https://www.ncnk.org/resources/briefing-papers/all-briefing-papers/china-north-korea-relations); Michael Schuman, "P'yŏngyang's China Connection: Beijing enforces some U.N. sanctions, but Chinese business still helps to preserve North Korea's government," *USNews* (Sept. 19, 2017, 1:46 p.m). https://www.usnews.com/news/best-countries/articles/2017-09-19/how-china-keeps-north-koreas-economy-afloat); Simon Denyer, "On China's border with North Korea, a constricted economic lifeline is still a lifeline," *Washington Post* (September 28, 2017, 6:29 AM EDT). https://www.washingtonpost.com/world/asia_pacific/on-chinas-border-with-north-korea-a-reduced-trade-lifeline-is-still-a-lifeline/2017/09/28/bbc6eefe-a2c4-11e7-b573-8ec86cdfe1ed_story.html; Todd Rosenblum, "How to persuade China to abandon North Korea," *Politico* (July 18, 2017 05:25 AM EDT). https://www.politico.com/agenda/story/2017/07/18/china-north-korea-american-troops-removal-000476/; Prof Kerry Brown (King's

College London), "How much leverage does China have over North Korea?" *BBC* (5 September 2017). https://www.bbc.com/news/world-asia-41152824; Catherine Mercier. "Bridge linking North Korea to China a trade lifeline" *CBS News* (April 10, 2013,1:47AMEDT).https://www.cbc.ca/news/world/bridge-linking-north-korea-to-china-a-trade-lifeline-1.1370440.

10 While accusations of the DPRK violating economic sanctions persist, it's important to note that, as of December 2023, only one individual—Singaporean businessman Kwe Kee Seng—has been indicted by the United States for such offenses. Kwe Kee Seng reportedly faces charges related to fuel deliveries to the DPRK, ship-to-ship transfers, and money laundering through front companies (VoA News, "Suspect in N. Korea Sanctions violation in Singapore, Police Say," *Voice of America*, (November 5, 2022). https://www.voanews.com/a/suspect-in-n-korea-sanctions-violation-in-singapore-police-say-/6822239.html. It's noteworthy that, to date, no Chinese entities or individuals have been officially accused by the United States of sanctions violations against the DPRK.

11 With the COVID-19 pandemic subsiding in 2023, the DPRK embarked on a phased relaxation of its strict border closure measures. This began in June with the repatriation of DPRK citizens residing abroad, followed by the welcoming of delegations from China and Russia in July. The most significant step came on September 25, 2023, when the DPRK fully reopened its borders to foreign nationals, marking the first such easing since the pandemic's inception.

12 Michael Lee, Jin-woo Jeong, Yeong-gyo Chung, "North Korea spends money it needs for food on missiles" *Korea JoongAng Daily* (December 12, 2022, 19:01). https://koreajoongangdaily.joins.com/2022/12/12/national/northKorea/Korea-North-Korea-food-insecurity/20221212190148616.html.

13 Wonju Yi, "N. Korean leader celebrates completion of major housing project in Pyongyang" *Yonhap News Agency* (April 12, 2022, 09:30). https://en.yna.co.kr/view/AEN20220412002000325.

14 Soo-yeon Kim, "(LEAD) N. Korean leader celebrates completion of building more new homes in Pyongyang," *Yonhap News Agency* (April 17, 2023, 11:29). https://en.yna.co.kr/view/AEN20230417000751325.

15 Pyŏngyŏp Cho'e, CEO of INEXHOUSING Co., Ltd., brings valuable experience in both commercial and non-commercial development in the Republic of Korea (ROK). Based on this expertise, he estimates that a similar project in the Seoul Metropolitan Area would require at least 1 trillion Korean wŏn (approximately 770 million USD). However, in the DPRK, lower costs for labor, building materials, and land lead to significantly reduced overall expenses. While specific construction costs remain unclear due to limited data, insights from Cho'e and ongoing projects suggest that the DPRK possesses sufficient financial capability to undertake and complete these developments as planned.

16 Most works focused on the DPRK economy originating from ROK primarily rely on these sources. Among the notable works in English that extensively employ these sources, the following are considered highly representative: Stephen Haggard, Marcus Noland, *Famine in North Korea: Markets, Aid, and Reform*, (New York: Columbia University Press, 2007); Stephen Haggard, Marcus Noland, *Witness to Transformation: Refugee Insights into North Korea* (Washington, DC: Peterson Institute for International Economics, 2010); Byung-Yeon Kim, *Unveiling the North Korean Economy: Collapse and Transition* (Cambridge: Cambridge University Press, 2017).

17 Song and Denney. "Studying North Korea through North Korean migrants: lessons from the field," *Critical Asian Studies* (2019), vol. 51, no. 3, pp. 453–455.

18 The DPRK, as a socialist state, meticulously plans its economy under the Workers' Party of Korea's guidance. This planning relies heavily on internal data gathered by various party and state organs. However, the regime rarely shares any economic statistics beyond limited portions of the national budget, often omitting even those

when unfavorable. This lack of transparency makes quantitative analysis of the DPRK's economy challenging.

Fortunately, despite the opacity, a wealth of qualitative data exists in the form of official pronouncements by DPRK leaders. Analyzing these materials, like the extensive '*Complete Works of Kim Il Sung*' and '*Selected Works of Kim Jong Il*,' alongside publications like *Rodong Sinmun* and *Chosun Central Yearbook*, can offer valuable insights. Additionally, cross-referencing these sources with rare glimpses of reality, such as seeking humanitarian aid during the "Arduous March" or implementing a full border closure during the COVID-19 pandemic, can further illuminate the economic situation.

By diligently examining these qualitative sources and going beyond customary approaches, researchers can bridge the information gap and gain deeper understanding of the complexities of the DPRK's economy.

19   Although the DPRK halted publication of comprehensive economic statistics in 1962, valuable economic insights remain accessible through the *CCY*, an annual publication dating back to 1949. Despite the absence of broader economic indices, the *CCY* reveals crucial information related to national budget revenue, expenditure, and even itemized breakdowns (including defense spending). This makes the *CCY* not just a useful cross-reference for the words and activities of the supreme leaders, but an essential piece of the puzzle in deciphering the DPRK's economic landscape.

Unfortunately, our utilization of the *CCY* is restricted to the 2018 edition. The DPRK inexplicably withheld distribution of any materials referencing the *CCY* outside its borders in 2019, a year before its pandemic-related closure. As a result, our analysis of the DPRK's economic construction and management system using the *CCY* is limited to data up to 2017.

20   Published since 1946, *Kŭlloja* offers a unique glimpse into the DPRK's economic realities and the effectiveness of its policies. Its articles showcase progress in construction projects, highlight obstacles encountered, and even criticize misconduct by responsible officials. However, its potential for research is severely limited. Since 1994, access has been restricted solely to high-ranking Party members, effectively locking away this valuable resource for scholars and researchers.

21   *KUAB* and *ER* stand as the DPRK's sole economic journals, offering valuable insights into the nation's economic landscape since their founding in 1954 and 1956, respectively. While primarily focusing on qualitative analysis, these journals provide unique glimpses into the country's economic realities.

The DPRK's definition of economics, as outlined in the 1985 "Dictionary of Economy Volume 1," emphasizes extracting general theories from real-world phenomena (p. 116). This necessitates grounding in objective data, which this study seeks to achieve by analyzing these crucial economic journals.

Interestingly, a distinct pattern emerges upon closer examination. *KUAB* features primarily longer, in-depth articles (averaging 5,200 words) by academics affiliated with Kim Il Sung University and its institutes. In contrast, *ER* showcases shorter (around 2,800 words) research papers by researchers from the Academy of Social Sciences, offering broader perspectives. Notably, *KUAB*'s 2016, volume 61, issue 4, contains only 20 articles, while *ER*'s 2016, issue 4 features 44 articles. This suggests that *KUAB* focuses on deep dives into specific topics, whereas *ER* offers a wider range of viewpoints on various economic issues.

1 Ch'ŏllima Movement, Taean System, and Centralized Planning

1.1 The Strategy of Prioritizing Heavy Industry and the Pyŏngjin (Parallel) Route

Following the armistice in 1953, the Democratic People's Republic of Korea (DPRK) embarked on an arduous path of economic development, guided by the principle articulated by Kim Il Sung: "the strategy of prioritizing heavy industry and simultaneous development of light industry and agriculture." This strategic blueprint was adopted at the Sixth Plenary Session of the Central Committee of the Workers' Party of Korea (WPK) on August 5, 1953, marking a pivotal moment in the nation's economic trajectory. Articulating the rationale behind this approach, Kim Il Sung elucidated the imperative of advancing the light industry and agriculture in tandem while ensuring the paramount recovery and expansion of heavy industry during the postwar phase of economic reconstruction. This, he argued, was essential for solidifying the country's economic foundations and expediting the improvement of living standards.[1]

In essence, the strategy sought to accord priority to the growth of heavy industry, thereby establishing a self-reliant economic base capable of providing the necessary impetus for the development of light industry and agriculture. By laying a sturdy groundwork through the cultivation of heavy industry, the DPRK aimed to consolidate its economic independence and subsequently harness the resulting momentum to propel the production of vital goods essential for advancing other sectors. This carefully crafted approach initially yielded notable successes for the DPRK, elevating its economic prowess to commendable heights.

Following the adoption of the strategy prioritizing heavy industry alongside the simultaneous development of light industry and agriculture, the DPRK experienced a period of notable economic achievements. During the Three-Year Plan from 1954 to 1956, focused on industrial recovery, the DPRK surpassed prewar levels of production, registering an impressive average annual growth rate of 41.7%. Notably, the industrial sector's resurgence was complemented by a remarkable grain output of 2.87 million tons.[2] Subsequently, during the five-year plan from 1957 to 1961, designed to establish the groundwork

DOI: 10.4324/9781003481737-2

for industrialization and address fundamental issues of sustenance and shelter, the DPRK outperformed its targets, attaining an annual industrial growth rate of 36.6%—two years ahead of schedule.[3]

However, the challenges emerged during the implementation of the First Seven-Year Plan. This period coincided with a series of security crises, including a military coup against communism in the Republic of Korea (ROK) in 1961, the Cuban Missile Crisis in 1962, and the Tonkin Gulf Incident, which witnessed heightened American military intervention in the Vietnam War in 1964.[4] In response to these turbulent events, the Second Party Representative Conference adopted the Pyŏngjin (Parallel) Route in October 1966, aiming to concurrently develop the economy and bolster national defense capabilities.[5] This policy directive, calling for increased investment in the national defense sector to strengthen national security, inevitably skewed investment toward heavy industry, which served as the bedrock for national defense infrastructure. As a consequence, this disproportionate focus on heavy industry resulted in surplus production of capital goods and a shortage of consumer goods, thereby disrupting the delicate equilibrium between "Ch'ukchŏkkwa Sobi" (accumulation and consumption).

Under the Parallel Route, the DPRK pursued a self-defense strategy known as the "Kunsahwabangch'im" (Self-Defense Militarization Policy), with the aim of arming the entire nation, fortifying the country, and establishing a system capable of generating and stockpiling military supplies across all sectors of the civilian economy. It is important to note that such an endeavor could not be accomplished instantaneously but, rather, necessitated a gradual implementation process. Moreover, the establishment of a system producing military supplies within all sectors of the civilian economy involved adjusting the proportion of such supplies within the existing budgetary allocations, rather than allocating separate funds exclusively for this purpose. Accordingly, defense spending in 1964, 1965, and 1966 accounted for approximately 11.8% to 28.6% of total expenditures.[6]

However, the pronounced bias toward heavy industry investment, which gained momentum in 1964, entailed corresponding budget cuts in sectors other than heavy industry,[7] which served as the foundation for national defense-related construction. The DPRK has adhered to a developmental strategy for its consumer goods industry, emphasizing the establishment and operation of medium-sized and small-scale local enterprises in conjunction with large-scale central industries.[8] Approximately half of the total production value of the light industry was attributed to these local enterprises.[9]

However, the adverse effects of governmental measures, such as the reduction of budgetary allocations for light industry and local areas, as well as a decrease in investments in these sectors, have been notable. This downturn had a detrimental impact on the overall production of consumer goods. Specifically, the growth rate in the total distribution of consumer goods plummeted from 13% in 1962 to a mere 3% in 1963, and the proportion of local industries within the total Kukkagŏraesuipkŭm (State Transaction Revenue) experienced a decline, dropping from 51.3% in 1962 to 45.6% in 1963.[10] These developments underscore the challenges and consequences associated with shifts in governmental policies and resource allocations on the consumer goods industry in the DPRK during this period.

The DPRK has not officially disclosed the precise proportion of local industries in the overall volume of distributed consumer goods and State Transaction Revenue since 1963. This lack of transparency might stem from the fact that the performance of these sectors has been lackluster and progressively deteriorating since that time. As Kim Il Sung elucidated while expounding on the rationale behind the Parallel Route, the DPRK persisted in following this path of economic and national defense construction "as long as there is a threat of war by imperialism."[11] Regrettably, adhering to this Route further exacerbated the imbalances among different economic sectors and had a demoralizing effect on DPRK peasants and workers, as the backward trajectory sacrificed the production of consumer goods, failing to satisfy the material incentives of the workers and negatively impacting labor productivity.[12]

The insufficiency of consumer goods production placed significant constraints on the smooth functioning of the economy. The excessive allocation of resources to national defense resulted in a severe imbalance between industrial sectors, raising concerns even among officials in the heavy industry sector. However, the supreme leader at the time, Kim Il Sung, swiftly dismissed and rebuffed their apprehensions, citing past experience.[13]

In the pursuit of enhancing national defense, the DPRK heightened resource allocation, with a particular emphasis on heavy industry, exacerbating the existing predicament of resource shortages. This challenge had already reached a critical level due to the successful implementation of the Ch'ŏllima Movement during the initial five-year plan under the leadership of Kim Il Sung. The Ch'ŏllima Movement was initiated when Kim Il Sung personally visited work sites, connecting with the masses and inspiring them to elevate production and foster innovation. The enthusiastic response from the masses led to large-scale production and innovation initiatives, resulting in remarkable economic growth.

The Five-Year Plan (1957–1961) witnessed an impressive average industrial production growth rate of 36.6%. However, while the Ch'ŏllima Movement effectively fueled the morale of the masses to amplify production and innovation, it fell short in providing adequate incentives for efficient resource utilization. This deficiency inevitably resulted in mismanagement and wastage of resources, further complicating the resource shortage issue.

The DPRK's factories and enterprises, as Kim Il Sung highlighted, operated in a bureaucratic manner, disregarding the nation's overall interests, and resulting in the squandering of vast resources. Illustratively, only one-third of the total coal production in the DPRK was utilized efficiently, while the extent of energy waste remained unknown.[14] The severity of this resource shortage had reached a stage where it could no longer be overlooked. To effectively implement the Parallel Route, which aimed to concentrate resources in the heavy industry sector, measures were imperative to address the issue of resource mismanagement.

Kim Il Sung sought the solution in the form of a centralized command planning system known as the Unified and Detailed Planning System (UDPS). During the Party Congress of the National Planning Commission on September 23, 1965, he identified planning as the most significant problem plaguing the DPRK economy. He emphasized the need for remedial action and said the following:

> The paramount concern in overseeing our nation's economy today lies in the imperative to enhance planned projects decisively … In a socialist society characterized by the collective ownership of all means of production, the functionality of the economy hinges on effective planning. The trajectory of a socialist economy, therefore, can only unfold in a methodical and strategic manner through robust planning …
>
> A litany of deficiencies, including the inability to normalize production in the industrial sector, unwarranted wastage, and the failure to elevate the populace's standard of living to a desirable level, can be predominantly attributed to suboptimal performance in planned projects. Addressing these challenges necessitates a renewed commitment to refining and fortifying the planning processes, as they constitute the linchpin for a thriving socialist economy.[15]

As he continued his address, Kim Il Sung highlighted two significant contradictions within the existing planning system. The first contradiction centered on the conflicting demands between the State planning agency and producers. The former sought increased production with reduced support, while the latter requested more support despite decreasing production. This fundamental contradiction manifested as a clash between the bureaucracy and subjectivism of the State planning agency and the departmentalism and localism of the producers.

The second contradiction revolved around the fact that the State planning agency possessed knowledge of the overall national economy and its prospects but lacked insights into the specific reality and production reserves. Conversely, producers were well acquainted with the specific reality and reserves of their enterprises but lacked awareness of the broader national economic situation and overall prospects for economic development.

Kim Il Sung argued that resolving these two contradictions would pave the way for the formulation of scientific and feasible plans. He concluded that for successful economic planning, it was imperative to implement the 'mass line' in planning. This involved eliminating the subjectivism and bureaucracy within State planning agency, strengthening Party leadership and control over planning, and eradicating the departmentalism and localism inherent among producers. Kim Il Sung emphasized that achieving the unity of planning was the only viable solution to address these challenges effectively.[16]

Central to Kim Il Sung's conclusion is the assertion that embracing the "mass line" in planning can rectify two critical flaws inherent in the current system: the subjective tendencies of national planning agencies and the self-serving behavior of individual institutions and localities. But what exactly is this "mass line" he proposes?

The "mass line," in this context, signifies the inclusion of the collective will and aspirations of the masses in the decision-making and implementation of the planned economy. Kim Il Sung's conclusion emphasizes that when the planned economy project adheres to the principles of the mass line, it can overcome the inherent problems and challenges associated with the existing planned economy system, particularly those stemming from bureaucratic tendencies and local self-interest.

Kim Il Sung's Ch'ŏllima Movement, which began with his visit to the Kangsŏn Steel Mill and on-site guidance, spread nationwide and produced tremendous results in terms of increased production. However, as was pointed out earlier, the Ch'ŏllima Movement was aimed at increasing production rather than efficiency, which led to resource overuse and waste, exacerbating the problem of resource scarcity.[17]

Moreover, the management system of factories and enterprises, operating under the "Chibaeinyuilgwallije" (Manager Monolithic Management System), proved counterproductive in addressing resource scarcity. Under this system, managers' compensation was based on the production volume of their respective factories or enterprises, incentivizing them to report lower production capacities to the State planning agency to secure more resources from the State. This pervasive behavior only served to exacerbate the already pressing issue of resource scarcity.

For Kim Il Sung, the issue of squandering resources through the improper use of materials became particularly pressing. The Ch'ŏllima Movement itself was initiated in response to a significant reduction in aid from the Soviet Union. Faced with dwindling external support and the ensuing resource shortage, the DPRK pivoted toward a self-reliance strategy in economic construction, giving rise to the Ch'ŏllima Movement. While the movement did lead to increased production, the pervasive practices of resource waste and overuse compounded the existing resource scarcity problem. Consequently, Kim Il Sung found it imperative to address and rectify this issue, no longer able to overlook the detrimental impact of such practices on the nation's resources.

During the enlarged meeting of the Fourth Central Committee of the WPK in November 1961, Kim Il Sung proposed tasks to enhance the level of economic guidance provided by production and management agencies, with the goal of fundamentally improving enterprise management and operations. Subsequently, he embarked on a project to restructure the industry's management system. In December of the same year, Kim Il Sung visited the Taean Electrical Machinery Factory twice, where he convened meetings with the factory's Party and administrative councils to discuss general issues pertaining to its management and operation. Building upon these initiatives, he implemented groundbreaking measures to establish a fundamentally new industrial management system known as the "Taean System," which reflected his unwavering emphasis on the mass line approach.

1.2 Taean System and Unified and Detailed Planning System

The Taean System is a complementary and expanded application of the "Ch'ongsan-ri Method,"[18] which was applied to cooperative farms, to factories and enterprises. The most notable departure from previous operational systems in factories and enterprises under the Taean System was the transition from a sole manager-dominated structure to a collective management and operating system led by the factory or enterprise Party committee. Consequently, this shift bolstered Party leadership and control in the management and operation of factories and enterprises, facilitating the establishment of a mechanism to unify Party policies for each individual factory and enterprise.

This transformation holds significant implications for the Kyehoegŭi Irwŏnhwach'egye (Unified Planning System), which entails cohesive planning and implementation at the national level. Under the previous "Manager Monolithic Management System," managers would report the production capacity of their respective factories or enterprises to the National Planning Commission through the relevant provincial or Administrative Bureau. Following specific negotiations,[19] the manager would receive the annual production plan for the factory or enterprise and a material allocation letter, enabling them to enter into contracts with other factories or enterprises and secure necessary materials.[20]

In contrast, the Taean System[21] operated on the principle of top-to-bottom assistance, wherein each bureau would have a materials manager responsible for procuring required materials from the materials managers of other bureaus. These materials would then be directly supplied to the factories and enterprises under the purview of the respective bureau.

Additionally, the principle of collective guidance was emphasized, leading to the establishment of material supply departments within factories and enterprises. These departments, overseen by deputy managers under the guidance of the factory or enterprise Party committees, played a pivotal role in enhancing the unified management of material supply and utilization. The operationalization of the Taean System was further solidified by a Cabinet decision in November 1963, which institutionalized its application across all plants and enterprises.[22] This decision provided the necessary institutional framework to effectively realize the practical implementation of unified planning.

As observed earlier, the Taean System was specifically designed to facilitate the implementation of the mass line and promote integrated planning within its framework. Therefore, it would be inaccurate to perceive the integration of the planning system as akin to a Stalinist centrally planned command system. The fundamental principle of the Taean System is to reject bureaucratic tendencies in economic operations and management, instead embracing the mass line approach. This involves engaging with the masses to understand the reality on the ground and guiding their cooperation in advancing economic projects. It is challenging to equate such an approach with a "command system."

A more appropriate perspective would characterize it as a "cooperative system," involving active dialogue with the masses to address project challenges and foster their collaboration. Thus, if we were to assign a name to the essence of the integrated planning system,[23] a "centrally guided cooperative system" would be a more fitting description.

Had the economic planning system of the DPRK solely ended with unified planning, there would be no significant issue in labeling it the centrally guided cooperative system and classifying it as a new economic system. However, Kim Il Sung's vision for a new planning system extended beyond the Unified Planning System. On September 23, 1965, Kim Il Sung instructed the Party Congress of the National Planning Commission to implement a "Sebuhwach'egye" (Detailed Planning System) in addition to the existing framework. In Kim Il Sung's perspective, the DPRK's planning suffered from a lack of scientific calculation and specificity, resulting in an inability to comprehensively cover all sectors of the economy. This flawed planning approach led to low rates of equipment utilization, impeded production normalization, and presented substantial shortcomings in economic development.

Kim Il Sung criticized the situation, pointing out that the DPRK's planning only focused on overall quantities, such as a few tons of ore, steel, cement, cars, and tractors, without detailed plans for essential components like bolts and toothed wheels. This absence of detailed planning invariably led to material and resource waste due to underutilization of facilities and insufficient availability of parts required for finished products. Consequently, production and construction inevitably suffered.[24]

For Kim Il Sung, the most pressing issue in the DPRK economic development was the scarcity of resources. In such circumstances, the compounding of material and resource waste due to deficiencies in planning caused by the absence of detailed plans was wholly unacceptable. Kim Il Sung maintained a firm and uncompromising stance on this matter. When certain members of the State Planning Commission argued that it was physically challenging to formulate detailed plans for all aspects of production, Kim Il Sung vehemently criticized their viewpoint, expressing the following.

> It appears that some officials within the State Planning Commission harbor thoughts along the lines of, "How can we excel in detailed planning beyond the capacity of other nations?" However, we must scrutinize the notion that we are limited by what others cannot achieve. Furthermore, there seems to be hesitancy among certain officials regarding detailed planning, citing the substantial number of plan indicators, exceeding 10,000. Yet, the abundance of indicators should not deter us; rather, it underscores the necessity of our commitment to comprehensive planning. Currently, despite our increased production of cloth, there remains a shortage, preventing the creation of adequate clothing for children.

Similarly, the production of numerous tractors and cars is hindered by the inability to use them effectively due to the lack of spare parts—a consequence of our deficiency in detailed planning. Even if the number of plan indicators exceeds tens of thousands, we must persist in detailed planning. If the sheer volume makes it impractical to complete within a day or two, we should dedicate the required time, be it one, two months, or a year. Should the State Planning Commission face a shortage of officials, proactive recruitment from factories and enterprises becomes imperative to surmount this challenge.[25]

As a result of Kim Il Sung's directive, the "Unified Detailed Planning System" (UDPS) became the officially sanctioned economic planning system of the DPRK in 1965. The addition of the Unified Planning System, which centralized and managed planning at the national level, and the Detailed Planning System, which meticulously covered all sectors, factories, and enterprises while ensuring close interconnections, transformed the DPRK's economic planning system into a manifestation of a centrally planned command system.[26]

However, implementing such a centrally planned command system proved exceedingly challenging, if not impossible, due to the staggering number of variables that required calculation and control at the national level. In contemporary times, supercomputers powered by artificial intelligence might be capable of handling and computing an array of variables, assisting in the planning process. Nevertheless, during that era, neither the DPRK nor any other country possessed supercomputers capable of utilizing artificial intelligence. Even if such technology had been available, attempting to execute a detailed plan that seamlessly integrated all facets of production, distribution, and consumption would have been unfeasible due to the inherent uncertainty within the economy. Just as predicting and controlling the weather and natural disasters remain elusive, attempting to create a comprehensive plan to control uncertainty in the economy and the natural world would be undesirable and impractical.

So why was Kim Il Sung so unwavering in his pursuit of the UDPS? As discussed, and examined earlier, the issue of resource scarcity in the DPRK had reached a critical level that could no longer be ignored. As the supreme leader, it was imperative for Kim Il Sung to devise a solution to this pressing problem. Another factor that drove Kim Il Sung's unwavering commitment to the UDPS was his belief in the superiority of the socialist economy and the means to achieve it, coupled with his ideal vision of a socialist economic system grounded in collectivism. Kim Il Sung held the conviction that in a socialist society where the means of production are collectively owned, as opposed to a capitalist society where they are privately owned, the economy could develop in a planned and balanced manner.

In this context, planned economic development entails identifying and utilizing all productive factors, such as resources, production equipment, and the labor force, existing or potentially available in society, to avoid idleness or waste. Moreover, the concept of "balance" in economic development encompasses the broader equilibrium between "accumulation and consumption," as well as more specific balances between industry and agriculture, heavy industry and light industry, and production and services. Kim Il Sung argued that to achieve planned and balanced economic development, unified and detailed plans were indispensable. However, he acknowledged the presence of two significant challenges that hindered the successful implementation of such planning initiatives, impeding the planned and balanced development of a socialist economy.

As observed, one issue lies in bureaucratic planning, which is rooted in the subjective desires of the central authorities. Consequently, it lacks objectivity and fails to acknowledge the untapped potential within the economy. Another problem arises when producers prioritize their own interests, the interests of their enterprises, or the interests of their counties over the welfare of the entire nation. These individuals aim to achieve recognition by minimizing their planning efforts, but they overlook the benefits that can be derived from producing a little more for the country. Such self-centered behavior results in wastage of resources and subpar production.[27]

Kim Il Sung contends that addressing various challenges can be effectively achieved through strategic planning within the framework of the Taean System, rooted in the principles of the "Hyŏngmyŏngjŏkkunjungnosŏ" (Revolutionary Mass Line). Specifically, he advocates for direct collaboration between the State Planning Commission and factory committees, along with laborers at production sites. This collaborative effort, guided by the mass line, aims to develop more objective plans that faithfully mirror the realities on the ground. Furthermore, Kim Il Sung emphasizes that the implementation of a robust Taean System within factories and enterprises, characterized by strict adherence to the Party's policies and guidelines, serves as a potent mechanism to minimize the prevalence of departmentalism or local selfishness. In his view, this adherence contributes to fostering an environment where production sites operate harmoniously and efficiently.

Kim Il Sung firmly believes that planning within the Taean System framework is indispensable for overcoming challenges such as bureaucratic centralism and the detrimental effects of departmentalism or local selfishness at production sites. By doing so, he envisions the cultivation of a balanced economic development landscape. This overarching argument, founded on his unwavering belief in the Taean System, reflects his idealistic vision of communism, where collective efforts and adherence to a common ideology propel socioeconomic progress. Kim Il Sung's argument encompasses an idealized conception of communism, which can be summarized as follows:

> In a capitalist society, individuals engage in fierce competition and strive to overcome each other, solely driven by the pursuit of personal well-being. However, the essence of a socialist society is starkly different—here, the collective thrives, and everyone enjoys a shared prosperity. The

goal of building socialism is not for personal aggrandizement but to forge a harmonious coexistence, where people can work and live well together.

In the tapestry of a socialist society, individuals cultivate comradely relationships, offering mutual assistance, bound by shared interests and common goals. Each person contributes to the collective good, and, reciprocally, the collective endeavors for the well-being of every individual. This symbiotic relationship gives rise to a harmonious and united societal family. Within such a framework, selfishness and egotism find no place, as the spirit of collectivism prevails. It is through this collective spirit that we can construct and thrive in a socialist society, where the synergy of shared efforts leads to a more equitable and fulfilling way of life.[28]

The Taean System emerged as a distinctive model of socialist economic operation in the DPRK, embodying the principle of "Hananŭn chŏnch'erŭl wihayŏ, Chŏnch'enŭn hanarŭl wihayŏ" (One for All, and All for One) within the economy.[29] Essentially, Kim Il Sung endeavored to construct an economic framework through the Taean System that would align with his idealized vision of communism.[30] His objective was to steer clear of subjective and bureaucratic practices within the central apparatus (the whole), while ensuring that each factory or enterprise could transcend self-interest and consider the broader interests of society (the one for the sake of the whole). This approach aimed to foster a state of "unified and detailed planning," ultimately fostering prosperity in economic development.[31]

However, one must acknowledge the fundamental challenge inherent in planned economies of this nature, a point even recognized by Kim Il Sung himself.[32] Nevertheless, his formative experience in leading the Kangsŏn Steel Mill, which served as the genesis of the Ch'ŏllima Movement, appears to have profoundly influenced his belief in the transformative potential of correctly implementing the mass line and unleashing the latent power residing within the masses, enabling the achievement of the seemingly insurmountable. Kim Il Sung underscored the necessity of introducing a Detailed Planning System into the economy and articulated the following sentiment.

Every element, including equipment capacity, the country's resources and materials, funds, and the workforce, demands careful consideration during the planning phase. Remarkably, **even the intangible factor of people's consciousness, challenging to quantify, becomes a crucial consideration** (emphasis added). A high level of consciousness among the populace can amplify the effectiveness of equipment with somewhat limited capacity, resulting in increased production. A compelling illustration of this synergy is evident in the Kangsŏn Steel Mill, where, in 1957, workers demonstrated exceptional patriotic enthusiasm, enabling them to produce 120,000 tons of steel from a nominal capacity of 60,000 tons—a testament to the transformative power of heightened collective consciousness in the planning process.[33]

Let us now delve into the circumstances surrounding the Kangsŏn Steel Mill, an event that held great significance in shaping Kim Il Sung's perception.

In 1956, during the August Plenum of the Central Committee of the Workers' Party, a dissenting group comprising Ch'angik Ch'oe, Ch'angok Pak, Konghŭm Yun, and others emerged, vehemently opposing both the policy of giving investment priority to heavy industry and the burgeoning cult of personality surrounding Kim Il Sung. Their audacious endeavor took the form of a political coup (also known as the "8wŏlchongp'asagŏn (August Sectarian Incident)," yet their aspirations were swiftly quelled by the loyalists of Kim Il Sung, resulting in their ultimate failure. It is worth noting that the coup leaders were known for their active support of the Soviet Union's "COMECON"[34] policy, as well as their affiliation with the anti-Stalin movement within the Soviet Union, thereby suggesting a connection to the Soviet realm.

Following the unsuccessful anti–Kim Il Sung coup and the subsequent punishment of the coup leaders, the Soviet Union responded by curtailing its assistance to the DPRK, reducing it by more than 50% of the initially envisaged postwar recovery period. During the period from 1954 to 1956, the DPRK had received a substantial sum of US$367.5 million in aid from the Soviet Union as part of the postwar reconstruction efforts. However, in the aftermath of the so-called "August Sectarian Incident," aid from the Soviet Union underwent a precipitous decline, with the DPRK receiving a mere US$156 million between 1957 and 1960.[35]

The sharp downturn in Soviet aid dealt a severe blow to the DPRK's economy. It stemmed from the fact that a significant portion of the capital required to realize the policy of giving investment priority to heavy industry hinged upon foreign assistance, primarily emanating from the Soviet Union. Sustained external aid was indispensable to uphold the tenets of the policy. Though the prospect of continued support from the Soviet Union was now unattainable, Kim Il Sung, at the Plenary Meeting of the Central Committee in December 1956, made it resolutely clear that he would not relinquish his commitment to the policy of giving investment priority to heavy industry.

On December 28 of that year, he journeyed to the Kangsŏn Steel Mill, where he convened a gathering with the managers and vice managers. Inquisitively, Kim queried whether they could surpass the planned steel production by an additional 10,000 tons in the following year. Regrettably, the managers responded with trepidation, citing the mill's existing allocation of 60,000 tons as its maximum production capacity. Faced with this quandary, Kim Il Sung resolved to directly address the workers, assembling them within a warehouse-like structure, and delivering a speech wherein he proclaimed the following sentiments.

The prevailing circumstances in our nation are undeniably challenging. As we embark on the implementation of the upcoming First Five-Year Plan from the next year, we find ourselves grappling with significant shortages in funds, resources, and equipment. Compounding these challenges are the persistent opposition from anti-party and anti-revolutionary elements, the pressures exerted by revisionists, and renewed threats of invasion from reactionary forces in the US and south Korea. In these testing times, our reliance rests solely on the shoulders of the working class.

The critical role of the working class becomes even more pronounced, considering the dire situation we face. A modest increase, such as producing an additional 10,000 tons of steel beyond the original plan, could have a profound impact, fortifying our nation and allowing it to stand tall amid these adversities.[36]

According to Kim Il Sung, as his speech reached its climax, the atmosphere filled with the resounding chorus of enthusiastic workers. Their joyous voices echoed with unwavering determination as they pledged to produce steel without hesitation, following the imperatives of the Party. Kim Il Sung recounted how they tapped into their inner reserves and embarked on an extraordinary endeavor, surpassing conventional limits by achieving an astounding 120,000 tons of steel from a blast furnace initially designed for a modest capacity of 60,000 tons. The remarkable news of Kangsŏn Steel Mill's achievement spread rapidly, igniting a nationwide surge of inspiration among countless factories and enterprises. Kim Il Sung affirmed that this transformative event marked the beginning of what he called the Ch'ŏllima Movement, a powerful symbol of the socialist construction drive within the DPRK.[37]

The encounter at the Kangsŏn Steel Mill profoundly impressed upon Kim Il Sung the intrinsic significance of political endeavors in the realm of economic construction. It underscored the paramount value of engagement with the populace. Kim recognized that a unified and politically enlightened collective possessed the capacity to generate a synergistic force that eluded facile quantification and transcended individual contributions. However, it is crucial to acknowledge the element of exaggeration inherent in such perceptions.

As evidenced by Kim Il Sung's reference to the Kangsŏn Steel Mill, he emphasized that "even the ideological consciousness of people, which is difficult to measure, must be taken into account when planning," contending that "even in the presence of deficient equipment capacity, a heightened level of ideological consciousness among the people empowers them to utilize the same resources more effectively, yielding greater productivity."[38] Nevertheless, as previously analyzed, the comprehensive inclusion of all material factors within planning endeavors remains an unattainable feat, rendering it beyond the purview of science to demand the integration of the immeasurable dimension of ideological consciousness into planning frameworks.

The centralized planning system adopted in the DPRK, arising against this backdrop, confronted the bureaucratic imperative, thus impeding its original aspiration of curbing resource misallocation, averting wastage, and ensuring the efficient and balanced utilization of resources to execute a harmonized and coordinated economy. Consequently, the State Planning Commission endeavored to refine the detailed planning system, infusing it with a more pragmatic orientation. However, Kim Il Sung's censure echoed forth, reaffirming his unwavering commitment to the meticulous planning policy.

> Individuals within the planning department who lack a profound understanding of socialist economic law and planning theory manifest diverse biases in their approach to planning projects. Notably, there is a failure to incorporate the Party's revolutionary mass line and the policy of unified and detailed planning. Some planning officials go as far as doubting the feasibility of detailed planning, opting for passivity rather than actively pursuing it. This mindset often leads to a reliance on outdated methods and a tendency to engage in planning subjectively and formalistically.[39]

Moreover, the escalating partiality toward heavy industry investments, spurred by the imperative of concurrent development of economy and defense, has engendered a pernicious confluence of excessive production of capital goods and debilitating scarcities in consumer goods. This disquieting state of affairs has given rise to a palpable disjunction between the imperatives of accumulation and the requirements of consumption, further exacerbating the pervasive apathy toward production among the toiling masses of workers and farmers within the DPRK.

Consequently, the conundrum of the "accumulation and consumption" imbalance has entrenched itself as a chronic predicament plaguing the DPRK.[40] Furthermore, as the nation's economy burgeons, the very foundations of the centralized planning system, predicated upon the bedrock of unified and detailed planning, confront an ever more arduous set of trials. The passage of time has unveiled an intricate web of challenges that render the task of detailed planning an increasingly daunting endeavor.[41]

1.3 Efforts to Correct the Imbalance between "Accumulation and Consumption"

1.3.1 *Fostering Light Industry*

Consumption goods production remained a persistent challenge that could not be overlooked. In response, the DPRK devised strategic measures by establishing independent units, branch factories,[42] within large factories and enterprises dedicated to the production of consumer goods. Concurrently, local governments were encouraged to independently manufacture the consumer goods essential for their communities. Kim Il Sung termed this self-reliant initiative the "Pun'gongjangch'egye" (Branch Factory System, BFS).[43]

The BFS aimed to bolster consumption goods production, presenting a more pragmatic approach compared to the existing light industry system. It empowered local governments or "Worker District"[44] to create consumer goods using regional resources or reserves leftover from the production process, ensuring self-sufficiency and cost-effectiveness without imposing substantial financial burdens on the central government. Despite its merits, the BFS had inherent limitations. It struggled to make a substantial impact on increasing consumption goods production to meet burgeoning demands. As highlighted by Kim Il Sung, the BFS operates on the principle of large, centrally governed factories with robust technical foundations assisting smaller- and medium-sized factories in the same region or province that possess comparatively weaker technical capabilities. The effectiveness of this system hinges on the accurate comprehension of the circumstances surrounding the smaller factories by the centrally operated counterparts. It is crucial for these larger entities to adeptly offer the necessary managerial and operational expertise. Ultimately, the success of this system relies heavily on institutional regulation and implementation to ensure its effectiveness.

Achieving a breakthrough in consumer goods production proves to be a formidable task when relying solely on the intent and will of the Party, without the necessary institutional support and material investment. In other words, establishing branching factories alone is insufficient to meet people's consumption needs without the requisite institutional support and material investment.

However, following Kim Il Sung's directives to establish and fortify the BFS, these facilities proliferated across the nation, reminiscent of bamboo shoots after rainfall. Despite their initial inability to fulfill their intended purpose of meeting consumers' demands due to a lack of requisite institutional support and material investment, they inadvertently served as catalysts for the advancement of the "8wŏl3il inminsobip'um saengsanundong (August 3rd People's Movement for the Production of Consumer Goods, also known as the 8·3 Movement)," initiated and guided by Kim Jong Il in 1984.

Moreover, as the "8·3 Movement" proliferated nationwide and enriched based on these factories, it laid the groundwork for the reinforcement and expansion of farmers' markets, providing a means for people to somewhat alleviate the hardships of sustaining themselves during the challenging period of the "Arduous March" from the mid-1990s onward.

In Section 1.1, where we explored augmented defense spending due to the implementation of the Parallel Route—a strategy advocating simultaneous development of the economy and defense—the balance between "accumulation and consumption" shifted toward "accumulation." This shift was propelled by increased investment in heavy industry, a prerequisite for fulfilling the goals of the Parallel Route. The question arises: did this practice change after the conclusion of the Parallel Route?

Table 1.1 National Defense as a Share of National Budget Expenditures (1960–1995)

Year	1960	1961	1962	1963	1964	1965	1966	1967	1968
National Defense Expenditure/ National Budget (%)	3.1	2.5	2.1	2.2	NR	NR	NR	30.4	32.4
Year	1969	1970	1971	1972	1973	1974	1975	1976	1977
National Defense Expenditure/ National Budget (%)	31.0	29.2	31.2	17.0	15.4	16.1	16.4	16.7	15.7
Year	1978	1979	1980	1981	1982	1983	1984	1985	1986
National Defense Expenditure/ National Budget (%)	15.9	15.1	14.6	14.8	14.8	14.7	14.6	14.4	14.0
Year	1987	1988	1989	1990	1991	1992	1993	1994	1995
National Defense Expenditure/ National Budget (%)	13.3	12.2	12.0	12.0	12.1	11.4	11.5	11.4	NR

Source: author.

Note: NR (Not Reported).
Table 1.1 is compiled data spanning the years 1961 to 1996, obtained from *CCY*.

As highlighted in Table 1.1, a significant transformation in defense expenditures becomes apparent, starting in 1972 with a reduction from over 30% of total expenditures to approximately 17%. This pattern persisted until the onset of the "Arduous March" in earnest in 1994, with defense expenditures fluctuating between 11% and 16% of total expenditures.

Between 1967 and 1971, following the establishment of the Parallel Route at the Party Congress in October 1966, the DPRK consistently allocated more than 30% of total expenditures to defense. This increase was attributed to the implementation of the Self-Defense Militarization Policy, rooted in the Parallel Route. Key components of this policy included the "Chŏninminŭi mujanghwa" (Arming of the Entire People), "Chŏn'gugŭi yosaehwa" (Fortification of the Entire Country), "Chŏn'gunŭi kanbuhwa" (Officerization of the Entire Armed Forces), and "Chŏn'gunŭi hyŏndaehwa" (Modernization of the Entire Armed Forces).[45]

Before the initiation of the Parallel Route, defense spending accounted for a mere 2–3% of total expenditures, covering essential operating costs to sustain and manage the military. This prompts the inference that the expenses associated with establishing, sustaining, and operating a system capable of producing military supplies across all sectors of the civilian economy formed the disparity between the proportion of defense spending in total expenditures from 1973 to 1994 (ranging between 11% and 16%) and the baseline operating cost. In essence, this analysis suggests that the DPRK allocated an additional 9–14% of the total budget annually from 1973 to 1994 to develop and manage a system capable of producing military supplies from all sectors of the economy, including the civilian sector, after fulfillment of the key components of the Self-Defense Militarization Policy.

Recognizing that the additional 9–14% of the total budget was not merely rhetorical but genuinely allocated to investments across all sectors of the economy, specifically to support the production of military supplies in line with the Self-Defense Militarization Policy, it is reasonable to presume that a substantial portion of this supplementary budget was directed toward heavy industry. This inference is grounded in the fact that the majority of munitions were produced within this sector. Consequently, light industry faced a dearth of investment, leading to a decline in its overall performance.

This perspective finds validation in Kim Il Sung's acknowledgment during the Six-Year Plan period (1971–1976), where he identified the underdevelopment of light industry as a critical challenge. Emphasizing the urgency of fortifying investments in light industry, Kim Il Sung advocated for the establishment of numerous domestic light industry factories. Furthermore, he expressed a willingness to acquire factories from foreign countries if necessary, underscoring the paramount importance of nurturing the growth of the light industry sector.[46]

Moreover, during a conversation with a delegation of scientists from the "Cheiltongp'o" (Korean diaspora in Japan), Kim Il Sung expressed that the country was heavily investing in and directing its efforts toward the light and chemical industries, which directly impacted people's lives. He highlighted the vigorous endeavors undertaken to augment the quantity and variety of light industrial products and enhance their quality.[47] He expressed confidence that with effective implementation of this endeavor for two to three years, the country would be able to adequately supply the people with high-quality light industrial products, thereby significantly improving their living standards.[48]

In essence, investment in the light industry witnessed an increase from 1972 onward compared to the preceding period (1963–1971). Regrettably, no DPRK document, including the *CWK* and *CCY*, provides specific indications regarding the proportion of the total budget allocated to the light industry or the amount of investment. Nonetheless, Kim Il Sung consistently underscored that investment in the light industry during the Six-Year Plan exceeded that of the initial Seven-Year Plan. In an October 1975 conversation with Australian journalist Burchett, he even asserted that investment in the light industry during the Six-Year Plan had surged to such an extent that it facilitated the possibility of completing the plan ahead of schedule.[49]

To ascertain the extent of the increase, let us examine the data. During the Six-Year Plan period from 1971 to 1976, the average proportion of defense expenditures in total expenditures stood at 18.8%. In comparison, during the Second Six-Year Plan period spanning from 1978 to 1984, the average share of defense expenditures in total expenditures decreased to 14.9%. This represents a difference of 3.9%. If the DPRK had not allocated any additional investment to sectors other than the light industry during these two periods, the entirety of the 3.9% difference would have been directed toward investment in the light industry.

Nonetheless, as Kim Il Sung emphasized, the DPRK sought to establish an industrial structure and system that could domestically produce raw materials and resources for the light industry, aligning with the objective of building a self-reliant economy.[50] Consequently, to foster the development of the textile industry, a prominent component of the light industry, it was imperative to expedite the production of the 2·8 Vinylon Plant within the chemical industry, as it served as a crucial source of raw materials for the textile sector.

Moreover, ensuring the smooth operation of the 2·8 Vinylon Plant necessitated a steady supply of coal, the primary raw material for vinylon[51] production. Simultaneously, support had to be provided to the power industry to facilitate uninterrupted operations. Given these considerations, it can be inferred that a portion of the 3.9% of the total expenditure mentioned earlier would have been allocated to the light industry, while the remaining portion would have been directed toward heavy industries such as the chemical industry. Kim Il Sung's subsequent remarks imply a greater emphasis on heavy industry in the allocation of resources.

> While our current garment supply falls short of the highest quality, a vision for the future unfolds. Over the next three years, a strategic plan will propel both the chemical and textile industries forward, weaving a path toward substantially increased production of exquisite garments. Building upon proven successes, the establishment of light industrial factories emerges as a relatively attainable objective. Through a focused effort, numerous facilities can rise, demonstrably elevating the living standards of our people …

> The most formidable challenge lies in forging a robust defense industry. Undeterred, our commitment remains resolute. Just as we have prioritized the development of heavy industry in the past, so too will we persist in this endeavor. We recognize that a solid foundation in heavy industry eases the path for light industry to flourish, solidifying our vision for a well-rounded and prosperous industrial landscape.[52]

The division of total investment between heavy and light industries in the overall industrial sector was estimated to be approximately 60% and 40%, respectively.[53] This allocation differed from the distribution observed during the initial eight years of the Parallel Route, where heavy and light industries accounted for 80% and 20% of total investment in the industry, respectively.[54] The increase in investment in the light industry during this period allowed the Six-Year Plan's targets for light industry output to be achieved, leading to an overall rise in the production of consumer goods within the DPRK. However, the quality of these goods remained subpar and failed to adequately satisfy the growing consumer demand.[55]

As previously highlighted, a significant challenge emerged in the pursuit of constructing a self-reliant economy. The imperative to advance heavy industry for the development of light industry became apparent. Consequently, the elusive objective of achieving a balance between "accumulation and consumption" was hindered by a skewed investment focus on heavy industry. This persistent imbalance had detrimental effects, causing a decline in workers' motivation for labor. The DPRK economy found itself entrenched in the challenging terrain of the law of diminishing returns, where the increase in physical investment in heavy industry did not proportionally translate into a corresponding increase in production.

1.3.2 *Local Budget System and Local Industrial Factories*

To address the challenge of balancing "accumulation and consumption," the DPRK introduced the "Chibangyesanje" (Local Budget System) in 1973, granting localities more control over their economic affairs. During the Fifth Session of the Supreme People's Assembly on April 8, 1975, Kim Il Sung emphasized the importance of boosting local budget revenues for the smooth implementation of the Local Budget System. He identified the rapid development of local industries as the most effective means of increasing local budget revenues. Furthermore, he highlighted that the development of local industries was not only crucial for revenue generation but also instrumental in accelerating the production of essential goods and revitalizing the local economy.[56]

Five years later, on March 26, 1980, during a meeting of the Political Bureau of the Central Committee of the WPK, Kim Il Sung once again underscored the pivotal role of local industry in consumption. He emphasized that the primary focus in setting local budgets should be on increasing revenue. To achieve this, Kim Il Sung highlighted the necessity of ensuring the normal operation of "local industrial factories" to produce a diverse range of life necessities, which could then be sold to the public.

In pursuit of enhanced local budget revenue, Kim Il Sung outlined the importance of assigning clear foreign currency earning tasks to the Cabinet, empowering provinces to generate income independently. This, he believed, would enable provinces to procure their own raw materials for light industry. Notably, Kim Il Sung stressed that provinces should refrain from increasing the contributions they make to the State from their local budgets. Instead, he advocated for utilizing the earned funds to spur local economic development and improve the quality of life for the populace.[57]

In this context, Kim Il Sung perceived the advancement of local industry as a viable strategy to rectify the imbalance between "accumulation and consumption." Demonstrating a commitment to augment local autonomy, he actively supported measures to boost local industry. Provinces, in turn, responded by making sustained endeavors to develop their local industries, beginning in 1973. However, it seems that the State Planning Commission intervened in these initiatives by the provinces, as they were conducted outside the framework of the UDPS.

Kim Il Sung's response to this matter is encapsulated in his address during the Planning Sector Officials' Conference on July 10 and 11, 1974. While acknowledging significant progress in rectifying the imbalance between "accumulation and consumption" during the Six-Year Plan period, he stressed the ongoing need for sustained efforts to achieve a harmonious equilibrium between the two. Providing guidance for drafting the Second Seven-Year Plan, Kim Il Sung reiterated that, akin to the Six-Year Plan, the paramount objective was to strike a balance between "accumulation and consumption," emphasizing the importance of increasing consumption while aligning it with accumulation. He said that the principle of unified and detailed planning should also be followed in drawing up the Second Seven-Year Plan, and said the following:

> Unified planning should not stifle local creativity. We should actively encourage local creativity … Only by letting the provinces actively exercise their creativity in developing daily necessities and food production and expanding the network of convenience services can we improve people's living standards more quickly. I think our planners think too narrowly about the Unified Planning System, but giving the provinces creativity is in no way contradictory to the Unified Planning System.

> If we give direction to the provincial planning agencies to make provincial plans and then put them into the country's sole planning system, we will realize the unification of planning. Furthermore, in preparing this outlook plan, we should not make plans crudely but realize the details of the plan intelligently. To realize the plan's details thoroughly, we must know all the production reserves and potentials to put everything together in detail.[58]

As illustrated earlier, Kim Il Sung advocated for granting provinces the flexibility to exercise "creativity" in their economic activities, emphasizing that this did not contradict the Unified Planning System but should be actively encouraged. However, the nature of planning being ex ante, with the current year's plan prepared in the previous year, presented challenges in incorporating the utilization of idle materials, resources, and internal resources in the provinces.

Kim Il Sung's concept of "creativity" in the provinces emphasized their capacity to recognize and mobilize dormant resources to manufacture and distribute essential consumer goods within their respective regions. However, due to the unpredictable nature of these resources, precise planning for them proved to be challenging. For instance, it was conceivable that a county might unexpectedly come across idle resources and establish a food factory during a period already planned. Nonetheless, it was impractical to anticipate such occurrences and include them in the province's plan in advance, despite the efforts made by local planning organizations.

Moreover, this local "creativity" could not align seamlessly with the Detailed Planning System since it relied on material motivations and, as Kim Il Sung acknowledged, required encouragement as "political work" precisely because the outcomes could not be precisely determined in advance. As local governments assumed an increasingly prominent role in the economy, realizing the objectives of the UDPS became an even more intricate task.

The implementation of the Local Budget System, which enhanced local autonomy, further contributed to the divergence from the UDPS. Localities were encouraged to invest their own funds into local industrial plants to cater to local consumption demands, and these plants operated outside the established planning system, especially small- and medium-sized local plants. Consequently, as the portion of the economy operating beyond the purview of the UDPS expanded, the overall scope of the system within the economy diminished.

Just as Kim Il Sung was becoming confident that the development of local industry was resolving the chronic imbalance between "accumulation and consumption,"[59] he announced a plan for economic construction that would decisively worsen the balance between "accumulation and consumption."

1.4 Return to the Policy of Prioritizing Heavy Industry: The Ten Grand Goals of Socialist Economic Construction

In October 1980, the DPRK held its Sixth Party Congress, at which Kim Il Sung announced the Sahoejuŭigyŏngjegŏnsŏrŭi 10tacjŏnmangmokp'yo (Ten Grand Goals of Socialist Economic Construction, Ten Grand Goals) as follows.

> We must develop production in all sectors of the People's Economy at a high rate, producing 100 billion kilowatt-hours of electricity, 120 million tons of coal, 15 million tons of steel, 1.5 million tons of colored metals, 20 million tons of cement, 7 million tons of chemical fertilizers, 1.5 billion meters of cloth, 5 million tons of fishery products, 15 million tons of grain, and reclaim 300,000 square kilometers of reclaimed land in the next 10 years. These are the "Ten Grand Goals" of socialist economic construction that we must reach in the 1980s.[60]

Kim Il Sung also acknowledged that the "Ten Grand Goals" were grandiose, but in reality, they were not just grandiose objects but also impossible targets to realize. Nevertheless, talking about the Second Seven-Year Plan (1978–1984), Kim Il Sung made the following predictions about the results of the Second Seven-Year Plan.

> By 1984, electricity production will reach 56-60 billion kilowatt hours. The annual coal production during the Second Seven-Year Plan will be 70-80 million tons … Colored metals will top 1 million tons … Steel production will be 7.4 to 8 million tons … Cement production will reach 12 to 13 million tons in 1984 … Textile production should reach 800 million meters in 1984 … In 1984, we will increase the production of aquatic products to 3.5 million tons … In the second Seven-Year

period … We will seize 10 million tons of grain highlands … We will concentrate our efforts on new targets and make 100,000 hectares of a tideland reclamation project.[61]

As evident from Kim Il Sung's projections, the targets set forth in the Ten Grand Goals surpassed the sector-specific objectives of the Second Seven-Year Plan by approximately 40–50%. These ambitious goals were envisioned as future benchmarks for the socialist economic construction in the 1980s. Their attainment depended not only on the successful implementation of the Second Seven-Year Plan but also on achieving a higher growth rate during the subsequent Seven-Year period (1987–1993).

Despite continuous critiques by Kim Il Sung regarding the ineffective implementation of the UDPS, leading to exacerbated resource shortages and imbalances between "accumulation and consumption," his experience at the helm of the Kangsŏn Steel Works in December 1956 appeared to have left a lasting impression. Kim Il Sung perceived the remarkable production increase achieved during the Ch'ŏllima Movement as replicable with effective political work and, thus, conceptualized the Ten Grand Goals.

However, the complexities in the DPRK suggested otherwise. As outlined earlier, the sustained imbalance between "accumulation and consumption" had dampened workers' motivation and production levels, while internal reserves were depleting due to increased mass mobilization akin to the Ch'ŏllima Movement. In such circumstances, the primary avenue for enhancing productivity was through technological innovation.

Acknowledging the crucial role of technological innovation, the DPRK had been advocating the three revolutions of Sasang (Thought), Gisul (Technology), and Munwha (Culture) since 1970. Integrating these revolutions into the People's Regime, they argued, was an imperative step toward building a communist society. However, despite sustained efforts, significant achievements for over two decades were predominantly observed only in the realm of ideology and culture, a fact even Kim Il Sung acknowledged.[62]

The DPRK aspired to fulfill the Ten Grand Goals and fortify the foundations of its self-reliant economy, with the ultimate aim of joining the ranks of advanced nations.[63] However, a paradox emerged: the more the DPRK pursued the Ten Grand Goals without adequate technological innovation, the weaker its self-reliant economy's foundation became.

Key raw materials like coke for the metal industry and crude oil for the chemical (fertilizer) industry and transportation were entirely reliant on imports, underscoring the vulnerability of the self-reliant economy to even minor external shocks. While advanced technology could potentially substitute for coke and crude oil, the DPRK had not yet acquired such capabilities. Consequently, as the pursuit of the Ten Grand Goals intensified, the country's dependence on external markets grew, exacerbating the fragility of its self-reliant economy.

The Ten Grand Goals required the seamless integration and high interdependence of all sectors within the economy. Implementation of these goals led to a greater degree of self-sufficiency within the economic structure. Notably, the interdependence between electricity, coal, metals, railroads, and transportation sectors was set to intensify under the Ten Grand Goals.[64] When circumstances favored them, these sectors could generate a virtuous cycle of synergy and mutual enhancement. However, they could also spiral into a vicious cycle if issues within one industry propagated and amplified across other sectors, akin to a domino effect.

Despite earnest efforts to implement the Ten Grand Goals during the Second Seven-Year Plan (1978–1984), the outcome deviated from Kim Il Sung's expectations. In his 1985 New Year's address, he omitted mentioning the achievements of the Second Seven-Year Plan.[65] Instead, he briefly acknowledged progress in economic construction, highlighting the significant strides made during the 80nyŏndaesoktot (80s Speed Movement) and the agricultural sector's production of 10 million tons of grain.[66]

The plan not only fell short of its intended outcomes but also revealed the shortcomings of the UDPS, which struggled to adapt as the economy expanded without substantive progress. The situation was further compounded by the disproportionate and extensive investment in the heavy industry sector to fulfill the Ten Grand Goals, necessitating modifications for sustainable progress.

1.5 Rationalization of Planning: The Independent Accounting System and the United Enterprises System

Reflecting on the DPRK's status as a socialist society in transition, Kim Il Sung emphasized the importance of managing and operating the socialist economy within the framework of the "Tongnipch'aesanje" (Independent Accounting System, IAS). Implementing this system was considered a fundamental principle for a socialist society. Kim Il Sung proposed that the most suitable entities for implementing the IAS were the Administrative Bureau or United Enterprises, outlining the rationale as follows:

> The landscape has shifted significantly since the introduction of the new economic management system … The People's Economy thrives, teeming with factories and enterprises. Yet, ensuring a seamless flow of materials to fuel this growth presents a complex challenge. Coordinating joint production across diverse entities and ensuring timely deliveries of materials and collaborative products adds further layers of complexity … The sheer multitude of factories across the nation makes direct communication between the State Planning Commission and individual entities a monumental task, hindering accurate matching and timely delivery of materials …

Nevertheless, the socialist economic management system demands adherence to its core principles ... To navigate these complexities in material security, cooperative production, and transportation, strategic solutions are imperative. My initial considerations propose a judicious reorganization of Bureaus and United Enterprises, coupled with the implementation of an IAS within these entities. Furthermore, extending the IAS to individual factories and enterprises holds the potential to streamline operations and effectively address the challenges at hand.[67]

In essence, the UDPS was initially conceived to oversee the comprehensive coordination of the country's production, distribution, and consumption sectors. However, since the country is too large a unit, it became imperative to strategically segment and administer the scale of the plan, aiming for heightened efficiency and rationalization. The adoption of the Administrative Bureau or United Enterprise as the designated planning unit emerged as a judicious approach to implement this strategy.

This strategic division of planning units finds justification in the acknowledgment that the DPRK is currently navigating a transitional phase within its socialist societal framework. Recognizing this, the tailored approach of designating Bureaus and United Enterprises aligns with the evolving needs of a nation undergoing dynamic changes, emphasizing the adaptability required to navigate its unique socioeconomic trajectory.

Kim Il Sung's critique of the existing planning system goes beyond the need for rationalization. It points to the persistent problem of the chronic imbalance between "accumulation and consumption," which stems from the disproportionate investment in the heavy industry sector. During the Sixth Plenary Session of the Central Committee of the Workers' Party of Korea on December 10, 1984, Kim Il Sung directed his criticism at the State Planning Commission, stating:

> The People's Economic Plan for the following year, which was originally set by the State Planning Commission, was too ambitious. The original plan set by the State Planning Commission predicted that the total industrial production volume would increase to 118% the following year. However, after discussing it at the subcommittee meetings, it was lowered to 112%. However, this is not a low number at all. It would be a great achievement to increase the total industrial production volume by 12% in one year under the current conditions in which the country's economic scale has grown.[68]

Building upon Kim Il Sung's vision, the initial plan for 1985 aimed for a monumental 118% surge in total industrial production. However, recognizing the ambitiousness of this target, subcommittee discussions brought it down to a still-daunting 112%.

Even this revised figure raises eyebrows. The post–Second Seven-Year Plan, with its average annual growth target of 18%, provides context. Yet even that was deemed unrealistic, highlighting the challenges of applying a blanket percentage to the country's burgeoning economy. The adjusted 12% target, while seemingly more moderate, still faces significant hurdles.

What becomes evident from the above analysis is that the average annual industrial production rate did not reach the projected 18% during the Second Seven-Year Plan and fell even below the revised target of 12%. This underperformance suggests that the DPRK has reached a stage where further increases in productivity are unattainable without simultaneously enhancing workers' incentives. During the same meeting, Kim Il Sung stressed the pressing need for normalizing electricity production at the current stage of economic development and emphasized the importance of expanding coal production to achieve this objective. In emphasizing the interdependence of these goals, he articulated his point as follows:

> Addressing the pressing issue of enhancing the production of people's consumption goods is paramount in our current national context. The key lies in generating a substantial quantity of high-quality people's consumer goods, a measure essential for elevating the living standards of our citizens, advancing the material well-being of workers, and successfully implementing an IAS. This endeavor is intricately linked to the broader challenges of refining socialist economic management and effectively realizing the goals set forth by the IAS.
>
> The significance of amplifying the production of people's consumer goods becomes evident in its direct impact on the quality of socialist economic management and the successful execution of an IAS. For the working population, the ability to spend their hard-earned money on desired items in stores is crucial for fostering tangible material interests. The mere accumulation of wealth becomes inconsequential if individuals cannot find the necessary products in stores, rendering money as nothing more than paper.
>
> Presently, there is a scarcity of clothing and a shortage of desirable items in stores. Despite the considerable earnings of our diligent workers, the limited availability of goods diminishes the practical value of their income. It is essential to recognize that the earnest commitment and loyalty of our people to the Party often result in their silent endurance of inconveniences in their lives. To address these issues effectively, an immediate and focused effort towards bolstering the production of people's consumption goods is indispensable.[69]

What is noteworthy about Kim Il Sung's address is his recognition of the paramount importance of enhancing workers' material motivation in the current stage of the DPRK's economic construction. He identifies the IAS as a means to ensure that workers' material incentives are adequately provided for.

To enable the effective functioning of the IAS within factories and enterprises, it is imperative to boost workers' motivation. This can be achieved by compensating them for their labor in accordance with the socialist principle of distribution. Consequently, the IAS emerged as a pivotal aspect in the management of the DPRK's economy.

Furthermore, this implies the imperative that all factories and enterprises should be managed and operated in accordance with this principle. Kim Il Sung, in the subsequent discourse, underscored the necessity of addressing systemic issues contributing to unnecessary waste in people's lives. He emphasized the need to eliminate the practice of "averageism," which entails the equal distribution of resources to everyone through State supply channels.[70] Using the example of clothing, Kim Il Sung highlighted the excessive provision of free clothing by the State as a source of wastefulness. This, he contended, is not confined to the realm of apparel but extends across various sectors. He decried this as a significant issue and asserted that rectifying such practices is essential for overall societal improvement.

In pursuit of enhancing people's lives, Kim Il Sung advocated for the establishment of dedicated workplaces and work teams within factories and enterprises for essential goods. He also proposed the creation of numerous supplementary jobs and household work teams in rural areas. The objective is to augment both the variety and quantity of people's consumer goods while fostering the development of convenience service businesses. He provides specific directives in the following manner:

Initiating a movement to establish 10,000 new workplaces, workgroups, home-work groups, and side work groups would be a commendable endeavor ... Currently, the country boasts around 3,000 cooperative farms, suggesting the potential to organize one side business group per farm, totaling 3,000 such groups. Expanding on this idea, envisioning the formation of additional side business groups in county seats is plausible.

For instance, small counties might accommodate around 30 side business groups, while larger counties could support 50-60 such groups ... The envisaged scenario of having 50 side business groups in each county promises a vibrant and bustling farmers' market. Over the span of a year or two, this strategic expansion is anticipated to yield a substantial increase in local budget revenue. Consequently, such an upswing in economic activity will contribute to a substantial improvement in the people's living standards, marking a noteworthy step forward.[71]

Kim Il Sung's aforementioned remarks were not mere instructions; they were conclusions reached at a Plenary Meeting of the Party Central Committee, making them a matter of utmost importance to be implemented. Based on these conclusions, the future economic system of the DPRK was slated to transition from a centrally planned model represented by the Unified and Detailed Planning System to a United Enterprise System.[72]

Under this new system, each sector or associated enterprise would have its own internal market, with material procurement and production primarily occurring through contracts. Remuneration would be distributed based on contribution, adhering to the principles of socialist distribution. Furthermore, as the movement to increase the production of consumer goods gained momentum and spread, spearheaded by Kim Jong Il's initiative on August 3, 1984 (8·3 Movement), the farmers' market underwent a transformation beyond its original scope. It became a space where a significant portion of the people's consumption goods was exchanged.

In November 1985, approximately a year after the 10th Plenum of the 6th Central Committee of the Party, which mandated the normalization of production by effectively implementing the IAS, Kim Il Sung ordered the introduction of the "Ryŏnhapkiŏpsoch'egye" (United Enterprise System, UES)[73] throughout the industry. This decision was made during a meeting of the Political Bureau of the Central Committee of the WPK. Kim Il Sung's choice to introduce the UES aimed to ensure the proper implementation of the IAS and was informed by his own experiences.

In a discussion with the Political Bureau, Kim Il Sung reflected on his experiences during his time as Cabinet head before the 1972 "Chusŏkche" (Presidential System), an Administrative Bureau existed. It saw successful implementation of the IAS, exceeding annual planning targets. However, with the Presidential System—Kim Il Sung overseeing overall affairs, Kim Jong Il leading the Party, and a Premier for the economy—things went awry. Cabinet officials, wielding centralized control, issued a barrage of regulations and directives, stifling factory and enterprise creativity. This, according to Kim Il Sung, clashed with the "Socialist Economic Law" and hampered economic performance.[74]

However, as Kim Il Sung acknowledged, when he headed the Cabinet, the DPRK's economy was relatively small, allowing for personal leadership, administration, and supervision of the proper implementation of the IAS. In the 1980s, the DPRK's economy had grown significantly in size and complexity compared to the 1950s and 1960s. Consequently, it became impractical for an individual or a small group of officials to manage it all. A system with inherent mechanisms to reduce resource waste in production and increase workers' motivation was deemed necessary.

The United Enterprises were structured in a manner where the "Chŏngmuwŏn" (Administrative Council) assumed responsibility for administrative aspects, including the reception of macro-planning and indices. However, it was the Party Committee of the United Enterprise that played a central role in "guiding"[75] and overseeing both the parent enterprises and other entities operating within the United Enterprises. Essentially, the parent enterprise was entrusted with devising micro-planning and indices through negotiation, and subsequently implemented the moderately flexible planning process by utilizing internal markets within the United Enterprise. This arrangement aimed to effectively address the challenges posed by scale and scope inherent in the UDPS.

Moreover, the UES was instrumental in minimizing production waste and fueling the material motivation of workers. This was achieved by enabling socialist distribution among workers through the implementation of a double IAS. Under this system, all enterprises within the United Enterprise operated in accordance with the principles of socialist distribution, ensuring that workers' contributions were duly recognized and rewarded.

Approximately a year after implementing the UES, Kim Il Sung turned his attention to addressing the issue of enhancing the production motivation of workers and farmers. He emphasized that the challenge of increasing workers' motivation to produce should not be approached by simply offering them more money, as seen in other countries. Instead, he advocated for a solution that was aligned with the conditions of the DPRK. To this end, Kim Il Sung proposed the "Kyŏnggongŏp'yŏngmyŏng" (Light Industry Revolution) and the "Pongsahyŏngmyŏng" (Service Revolution) as vital avenues for boosting workers' production motivation.

Kim Il Sung believed that if stores were abundantly stocked with goods and workers could purchase whatever they needed at any time with the money they earned, their dedication to work would intensify. He argued that workers would strive to acquire additional quality products, thereby further fueling their motivation to contribute to production.

In the case of the peasants, Kim Il Sung suggested that increasing their production motivation necessitated bringing a wide range of goods to rural areas for sale. He stated, "Let us supply an ample quantity of goods to the rural shops and make them available for purchase." By doing so, he believed that the peasants would be better equipped to engage in farming and actively participate in commercial activities. Therefore, Kim Il Sung emphasized the importance of driving workers' and peasants' motivation to produce through the Light Industry Revolution and the Service Revolution.[76]

The Light Industry Revolution and the Service Revolution, initiated by Kim Il Sung during the Supreme People's Assembly, facilitated the widespread adoption of the 8·3 Movement. This movement, which had been in progress since 1984, was expanded and deepened across the entire country. Furthermore, the existing system of branch factories was strengthened and extended, reaching even the most fundamental economic and administrative units in the DPRK, namely the counties. As a result, a multitude of branch factories, workplaces engaged in the production of daily necessities, and household sideline work groups were established, collectively known as "Chibangsanŏpkongjang" (Local Industrial Plants).

It is important to note that these Local Industrial Plants were not initially organized within centrally controlled planned sectors.[77] Rather, they operated outside the bounds of the planned economy. The 8·3 Movement, operated by utilizing by-products, idle resources, and available labor, also operating independently of the central planning system.

The conclusions reached by Kim Il Sung during the Sixth Plenum of the Central Committee of the WPK on December 10, 1984, had a profound impact on the economic structure and system of the country. Several key transformations were introduced. Firstly, the previously centralized planning system was relaxed, paving the way for the implementation of the UES. Under this new system, macro-planning responsibilities were assigned to the State, while micro-planning was entrusted to United Enterprises. This division of planning authority aimed to achieve a more efficient and flexible economic framework.

Moreover, in order to boost the production motivation of workers and peasants, emphasis was placed on promoting the growth of the light industry and service industry, with a focus on increasing the production of consumer goods. As a result, a proliferation of Local Industrial Plants emerged, operating independently from centralized planning. These plants harnessed local resources, materials, and idle labor to spur economic activity.

The nationwide spread of the 8·3 Movement, originating in P'yŏngyang, played a pivotal role in this transformation. It led to the establishment of numerous small- and medium-sized light industrial factories and service enterprises throughout the country. Consequently, the proportion of the economy operating outside the planned sector expanded significantly compared to the era of the UDPS. Overall, these changes signaled a shift toward a more decentralized and dynamic economic system, with increased emphasis on local initiatives and the production of consumer goods.

Kim Il Sung consistently voiced his criticism of the members of the Chŏngmuwŏn for their role in wasteful economic construction and their contribution to the demotivation of workers and peasants; his unwavering determination to achieve the Party's economic construction goals was evident as he emphasized the need to employ any means necessary, apart from resorting to capitalist methods.[78] Furthermore, he placed great importance on securing the essential raw materials, materials, and technology required for economic construction through foreign trade.[79]

Kim Il Sung's early interest in foreign trade led to the introduction of trade at the provincial level, commencing in 1970. Each province established its own import and export companies,[80] thereby facilitating trade through the committees and departments of the Administrative Council. These entities were granted autonomy to utilize the foreign currency earned to procure necessary goods for the factories and enterprises under their management, free from interference by the Administrative Council, the State Planning Commission, or the Ministry of Trade.[81] This right to engage in trade was also extended to United Enterprises, albeit with certain limitations. These enterprises were permitted to partake in foreign trade under the supervision of the Administrative Council, with a portion of the foreign currency earned allocated for the acquisition of goods from international markets.[82]

As the DPRK fell short of satisfactory results during the Second Seven-Year Plan, Kim Il Sung introduced the UES to minimize resource waste prevalent in the UDPS.[83] Furthermore, he revitalized the light industry to significantly increase consumer goods production and bolster the production motivation of workers and peasants. The development of foreign trade was pursued to overcome the inefficiencies of a self-sufficient economy. Following the conclusion of the Second Seven-Year Plan, the DPRK had a two-year buffer period (1985–1986) before embarking on the Third Seven-Year Plan, which spanned from 1987 to 1993.

The Third Seven-Year Plan was crafted with the paramount objectives of resolutely advancing "Chuch'ehwa" (Subjectivation), "Hyŏndaehwa" (Modernization), and "Kongŏp'wa" (Industrialization) within the economy. Its overarching goal was to lay the groundwork for a robust material and technological infrastructure, paving the way for the triumphant achievement of socialism's Ten Grand Goals for economic construction, as articulated by the Sixth Party Congress.

This comprehensive plan outlined ambitious targets, including a 1.9-fold augmentation in industrial production and a more than 1.4-fold increase in agricultural output. The vision behind these targets was to propel the nation toward socio-economic prosperity, aligning with the broader objectives set forth by the political leadership.[84] Notably, Kim Il Sung identified the paramount importance of developing science and technology, fortifying the movement of technological innovation, and energetically driving the technological revitalization of the People's Economy as pivotal factors in executing the Third Seven-Year Plan.[85]

Kim Il Sung recognized a pivotal shift was needed. The prior strategy of relying on external resources—injecting materials and labor—had reached its limits for sustaining economic growth. Instead, he envisioned a bolder path: propelling economic advancement through technological innovation fueled by scientific progress. This audacious approach was conceived as a solution to the "Arduous March," the nation's most formidable economic challenge. This vision transcended Kim Il Sung's lifetime, becoming the cornerstone of Kim Jong Il's leadership and economic development strategy.

Although the targets established for the Third Seven-Year Plan were more conservative compared to those of the Second Seven-Year Plan, realizing a 1.9-fold increase in industrial production over the span of seven years would require maintaining an average annual industrial growth rate of 9.6%. The target for agricultural production also appeared exceedingly challenging, given that the DPRK had not reached the milestone of 10 million tons of grain production even by the year 1990.

However, the ambitious goal was set based on the belief that, through the full implementation of the UES in the industry, the comprehensive promotion of light industry, and the revitalization of trade in various dimensions, the inherent problems of the DPRK economy could be overcome, leading to a high level of economic growth once again.

The plans of the DPRK were dampened by the collapse of the Soviet Union during the Third Seven-Year Plan. However, what cannot be overlooked is the fact that for about a decade, the structure and system of the DPRK economy were moving away from the centrally planned economic system, as the country organized the entire industry into a system of United Enterprises and implemented policies to revitalize light industry and trade in a multifaceted manner.

Notes

1 Kim Il Sung, "Modŭn kŏsŭl chŏnhuinmin'gyŏngjebokkubalchŏnŭl wihayŏ: Chosŏllodongdang chungangwiwŏnhoe che6ch'ajŏnwŏnhoeŭiesŏ han pogo (1953nyŏn 8wŏl 5il)" (Report Delivered at the 6th Plenary Session of the Central Committee of the WPK, (August 5, 1953)), *Kimilsŏngjŏnjip 16* (*CWK16*) (P'yŏngyang: WPK Publishing House, 1997), p. 24.

2 Kim Il Sung, "3kaenyŏninmin'gyŏngjegyechoekshirhaengch'onghwarŭl charhalte taehayŏ: Chosŏnminjujuŭiinmin'gonghwagung naegang che3ch'ajŏnwŏnhoeŭiesŏ han kyŏllon (1957nyŏn 4wŏl 6il)" (Conclusions on the Successful Execution of the Three-Year Plan for the Development of the People's Economy, (April 6, 1957)), *CWK 20* (P'yŏngyang: WPK Publishing House, 1998), p. 191.

3 Kim Il Sung, "Chosŏllodongdang che4ch'adaehoesŏ han chungangwiwŏnhoe-saŏpch'onghwabogo (1961nyŏn 9wŏl 11il)" (Report on the Work of the Central Committee Delivered at the 4th Congress of the WPK, (September 11, 1961), *CWK 27* (P'yŏngyang: WPK Publishing House, 1999), pp. 334–335.

4 This series of incidents has raised concerns for the DPRK, especially with approximately 50,000 U.S. soldiers stationed in the ROK between the 38th demilitarized zone. The Korean War, having only reached a temporary armistice in 1953, remains unresolved. Notably, the conflict persists as no permanent peace agreement has been established, and nearly 30,000 U.S. soldiers continue to be stationed in the ROK.

5 Although the Parallel Route was officially adopted at the Second Party Representative Conference in October 1966, significant defense investments had been made since 1964. In his October 1963 speech at the Kim Il Sung Military College graduation ceremony, Kim Il Sung emphasized the need to boost defense spending, a sentiment reflected in the 1964 budget. He stated,

> We must thoroughly implement the Self-Defense Militarization Policy advocated by the Party. For this purpose, the entire people must be armed ... Second, we must fortify the entire country. We do not have atomic bombs, but we should be able to fight and withstand any enemies having atomic bombs ... We must dig tunnels everywhere. We must build many factories underground ....
>
> We must prepare all sectors of the economy, including the machinery and metal industries so that they can serve in the war when it breaks out ... At the same time, we must prepare reserves that can be used in case of war ... and the entire economy can be mobilized for the war.
>
> (Kim Il Sung, "Uri inmin'gundaerŭl hyŏngmyŏnggundaero mandŭlmyŏ kukpangesŏ chawiŭi pangch'imŭl kwanch'ŏrhaja (palch'wi): Kimilsŏnggunsadaehang che7kijorŏpshigesŏ han yŏnsŏl (1963nyŏn 10wŏl 5il)" (Let Us Make Our People's Army a Revolutionary Army and Adhere to the Policy of Self-Defense in National Defense (extract): Speech at the Seventh Graduation Ceremony of the Kim Il Sung Military College (October 5, 1963)), *CWK 32* (P'yŏngyang: WPK Publishing House, 2000), pp. 13–17)

6 After the First Five-Year Plan was implemented, the proportion of heavy and light industry in total industrial sector spending increased and decreased by 3% to 6%, respectively (T'aesŏp I, "Puk'anŭi chiptanjuŭijŏk palchŏnjŏllyakkwa suryŏngch'eje hwangnip" (The DPRK's Collectivist Development Strategy and the Establishment of the 'Suryŏng' System) (Sŏultaehakkyo chŏngch'ihakkwa paksanonmun, 2000 (Ph.D. dissertation, Department of Political Science, Seoul National University, 2000)), p. 202).

Considering the industrial sector comprises 60% of total spending, the additional investment in heavy industry constitutes approximately 1.8–3.6% of the overall budget. Constructing immediate-use facilities like underground shelters and military installations requires an annual allocation of 1–2% of the total budget.

Moreover, establishing a system for major ordinary heavy industry factories to produce military supplies incurs an estimated expense of at least 10–20% of total heavy industry investment. By summing up these additional costs ((1.8% to 3.6%) + (2% to 4%) + (6% to 18%)) and incorporating them into the existing Defense budget (2–3% of the total budget), it can be estimated that defense spending from 1964 to 1966 ranged from 11.8% to a maximum of 28.6%.

7 However, investment in rural areas increased after Kim Il Sung's "Rural Thesis" was announced in 1964. In 1964, rural investment was 2.32 times higher than in 1960 (Sŏngmuk O, "Nongŏm saengsallyŏge sangŭnghayŏ kwalli unyŏng sujunŭl chegohaja (Let's Improve Management and Operational Standards in Line with Agricultural Productivity)," *Kŭlloja* (1966), vol. 1, no. 1, p. 13).

8 Ch'angsŏk Kim emphatically asserts the WPK's steadfast dedication to a distinctive industrial construction policy, stating, "Our unique approach entails the concurrent development of small to medium-sized local industries alongside large-scale central industries. This policy has not only been unwaveringly championed by our Party but has also been unequivocally validated through practical implementation" (Ch'angsŏk Kim, "Tangŭi kyŏnggongŏp'yŏngmyŏngbangch'im kwanch'ŏlgwa ilgundŭrŭi kyŏngjejojiksaŏp" (The Implementation of the Party's Industrial Revolution Policy and the Economic Organizational Business of the Workers)), *Kŭlloja* (1992), no. 3, p. 48).

9 According to the *Rodong Sinmun*, the proportion of local industry in total consumer goods production increased from 13% in 1956 to 51% in 1962 (Central Statistical Bureau, DPRK, "1962nyŏn kyŏngje kyehoeng shirhaenge kwanhan chungangt'onggyegung podo" (Central Statistical Bureau Report on the Implementation of the 1962 Economic Plan), *Rodong Sinmun* (January 17, 1963).

10 T'aesŏp I, "Puk'anŭi chiptanjuŭijŏk palchŏnjŏllyakkwa suryŏngch'eje hwangnip" (The DPRK's Collectivist Development Strategy and the Establishment of the 'Suryŏng' System) (Sŏultaehakkyo chŏngch'ihakkwa paksanonmun, 2000 (Ph.D. dissertation, Department of Political Science, Seoul National University, 2000), p. 201.

11 In the exact phrasing of Kim Il Sung:

It is misguided to exclusively prioritize defense construction while neglecting economic development, under the assumption that everything will be obliterated in the event of war. Conversely, concentrating solely on economic advancement without adequately fortifying the national defense force due to a prevailing sense of peace is equally erroneous … The prevention of war is, at best, a possibility, and in the enduring presence of imperialism, an absolute guarantee of peace remains elusive. The specter of war persists, ready to materialize at any moment

(Kim Il Sung, "Hyŏnjŏngsewa uri tangŭi kwaŏp:
Chosŏllodongdangdaep'yojahoeesŏ han pogo (1966nyŏn 10wŏl 5il) (Current
Situation and the Tasks of Our Party: Report to the Congress of Delegates of the
WPK (October 5, 1966)), *CWK 37* (P'yŏngyang: WPK Publishing House,
2001), pp. 268–269)

12 In the exact words of Kim Il Sung:

There are not many good products in rural stores now, so farmers cannot buy the products they want even if they have money. How can we increase the enthusiasm for farmers' production … If there are no products in rural stores, farmers cannot use their money, so they do not try to produce more grains or sell surplus grains.

(Kim Il Sung, "Hyŏnjŏngsewa uri tangŭi kwaŏp:
Chosŏllodongdangdaep'yojahoeesŏ han pogo (1966nyŏn 10wŏl 5il)" (To Send
More Various Products to Rural Areas: A Speech at the Textile Industry Workers'
Conference (January 11, 1967)), *CWK 38* (P'yŏngyang: WPK Publishing House,
2001), pp. 58–59)

13 The subsequent narrative encapsulates Kim Il Sung's retrospective insights and identifies a looming challenge:

During the initial pursuit of heavy industry development, concomitant with the simultaneous advancement of light industry and agriculture as the fundamental tenets of our post-armistice economic construction, we faced numerous disruptive and opposing elements ....

In the years 1957 and 1958, amid the inception of the Ch'ŏllima Movement, a surge of disruptive, passive, and conservative elements surfaced within our ranks. Can it be asserted that these elements have vanished entirely from our midst today? Such an assertion eludes us.

Upon scrutinizing the plans presented by the National Planning Commission, the Metallurgical Industry Bureau, the Light Industry Bureau, and the Chemical Industry Bureau during the spring Cabinet Council meeting, it became apparent that passive elements persisted among the economic officials.

> (Kim Il Sung, "Tangmyŏnhan kyŏngjesaŏbesŏ hyŏngmyŏngjŏng taegojorŭl irŭk'imyŏ rodonghaengjŏngsaŏbŭl kaesŏn'ganghwahalte tachayŏ: Chosŏllodongdang chungangwiwŏnhoe che4ki che16ch'a chŏnwŏnhoeŭiesŏ han kyŏllon (1967nyŏn 7wŏl 3il)" (On the Revolutionary Upturn in Current Economic Projects and Strengthening and Improving Party Administration: Conclusions from the 16th Plenary Meeting of the 4th Central Committee of the WPK (July 3, 1967)), *CWK 39* (P'yŏngyang: WPK Publishing House, 2001), p. 157)

14 Kim Il Sung, "Chosŏllodongdang chungangwiwŏnhoe che4ki che11ch'ajŏnwŏn-hoeŭiesŏ han kyŏllon (1965nyŏn 7wŏl 1il)" (Conclusions at the Fourth Plenary Session of the 11th Central Committee of the WPK (July 1, 1965)), *CWK 35* (P'yŏngyang: WPK Publishing House, 2001), pp. 353–354.

15 Kim Il Sung, "Inmin'gyŏngjegyehoegŭi irwŏnhwa, sebuhwaŭi widaehan saenghwal-lyŏkŭl namgimŏpshi parhwihagi wihayŏ: Kukkagyehoegwiwŏnhoedangch'onghoeesŏ han yŏnsŏl (1965nyŏn 9wŏl 23il)" (Speech at the National Planning Commission Meeting to Fully Display the Great Vitality of the Unification and Detailed Planning of the People's Economic Plan (September 23, 1965)), *CWK 35*, pp. 437–438.

16 Kim Il Sung, "Inmin'gyŏngjegyehoegŭi irwŏnhwa, sebuhwaŭi widaehan saenghwal-lyŏkŭl namgimŏpshi parhwihagi wihayŏ: Kukkagyehoegwiwŏnhoedangch'onghoeesŏ han yŏnsŏl (1965nyŏn 9wŏl 23il)" (Speech at the National Planning Commission Meeting to Fully Display the Great Vitality of the Unification and Detailed Planning of the People's Economic Plan (September 23, 1965)), *CWK 35*, p. 450.

17 The challenge of inefficiency and subsequent wastage stemming from the Ch'ŏllima Movement reached a critical juncture that even its originator, Kim Il Sung, could not overlook. Consequently, he addressed the issue and advocated for its resolution in the following manner:

> In economic operations, the crucial imperative lies in discarding the Ch'ŏllima Movement approach and transitioning towards normalized production and construction. In the immediate aftermath of the armistice, we employed the Ch'ŏllima method for the restoration and construction of factories. Undoubtedly, this approach was deemed appropriate under the prevailing circumstances, allowing for the swift construction of numerous facilities.
>
> However, due to the hurried nature of these constructions, many areas were left incomplete. Furthermore, the 2·8 Electric Cable Factory suffered from substandard equipment, impeding our ability to normalize production. Similar deficiencies exist in various other sectors, where possession of one element is often accompanied by a lack of another, resulting in our inability to ensure proper production
>
> (Kim Il Sung, "Tangsaŏpkwa kyŏngjesaŏbesŏ nasŏnŭn myŏtkaji kwaŏbe tachayŏ: Tangjungangwiwŏnhoe pubujangisangilgundŭrap'esŏ han yŏnsŏl (1963nyŏn 1wŏl 3il)" (On Some Tasks in Party Work and Economic Work: Speech Delivered to those above the Deputy Director level of the Party Central Committee (January 3, 1963)), *CWK 30* (P'yŏngyang: WPK Publishing House, 2000), pp. 168–169)

18 An editor from *Rodong Sinmun* introduces the Ch'ongsan-ri Method as a ground-breaking approach to Party work, breaking free from the constraints of bureaucracy and formalism. This innovative method diverges from conventional top-down directives, opting instead to harness the power of mass mobilization. The editor elucidates, "This method addresses issues by delving into the grassroots, extending assistance, and comprehending their distinct realities." He emphasizes, "By empowering and organizing the masses, it guarantees the efficient implementation of Party policies," thereby underscoring the method's transformative impact" (P'yŏnjippu (Editorial Office of *Rodong Simun*), "Ch'ŏngsan-ri pangbŏbŭn sahoejuŭi kŏnsŏrŭl ch'okchinhanŭn wiryŏk'an mugiida" (Ch'ŏngsan-ri Method is a Powerful Weapon for Promoting Socialist Construction), *Kŭlloja* (1963), no. 8, pp. 10–12).

19 The outcome of these negotiations would inevitably depend on the so-called power or ability of the manager. The ability of the proprietor depended on his ability to influence the official in charge of the province or bureau to which his factory or enterprise belonged, to obtain material allocations in favor of his factory or enterprise.

20 Through this system, the factory or enterprise would receive an allocation of annual production plans and a material allocation plan accordingly, which they would use to contract with other factories or enterprises and secure materials directly.

21 Kim Il Sung championed the Taean System as a transformative force across all sectors. He described it as a "functional framework where leaders empower those at the grassroots." He emphasized the system's alignment with the "mass line," a core principle prioritizing the needs and experiences of the people. Implementing the Taean System, he declared, meant "moving away from bureaucracy" and creating a business environment rooted in the "mass line" principles (Kim Il Sung, "Tangsaŏpkwa kyŏngjesaŏbesŏ nasŏnŭn myŏtkaji kwaŏbe taehayŏ: Tangjungangwiwŏnhoe pubujangisang ilgundŭl ap'esŏ han yŏnsŏl (1963nyŏn 1wŏl 3il)" (On Some Tasks in Party Work and Economic Work: Speech Before the Vice-Chairmen and Members of the Party Central Committee (January 3, 1963)), *CWK 30*, p. 174).

22 Kim Il Sung, "Saeroun kyŏngje kwalli ch'egyerŭl naeol te taehayŏ (1961nyŏn 12wŏl 15il)" (On Coming Up with a New System of Economic Management (December 15, 1961)), *CWK 28* (P'yŏngyang: WPK Publishing House, 1999), pp. 235–236.

23 Kim Il Sung unveiled a unique planning system, presenting it as a creative adaptation of Marxist-Leninist principles to his country's specific situation. He emphasized its rejection of both rigid dogma and uncritical empiricism. "I studied the works of Marx, Engels, and Lenin, and planning systems elsewhere," he explained, "but found none that truly fit our needs. So, we developed a system based on Marxist-Leninist principles, adapted to our reality."

He further described the system as a manifestation of the Ch'ŏngsan-ri Method and the Taean System, emphasizing its core strengths: balancing centralized leadership with local initiative, and upholding the "mass line" while maintaining proletarian dictatorship. He concluded by declaring it the "most potent and effective approach" for his nation (Kim Il Sung, Speech at the National Planning Commission Meeting to Fully Display the Great Vitality of the Unification and Detailed Planning of the People's Economic Plan, (September 23, 1965), *CWK 35* pp. 451–452).

24 Kim Il Sung,Speech at the National Planning Commission Meeting to Fully Display the Great Vitality of the Unification and Detailed Planning of the People's Economic Plan (September 23, 1965), *CWK 35*, pp. 453–454.

25 Kim Il Sung, "Tangsaŏbŭl kanghwahamyŏ naraŭi sallimsarirŭl alttŭrhage kkurilte taehayŏ: Chosŏllodongdang chungangwiwŏnhoe che4ki che12ch'ajŏnwŏnhoeŭiesŏ han kyŏllon (1965nyŏn 11wŏl 15t'on17il)" (On Strengthening Our Enterprise and Thoroughly Organizing Our Country's Economy: Concluding Speech at the Fourth Plenary Meeting of the 4th Central Committee of the WPK (November 15–17, 1965), *CWK 35*, pp. 235–236.

26 This system aligns with a "command" economic model, as evidenced by Kim Il Sung's words: "Imagine the metal industry needs to produce 1,000 goods based on public needs. We turn that into a national, legally-binding obligation for them. Similarly, 500 chemicals for the chemical industry, 10,000 light industry products—all become legal mandates" (Kim Il Sung, "Inmin'gyŏngjegyehoegŭi irwŏnhwa, sebuhwaŭi widaehan saenghwallyŏkŭl namgimŏpshi parhwihagi wihayŏ (1965nyŏn 9wŏl 23il)" (To Give Full Play to the Great Living Force of Unification and Refinement of the People's Economic Plan (September 23, 1965)), *CWK 35*, pp. 457–458).

27 Kim Il Sung, "Chidoilgundŭrŭi tangsŏng, kyegŭpsŏng, inminsŏngŭl nop'imyŏ inmin'gyŏngjeŭi kwalliunyŏngsaŏbŭl kaesŏnhalte taehayŏ: Chosŏllodongdang chungangwiwŏnhoe che4ki che10ch'ajŏnwŏnhoeŭiesŏ han kyŏllon (1964nyŏn 12wŏl 19il)" (On Raising the Party, Class and People's Character of the Leaders and Improving the Work of Managing the People's Economy: Conclusions at the Tenth Plenary Session of the Fourth Central Committee of the WPK (December 19, 1964)), *CWK 33* (P'yŏngyang: WPK Publishing House, 2001), pp. 466–467.

28 Kim Il Sung, "Ch'ŏngsonyŏn'gyoyangesŏ kyoyugilgundŭrŭi immue taehayŏ: Chŏn'gukkyoyugilgunyŏlsŏngjadaehoeesŏ han yŏnsŏl (1961nyŏn 4wŏl 25il)" (On the Duty of the Educators in the Youth Education: Speech Delivered at the National Assembly of the Educators (April 25, 1961)), *CWK 27* (P'yŏngyang: WPK Publishing House, 1999)), p. 97.

29 To the extent that the phrase "One for All, and All for One" is stated in Article 49 of Chapter 4 (Basic Rights and Duties of the People) of the Socialist Constitution, as amended at the Fifth Plenary Session of the Supreme People's Assembly on December 27, 1972, it is no longer just an ideal, but a task and goal that must be realized and achieved in the DPRK.

30 In the precise words of Kim Il Sung: "The Taean System constitutes a fundamentally different and superior management system compared to the previous one, incorporating numerous elements of communist enterprise management. This innovative work system brilliantly embodies the core collectivist and communist principle of 'One for All, and All for One" (Kim Il Sung, "Taeanŭi saŏpch'egyerŭl tŏung palchŏnshik'ilte taehayŏ: Taeanjŏn'gigongjangdangwiwŏnhoe hwaktaehoeŭiesŏ han yŏnsŏl (1962nyŏn 11wŏl 9il)" (On Further Developing the Alternative Business System: Speech at the Enlarged Meeting of the Party Committee of the Taean Electric Factory (November 9, 1962)), *CWK 30*, p. 2).

31 The Party's central role in the DPRK's economy is undeniable. The National Planning Commission, under Party leadership, actively collaborates with production sites and factory committees, ensuring top-down guidance aligns with Party policies. This prevents departmentalism, prioritizing individual over collective interests, and promotes the "One for All, All for One" ethos. Party members focus on political, organizational, and propaganda work, cultivating the workforce and enforcing policies through people-centric initiatives.

Their role avoids interfering with administrative and economic matters. Understanding this dynamic is crucial when analyzing the DPRK's economic system. While they claim adherence to socialist principles, the key question lies in whether the Party's role in economic construction has evolved.

If the Party remains central, the DPRK aligns with socialist collectivism. However, any shift toward politics and economics diverging, like China, or politics subordinating to economics, like some former socialist states, would challenge this classification. This complex issue will be explored further in Chapters 2 and 3.

32 He stated, "There is no doubt that planned economy is a very difficult and complex task. Although we have been running a planned economy for almost 20 years, we still have not been doing it well" (Kim Il Sung, "Chidoilgundŭrŭi tangsŏng, kyegŭpsŏng, inminsŏngŭl nop'imyŏ inmin'gyŏngjeŭi kwalliunyŏngsaŏbŭl kaesŏnhalte taehayŏ: Chosŏllodongdang chungangwiwŏnhoe che4ki che10ch'a chŏnwŏnhoeŭiesŏ han kyŏllon (1964nyŏn 12wŏl 19il)" (On Improving the Management

and Operation of the People's Economy by Raising the Party, Class, and Popular Nature of the Leading Cadres: Conclusion of the Fourth Plenary Meeting of the Central Committee of the WPK (December 19, 1964)), *CWK 33*, p. 464.

33 Kim Il Sung, "Chidoilgundŭrŭi tangsŏng, kyegŭpsŏng, inminsŏngŭl nop'imyŏ inmin'gyŏngjeŭi kwalliunyŏngsaŏbŭl kaesŏnhalte taehayŏ: Chosŏllodongdang chungangwiwŏnhoe che4ki che10ch'a chŏnwŏnhoeŭiesŏ han kyŏllon (1964nyŏn 12wŏl 19il)" (On Improving the Management and Operation of the People's Economy by Raising the Party, Class, and Popular Nature of the Leading Cadres: Conclusion of the Fourth Plenary Meeting of the Central Committee of the WPK (December 19, 1964)), *CWK 33*, pp. 464–465.

34 Comecon, byname of Council for Mutual Economic Assistance (CMEA), also called (from 1991) Organization for International Economic Cooperation, organization established in January 1949 to facilitate and coordinate the economic development of the eastern European countries belonging to the Soviet bloc. (*Britanica*: https://www.britannica.com/topic/Comecon).

35 Phillip H. Park, *Self-Reliance or Self-Destruction?* (New York: Routledge, 2001), p. 41.

36 Kim Il Sung, "Naebuyebirŭl ch'oedaehanŭro tongwŏnhayŏ tŏ manŭn kangjaerŭl saengsanhaja: Kangsŏnjegangso chidoilgun min mobŏmnodongjadŭrŭi hyŏbŭihoeesŏ han yŏnsŏl (1956nyŏn 12wŏl28il)" (Let's Produce More Steel by Mobilizing Internal Reserves to the Maximum: Speech at a Meeting of the Leaders and Model Workers of the Kangsŏn Steel Mill (December 28, 1956)), *CWK 10*, p. 270.

37 Kim Il Sung, "Naebuyebirŭl ch'oedaehanŭro tongwŏnhayŏ tŏ manŭn kangjaerŭl saengsanhaja: Kangsŏnjegangso chidoilgun min mobŏmnodongjadŭrŭi hyŏbŭihoeesŏ han yŏnsŏl (1956nyŏn 12wŏl28il)" (Let's Produce More Steel by Mobilizing Internal Reserves to the Maximum: Speech at a Meeting of the Leaders and Model Workers of the Kangsŏn Steel Mill (December 28, 1956)), *CWK 10*, pp. 270–272.

38 Kim Il Sung. His Conclusion of the Fourth Plenary Meeting of the Central Committee of the WPK (December 19, 1964). op. cit., pp. 464–465.

39 Kim Il Sung, "Kiŏpkwallirŭl chŏnggyuhwahagi wihan kyoyuksaŏbŭl charhalte taehayŏ: Inmin'gyŏngjedaehakch'angnim 20tol kinyŏmbogohoeesŏ han yŏnsŏl (1966nyŏn 6wŏl 30il)" (On Managing a Sound Job in Educational Work to Regularize Enterprise Management: Speech at the Report on the 20th Anniversary of the Establishment of the People's University of Economics (June 30, 1966)), *CWK 37*, pp. 22–23.

40 Kim Il Sung acknowledged the need for balance in the DPRK's economy:

> We have achieved an industrial base, but our people's standard of living lags behind, and light industry trails heavy industry. Building a socialist economy requires a harmonious balance between accumulation and consumption, ensuring both the production of essential goods and consumer goods. Without this balance, expanding production and improving living standards become difficult
>
> (Kim Il Sung, "Chibanggongŏbŭl palchŏnshik'yŏ inminsobip'umsaengsanesŏ saeroun chŏnhwanŭl irŭk'ija: Chŏn'gukchibangsanŏbilgundaehoeesŏ han yŏnsŏl (1970nyŏn 2wŏl 27il)" (Let's Develop Local Industry and Create a New Transition in the Production of Consumer Goods: Speech at the Nationwide Conference of Local Industrial Workers (February 27, 1970)), *CWK 44* (P'yŏngyang: WPK Publishing House, 2002), p. 261)

41 Kim Il Sung's subsequent criticisms highlight the enduring issue that, despite the prolonged implementation of the UDPS, the planned projects are not being executed correctly:

> Our policy of centralizing and detailing plans represents a superior approach, allowing us to manage and operate a socialist economy with utmost scientific

precision and rationality. Regrettably, the proper implementation of this policy is lacking, leading to a misalignment between supply and demand in material supply plans and inducing confusion in the overall material supply process

(Kim Il Sung, "Inmin'gyŏngjeŭi kyehoekkyuryurŭl kanghwahamyŏ sahoejuŭi-gyŏngjegŏnsŏresŏ saeroun angyangŭl irŭk'ilte taehayŏ: Chosŏllodongdang chungangwiwŏnhoe che5ki che19ch'ajŏnwŏnhoeŭiesŏ han kyŏllon (1979nyŏn 12wŏl 12il)" (On strengthening the Planning Rules of the People's Economy and Creating a New Upsurge in Socialist Economic Construction: A Conclusion at the 19th Plenary Meeting of the 5th Central Committee of the WPK (December 12, 1979)), *CWK 70* (P'yŏngyang: WPK Publishing House, 2007, p. 490)

I have already emphasized the need to unify and detail the plan and to thoroughly implement it for some time now. However, the failure to precisely carry out the unification and detailing of the plan is causing significant obstacles to the planned development of the country's economy

(Kim Il Sung, "Chŏngmuwŏn ch'aegimilgundŭrŭi yŏk'arŭl nop'yŏ tangŭi kyŏngjejŏngch'aekŭl ch'ŏlchŏhi kwanch'ŏrhaja: Chosŏnminjujuŭiinmin'gonghwagung chŏngmuwŏn ch'aegimilgunhyŏbŭihoeesŏ han yŏnsŏl (1980nyŏn 3wŏl 5il)" (Let Us Raise the Role of Responsible Officials of the Central Committee and Thoroughly Implement the Party's Economic Policies: Speech at the Meeting of Responsible Officials of the Central Committee (March 5, 1980)), *CWK 71* (P'yŏngyang: WPK Publishing House, 2007), p. 76)

The gravity of subjectivism, bureaucratic formalism, and schematism issues among the members of the National Planning Commission becomes evident when scrutinizing their planning projects, which lack a solid foundation of intelligent data. Without essential data for planning, committee members tend to propose planning figures without concrete comparisons, leading to the absence of a tangible and well-grounded plan

(Kim Il Sung, "Inmin'gyŏngjegyehoek'wasaŏbŭl kaesŏn kanghwahalte taehayŏ: Chŏngmuwŏn min kukkagyehoegwiwŏnhoe ch'aegimilgundŭlgwa han tamhwa (1982nyŏn 12wŏl 2il)" (On Strengthening and Improving the Planning of the People's Economy: A Talk with Responsible Officials of the Central Committee and National Planning Commission (December 2, 1982)), *CWK 76* (P'yŏngyang: WPK Publishing House, 2008), p. 525)

42 Kim Il Sung offered a detailed insight into the operations of branch factories, citing the Sakchu Textile Factory and the Sup'ung Textile Factory as exemplary models of such branched facilities.

"Before implementing the branch factory system nationwide, the Party initiated a trial version with the Kusŏng Textile Factory as the parent facility and the Sakchu Textile Factory and the Sup'ung Textile Factory as branch factories. Through consistent efforts, engineers, and technicians from the Kusŏng Textile Factory actively engaged with the branch factories, offering solutions to challenges and providing essential technical support. Consequently, the Sakchu Textile Factory and the Sup'ung Textile Factory underwent significant transformations in a remarkably short period. Initially a modest facility, the Sakchu Textile Factory has evolved into a formidable producer of woven shoe fabrics.

Similarly, the Sup'ung Textile Factory, initially a small enterprise run by individuals who had rented a warehouse at the Sup'ung Power Plant and set up a few looms, received valuable assistance from the Kusŏng Textile Factory. Timely repairs and upgrades to equipment resulted in its transformation into a prominent facility producing high-quality cloth today" (Kim Il Sung, "7kaenyŏn'gyehoegŭi chungyo kojidŭrŭl chŏmnyŏnghagi wihayŏ ch'ŏllimaŭi kisero ch'ongdolgyŏk'aja:

Chosŏllodongdang chungangwiwŏnhoe che4ki che17ch'ajŏnwŏnhoeŭi hwaktaehoeŭiesŏ han kyŏllon (1968nyŏn 4wŏl 25il)" (Let's Make a Full-Frontal Assault
with the Momentum of the Ch'ŏllima to Capture the Important Heights of the
Seven-Year Plan: Conclusions at the Enlarged Session of the Fourth Plenum of the
17th Central Committee of the WPK (April 25, 1968)), *CWK 40* (P'yŏngyang:
WPK Publishing House, 2001), p. 303).

43 The initial reference to a branch factory surfaced in Kim Il Sung's concluding
remarks on August 8, 1962, during the Ch'angsŏng Joint Meeting of the Local
Party and Economic Workers' Group. Subsequently, the first mention of the BFS
was introduced by Kim Il Sung on April 25, 1968, during his concluding remarks
at an expanded meeting of the Fourth Plenum of the 17th Central Committee of
the WPK.

The BFS aimed to enhance consumption and production through smaller
branches, encompassing factories, worker districts in cities, and even local household workshops operated by provinces and counties as part of this nationwide initiative. Kim Il Sung underscored the imperative of enhancing the role of local
industrial management committees in regional industry, stating,

In tandem with the development of local industries, we should establish more
household work groups. It is a misconception among our cadres that goods can
only be produced by establishing factories. This notion is flawed. Simple daily
necessities and foodstuffs can also be manufactured in household work groups ...
Our focus should not solely be on constructing large factories; instead, we should
establish numerous household work groups, providing them with small materials,
including yarn, to craft various consumer goods

(Kim Il Sung, "Tangsaŏbŭl kanghwahamyŏ naraŭi sallimsarirŭl alttŭrhage
kkurilte taehayŏ: Chosŏllodongdang chungangwiwŏnhoe che4ki che12ch'ajŏnwŏnhoeŭiesŏ han kyŏllon (1965nyŏn 11wŏl 15t'on17il)" (On Strengthening Party
Work and Making the Country's Living Affordable: Conclusions at the Fourth
Plenary Session of the Twelfth Central Committee of the WPK (November 15–17,
1965)), *CWK 36* (P'yŏngyang: WPK Publishing House, 2001), pp. 119–120)

44 Established in 1952, workers districts are unique administrative units in the DPRK,
typically encompassing factories, mines, farms, and public facilities in a single community. These districts, with a minimum population of 400 adults (65% being
workers), aimed to improve labor management and efficiency.

Initially, 41 Worker Districts were established, and according to a March 2002
announcement by the ROK's Ministry of Unification, they are distributed as follows:
ten in P'yŏngyang, twenty-nine in South P'yŏngan Province, thirty-one in North
P'yŏngan Province, seventeen in Chagang Province, sixty-six in Yanggang Province,
thirty-two in South Hamgyong Province, thirty-two in North Hamgyong Province,
forty-four in Hamgyong Province, ten in South Hwanghae Province, seven in North
Hwanghae Province, and seven in Gangwon Province. In total, there are two hun-
dred fifty-five labor districts across the nation (NKChosun, *Nodongja-gu* (*Worker
District*): https://nk.chosun.com/bbs/view.html?idxno=3671&sc_category=).

45 The following statement by Kim Il Sung confirms the estimation.
"The Party Congress held in 1966, in response to the situation created, laid
down the line of moving forward in economic and national defense construction in
tandem, and accordingly, we have made a lot of additional investment in implementing the policy of Arming of the Entire People, Fortifying of the Entire Country,
Officerization of the Entire Armed Force, and Modernization of the Entire Armed
Force" (Kim Il Sung, "Chibanggongŏbŭl palchŏnshik'yŏ inminsobip'umsaengsanesŏ saeroun chŏnhwanŭl irŭk'ija: Chŏn'gukchibangsanŏbilgundaehoeesŏ han

yŏnsŏl (1970nyŏn 2wŏl 27il)" (Let's Develop Local Industry and Create a New Transition in the Production of Consumer Goods: Speech at the National Conference of Local Industry Workers (February 27, 1970)), *CWK 44*, p. 264.

46　Kim Il Sung, "Chosŏllodongdang chungangwiwŏnhoe che5ki che3ch'ajŏnwŏn-hoeŭiesŏ han kyŏllon (1971nyŏn 11wŏl 18il, 23il)" (Conclusions at the Third Plenary Session of the Fifth Central Committee of the WPK (November 18 and 23, 1971)), *CWK 47* (P'yŏngyang: WPK Publishing House, 2003), p. 456.

47　Kim Il Sung, "Techaeilbonjosŏnin'gwahakchadŭrŭn uri naraŭi kwahakkisulbal-chŏne chŏkkŭng ibajihayŏya handa: Chaeilbonjosŏnin'gwahakchadaep'yodan'gwa han tamhwa (1972nyŏn 12wŏl 16il)" (Korean Scientists in Japan Should Make Active Contributions to the Development of Science and Technology in Our Country: A Discourse with a Delegation of Korean Scientists in Japan (December 16, 1972)), *CWK 50* (P'yŏngyang: WPK Publishing House, 2003), p. 149.

48　Kim Il Sung, driven by a steadfast commitment to elevate the standard of living, pursued unprecedented measures, including the facilitation of trade at the provincial level. In his address to the National Conference of Local Industry Workers on February 27, 1970, Kim Il Sung underscored the necessity of obtaining facilities for consumer goods production or essential raw materials, even if not domestically available in the DPRK, expressing a readiness to absorb foreign currency costs.

To expedite this initiative, he proposed the direct allocation of 10% of foreign currency earnings from local industries to the trade sector, bypassing the State Planning Commission. This allocation would be earmarked for procuring vital facilities and materials for local industrial plants. Recognizing the need for efficiency, Kim Il Sung emphasized the appointment of a provincial import and export manager to streamline the process, citing the existing strain on the Ministry of Trade.

He voiced concern over the Ministry's potential arbitrary halting of orders from local industrial plants. To address these concerns, he advocated for the establishment of provincial-level trading with other countries, specifying that import and export companies in the provinces should exclusively handle consumer goods produced by provincial industrial plants, subject to approval from the Cabinet before forging international connections (Kim Il Sung. His Speech at the Nationwide Conference of Local Industrial Workers (February 27, 1970). op. cit., pp. 279–280).

49　Kim Il Sung, "Osŭt'ŭrallia chakkaimyŏ kijain wŏlp'ŭredŭ pŏch'et'ŭwa han tamhwa (1975nyŏn 10wŏl 21il)" (Discourse with Australian author and journalist Wilfred Burchett (October 21, 1975)), *CWK 58* (P'yŏngyang: WPK Publishing House, 2005), pp. 111–112.

50　Kim Il Sung. Let's Develop Local Industry and Create a New Transition in the Production of Consumer Goods: Speech at the National Conference of Local Industry Workers (February 27, 1970), *CWK 44*, p. 282.

51　Vinylon, or Vinalon, is a synthetic fiber made from polyvinyl alcohol (PVA) and formaldehyde. Developed in Japan in 1939, it wasn't until North Korea's Ri Sung-ki discovered a way to produce PVA domestically from coal and limestone that it became relevant for their economy. In 1961, North Korea built "Vinylon City" in Hamhung to mass-produce the fiber. Due to its widespread use, Vinylon became known as "Juche textile," symbolizing the country's self-reliance philosophy. While most commonly used as a textile, vinylon also has non-fibrous applications, mainly as an insulating material for electrical wires (academic-accelerator: https://academic-accelerator.com/encyclopedia/vinylon).

52　Kim Il Sung. "Ch'ongnyŏnjojikŭl tŏung kanghwahalte taehayŏ: Chaeilcho-sŏninch'uk'adan'gwa han tamhwa (1972nyŏn 6wŏl 14il) (On Further Strengthening the General Organization of the WPK: A Discourse with the Congratulatory Delegation of the Korean People of Japan (June 14, 1972)), *CWK 49* (P'yŏngyang: WPK Publishing House, 2003), p. 103.

53 Central Bureau of Statistics, DPRK, "1963nyŏn kyŏngje kyehoegŭi ihaenge kwan-han chungang t'onggyegugŭi pogo" (Report of the Central Bureau of Statistics on the Implementation of the 1963 Economic Plan), *Rodong Simun* (January 18, 1964).

54 Phillip H. Park, *Self-Reliance or Self-Destruction?* (New York: Routledge, 2001), p. 51.

55 Despite recent growth in light industry, Kim Il Sung acknowledged the ongoing challenge of balancing "accumulation and consumption":

> While advancements in light industry pave the way for increased consumption, we haven't yet achieved the ideal balance between investment and consumer goods production. Though the Six-Year Plan made significant strides, our efforts must continue to ensure seamless harmony between these two aspects
>
> (Kim Il Sung, "Che2ch'a7kaenyŏn'gyehoeng chaksŏngbanghyange taehayŏ: Kyehoekpumunilgunhyŏbŭihoeesŏ han yŏnsŏl (1974nyŏn 7wŏl 10t'on11il)" (On the Direction of the Work on the Second Seven-Year Plan: Speech at the Joint Military Council of the Planning Department (July 10–11, 1974)), *CWK 55* (P'yŏngyang: WPK Publishing House, 2004), p. 15)

56 Kim Il Sung, "Chibangyesanjerŭl tŏung palchŏnshik'ilte taehayŏ: Chosŏn-minjujuŭiinmin'gonghwagung ch'oegoinminhoeŭi che5ki che5ch'ahoeŭiesŏ han yŏnsŏl (1975nyŏn 4wŏl 8il)" (On Further Developing the Local Budget System: Speech at the Fifth Session of the Supreme People's Assembly of the DPRK (April 8, 1975)), *CWK 57* (P'yŏngyang: WPK Publishing House, 2003), pp. 3–10.

57 Kim Il Sung, "Orhae kukkayesanŭl paroseulte taehayŏ chosŏllodongdang chun-gangwiwŏnhoe chŏngch'iwiwŏnhoeesŏ han yŏnsŏl (1980nyŏn 3wŏl26il)" (On Setting the State Budget Right This Year: Speech at the Political Commission of the Central Committee of the WPK (March 26, 1980)), *CWK 71*, p. 71.

58 Kim Il Sung, "Orhae kukkayesanŭl paroseulte taehayŏ chosŏllodongdang chun-gangwiwŏnhoe chŏngch'iwiwŏnhoeesŏ han yŏnsŏl (1980nyŏn 3wŏl26il)" (On Setting the State Budget Right This Year: Speech at the Political Commission of the Central Committee of the WPK (March 26, 1980)), *CWK 71*, p. 50.

59 By 1980, Kim Il Sung expressed confidence in the growth of local industry, outlin-ing its progress in a speech to the National Conference of Local Industry Officials:

> When we began integrating large-scale central industry with local industry, it was in its infancy. Many officials saw it as a daunting task ... Through dedication and hard work, Party organizations and workers across the nation embarked on a sig-nificant expansion. Notably, Conference of Local Party and Economic Officials in August 1962 and the National Conference of Local Industrial Officials in February 1970 provided major boosts. Since then, the number of local industrial plants has nearly doubled, averaging over 18 per county ....
>
> Initially, local industry produced basic goods. Now, it offers a diverse range of daily necessities, significantly contributing to national output ... It can be deemed a miracle that we have successfully erected nearly 4,000 modern local industrial plants within a short timeframe, commencing from ground zero—where all indig-enous handicrafts were obliterated during the Japanese colonial rule and the after-math of war left everything in ruins. This achievement stands as a testament to our resilience and determination to independently secure the production of essential items for the people's sustenance, clothing, and daily living needs.
>
> (Kim Il Sung, "Chibanggongŏbŭl tŏung palchŏnshik'ija: Chŏn'gukchibangsanŏbilgundaehoeesŏ han yŏnsŏl (1980nyŏn 6wŏl 30il)" (Let's Further Develop Local Industry: Speech at the National Conference of Local Industry Workers (June 30, 1980)), *CWK 71*, pp. 379–381)

60   Kim Il Sung, "Chosŏllodongdang che6ch'adaehoeesŏ han chungangwiwŏnhoe-saŏpch'onghwabogo (1980nyŏn 10wŏl 10il)" (Report on the Generalization of the Work of the Central Committee Made at the Sixth Congress of the WPK (October 10, 1980)), *CWK 72* (P'yŏngyang: WPK Publishing House, 2007), p. 295.

61   Kim Il Sung, "Chosŏnminjujuŭiinmin'gonghwagung inmin'gyŏngje palchŏn che2ch'a7kaenyŏn   (1978–1984)   kyehoege   taehayŏ: Chosŏnminjujuŭiinmin'gonghwagung ch'oegoinminhoeŭi pŏmnyŏng ch'oegoin-minhoeŭi che6ki che1ch'ahoeŭiesŏ ch'aet'aeng (1977nyŏn 12wŏl 17il)" (On the Second Seven-Year (1978–1984) Plan for the Development of the People's Economy of the DPRK: Decree of the Supreme People's Assembly of the DPRK Adopted at the First Session of the Sixth Supreme People's Assembly (December 17, 1977)), *CWK 65* (P'yŏngyang: WPK Publishing House, 2006), pp. 423–430.

62   Kim Il Sung, "Urugwai 3wŏl26irundong taep'yodan'gwa han tamhwa (1993nyŏn 2wŏl 20il)" (Discourse with the Delegation of the March 26 Movement in Uruguay (February 20, 1993)), *CWK 93* (P'yŏngyang: WPK Publishing House, 2011), p. 48.

63   Kim Il Sung, Report on the Generalization of the Work of the Central Committee Made at the Sixth Congress of the WPK (October 10, 1980), *CWK 72*, p. 294.

64   In the intricate machinery of the DPRK economy, the electricity industry acts as the heart, pumping lifeblood to every corner. Coal, the fuel that keeps this heart beating, flows from the mines, nurtured by the mining and machinery industries that provide the muscle. This lifeblood sustains not only the electricity industry but also the metal industry, a vital cog that supplies the very rails upon which resources like coal and minerals travel back to the metal industry itself. Efficient rail transportation, the lubricant of this system, ensures smooth delivery between all, fostering the collective development of each vital organ. This interconnected dance, from the electricity that sparks everything to the coal that feeds it, and from the metal that builds to the rails that transport, demonstrates the delicate balance upon which the DPRK economy rests.

65   While Kim Il Sung claimed the Second Seven-Year Plan (1978–1984) achieved a goal of 10 million tons of grain production, evidence suggests otherwise. An analysis of his later statements contradicts this claim. For example, on May 28, 1990, during the First Plenary Session of the Ninth Workers' Party Congress, he acknowledged,

With current land resources, we can reach 10 million tons of grain if we intensify agriculture as prescribed by the Chuch'e system. This would provide food security, 3 million tons for livestock feed, and reserves. We must vigorously strive to meet this goal this year

(Kim Il Sung. "Chunganginminwiwŏnhoewa chŏngmuwŏnŭi saŏppanghyange taehayŏ chosŏnminjujuŭiinmin'gonghwagung chunganginminwiwŏnhoe cheqki che1ch'ahoeŭi, chŏngmuwŏn cheqki che1ch'a chŏnwŏnhoeŭiesŏ han yŏnsŏl (1990nyŏn 5wŏl 28il)" (Speech on the Work Direction of the Central People's Committee and the Politburo at the First Session of the Ninth Plenary Session of the Central People's Committee of the DPRK and the First Plenary Session of the Ninth Politburo (May 28, 1990), *CWK 89* (P'yŏngyang: WPK Publishing House, 2010), p. 266)

Over six years after the conclusion of the Second Seven-Year Plan, Kim Il Sung continued to advocate for the production of 10 million tons of grain, as outlined earlier. This persistent endorsement implies that the claim of attaining 10 million tons of grain production during the Second Seven-Year Plan was far from accurate.

66   Kim Il Sung, "Shinnyŏnsa (1985nyŏn 1wŏl1il)" (New Year's Address (January 1, 1985)), *CWK 81* (P'yŏngyang: WPK Publishing House, 2010), p. 7.

67   Kim Il Sung, "Tongnipch'aesanjerŭl paro shilshihanŭndesŏ nasŏnŭn myŏtkaji munjee taehayŏ: Chosŏnminjujuŭiinmin'gonghwagung chŏngmuwŏn sangmuhoeŭiesŏ han yŏnsŏl (1984nyŏn 11wŏl 13il)" (On Some Problems in the Immediate Implementation

of the IAS: Speech at the Presidium of the Politburo of the DPRK (November 13, 1984)), *CWK 80* (P'yŏngyang: WPK Publishing House, 2009), pp. 328–329.

68 Kim Il Sung, "Chosŏllodongdang chungangwiwŏnhoe che6ki che10ch'ajŏnwŏn-hoeŭiesŏ han kyŏllon (1984nyŏn 12wŏl 10il)" (Conclusions at the Tenth Plenary Session of the Sixth Central Committee of the WPK (December 10, 1984)), *CWK 80*, p. 423.

69 Kim Il Sung, "Chosŏllodongdang chungangwiwŏnhoe che6ki che10ch'ajŏnwŏn-hoeŭiesŏ han kyŏllon (1984nyŏn 12wŏl 10il)" (Conclusions at the Tenth Plenary Session of the Sixth Central Committee of the WPK (December 10, 1984)), *CWK 80*, p. 328.

70 Kim Il Sung admonished the excessive provision of free clothing by the State, identifying it as a source of wastefulness. He contended that this issue extends beyond the realm of clothing, emphasizing its broader implications as a significant problem affecting various sectors (Kim Il Sung, "Chosŏllodongdang chungangwiwŏnhoe che6ki che10ch'ajŏnwŏnhoeŭiesŏ han kyŏllon (1984nyŏn 12wŏl 10il)" (Conclusions at the Tenth Plenary Session of the Sixth Central Committee of the WPK (December 10, 1984)), *CWK 80*, p. 431).

71 Kim Il Sung, "Chosŏllodongdang chungangwiwŏnhoe che6ki che10ch'ajŏnwŏn-hoeŭiesŏ han kyŏllon (1984nyŏn 12wŏl 10il)" (Conclusions at the Tenth Plenary Session of the Sixth Central Committee of the WPK (December 10, 1984)), *CWK 80*, pp. 433–434.

72 This system operates as a conglomerate of factories and enterprises functioning collectively within a unified entity known as the United Enterprise. As described by a high-ranking Party official, the system operates under centralized planning, with each United Enterprise crafting comprehensive plans for itself and its subsidiaries. This grants them substantial autonomy in managing their operations and those of their subordinate entities. Importantly, this official emphasized that each United Enterprise holds full responsibility before the Party and the State for production, finances, and legal matters concerning itself and its subsidiaries (Chinsŏng Ch'oe, "Ryŏnhapkiŏpsoŭi ch'angsŏrŭn widaehan taeanŭi saŏpch'egeŭi yogurŭl ch'ŏlchŏhi kwanch'ŏrhagi wihan hoekkijŏng choch'i" (The Establishment of United Enterprise is a Groundbreaking Measure in Carrying Out the Demands of the Great Taean System), *Kŭlloja* (1974), no. 12, p. 39).

73 1973 saw the birth and experimentation of the United Enterprise concept. During a February 10th lecture to the industrial sector's "Three Revolutionary Teams," Kim Il Sung expressed frustration. Despite years under the Taean System, a reliable material supply system remained elusive. Factories and businesses struggled with material shortages, leading to inefficiencies and waste. To address these challenges and improve economic guidance within the Taean framework, Kim Il Sung implemented two key measures.

First, he streamlined the Administrative Council by merging and eliminating departments, creating a leaner governing body. Second, he consolidated businesses within the same sector into "Management Bureaus" or "United Enterprises." This aimed to establish a more accountable and efficient system for material distribution. These changes were designed to rectify bottlenecks and enhance overall economic performance (Kim Il Sung, "Kongŏppumunesŏ sasang, kisul, munhwaŭi 3taehyŏng-myŏngŭl himitke pŏllilte taehayŏ: Kongŏppumun3taehyŏngmyŏngsojowŏndŭrŭl wihan kangsŭbesŏ han yŏnsŏl (1973nyŏn 2wŏl 10il)" (On Vigorously Waging the Third Revolution in Thought, Technology, and Culture in the Industrial Sector: Speech at a Course for Members of the Third Revolution in the Industrial Sector (February 10, 1973)), *CWK 51* (P'yŏngyang: WPK Publishing House, 2003), pp. 41–42).

74 Kim Il Sung, "Ryŏnhapkiŏpsorŭl chojik'amyŏ chŏngmuwŏnŭi saŏm ch'egyewa pang-bŏbŭl kaesŏnhalte taehayŏ: Chosŏllodongdang chungangwiwŏnhoe chŏngch'ig-uk'oeŭiesŏ han yŏnsŏl (1985nyŏn 11wŏl 19il)" (On Organizing United Enterprises

and Improving the Business System and Methods of Administrative Council Staffs: Speech at the Political Bureau Meeting of the Central Committee of the WPK (November 19, 1985)), *CWK 82* (P'yŏngyang: WPK Publishing House, 2009), pp. 450–460.

75 Within the UES, "guiding" refers to the United Enterprise's role in formulating its own plans under the overall direction of the National Planning Commission. These plans are then distributed to affiliated factories and enterprises, with adjustments made as needed to ensure alignment with national goals. Additionally, the United Enterprise can engage in economic transactions with other entities directly, further contributing to economic activity (Ch'ŏlsik Kim, "Uri nara ryŏnhapkiŏpsonŭn sahoejuŭigiŏpsojojigŭi saeroun hyŏngt'ae" (Our "United Enterprise" is a New Form of Socialist Enterprise Organization), *Kŭlloja*, no. 2, 1985, p. 71).

This approach differed from the UDPS, which possessed a command-oriented nature, with the final decision on planning projects resting in the hands of the National Planning Commission.

76 Kim Il Sung. Conclusions at the Tenth Plenary Session of the Sixth Central Committee of the WPK (December 10, 1984), *CWK 80*, p. 431.

77 This is affirmed by the following statement from Kim Il Sung:

Historically, attempts to consolidate these factories under centralized oversight yielded less success compared to direct provincial supervision. The zenith of local industry output, witnessed during the Ch'angsŏngyŏnsŏk Conference, coincided with direct provincial involvement. However, a decline ensued with the shift to central supervision.

Reflecting on this historical perspective, it is imperative to reassess the approach by creating conditions for provinces to exert influence on local industry and nurturing regional creativity. Empowering provinces to lead local industries and fostering local ingenuity has the potential to rekindle historical peaks in output, thereby contributing to overall economic growth and national vitality.

(Kim Il Sung, "Chibanggongŏbŭl palchŏnshik'yŏ inminsobip'umsaengsanesŏ saeroun chŏnhwanŭl irŭk'ija: Chŏn'gukchibangsanŏbilgundaehoeesŏ han yŏnsŏl (1970nyŏn 2wŏl 27il)" (Let's Develop Local Industry and Create a New Transition in the Production of Consumer Goods: Speech at the National Conference of Local Industry Workers (February 27, 1970)), *CWK 44*, pp. 285–286)

78 Kim Il Sung, "Taeanŭi saŏpch'egyerŭl ch'ŏlchŏhi kwanch'ŏrhayŏ kongjanggwalliunyŏngŭl kaesŏnhaja: Chosŏllodongdang chungangwiwŏnhoe che6ki che3ch'ajŏnwŏnhoeŭiesŏ han kyŏllon (1981nyŏn 4wŏl 2il)" (Improving Factory Management Operations by Thoroughly Implementing the Taean System: Conclusions at the Third Plenary Session of the Sixth Central Committee of the WPK (April 2, 1981), *CWK 73* (P'yŏngyang: WPK Publishing House, 2007), pp. 194–195; Kim Il Sung, "Chŏngmuwŏnŭi saŏppanghyange taehayŏ: Chosŏnminjujuŭiinmin'gonghwagung chŏngmuwŏn che1ch'a chŏnwŏnhoeŭiesŏ han yŏnsŏl (1982nyŏn 4wŏl 6il)" (On the Work Direction of the Chŏngmuwŏn: Speech at the First Plenary Session of the Chŏngmuwŏn of the DPRK (April 6, 1982)), *CWK 75* (P'yŏngyang: WPK Publishing House, 2008), p. 261; Kim Il Sung's earlier speech (November 13, 1984), *CWK 82*, pp. 357–359.

79 In the precise words of Kim Il Sung:

The current landscape of our country's economic advancement, coupled with the ongoing trajectory of global economic development, underscores the pressing need for an intensified focus on the expansion of foreign trade. At present, our nation's economy stands unparalleled in its magnitude, boasting a remarkably intricate sectoral structure and reaching a pinnacle in technical equipment sophistication. Consequently, the demand for a diverse array of raw materials and resources across different sectors of the People's Economy has surged, reaching substantial volumes.

In the absence of a concerted effort to enhance foreign trade, there exists a critical risk of inadequately meeting the material and raw material requisites of the diverse sectors within the People's Economy. Recognizing this imperative, the further development of foreign trade emerges not only as a strategic necessity but as an indispensable means to effectively ensure the fulfillment of the extensive and varied material needs crucial for sustaining the robust functioning of our multifaceted economy

(Kim Il Sung, "Taeoemuyŏkŭl tagak'wa, tayanghwahalte taehan tangŭi pangch'imŭl ch'ŏlchŏhi kwanch'ŏrhaja: Muyŏkpumun ch'aegimilgundŭlgwa han tamhwa (1984nyŏn 2wŏl 13il)" (Thoroughly Implementing the Party's Policy on Diversifying and Diversifying Foreign Trade: A Discourse with the Workers in Charge of the Trade Sector (February 13, 1984)), *CWK 79* (P'yŏngyang: WPK Publishing House, 2009), p. 152

80 These import-export firms were limited to handling consumer goods exclusively from Local Industrial Plants, and any international connections required approval from the Cabinet. This arrangement is evident in the statements made by Kim Il Sung in the following speech:

I believe it's crucial for each province to appoint its own import-export commissioner to optimize the efficiency of this trade. Presently, the Ministry of Trade bears the responsibility for managing international trade, a task that proves burdensome, and it has the authority to arbitrarily suspend orders from local industrial plants. This issue could be rectified by empowering each province with its own import-export company, granting them the autonomy to engage in international trade independently

(Kim Il Sung, "Chibanggongŏbŭl palchŏnshik'yŏ inminsobip'umsaengsanesŏ saeroun chŏnhwanŭl irŭk'ija: Chŏn'gukchibangsanŏbilgundaehoeesŏ han yŏnsŏl (1970nyŏn 2wŏl 27il)" (Let's Develop Local Industry and Create a New Transition in the Production of Consumer Goods: Speech at the Nationwide Conference of Local Industrial Workers (February 27, 1970)), *CWK 44*, pp. 270–280)

81 Kim Il Sung, "Kyŏnggongŏbŭl palchŏnshik'imyŏ inminbongsasaŏbŭl kaesŏnhalte taehayŏ: Kyŏnggongŏppumun'gwa inminbongsabumun ch'aegimilgunhyŏbŭihoeesŏ han yŏnsŏl (1979nyŏn 11wŏl 3il)" (On Developing Light Industry and Improving People's Service Work: Speech to the Staffs in Charge of Light Industry and People's Service Work (November 3, 1979)), *CWK 70*, p. 397.

82 Kim Il Sung, "Kyŏnggongŏbŭl palchŏnshik'imyŏ inminbongsasaŏbŭl kaesŏnhalte taehayŏ: Kyŏnggongŏppumun'gwa inminbongsabumun ch'aegimilgunhyŏbŭihoeesŏ han yŏnsŏl (1979nyŏn 11wŏl 3il)" (On Developing Light Industry and Improving People's Service Work: Speech to the Staffs in Charge of Light Industry and People's Service Work (November 3, 1979)), *CWK 70*, pp. 480–482.

83 Kim Il Sung's implementation of the UES transcended a mere effort to address inefficiencies within the DPRK's socialist economic model. Delving into the intricacies of Kim Il Sung's address to economists regarding the UES reveals it to be a distinctively the DPRK response to the challenges posed by socialist countries contemplating the adoption of capitalist economic paradigms and transitioning from socialist to capitalist economic systems. In conveying his message to economists, Kim Il Sung articulated the following sentiments:

Several nations profess their acceptance of capitalist enterprise management practices; however, the implementation of such methods requires factories and enterprises to independently resolve all fuel and material needs for production. This poses a formidable challenge, particularly for large-scale facilities. While smaller, local industrial factories with minimal raw material requirements might find it feasible to adopt capitalist management approaches, the same cannot be easily achieved for extensive enterprises heavily reliant on resources such as iron ore, coal, and heavy oil. Not a few socialist countries are accepting market economies, but if we accept market economies, we will ruin socialist construction.

We must never accept market economies. Regardless of the economic management strategies adopted by other nations, we must prioritize propelling our United Enterprises to deliver rapid, impactful results. Simultaneously, we must enhance and refine the IAS and socialist labor compensation structure within these United Enterprises. In essence, we are urged to perpetuate the faithful implementation of the principles and methodologies of socialist economic management as articulated by our Party.

Moreover, we are called upon to continually deepen and perfect the IAS of State-owned enterprises, aligning it with the Taean System and in harmony with the Socialist Economic Law, all while remaining attuned to the evolving realities of our nation

(Kim Il Sung, "Sahoejuŭigyŏngjeŭi ponsŏnge matke kyŏngjegwallirŭl charhalte taehayŏ: Kyŏngjehakchadŭlgwa han tamhwa (1990nyŏn 4wŏl 4il)" (On Managing the Economy Well in accordance with the Nature of the Socialist Economy: A Discourse with Economists (April 4, 1990)), *CWK 89*, pp. 152–153)

Kim Il Sung's introduction of the UES was, fundamentally, a well-thought-out strategy with a dual purpose: challenging the sustainability of privately owned enterprises susceptible to unrestricted competition and potential capitalist influences infiltrating socialist nations. The UES addressed perceived shortcomings within private enterprises through two distinct approaches.

Firstly, it contested the conventional belief that individual profit is the primary driver of optimal performance, emphasizing instead the significance of collective management and cooperation. This approach aimed to enhance enterprise viability within a socially responsible framework. Secondly, the UES served as a protective measure for the socialist country against the perceived 'threat' of capitalism. By presenting a potentially superior model grounded in principles of cooperation and operational efficiency, Kim Il Sung sought to demonstrate the enduring relevance and success of socialism in the contemporary world.

84 Kim Il Sung, "Sahoejuŭiŭi wanjŏnhan sŭngnirŭl wihayŏ: Chosŏnminjujuŭiinmin'gonghwagung ch'oegoinminhoeŭi chepki che1ch'ahoeŭiesŏ han shijŏngyŏnsŏl (1986nyŏn 12wŏl 30il)" (For the Complete Victory of Socialism: Administrative Policy Speech Delivered at the First Session of the Eighth Supreme People's Assembly of the Democratic People's Republic of Korea (December 30, 1986)), *CWK 84* (P'yŏngyang: WPK Publishing House, 2009), pp. 581–582.

85 Kim Il Sung's words echoed the crucial role of accelerating scientific and technological progress in building a socialist future for the DPRK. He recognized the dire need for this development, stating that without it, fulfilling ambitious plans and elevating the economy would be impossible. He urged "great efforts" to tackle technological challenges and reach the world's scientific level, emphasizing the critical role of stronger Party and State support for research and innovation initiatives.

Furthermore, he pinpointed key industries like mechanics, microelectronics, and robotics as essential for laying the foundation of a modernized economy, ensuring smooth production of various modern elements and devices necessary for its transformation (Kim Il Sung, "Sahoejuŭiŭi wanjŏnhan sŭngnirŭl wihayŏ: Chosŏnminjujuŭiinmin'gonghwagung ch'oegoinminhoeŭi chepki che1ch'ahoeŭiesŏ han shijŏngyŏnsŏl (1986nyŏn 12wŏl 30il)" (For the Complete Victory of Socialism: Administrative Policy Speech Delivered at the First Session of the Eighth Supreme People's Assembly of the Democratic People's Republic of Korea (December 30, 1986)), *CWK 84* (P'yŏngyang: WPK Publishing House, 2009), p. 236).

Bibliography

Academic-accelerator. 'Vinylon,' accessed April 9, 2022. https://academic-accelerator. com/encyclopedia/vinylon.

Britanica. "Comecon," accessed June 25, 2018. https://www.britannica.com/topic/ Comecon.

Central Statistical Bureau, DPRK. "1962nyŏn kyŏngje kyehoeng shirhaenge kwanhan chungangt'onggyegung podo" (Report of Central Statistical Bureau on the Implementation of the 1962 Economic Plan), *Rodong Sinmun* (January 17, 1963).

Central Statistical Bureau, DPRK. "1963nyŏn kyŏngje kyehoegŭi ihaenge kwanhan chungang t'onggyegugŭi pogo" (Report of the Central Bureau of Statistics on the Implementation of the 1963 Economic Plan), *Rodong Simun* (January 18, 1964).

Ch'oe, Chinsŏng. "Ryŏnhapkiŏpsoŭi ch'angsŏrŭn widaehan taeanŭi saŏpch'egeŭi yogurŭl ch'ŏlchŏhi kwanch'ŏrhagi wihan hoekkijŏng choch'i" (The Establishment of United Enterprise is a Groundbreaking Measure in Carrying Out the Demands of the Great Taean System), *Kŭlloja* (1974), no. 12, pp. 38–39.

The Chosun Central News Agency. *Chosun Central Yearbook (CCY) 1961–1996.* P'yŏngyang: Worker's Party of Korea Publishing House, 1962–1997.

T'aesŏp, I. "Puk'anŭi chiptanjuŭijŏk palchŏnjŏllyakkwa suryŏngch'eje hwangnip" (The DPRK's Collectivist Development Strategy and the Establishment of the 'Suryŏng' System) (Sŏultaehakkyo chŏngch'ihakkwa paksanonmun, 2000), Ph.D. dissertation, Department of Political Science, Seoul National University, 2000.

Kim, Ch'angsŏk. "Tangŭi kyŏnggongŏp'yŏngmyŏngbangch'im kwanch'ŏlgwa ilgun-dŭrŭi kyŏngjejojiksaŏp" (The Implementation of the Party's Industrial Revolution Policy and the Economic Organizational Business of the Workers), *Kŭlloja* (1992), no. 3, p. 47–49.

Kim, Ch'angsŏk. "Uri nara ryŏnhapkiŏpsonŭn sahoejuŭigiŏpsojojigŭi saeroun hyŏngt'ae" (Our 'United Enterprise' is a New Form of Socialist Enterprise Organization), *Kŭlloja* (1985), no. 2, pp. 70–71.

Kim, Il Sung. "Naebuyebirŭl ch'oedaehanŭro tongwŏnhayŏ tŏ manŭn kangjaerŭl sae-ngsanhaja: Kangsŏnjegangso chidoilgun min mobŏmnodongjadŭrŭi hyŏbŭihoeesŏ han yŏnsŏl (1956nyŏn 12wŏl28il)" (Let's Produce More Steel by Mobilizing Internal Reserves to the Maximum: Speech at a Meeting of the Leaders and Model Workers of the Kangsŏn Steel Mill (December 28, 1956)), *Kimilsŏngjŏnjip 10 (CWK 10)*, P'yŏngyang: WPK Publishing House, 1994.

Kim, Il Sung. "Modŭn kŏsŭl chŏnhuinmin'gyŏngjebokkubalchŏnŭl wihayŏ: Chosŏllodongdang chungangwiwŏnhoe che4ch'ajŏnwŏnhoeŭiesŏ han pogo (1953nyŏn 8wŏl 5il)" (Report Delivered at the 6th Plenary Session of the Central Committee of the WPK, (August 5, 1953)), *CWK 16*, P'yŏngyang: WPK Publishing House, 1997.

Kim, Il Sung. "3kaenyŏninmin'gyŏngjegyehoeckshirhaengch'onghwarŭl charhalte tae-hayŏ: Chosŏnminjujuŭiinmin'gonghwagung naegang che3ch'ajŏnwŏnhoeŭiesŏ han kyŏllon (1957nyŏn 4wŏl 6il)" (Conclusions on the Successful Execution of the Three-Year Plan for the Development of the People's Economy, (April 6, 1957)), *CWK 20*, P'yŏngyang: WPK Publishing House, 1998.

Kim, Il Sung. "Chosŏllodongdang che4ch'adaehoeesŏ han chungangwiwŏnhoe-saŏpch'onghwabogo (1961nyŏn 9wŏl 11il)" (Report on the Work of the Central Committee Delivered at the 4th Congress of the WPK, (September 11, 1961), *CWK 27*, P'yŏngyang: WPK Publishing House, 1999a.

Kim, Il Sung. "Saeroun kyŏngje kwalli ch'egyerŭl naeol te taehayŏ (1961nyŏn 12wŏl 15il)" (On Coming Up with a New System of Economic Management (December 15, 1961)), *CWK 28*, P'yŏngyang: WPK Publishing House, 1999b.

Kim, Il Sung. "Tangsaŏpkwa kyŏngjesaŏbesŏ nasŏnŭn myŏtkaji kwaŏbe taehayŏ: Tangjungangwiwŏnhoe pubujangisangilgundŭrap'esŏ han yŏnsŏl (1963nyŏn 1wŏl 3il)" (On Some Tasks in Party Work and Economic Work: Speech Delivered to those above the Deputy Director level of the Party Central Committee (January 3, 1963)), *CWK 30*, P'yŏngyang: WPK Publishing House, 2000a.

Kim, Il Sung. "Uri inmin'gundaerŭl hyŏngmyŏnggundaero mandŭlmyŏ kukpangesŏ chawiŭi pangch'imŭl kwanch'ŏrhaja (palch'wi): Kimilsŏnggunsadaehang che7kijorŏpshigesŏ han yŏnsŏl (1963nyŏn 10wŏl 5il)" (Let Us Make Our People's Army a Revolutionary Army and Adhere to the Policy of Self-Defense in National Defense (extract): Speech at the Seventh Graduation Ceremony of the Kim Il Sung Military College (October 5, 1963)), *CWK 32*, P'yŏngyang: WPK Publishing House, 2000b.

Kim, Il Sung. "Chidoilgundŭrŭi tangsŏng, kyegŭpsŏng, inminsŏngŭl nop'imyŏ inmin'gyŏngjeŭi kwalliunyŏngsaŏbŭl kaesŏnhalte taehayŏ: Chosŏllodongdang chungangwiwŏnhoe che4ki che10ch'ajŏnwŏnhoeŭiesŏ han kyŏllon (1964nyŏn 12wŏl 19il)" (On Raising the Party, Class and People's Character of the Leaders and Improving the Work of Managing the People's Economy: Conclusions at the Tenth Plenary Session of the Fourth Central Committee of the WPK (December 19, 1964)), *CWK 33*, P'yŏngyang: WPK Publishing House, 2001a.

Kim, Il Sung. "Chosŏllodongdang chungangwiwŏnhoe che4ki che11ch'ajŏnwŏnhoeŭiesŏ han kyŏllon (1965nyŏn 7wŏl 1il)" (Conclusions at the Fourth Plenary Session of the 11th Central Committee of the WPK (July 1, 1965)), *CWK 35*, P'yŏngyang: WPK Publishing House, 2001b.

Kim, Il Sung. "Inmin'gyŏngjegyechoegŭi irwŏnhwa, sebuhwaŭi widaehan saenghwally-ŏkŭl namgimŏpshi parhwihagi wihayŏ: Kukkagyechoegwiwŏnhoedangch'onghoesŏ han yŏnsŏl (1965nyŏn 9wŏl 23il)" (Speech at the National Planning Commission Meeting to Fully Display the Great Vitality of the Unification and Detailed Planning of the People's Economic Plan (September 23, 1965)), *CWK 35*, n.d.-a

Kim, Il Sung. "Tangsaŏbŭl kanghwahamyŏ naraŭi sallimsarirŭl alttŭrhage kkurilte taehayŏ: Chosŏllodongdang chungangwiwŏnhoe che4ki che12ch'ajŏnwŏnhoeŭiesŏ han kyŏllon (1965nyŏn 11wŏl 15t'on17il)" (On Strengthening Our Enterprise and Thoroughly Organizing Our Country's Economy: Concluding Speech at the Fourth Plenary Meeting of the 4th Central Committee of the WPK (November 15–17, 1965), *CWK 35*, n.d.-b

Kim, Il Sung. "Tangsaŏbŭl kanghwahamyŏ naraŭi sallimsarirŭl alttŭrhage kkurilte taehayŏ: Chosŏllodongdang chungangwiwŏnhoe che4ki che12ch'ajŏnwŏnhoeŭiesŏ han kyŏllon (1965nyŏn 11wŏl 15t'on17il)" (On Strengthening Party Work and Making the Country's Living Affordable: Conclusions at the Fourth Plenary Session of the Twelfth Central Committee of the WPK (November 15–17, 1965)), *CWK 36*, P'yŏngyang: WPK Publishing House, 2001c.

Kim, Il Sung. "Hyŏnjŏngsewa uri tangŭi kwaŏp: Chosŏllodongdangdaep'yojahoesŏ han pogo (1966nyŏn 10wŏl 5il)" (Current Situation and the Tasks of Our Party: Report to the Congress of Delegates of the WPK (October 5, 1966)), *CWK 37*, P'yŏngyang: WPK Publishing House, 2001d.

Kim, Il Sung. "Hyŏnjŏngsewa uri tangŭi kwaŏp: Chosŏllodongdangdaep'yojahoesŏ han pogo (1966nyŏn 10wŏl 5il)" (To Send More Various Products to Rural Areas: A Speech at the Textile Industry Workers' Conference (January 11, 1967)), *CWK 38*, P'yŏngyang: WPK Publishing House, 2001e.

Kim, Il Sung. "Tangmyŏnhan kyŏngjesaŏbesŏ hyŏngmyŏngjŏng taegojorŭl irŭk'imyŏ rodonghaengjŏngsaŏbŭl kaesŏn'ganghwahalte taehayŏ: Chosŏllodongdang chungangwiwŏnhoe che4ki che16ch'a chŏnwŏnhoeŭiesŏ han kyŏllon (1967nyŏn 7wŏl 3il)" (On the Revolutionary Upturn in Current Economic Projects and Strengthening and Improving Party Administration: Conclusions from the 16th Plenary Meeting of the 4th Central Committee of the WPK (July 3, 1967)), *CWK 39*, P'yŏngyang: WPK Publishing House, 2001f.

Kim, Il Sung. "7kaenyŏn'gyehoeŭi chungyo kojidŭrŭl chŏmnyŏnghagi wihayŏ ch'ŏllimaŭi kisero ch'ongdolgyŏk'aja: Chosŏllodongdang chungangwiwŏnhoe che4ki che17ch'ajŏnwŏnhoeŭi hwaktaehoeŭiesŏ han kyŏllon (1968nyŏn 4wŏl 25il)" (Let's

Make a Full-Frontal Assault with the Momentum of the Ch'ŏllima to Capture the Important Heights of the Seven-Year Plan: Conclusions at the Enlarged Session of the Fourth Plenum of the 17th Central Committee of the WPK (April 25, 1968)), *CWK 40*, P'yŏngyang: WPK Publishing House, 2001g.

Kim, Il Sung. "Chibanggongŏbŭl palchŏnshik'yŏ inminsobip'umsaengsanesŏ saeroun chŏnhwanŭl irŭk'ija: Chŏn'gukchibangsanŏbilgundaehoeesŏ han yŏnsŏl (1970nyŏn 2wŏl 27il)" (Let's Develop Local Industry and Create a New Transition in the Production of Consumer Goods: Speech at the Nationwide Conference of Local Industrial Workers (February 27, 1970)), *CWK 44*, P'yŏngyang: WPK Publishing House, 2002.

Kim, Il Sung. "Chosŏllodongdang chungangwiwŏnhoe che5ki che3ch'ajŏnwŏn- hoeŭiesŏ han kyŏllon (1971nyŏn 11wŏl 18il, 23il)" (Conclusions at the Third Plenary Session of the Fifth Central Committee of the WPK (November 18 and 23, 1971)), *CWK 47*, P'yŏngyang: WPK Publishing House, 2003a.

Kim, Il Sung. "Ch'ongnyŏnjojikŭl tŏung kanghwahalte taehayŏ: Chaeilcho- sŏninch'uk'adan'gwa han tamhwa (1972nyŏn 6wŏl 14il)" (On Further Strengthening the General Organization of the WPK: A Discourse with the Congratulatory Delegation of the Korean People of Japan (June 14, 1972)), *CWK 49*, P'yŏngyang: WPK Publishing House, 2003b.

Kim, Il Sung. "Techaeilbonjosŏnin'gwahakchadŭrŭn uri naraŭi kwahakkisulbalchŏne chŏkkŭng ibajihayŏya handa: Chaeilbonjosŏnin'gwahakchadaep'yodan'gwa han tam- hwa (1972nyŏn 12wŏl 16il)" (Korean Scientists in Japan Should Make Active Contributions to the Development of Science and Technology in Our Country: A Discourse with a Delegation of Korean Scientists in Japan (December 16, 1972)), *CWK 50*, P'yŏngyang: WPK Publishing House, 2003c.

Kim, Il Sung. "Che2ch'a7kaenyŏn'gyehoeng chaksŏngbanghyange taehayŏ: Kyehoekpumunilgunhyŏbŭihoeesŏ han yŏnsŏl (1974nyŏn 7wŏl 10t'on11il)" (On the Direction of the Work on the Second Seven-Year Plan: Speech at the Joint Military Council of the Planning Department (July 10–11, 1974)), *CWK 55*, P'yŏngyang: WPK Publishing House, 2004.

Kim, Il Sung. "Chibangyesanjerŭl tŏung palchŏnshik'ilte taehayŏ: Chosŏnmin- jujuŭiinmin'gonghwagung ch'oegoinminhoeŭi che5ki che5ch'ahoeŭiesŏ han yŏnsŏl (1975nyŏn 4wŏl 8il)" (On Further Developing the Local Budget System: Speech at the Fifth Session of the Supreme People's Assembly of the DPRK (April 8, 1975)), *CWK 57*, P'yŏngyang: WPK Publishing House, 2003d.

Kim, Il Sung. "Osŭt'ŭrallia chakkaimyŏ kijain wŏlp'ŭredŭ pŏch'et'ŭwa han tamhwa (1975nyŏn 10wŏl 21il)" (Discourse with Australian author and journalist Wilfred Burchett (October 21, 1975)), *CWK 58*, P'yŏngyang: WPK Publishing House, 2005.

Kim, Il Sung. "Chosŏnminjujuŭiinmin'gonghwagung inmin'gyŏngje palchŏn che2ch'a7kaenyŏn(1978–1984)kyehoege taehayŏ: Chosŏnminjujuŭiinmin'gong- hwagungch'oegoinminhoeŭipŏmnyŏngch'oegoinminhoeŭiche6kiche1ch'ahoeŭiesŏ ch'aet'aeng (1977nyŏn 12wŏl 17il)" (On the Second Seven-Year (1978–1984) Plan for the Development of the People's Economy of the DPRK: Decree of the Supreme People's Assembly of the DPRK Adopted at the First Session of the Sixth Supreme People's Assembly (December 17, 1977)), *CWK 65*, P'yŏngyang: WPK Publishing House, 2006.

Kim, Il Sung. "Chŏngmuwŏn ch'aegimilgundŭrŭi yŏk'arŭl nop'yŏ tangŭi kyŏngje- jŏngch'aekŭl ch'ŏlchŏhi kwanch'ŏrhaja: Chosŏnminjujuŭiinmin'gonghwagung chŏngmuwŏn ch'aegimilgunhyŏbŭihoeesŏ han yŏnsŏl (1980nyŏn 3wŏl 5il)" (Let Us Raise the Role of Responsible Officials of the Central Committee and Thoroughly Implement the Party's Economic Policies: Speech at the Meeting of Responsible Officials of the Central Committee (March 5, 1980)), *CWK 71*, P'yŏngyang: WPK Publishing House, 2007.

Kim, Il Sung. "Orhae kukkayesanŭl paroseulte taehayŏ chosŏllodongdang chungang-wiwŏnhoe chŏngch'iwiwŏnhoeesŏ han yŏnsŏl (1980nyŏn 3wŏl26il)" (On Setting the State Budget Right This Year: Speech at the Political Commission of the Central Committee of the WPK (March 26, 1980)), *CWK 71*, n.d.-c

Kim, Il Sung. "Inmin'gyŏngjegyehoek'wasaŏbŭl kaesŏn kanghwahalte taehayŏ: Chŏngmuwŏn min kukkagyehoegwiwŏnhoe ch'aegimilgundŭlgwa han tamhwa (1982nyŏn 12wŏl 2il)" (On Strengthening and Improving the Planning of the People's Economy: A Talk with Responsible Officials of the Central Committee and National Planning Commission (December 2, 1982)), *CWK 76*, P'yŏngyang: WPK Publishing House, 2008.

Kim, Il Sung. "Tongnipch'aesanjerŭl paro shilshihanŭndesŏ nasŏnŭn myŏtkaji munjee taehayŏ: Chosŏnminjujuŭiinmin'gonghwagung chŏngmuwŏn sangmuhoeŭiesŏ han yŏnsŏl (1984nyŏn 11wŏl 13il)" (On Some Problems in the Immediate Implementation of the IAS: Speech at the Presidium of the Politburo of the DPRK (November 13, 1984)), *CWK 80*, P'yŏngyang: WPK Publishing House, 2009a.

Kim, Il Sung. "Chosŏllodongdang chungangwiwŏnhoe che6ki che10ch'ajŏnwŏn-hoeŭiesŏ han kyŏllon (1984nyŏn 12wŏl 10il)" (Conclusions at the Tenth Plenary Session of the Sixth Central Committee of the WPK (December 10, 1984)), *CWK 80*, n.d.-d

Kim, Il Sung. "Shinnyŏnsa (1985nyŏn 1wŏl1il)" (New Year's Address (January 1, 1985)), *CWK 81*, P'yŏngyang: WPK Publishing House, 2010a.

Kim, Il Sung. "Sahoejuŭiŭi wanjŏnhan sŭngnirŭl wihayŏ: Chosŏnmin-jujuŭiinmin'gonghwagung ch'oegoinminhoeŭi chepki che1ch'ahoeŭiesŏ han shi-jŏngyŏnsŏl (1986nyŏn 12wŏl 30il)" (For the Complete Victory of Socialism: Administrative Policy Speech Delivered at the First Session of the Eighth Supreme People's Assembly of the Democratic People's Republic of Korea (December 30, 1986)), *CWK 84*, P'yŏngyang: WPK Publishing House, 2009b.

Kim, Il Sung. "Chunganginminwiwŏnhoewa chŏngmuwŏnŭi saŏppanghyange tae-hayŏ chosŏnminjujuŭiinmin'gonghwagung chunganginminwiwŏnhoe cheqki che1ch'ahoeŭi, chŏngmuwŏn cheqki che1ch'a chŏnwŏnhoeŭiesŏ han yŏnsŏl (1990nyŏn 5wŏl 28il)" (Speech on the Work Direction of the Central People's Committee and the Politburo at the First Session of the Ninth Plenary Session of the Central People's Committee of the DPRK and the First Plenary Session of the Ninth Politburo (May 28, 1990)), *CWK 89*, P'yŏngyang: WPK Publishing House, 2010b.

Kim, Il Sung. "Sahoejuŭigyŏngjeŭi ponsŏnge matke kyŏngjegwallirŭl charhalte tae-hayŏ: Kyŏngjehakchadŭlgwa han tamhwa (1990nyŏn 4wŏl 4il)" (On Managing the Economy Well in accordance with the Nature of the Socialist Economy: A Discourse with Economists (April 4, 1990)), *CWK 89*, n.d.-e

Sŏngmuk, O. "Nongŏm saengsallyŏge sangŭnghayŏ kwalli unyŏng sujunŭl chegohaja" (Let's Improve Management and Operational Standards in Line with Agricultural Productivity)," *Kŭlloja* (1966), vol. 1, no. 1, pp. 13–15.

Park, Phillip H. *Self-Reliance or Self-Destruction?: Success and Failure of the Democratic People's Republic of Korea's Development Strategy of Self-reliance 'Juche'*, New York: Routledge, 2001.

P'yŏnjippu (Editorial Office of *Rodong Simun*). "Ch'ŏngsan-ri pangbŏbŭn sahoejuŭi kŏnsŏrŭl ch'okchinhanŭn wiryŏk'an mugiida" (Ch'ŏngsan-ri Method is a Powerful Weapon for Promoting Socialist Construction), *Kŭlloja* (1963), no. 8, pp. 10–13.

2 Military-First Politics, CNC, and the Pursuit of Maximum Practical Benefits While Adhering to Socialist Principles Route

2.1 The Arduous March and Military-First Politics

At the 21st Plenum of the 6th Party Central Committee in 1993, the DPRK adopted a new economic construction strategy for the period until 1996. This strategy included a three-year buffer period, during which the country would "Nongŏpcheilchuŭi, Kyŏnggongŏpcheilchuŭi, Muyŏkcheilchuŭi pangch'imŭl ch'ŏlchŏhi kwanch'ŏl (Strictly Adhere to the Policy of Agriculture First, Light Industry First, and Trade First, also known as Three Sectors First Policy)." It aimed to develop and revitalize agriculture, light industry, and trade, which had already been implemented since the mid-1980s. The formalization of the "Three Sectors First Policy" was a response to the collapse of the Soviet Union and the Eastern Bloc socialist economies, with the goal of securing national survival while incorporating elements from the Third Seven-Year Plan.

The economic crisis in the DPRK emerged in the mid-1990s, and Kim Jong Il provided an explanation for its onset. He attributed the country's economic difficulties to "the imperialists' economic blockade and isolationist aggression against the DPRK. Additionally, the collapse of the world socialist market and the breakdown of economic cooperation with former socialist countries, along with ongoing natural disasters, worsened the economic conditions and people's livelihoods."[1]

It is important to note that U.S. economic sanctions against the DPRK have been in place since January 1949. Accordingly, these sanctions cannot be considered a direct cause of the hardships faced by the country. Similarly, while natural disasters like floods and cold-weather damages in the mid-1990s contributed to the economic crisis, they were secondary factors that exacerbated and deepened the existing challenges.[2]

The economic crisis in the DPRK can be primarily ascribed to the demise of the Soviet Union and the subsequent collapse of socialist markets. Despite the DPRK's efforts to establish a self-reliant economy driven by its own initiatives, it proved challenging to create a fully autonomous system capable of independently addressing all economic challenges. The nation encountered constraints, particularly in securing vital raw materials like coke and crude oil, which were not abundantly available from its domestic resources.

DOI: 10.4324/9781003481737-3

Furthermore, the prioritization of heavy industry in the DPRK's economic development led to a loss of comparative advantage for the raw materials and materials required for light industry production. Producing these materials domestically proved to be expensive, necessitating their importation through the market of socialist countries. However, with the downfall of the Soviet Union, a leading Socialist State and the DPRK's primary trading partner, and the subsequent market collapse in the Eastern Bloc socialist countries, the DPRK confronted an unprecedented economic crisis.

It is worth noting that while the DPRK pursued self-reliance, it was heavily reliant on external factors for certain critical resources and markets. The sudden disruption and loss of these external sources significantly contributed to the severity of the economic crisis faced by the country.

As illustrated in Table 2.1, the import figures for coke and crude oil in the DPRK exhibit a notable downturn starting in 1992 for coke and 1993 for crude oil. The substantial decrease in coke imports, crucial for the advancement of the metal industry, became particularly evident in 1992. Import levels plummeted to 425,000 tons in 1996, a mere one-third of the preceding year's quantity, and further declined to 270,000 tons in 1998, signaling a significant disruption in the regular operations of the metal industry since 1996. Crude oil imports followed a parallel trajectory, dwindling to half the average of the previous nine years from 1997 onward.

Given that naphtha, an essential byproduct of crude oil, serves as a critical raw material for urea production, which is in turn pivotal for the manufacturing of nitrogenous fertilizers, it can be asserted that the onset of severe food shortages occurred in 1995, the year following the sharp decline in crude oil imports in 1994.[3]

Chapter 1 highlighted the DPRK's struggles to secure external aid, especially from the Soviet Union, a crucial donor after the Korean War. This lack of assistance hampered the country's efforts to establish a self-reliant economy. Ironically, the DPRK's resulting economic structure, designed for self-sufficiency and minimal external dependence, became a double-edged sword. While achieving a degree of self-reliance, this very structure exacerbated the country's economic difficulties.

The intricacies of this self-reliant economic framework became apparent as various sectors became tightly interconnected. For instance, the extractive industry formed the foundation of the coal industry, the coal industry supported the chemical industry, and the chemical industry played a pivotal role in food production. Within this interconnected system, issues in one sector triggered a chain reaction, permeating throughout the entire economy. Problems in the extractive industry, for example, would cascade into the coal industry, affecting the chemical industry and, consequently, disrupting food production. This interdependence created a destructive cycle, amplifying the magnitude of the challenges faced by the country.

Moreover, for over a decade, the DPRK has pursued the ambitious objective of achieving substantial economic growth through the Ten Grand Goals.

Table 2.1 The DPRK's Import of Coke and Crude Oil (1988–1998)

Year	1988	1989	1990	1991	1992	1993	1994	1995	1996	1997	1998
Coke	194.2 (297.9)	168.9 (262.8)	182.0 (264.7)	204.7 (223.1)	149.3	175	160	120.2	42.5	31.7	27.0
Crude Oil	120.2 (184.2)	107.3 (201.2)	106.2 (147.2)	110.2 (152.2)	107.6 (126.6)	103.3	83.3	102.1	93.6	50.6	61.4

Source: author.

Unit: 10,000 ton.

Table 2.1 is compiled from the UN Comtrade Database, which does not encompass exports of coke and crude oil from the Soviet Union to the DPRK before the Soviet Union's collapse. Only in 2002 did the Russian Federation, the successor to the Soviet Union, resume exporting these commodities to the DPRK. Notably, JETRO (Japan External Trade Organization) possesses data on coke and crude oil exports from the Soviet Union to the DPRK for the years 1988 to 1991, a dataset absent in the UN Comtrade Database. Consequently, to derive the comprehensive amount of coke and crude oil exported to the DPRK during the specified period, it is imperative to augment the UN Comtrade Database with the relevant JETRO data, as indicated in the parentheses of Table 2.1.

This endeavor has primarily relied on the approach of extensive source of growth, which emphasizes augmenting production factors, namely labor and capital, rather than the intensive source of growth method, which prioritizes technological advancement. The excessive infusion of production factors has disrupted the delicate equilibrium between "accumulation and consumption" within the economy. Consequently, when the crisis struck, the impact and ramifications were bound to be magnified, intensifying the ensuing damage.

Understanding the economic impact on the DPRK requires close examination of its annual budgetary revenue, presented in *CCY*. This revenue acts as a snapshot of the country's financial inflows and comprises several key components. Among these, Kŏraesuipkŭm (State Transaction Revenue) and Kukkagiŏmniikkŭm (State Enterprise Profit Revenue) hold particular significance.

State Transaction Revenue arises from State-owned enterprises and production cooperatives that sell consumer goods. These entities add a fixed percentage to the original product price, passed on to consumers. In contrast, State Enterprise Profit Revenue represents a portion of an enterprise's net income, earned through business activities, that is mandatorily paid to the State.

Crucially, the combined sum of these two revenue sources directly mirrors the DPRK's national income. Since all enterprises in the country are State-controlled, analyzing this combined budget income serves as a critical gauge of overall economic health. Therefore, assessing the national budget becomes an indispensable tool for understanding the current state and potential trajectory of the DPRK's economy.

During a four-year span from 1994 to 1997, the DPRK refrained from disclosing its national budget revenues. However, in 1998, the country once again announced a total national budget revenue of 19.790 billion wŏn, which amounted to a mere 48.8% of the 1993 figure of 40.5712 billion wŏn. The 1999 edition of the *CCY* elaborates, "Although the scale of budgetary revenues and expenditures in 1998 has not yet reached the level of the early 1990s, budgetary revenues have increased by 100.4 percent compared to 1997."

It further emphasizes that "the achievement of a large increase in State budgetary revenues in 1998, which put the country's finances on a forward path, is an important achievement in the struggle to implement the national budget and victoriously unite the socialist forces."[4] These accounts suggest a significant decline in national budgetary revenues from 1994 to 1997. As a consequence, the total amount of national budget revenues in 1994 was likely less than half of the 1993 value, signifying a pronounced economic downturn in that year.[5]

The DPRK channels these revenues into various sectors of its economy, including coal, electricity, metals, and chemical industries, collectively known as the People's Economy. Additionally, a portion of the funds is allocated to social and cultural expenditures, with the aim of improving the well-being of the population. However, when national budget revenues decline, the capacity for investment diminishes accordingly. This reduction in investment disproportionately affects sectors that receive inadequate funding, resulting in a significant decrease in the DPRK's national income. Consequently, it is highly probable that the country's GDP[6] has plummeted by more than 50% since 1994 compared to 1993. Such an economic shock is a rare event in the annals of 20th-century history.

Prior to his passing, Kim Il Sung had put forth a new strategy for economic development, centered around three key sectors: agriculture, light industry, and trade. Of these sectors, special attention was given to trade. During the Twenty-first Plenary Session of the Sixth Central Committee of the Party, Kim Il Sung expressed regret that the DPRK was unable to sell its magnesium clinker blast furnace, a product that held a monopolistic position in the socialist market. The reason behind this failure lay in the insufficient operation of the Sŭngni Chemical United Enterprise due to the sharp decline in crude oil imports from the Soviet Union. Recognizing the disappearance of the socialist market, Kim Il Sung stressed the necessity of redirecting foreign trade to sell DPRK goods to other nations while procuring essential goods required for economic development.[7]

In the final meeting with the Committee responsible for the economic sector, which marked the last official gathering of Kim Il Sung's life, he emphasized the imperative of thoroughly implementing the Party's Revolutionary Economic Strategy to establish a new foundation for the construction of a socialist economy. He identified several challenges that needed to be addressed, seeking their resolution within this strategic framework.

> Foremost, we urgently need to address the power shortage issue ... To solve the power problem, constructing a heavy oil power plant is imperative ... Next, emphasis must be placed on revitalizing the chemical industry, ensuring the regular production of chemical fertilizers and vinylon. Adequate production and distribution of chemical fertilizers in the countryside are pivotal for addressing food shortages, aligning with the Party's agricultural policy. Establishing a robust farming system to solve the people's food problems necessitates a substantial output of chemical fertilizers ... Securing the production of stainless steel, essential for maintaining fertilizer plants, is crucial. Even if it requires foreign currency, we must guarantee its procurement.

> Additionally, normalizing cement production holds significance, **as surplus cement production can contribute to foreign currency earnings** (emphasis added) and drive construction projects forward ... Moving the People's Economy forward mandates the development of the metal industry and a substantial increase in steel production. Given steel's ubiquitous use across all economic sectors, its production is integral to progress. To optimize the performance of metal factories, we must address the coke problem strategically. Diversifying sources is imperative; reliance on a single country for coke is unsustainable. Exploring procurement options from various nations, such as Russia or Australia, ensures a more resilient supply chain for the steel industry's coke requirements.[8]

Ultimately, Kim Il Sung arrived at the conclusion that trade, particularly imports, should be utilized to develop the essential electric power, chemical, and metal industries, as well as to normalize cement production and increase foreign currency earnings through exports.

Under the monolithic leadership, Kim Il Sung's instructions transformed into immediate policies for implementation. His directives to normalize production in key sectors such as electric power, chemical, cement, and metal industries through trade were of utmost importance prior to his passing. Consequently, both the Party and all economic sectors shifted their focus toward trade.[9] However, faced with the collapse of the socialist economy and the ongoing blockade by the United States, expanding and facilitating external economic activities proved to be a challenging endeavor.

Furthermore, as the country emphasized trade, a socially recognized value emerged wherein individuals or units that generated the most money gained prominence. This propagated the prevalent practice of "mammonism," characterized by the pursuit of profit-driven activities. Kim Jong Il's quote sheds light on the prevailing reality within the DPRK during that period:

> Presently, certain units are suggesting the use of foreign currency earned within their units for personal purchases, reflecting a bias stemming from a lack of a proper understanding of socialist foreign trade principles ... Engaging in independent decisions regarding the export and import of goods reflects a capitalist trade methodology, contrary to the principles of socialist economic systems ...

> Some university graduates are expressing a preference for roles in the trade or joint venture sectors rather than pursuing careers in their respective majors. This shift indicates a prioritization of personal well-being over the commitment to serve the Party and the nation that has provided for their sustenance, clothing, and education. This ideological inclination poses a significant and potentially hazardous challenge that warrants careful consideration and corrective measures.[10]

Following Kim Il Sung's demise, the situation in the DPRK became increasingly serious and precarious, with internal turmoil shaking the system. After the failure of successive economic construction plans from the Second Seven-Year Plan to the Third Seven-Year Plan, beginning in the mid-1980s, the UDPS was gradually relaxed.

The full-fledged implementation of the IAS led to the establishment of United Enterprises, while various production organizations were encouraged across different regions and units to boost consumer goods production. Consequently, the unplanned sector's share in the overall economy experienced a significant increase. With each unit engaging in trade without central authorization, the Party's economic control weakened. Units within the economic sector became driven by their own institutional self-interest, pursuing their respective agendas.

Additionally, due to food shortages and inadequate distribution, people resorted to wandering in search of sustenance, leading to the rapid spread of spontaneous markets known as Changmadang.[11] These markets allowed people to exchange goods they had in relative abundance for survival.[12] Compounding the situation, Party cadres also joined this trend, exploiting their positions and authority to directly intervene in economic affairs. This phenomenon manifested as a widespread occurrence of "Party organizations and Party cadres taking over or hijacking administrative and economic projects." Kim Jong Il criticized this behavior, remarking:

> Certain Party organizations and cadres are presently involved in administrative and economic tasks without giving due consideration to internal Party affairs. In the preceding year, the Party deployed numerous cadres to pivotal economic sectors, such as coal and chemical industries. Unfortunately, they exhibited minimal interest or neglected internal Party responsibilities, concentrating solely on economic administration. This diversion of focus towards economic tasks weakens the emphasis on internal Party work. As Party cadres immerse themselves in addressing issues within economic spheres, gaps in Party operations emerge, posing a potential threat to the Party in the long run.[13]

Kim Jong Il perceived this behavior as a grave threat to the Party and an exceedingly precarious situation that could potentially lead to the collapse of the system, mirroring events in other socialist countries. He attributed the downfall of the Soviet Union and the socialist countries of the Eastern Bloc to their excessive emphasis on material and economic conditions, neglecting the vital task of reforming the ideological outlook of the masses. According to Kim Jong Il, they failed to bolster the revolutionary subject and enhance its role, ultimately overlooking the crucial role of thought in socialist construction.

In contrast, Kim Jong Il stressed the foundational role of ideological and political work in socialist development. He argued that educating the masses, nurturing their revolutionary enthusiasm, and encouraging their creative activism should constitute the fundamental framework for progress. With this perspective, he affirmed his commitment to overcoming the challenges faced by the DPRK by placing a strong emphasis on ideological and political work.[14]

However, as previously discussed, the Party itself became deeply entrenched in economic matters. The widespread phenomenon of the Party "taking over or substituting administrative and economic projects" prompted Kim Jong Il to identify an alternative organization capable of implementing his directives. This organization emerged as the military.

The collapse of the Soviet Union and the Eastern Bloc socialist states, along with the disintegration of the socialist economic bloc, created a national crisis. In response, Kim Jong Il, as the supreme leader, prioritized the building and strengthening of the military to safeguard the system .

He expressed his intention to overcome the country's crisis through ideological reform and political work, with ideology representing collectivism and ideological reform involving the unification of all people around the supreme leader through organizations dedicated to upholding and actualizing his ideology of collectivism. Political work entailed direct engagement and dialogue with the people, providing guidance, and instigating their adherence to Party decisions. It aimed to help individuals discover their abilities and employ them to the fullest for the collective good. The Party organizations were supposedly responsible for this task, but due to their ideological instability, Kim Jong Il assigned it to another organization. He chose the military, where these principles were deeply ingrained and reinforced by his special attention.[15]

2.2 Revolutionary Soldier Spirit and Kanggye Spirit

In the wake of Kim Il Sung's demise and the onset of the economic hardship known as the "Arduous March," Kim Jong Il directed a significant portion of his time and efforts toward providing field guidance to the military.[16] However, his involvement with the Armed Forces transcended mere caretaking. In the aftermath of the two failed Seven-Year Plans and the subsequent implementation of policies that expanded the market's role in the economy, matters of "Thought" and "Politics" were relegated to the periphery of society. The collapse of the Soviet Union and the socialist economic system further intensified the pressure for "Reform" and "Opening-up," causing even the ideological foundations of the Party organization to waver.

Amid these circumstances, Kim Jong Il sought to restore prominence to "Thought" and "Politics" by harnessing the Armed Forces, a concept referred to as "Military-First Politics."[17] Thus, it is essential to perceive Kim Jong Il's field guidance of the Armed Forces as an endeavor that surpasses the mere care and upkeep of military affairs. It aimed to establish an exemplar of conducting business with ideology and politics at the forefront, allowing society as a whole to derive valuable lessons and engender a system where ideology and politics regain their commanding position.

Within the sphere of his field guidance, Kim Jong Il accentuated the imperative of securing the primacy of ideas within economic activities, particularly in the realm of sustenance. In essence, economic pursuits ought to be anchored in the principles of Chuch'e ideology. This, in turn, entails the pursuit of economic self-reliance, wherein the nation endeavors to resolve its food and livelihood predicaments autonomously.

The concept of economic self-reliance had already taken root three decades earlier. However, in the aftermath of the economic hardships endured during the Arduous March, the nation's income plummeted to less than half its former glory, while the PDS struggled to meet the needs of the populace. Faced with the grim reality of survival, people, especially ones in the remote areas, resorted to wandering in search of sustenance, relying on the emergent market as they exchanged goods with others who possessed relatively more.

Given these dire circumstances, the notion of self-reliance in economic affairs seemed untenable to the people. To compound matters, the Party itself was experiencing a crisis, with a considerable faction within the central Party clamoring for "Reform" and "Opening-up," inspired by the examples set by the Soviet Union, Eastern Bloc socialist nations, and China.

In response to these deliberations, Kim Jong Il voiced his resolute opposition, asserting,

> Certain Party members are now engaging in economic discussions outside the purview of Party leadership, and this must not be permitted. It is an unwavering tenet of our Party that it assumes responsibility for all economic matters and the welfare of the people.[18]

Kim Jong Il made it abundantly clear that he adamantly rejected the notion of severing the intertwining threads of economics and politics. Additionally, there were suggestions to adopt the Chinese model, which advocated dismantling the People's Commune System in agriculture, replacing it with the Household Responsibility System, and incrementally implementing reforms in the industrial and service sectors. In response, Kim Jong Il heightened his vigilance and articulated the following words:

> I will staunchly resist the notions of "Kaehyŏk" (Reform) or "Kaebang" (Opening-up) for as long as I live. This is my unwavering commitment. Even when exploring strategies to address economic challenges, we must steadfastly adhere to socialist principles ... The endeavor of socialist construction demands the application of socialist methods grounded in collectivism.

> The development of socialist rural construction is inconceivable without maintaining fidelity to socialist principles ... In the ongoing struggle to eradicate capitalist ideas and exoticism, the focus must be on the cadre. It is the cadre who requires our attention. Party organizations must intensify their efforts with the cadres, fostering their awakening and bringing them to a heightened awareness of their responsibilities.[19]

In accordance with his directives, Kim Jong Il placed great emphasis on organizing the Armed Forces' material provisions, including food, as a means of fostering self-reliance. Naturally, such self-reliance could not be achieved at the platoon or company level but rather at the battalion level and above, contingent upon favorable locations for food production and supply procurement.

Nevertheless, regardless of unit size or geographic placement, Kim Jong Il mandated that all levels of the Armed Forces take responsibility for resolving their own economic challenges. While it was unrealistic to expect every unit to independently meet their main provisioning needs as instructed by Kim Jong Il, what truly mattered was the willingness and diligence exhibited in adhering to his guidance and striving to make it a reality.

Unwaveringly adhering to and executing Kim Jong Il's instructions and orders epitomized the "Hyŏngmyŏngjŏkkuninjŏngshin" (Spirit of the Revolutionary Soldier). To Kim Jong Il, the Armed Forces stood as the vanguard in confronting the myriad challenges faced by the nation, embodying the essence of Chosun (DPRK)-style collectivism by devoting their all to the supreme leader.

For Kim Jong Il, surmounting the crisis without this organizational foundation was simply inconceivable. Given that the guiding principle was to approach all endeavors, not solely economic construction, through the lens of unity centered around the supreme leader, the indomitable Spirit of the Revolutionary Soldier[20] emerged as a decisive factor in overcoming the most formidable crisis the country had encountered since its inception.

Kim Jong Il's vision extended beyond mere calls for a Revolutionary Soldier Spirit. In the face of the arduous and grueling Arduous March, he personally embarked on frontline inspections, ensuring that the army upheld its paramount role as a bastion of the revolution and the primary force driving it forward. Kim Jong Il took it upon himself to cultivate the commanders of divisions, regiments, and battalions within the DPRK Army, aiming to imbue the entire Armed Forces with the unwavering spirit of the "Revolutionary Soldier."[21] His objective was to form a core group of individuals who would wholeheartedly follow and support him, subsequently assuming leadership positions and exerting control over the army.

Remarkably, this approach employed by Kim Jong Il in his political endeavors mirrored the very method employed during the period referred to as "Tangŭi kich'och'uksŏng" (Building the Foundation of the Party). Kim Jong Il emerged as the successor to Kim Il Sung in the 1970s, he scoured every corner of the Party, seeking comrades who would stand by his side, ready to face life and death together. These loyal comrades played a pivotal role in forging the monolithic leadership of Kim Jong Il, unfailingly heeding his instructions and carrying out his orders without question.[22] Ultimately, Kim Jong Il resorted to the same method employed during the "Building the Foundation of the Party" era to establish a core group of unwavering loyalty within the military, employing their collective strength to overcome the nation's most profound crisis.

In accordance with Kim Jong Il's guidance, the Armed Forces units diligently endeavored to secure their own sustenance, engaging in activities such as cultivating beans, rearing goats, and cultivating home gardens for vegetables and greens. They aimed to set a commendable example for other social organizations, including factories, enterprises, and cooperative farms.[23] Moreover, Armed Forces units were dispatched to various regions across the country to spearhead extensive construction projects, ranging from power plants and roads to endeavors directly impacting the lives of the people, such as fish farms, duck factories, pig farms, and amusement parks.[24]

The accomplishments of these units swiftly became a testament to the soundness of Kim Jong Il's path toward self-reliance. Rooted in the resolute Revolutionary Soldier Spirit, characterized by wholehearted dedication to safeguarding the supreme commander's directives, their actions and deeds functioned as a protective shield against the so-called "imperialist challenge" from external forces and as a sharp sword to sever the budding materialistic selfishness within society.

Under the framework of the Military-First Politics, soldiers were assigned to participate in arduous labor and construction projects within the realm of economic development. However, their responsibilities extended beyond these endeavors. Kim Jong Il saw fit to dispatch veterans to labor-intensive sectors such as mines, cooperative farms, and challenging factory environments, in order to address labor shortages. Additionally, he entrusted them with leadership roles within primary Party organizations, assuming positions such as Party cell secretaries. This strategic deployment ensured the implementation and realization of his Military-First Politics from the grassroots level of the Party organization.[25]

The practice of deploying and assigning veterans to diverse segments of society commenced in 1998. Given that the average length of military service in the Korean People's Armed Forces spans seven to ten years, and the Armed Forces boast a strength of one to 1.2 million soldiers, it can be estimated that a minimum of 20% of these soldiers,[26] roughly between 200,000 and 240,000 individuals, were dispersed throughout various sectors of society, assuming leadership roles within the Party's primary organizations.

Bolstered by their support, Kim Jong Il possessed the necessary conditions to implement Military-First Politics from the grassroots level of social organization.[27] Consequently, Military-First Politics transcended being merely a political slogan, acquiring substantive significance and practical implications. Kim Jong Il's confidence in the ability of the People's Army to defend the regime seems to have been expressed in early 1997. On January 24, 1997, letter to participants in the All-Party Cadres' Conference, Kim Jong Il wrote,

> The People's Army has undergone significant strengthening and development, evolving into an invincible and triumphant force—a steadfast guardian of the Party, the revolution, the country, and its people … **The entire army stands united in defense of the Party, moving cohesively under the Party's directives and instructions. Politically, ideologically, and militarily, it stands ready to confront any injustice with unwavering resolve** (emphasis added) …

> We have laid the crucial political and ideological foundations necessary for the brilliant continuation and advancement of Comrade Kim Il Sung's remarkable achievements. Simultaneously, we have established firm military assurances to reliably defend our revolution and socialist homeland. This monumental accomplishment is the culmination of our unwavering struggle over the past two and a half years, marking a resounding victory for our cause.[28]

Amid Kim Jong Il's growing confidence in the country's defense, news reached him from the Chagang Province Party Committee, highlighting the construction of numerous small- and medium-sized power plants in the Kanggye area of Chagang Province. This development enabled the region to meet its own electricity demands.

Without delay, Kim Jong Il made a visit to the city of Kanggye, commending them for successfully resolving their electricity needs. Just as Kim Il Sung had visited the workers of Kangsŏn Steel Mill in December of 1956, inspiring them to initiate the Ch'ŏllima Movement, Kim Jong Il expressed his intent to utilize Kanggye as a model to achieve a breakthrough during the Arduous March. He underscored the importance of the entire nation learning from Kanggye's example and embracing the revolutionary spirit exhibited by its people.[29]

In conjunction with the revered Revolutionary Soldier Spirit, this emerging "Kanggye Jŏngshin" (Kanggye Spirit) was promoted and fervently encouraged by all sectors of society as an essential attribute to navigate the challenges of the Arduous March. However, the experiences witnessed in Chagang Province, often regarded as the birthplace of this remarkable Kanggye Spirit, offer valuable insights into the financial landscape of the DPRK at that time. These experiences shed light on the fact that the country not only independently resolved its electricity problem without relying on State assistance but also effectively mobilized internal reserves to address and utilize necessary machinery, raw materials, and supplies.

Crucially, important factories and enterprises continued operating through these concerted efforts.[30] As outlined in our earlier analysis, the national budget revenues during the Arduous March were less than half of their pre-March figures. Consequently, the State faced significant constraints in providing adequate budgetary support to nationally significant factories and enterprises,[31] leading to the cessation of budgetary assistance to the provinces.[32]

Kim Jong Il, recognizing the criticality of the military, directed a substantial portion of the national budget toward their needs. While ostensibly requiring the Armed Forces to be self-reliant in procuring their own food and necessities, he prioritized the food supply to the military, leveraging it as a means to showcase the power of self-reliance.[33] In this context, the achievements in Chagang Province served as concrete evidence of the validity of Kim Jong Il's self-reliance approach. It provided the basis for asserting the universality of the Revolutionary Soldier Spirit through the embodiment of the Kanggye Spirit. By emphasizing the significance of self-reliance, Kim Jong Il aimed to rectify the wavering Party, which had been affected by the winds of "Reform" and "Opening-up," and firmly establish "Military-First Politics" as a primary principle.

Reflecting upon the impact of the Kanggye Spirit, Kim Jong Il once remarked,

> Looking back, the Kanggye Spirit bestowed upon me immense strength during the most arduous phase of our revolutionary journey. It fortified my resolve and determination, enabling our people to march victoriously through the Forced March of the Arduous March. The memory of the Kanggye Spirit will forever remain etched in my mind .[34]

This remarkable experience in Chagang province not only validated Kim Jong Il's ideological stance but also propelled him to persistently adhere to his course and forge ahead.

As the promotion of the Revolutionary Soldier Spirit and the Kanggye Spirit spread across the nation, all organizations and groups were urged to learn from these ideals. Factories and enterprises commenced mobilizing their reserves and making concerted efforts to normalize production on their own. Provinces sought to address their electricity needs by constructing small- and medium-sized power plants at the provincial and county levels, drawing inspiration from Chagang province's success.[35]

These endeavors allowed Kim Jong Il to concentrate his resources on the defense industry, as well as strategically significant factories and enterprises, instead of dispersing the national budget during the challenging period of the Arduous March. With the national budget revenues more than halved, Kim Jong Il focused investments on areas that promised the greatest returns, with particular emphasis on science and technology.

2.3 Kim Jong Il's Strategy of Focus on Science and Technology

Initially, Kim Jong Il's ascent to the chairmanship of the National Defense Commission during the inaugural session of the 10th Supreme People's Assembly marked the official commencement of the "Military-First Politics" era. The DPRK's launch of its inaugural artificial satellite, *Kwangmyŏngsŏng-1*, further showcased its advancements in long-range missile production, demonstrating that its military capabilities had not wavered even amid the challenges of the Arduous March.

In 1998, Kim Jong Il declared it the year of the march to overcome the nation's economic difficulties, emphasizing the imperative to fortify the material and economic foundations as the bedrock of its political, ideological, and military prowess. This commitment was manifested in his focused attention on the economic sector, notably through his active involvement with the Sŏngjin Steel United Enterprise.[36]

In the DPRK, the supreme leader's field guidance goes beyond mere visitations or inspections. On-the-spot guidance, particularly in the economic sphere, serves the purpose of resolving immediate challenges in revolution and construction by providing specific guidance to production units. The objective is to create exemplary models that can be replicated across other sectors and units, enabling the implementation of Party policies by establishing a central link and propagating the model to various units.

For the DPRK, Sŏngjin Steel held pivotal significance in its endeavor to produce steel without relying on coke since the 1980s. In 1983, the enterprise accomplished the re-steelmaking process through the use of four rotary kilns, employing the Samhwa iron method, which amalgamates iron ore, anthracite coal, and cement as a binder and subjects it to rotary kiln treatment.[37] However, the enterprise's operations were severely hampered by power shortages during the Arduous March. Kim Jong Il's decision to provide on-the-spot guidance to Sŏngjin Steel was driven by several crucial factors.

Foremost, Sŏngjin Steel United Enterprise was deemed the most likely candidate to normalize production swiftly with concentrated investment and guidance. Moreover, Kim Jong Il's choice to offer guidance to this enterprise aimed to establish a demonstrative example of how to expedite the normalization of production. By doing so, other factories and enterprises could learn from this model and promptly achieve production normalization across all industrial sectors.

In the DPRK, the remarkable achievements of the "Sŏnggang" (Sŏngjin Steel) workers are widely acknowledged. They were inspired by the on-the-spot guidance of Kim Jong Il, which united them to restore normal production, laying a solid foundation for the country's normalization,[38] and this accomplishment is famously known as the "Sŏnggangŭi Ponghwa" (Torch of the Sŏnggang). However, it is important to note that the success of the "Torch of the Sŏnggang" was not solely a result of the workers' determination, instilled through Kim Jong Il's field guidance. Strategic investments, made despite the lack of capital in the country, also played a vital role in this accomplishment.

In the DPRK, it is widely acknowledged that Kim Jong Il made a pivotal decision at a crucial moment when the nation stood at a crossroads. The narrative unfolds as follows: In the late 1990s, the nation grappled with formidable challenges. Nevertheless, Kim Jong Il, in a poignant move, prioritized the long-term advancement of the industrial sector. In a deeply emotional moment, Kim Jong Il revealed that he faced the dilemma of using his foreign currency to procure food and support his people. Yet, with tears in his eyes, he chose to invest in acquiring cutting-edge equipment essential for the modernization and reconstruction of the industrial sector.[39]

Although the veracity of this claim is difficult to ascertain, Kim Jong Il succeeded in extrapolating the experience of Chagang Province, as discussed earlier, into a broader concept known as the Kanggye Spirit. This enabled him to legitimately advocate for self-revitalization not only in all provinces but also in all units, allowing him to concentrate investments in strategically significant areas without diluting the national budget. The primary objective of this approach was the Sŏngjin Steel United Enterprise. Kim Jong Il strategically selected and prioritized the economic reconstruction of factories and enterprises essential to the DPRK's development by initiating advancements in equipment and production technology. Through this strategic focus, he effectively implemented his strategy for rebuilding the DPRK economy.

In a speech to Party officials on January 1, 1999, Kim Jong Il declared,

> In the past year, our entire Party, soldiers, and people have elevated the flame of tirelessness, capable of surmounting the most arduous obstacles, and transformed the Arduous March into a march towards "Ragwŏn" (paradise) by firmly upholding the Party's rallying cry of "Ch'oehusŭngnirŭl wihan kanghaenggun ap'ŭro!" (Forward to the Final Victory!) and confronting challenges with unwavering spirit and indomitable determination.[40]

Kim Jong Il's remarks can be interpreted as follows within the context of our discussion thus far: By adhering to and advancing the Military-First Politics based on self-reliance, Kim Jong Il stabilized the wavering Party, reestablished the supremacy of his ideas, and commenced economic reconstruction. This point assumes great importance when considering the DPRK's trajectory in overcoming the challenges of the Arduous March because once the supremacy of ideas is firmly established and can be actively pursued, rebuilding the economy becomes a matter of increasing productivity.[41]

In 1997, Kim Jong Il embarked determinedly on a path, recognizing the crucial role of science and technology in the realm of economic development; to instill confidence in the public regarding the soundness and feasibility of his decision, he introduced, with a sense of conviction, the resounding slogan "Kangsŏngdaeguk Kŏnsŏl" (Building a Strong and Great Nation) in 1999.[42] At the core of this vision lay the conviction that science and technology wielded an unparalleled power as propellers of national strength and greatness. This emblematic slogan established the fundamental trajectory for economic construction and reconstruction within the DPRK. The aim was unequivocal: to fortify and revitalize the economy by augmenting productivity through the mastery of advanced scientific principles and technological prowess, all while keeping Military-First Politics at the vanguard of the nation's priorities.

Bolstered by this overarching mission, the guiding principle of economic construction became "the pursuit of maximum practical benefits while unwaveringly upholding the principles of socialism."[43] To uphold these principles was to tackle economic challenges through collective efforts and forge an economy founded upon self-reliance, enshrined within the tenets of Chuch'e Thought. Simultaneously, the pursuit of maximum practical benefits entailed maximizing efficiency at every turn. Hence, the aforementioned statement can be interpreted as an endeavor to construct (or reconstruct) the economy by augmenting productivity through the introduction and application of advanced science and technology, all within the framework of collectivism and the principle of self-reliance.

Recognizing the pivotal role science and technology played in strengthening the defense industry and facilitating the development of vital sectors such as metalworking, machinery, and chemicals, Kim Jong Il directed his attention and considerable investments toward their advancement. He discerned that these advancements formed the bedrock for the nation's journey toward self-reliance. Consequently, Kim Jong Il determined the focus of his investments, carefully selecting and prioritizing factories and enterprises that possessed strategic significance for the country's economic construction.

This approach to investing in factories and enterprises with strategic importance for economic construction (or reconstruction) was executed with heightened precision under the grand proposition of "Building a Strong and Great Nation." As illustrated in Table 2.1, on-the-spot guidance and subsequent State investments were judiciously directed toward factories within the metal industry, producing steel or magnesia clinker, and fertilizer factories within the chemical industry that yielded fertilizers.

Table 2.2 Factories and Enterprises with Strategic Significance in the DPRK Economic Construction (Reconstruction) That Kim Jong Il Did On-the-Spot Guidance (1998–2011)

Name	Date of On-the-Spot Guidance	Strategic Meaning
Sŏngjin Steel United Enterprise	(1998.03.13), (2005.12.15), (2007.08.07), (2010.09.04), (2010.12.19)	Chuch'e Steel (steel made by the DPRK's own resource and technology)
Hŭich'ŏn Machine Tools General Factory	(1998.06.01), (2003.07.01), (2007.01.19), (2009.05.09), (2010.03.10)	CNC (Computerized Numerical Control) Machine Tools
28 Vinylon United Enterprise	(1999.09.24), (2007.08.10), (2008.05.12), (2008.05.28), (2009.02.04), (2009.11.06), (2010.02.07), (2010.02.09), (2011.08.02), (2011.01.30), (2011.08.08), (2011.10.16), (2011.12.10)	Vinylon (a synthetic fiber made from polyvinyl alcohol synthesized from carbide derived from limestone and anthracite)
Hŭngnam Fertilizer United Enterprise	(2005.09.17), (2007.11.13), (2008.08.11), (2009.02.06), (2009.09.14), (2009.11.06), (2010.08.03), (2011.01.30), (2011.03.10), (2011.10.16)	Chuch'e Fertilizer (chemical fertilizer made by the DPRK's own resource and technology)
Ryongsŏng Machinery United Enterprise	(2001.04.11), (2002.06.07), (2005.09.16), (2006.11.13), (2007.08.10), (2009.02,04), (2010.05.21), (2010.08.03), (2011.01.30), (2011.03.10), (2011.04.24), (2011.10.16), (2011.12.10)	Large-scale machinery and tailored equipment required for each industry sector, including mining, power, chemicals, electronics, etc.
Kusŏng Machine Tools Factory	(2000.01.25), (2001.02.14), (2001.12.16), (2002.05.19), (2004.06.01), (2006.09.04), (2009.03.27)	CNC Machine Tools
Kimch'aek Steel United Enterprise	(2001.08.01), (2007.08.06), (2009.02.21), (2009.12.17), (2010.03.04), (2011.12.06)	Chuch'e Steel
Ragwŏn Machinery United Enterprise	(2001.10.23), (2004.05.17), (2005.01.14), (2007.02.21), (2007.06.07), (2008.11.24), (2009.02.08), (2009.09.14), (2010.02.25), (2010.06.18), (2011.07.06)	Large machinery (excavators and rotary drillers, automobile cranes, large oxygen separators) and tailored facilities

Source: author.

Table 2.2 is compiled from data spanning the years 1998 to 2011, obtained from the *CCY*.

Vinylon factories, responsible for primary raw materials in the light industry—such as cloth—also received special attention, alongside mining equipment, machinery, and machine tool factories producing Computerized Numerical Control (CNC) machines embedded with micro-processes. These CNC machines augmented the efficiency of various production mechanisms utilized within these factories, embodying the epitome of technological advancement.

Kim Jong Il assigned specific factories and enterprises with pivotal responsibilities to tackle pressing challenges across various industries. In the metal industry, a notable undertaking was entrusted to the Sŏngjin Steel United Enterprise: achieving steel and iron production without reliance on coke (Chuch'e Steel). As previously analyzed, the DPRK's economy had suffered a severe setback and stagnation due to the inability to procure coke.

To tackle this obstacle head-on, the Sŏngjin Steel United Enterprise, along with the Kimch'aek Steel United Enterprise, which received selective and prioritized investments, was tasked with successfully accomplishing the iron and steelmaking processes without the use of coke.[44] Secondly, a material known as carbide was utilized in the production of Chuch'e Fiber. However, this posed a predicament as carbide demanded substantial amounts of electricity.[45] Responding to this challenge, Kim Jong Il issued a directive to produce vinylon without relying on carbide.[46] Thirdly, faced with limitations in importing an adequate supply of crude oil, Kim Jong Il urged the Hŭngnam Fertilizer United Enterprise to find alternative means of producing fertilizer without relying on naphtha.[47]

Lastly, and of utmost significance, Kim Jong Il identified CNC technology as the linchpin for enhancing productivity through scientific and technological advancements, serving as the bedrock for achieving self-reliance. Accordingly, substantial investments were directed toward the development and widespread implementation of CNC technology across all industries—a grand endeavor known as CNCization.[48]

Now, the question arises: Why did Kim Jong Il perceive CNC technology as the vital catalyst for augmenting productivity in the realm of economic construction (or reconstruction), as well as being indispensable for achieving self-reliance? The answer lies in the transformative potential of CNC technology to revolutionize production processes. CNC technology, with its embedded computer micro-processes, enhances the efficiency and precision of machinery utilized in various industries. By harnessing CNC technology, the DPRK aimed to streamline manufacturing processes, increase output, and achieve higher levels of productivity. This focus on CNC technology was rooted in Kim Jong Il's vision of utilizing science and technology as the driving force for self-reliance, fortifying the nation's economic foundations, and reducing reliance on external sources.

As emphasized earlier, the realization of processes like the "Pik'oksŭhwagongbŏp" (non-coking process) in iron and steelmaking, the "Sŏkt'an'gasŭhwagongbŏp" (anthracite gasification process) for producing nitrogenous fuels from coal, and the enhancement of carbide production technology to derive vinylon from anthracite coal all hinged on the groundbreaking "Koon'gong-giyŏnsogisul" (hot air combustion technology).

This innovative approach involved employing high-temperature air to combust gaseous or liquid raw materials, thereby maintaining the furnace's internal temperature at the required level. This high-temperature air, derived from anthracite coal gasification, earned the designation "high-temperature air combustion technology by anthracite coal gasification." The technology comprised vital elements such as furnaces, heat storage bodies, high-speed change-over mechanisms, blowing and exhausting systems, and automatic control systems. Effectively organizing and operating such an intricate system demanded the integration of CNC technology.

In essence, CNC technology serves as an indispensable prerequisite for the initiation and fruition of the Chuch'e Steel, Chuch'e Fertilizer, and Chuch'e Fiber production systems. Furthermore, it proves crucial in the manufacturing of power generation equipment, large electric motors, and transformers required for power plants. Additionally, CNC technology plays a vital role in producing high-performance mining machines and related machinery essential for mining operations. Kim Jong Il, in his efforts to bolster the economy through the application of advanced science and technology for enhanced productivity, underscored the pivotal role of CNC technology. It functioned as a master key, unlocking opportunities for self-reliance and technological advancement in various sectors.

To fully grasp the benefits of CNC technology, we turn to Kim Jong Il's remarks during his on-the-spot guidance. On July 26, 2002, Kim Jong Il visited the Hŭich'ŏn Machine Tool General Factory, where he acknowledged that the factory's achievements in machine tool production stemmed from their unwavering commitment to technological reform, embracing advanced technology, and championing modernization.

Kim Jong Il assessed the factory's remarkable accomplishments as a testament to the efficacy and vitality of the Party's endeavors in science and technology. Underscoring the factory's significance as the "mother factory" of the country's machinery industry, he emphasized the importance of continuous improvement in product quality, relentless production growth, and active contributions to the country's economic development.[49]

Kim Jong Il's remarks on the Hŭich'ŏn Machine Tools General Factory carry two significant implications. Firstly, this factory specializes in the production of crucial machine tools integral to manufacturing machines, particularly those employing CNC technology—examples include numeric adjustable lathes, numeric vertical comprehensive processing lathes, and universal lathes. Secondly, the Hŭich'ŏn Machine Tools General Factory assumes the critical role of a "mother factory" within the machinery industry of the DPRK, with the responsibility of producing machines for various factories nationwide. The adoption of CNC technology has notably elevated the production efficiency of these machines compared to their predecessors.

Summarizing Kim Jong Il's statement, we understand that the Hŭich'ŏn Machine Tools General Factory has historically played and must continue to play a pivotal role as the parent entity within the DPRK's machinery industry, responsible for manufacturing production machines. With the advent of CNC technology, these machines now exhibit substantially improved production capabilities.

Intriguingly, this factory is also a home of the Ragwŏn Machinery United Enterprise, which procures machine tools from the Hŭich'ŏn Machine Tools General Factory. Standing as the sole United Enterprise in the DPRK specializing in essential equipment production, Ragwŏn Machinery excels in crafting critical mining excavators and large-scale oxygen separators. These separators play a vital role in gasifying coal for Chuch'e Fertilizer and Steel production, remarkably without relying on oil or coke. This distinctive enterprise has demonstrably played an exceptional role in the DPRK's economic reconstruction, earning it the coveted title of the nation's "only son factory" from Kim Jong Il himself.[50]

In essence, the provision of high-performance excavators by the Ragwŏn Machinery United Enterprise to coal mines facilitates the normalization of coal mining operations, ensuring an adequate supply of anthracite coal. Additionally, the supply of large oxygen separators to fertilizer and steel plants enables the production of Chuch'e Fertilizer and Chuch'e Steel through the anthracite coal gasification process.[51]

It is worth noting that the coordinating lathes and vertical comprehensive processing units responsible for manufacturing these machines at Ragwŏn rely on CNC technology, which is implemented and perfected at the Hŭich'ŏn Machine Tools General Factory. Only through CNC technology can numeric controlled coordinating lathes and numeric controlled vertical comprehensive processing units be produced, enabling the creation of high-performance excavators and large oxygen separators. Therefore, it is not an exaggeration to assert that CNC technology holds the key to the revitalization and reconstruction of the DPRK economy.

Kim Jong Il has dedicated significant efforts to nurturing and advancing CNC technology at the national strategic level. In a speech delivered on January 1, 2010, to responsible officials of the Party's Central Committee, he proudly proclaimed, "The year 2009 stands as a remarkable turning point in the construction history of the DPRK, marked by the triumphant launch of the Kwangmyŏngsŏng-2 satellite, the successful nuclear test, and the completion of the Chuch'e Steel production system." However, what truly fills him with immense pride is the fact that the DPRK's CNC technology has achieved world-class status. He joyfully declares that "the recognition garnered by our CNC technology stands out as the most exceptional accomplishment amidst the numerous achievements we accomplished in the preceding year." Continuing his statement, he added,

The memory of the day in 1994, spent in tears, remains vivid as I witnessed the unveiling of the first domestically produced CNC machine in April 1995 ... The inaugural sight of the Ryŏnha CNC machine was akin to discovering a precious treasure, infusing me with tremendous strength in the pursuit of building a robust nation ... The dedication of defense industry workers and Ryŏnha machinery developers blazed a trail in high-tech advancements, realizing the vision I had set forth and making significant contributions without a hint of speculation.

CNC technology stands as a cornerstone, indispensable for discussing the triumphant launch of our artificial satellite and, more broadly, the achievement of our formidable defense industry and military prowess ... Beyond its role in manufacturing, **CNC technology has become a linchpin in the realization of our national aspirations and capabilities** (emphasis added).[52]

Kim Jong Il emphasized that the successful launch of the artificial satellite and the formidable strength of the DPRK's defense industry and military capabilities were inconceivable without the pivotal role played by CNC technology. According to a DPRK documentary film on Kim Jong Il, orders for the development of CNCs were issued by him in the early 1990s,[53] a time when the country was on the brink of the Arduous March. This fact underscores the profound significance and implications encapsulated in Kim Jong Il's earlier quote.

The DPRK devoted a significant portion of its resources to developing CNC technology, primarily for the defense industry, with a specific focus on nuclear and long-range missile capabilities. Following the successful satellite launch test in August 1998 and the first nuclear test in October 2006, the DPRK expanded the application of CNC technology and increased investment not only in the defense industry but also in other heavy industries such as metals and chemicals. The advanced plant witnessed the culmination of over a decade of trial and error,[54] with the completion of the Chuch'e Steel production system in 2009. Subsequently, in the same year, the Chuch'e Fiber production system emerged,[55] followed by the Chuch'e Fertilizer production system at advanced plants in 2010.[56]

After more than a decade of strategic investment in strategically significant factories and enterprises, Kim Jong Il's vision for economic reconstruction in the DPRK began to bear fruit. The country had made significant strides in laying the essential groundwork necessary to overcome the severe economic crisis it had endured. It is important to note that this crisis was primarily triggered by the inability to import critical resources such as coke and crude oil. However, the development of systems capable of producing steel without coke and chemical fertilizers without crude oil underscored a notable achievement—the DPRK had established the foundations for bringing an end to the Arduous March and restoring normalcy to its production processes.

This significant shift in the DPRK's economic growth strategy emerged as a somewhat ironic consequence.[57] With the ability to produce vital commodities independent of external dependencies, the country embarked on a transition from an extensive source of growth strategy to an intensive source of growth strategy. In the former, growth is primarily driven by the increase in production factors, but over time, the growth rate slows down as it becomes subject to the law of diminishing returns. Conversely, in the intensive source of growth strategy, technological advancements and improvements take center stage, driving sustained growth.

In evaluating the veracity of the DPRK's advancements in overcoming the Arduous March and restoring production normalization, a fruitful avenue for analysis lies in examining the country's rice production and Chuch'e Fertilizer production, for which objective data is available. These sectors provide valuable insights into the concrete effects of the groundwork laid by the DPRK.

In 1994, the DPRK relied heavily on rice farming with imported crude oil-based fertilizers to achieve a total rice production of 317.7 million tons. It is worth noting that the country's fertilizer imports in 1993 were merely 0.28 million tons, indicating a limited reliance on imported fertilizers. Before the economic crisis hit, the DPRK required approximately 1.7 million tons of crude oil.[60] However, from 1994 to 2012, during the period leading up to the Arduous March, the country could secure an average annual amount of only about 780,000 tons of crude oil. Consequently, the average annual amount of crude oil secured by the country during this period amounted to only around 45% of the pre-crisis level.

Apart from fertilizer, the DPRK also refines and processes crude oil for various sectors such as military operations, civilian transportation, and agricultural machinery like tractors. While the specific allocation of crude oil across sectors remains unknown, reducing crude oil imports by over half inevitably impacts every sector reliant on it. However, it is likely that transportation and shipping experienced relatively smaller cuts compared to fertilizer, as the latter can be substituted with imported alternatives, whereas refining crude oil for gasoline lacks a viable substitute.

Accordingly, as depicted in Table 2.3, the DPRK has increased its fertilizer imports for food production since 1997, surpassing the pre-crisis levels. Notably, rice production in the country has exhibited steady growth since 2001, reaching 91% of its pre-Arduous March level in 2013 and, according to unofficial data, 93% in 2015. These developments highlight the resilience and adaptive measures undertaken by the DPRK to mitigate the challenges posed by reduced crude oil availability, ensuring the continued increase in rice production.[61]

In the context of the DPRK, the period following the Arduous March witnessed significant developments that reshaped the country's economic landscape. One notable aspect of this transformation was the establishment of the Chuch'e Fertilizer production system in 2010, although its immediate implementation did not guarantee immediate self-sufficiency in fertilizer production.

Table 2.3 The DPRK's Crude Oil and Fertilizer Imports (1993–2012) and Rice Production (1994–2015)

Year	1993	1994	1995	1996	1997	1998	1999	2000	2001	2002	2003
Imported Crude Oil	103.3	83.3	102.1	93.6	50.6	61.4	58.4	85.6	72.1	72.1	0.28
Imported Chemical Fertilizer	0.28	3.05	0.38	4.7	18.7	11.2	4.8	6.2	15.8	24.0	14.4
Year	1994	1995	1996	1997	1998	1999	2000	2001	2002	2003	2004
Rice Production	317.7	201.6	142.6	152.7	230.7	234.3	169.0	206.0	218.6	224.4	237.0
Year	2004	2005.	2006	2007	2008	2009	2010	2011	2012	2013	2014
Imported Crude Oil	77.0	126.9	127.9	103.2	60.5	68.7	52.8	52.6	53.3	57.8	53.9[58]
Imported Chemical Fertilizer	19.0	7.8	12.2	6.5	4.1	12.6	28.6	35.5	25.2	19.0	13.2
Year	2005	2006.	2007	2008	2009	2010	2011	2012	2013	2014	2015
Rice Production	258.3	247.8	187.0	286.2[59] (ud)	233.6	242.6	248.0	286.1	290.1	262.6 (ud)	294.8 (ud)

Source: author.

Note: ud—unofficial data.

Unit: 10,000 ton.

Table 2.3 presents compiled data spanning from 1993 to 2014, obtained from the UN Comtrade Database for crude oil and chemical fertilizer, and from FAOSTAT for rice production covering the years 1994 to 2015.

Since the fertilizer to be used in the current year is made from crude oil imported in the previous year, and fertilizer is usually applied intensively in spring and summer, it is assumed that the imported fertilizer to be applied in the current year was imported in the previous year.

Table 2.4 Total Supply of Chemical Fertilizer in the DPRK (2009–2016)

Year	Nitrogen Fertilizer	Phosphatic Fertilizer	Potassic Fertilizer	Total
2009	434,807	2,776	8,400	445,983
2010	475,100	11,402	12,314	498,816
2011	735,943	5,545	4,477	745,965
2012	686,517	21,460	18,650	726,627
2013	686,015	18,396	2,788	707,199
2014	727,993	18,977	2,700	749,670
2015	612,194	7,817	2,595	622,606
2016	837,171	11,911	930	850,012

Source: FAO/GIEWS, Special Alert No. 340.

Unit: 1 ton.
The data concerning the total supply of chemical fertilizer in the DPRK (2009–2016) were initially reported by the DPRK's Department of Agriculture and compiled by the Food and Agriculture Organization's (FAO) Global Information and Early Warning System on Food and Agriculture (GIEWS).

This point was emphasized by Kim Jong Un in a Plenum Meeting in March 2013, where he stressed the importance of localizing crucial resources and materials necessary for economic advancement.[62]

During this period, the DPRK made significant strides in the production of Chuch'e Fertilizer, utilizing its own materials and technology. By 2016, Chuch'e Fertilizer accounted for a substantial proportion, approximately 91.5%,[63] of the overall fertilizer supply. These statistics stand as a testament to the advanced stage of completion that the Chuch'e Fertilizer production system had achieved or was on the verge of attaining.

This is further supported by the data presented in Table 2.3, clearly illustrating the consistent growth in rice production from 2,480,000 tons in 2011 to 2,948,000 tons in 2014. Given the interconnected nature of industries within the DPRK, guided by the principle of self-reliance, the development of the Chuch'e Fertilizer system implied a broader normalization of production across all sectors.[64] Consequently, it can be inferred that the DPRK had indeed laid the groundwork for "production normalization" as claimed by the country since 2011. This achievement provided the necessary foundation for the

Table 2.5 The DPRK's Imported Chemical Fertilizer (2009–2016)

Year	2009	2010	2011	2012	2013	2014	2015	2016
Imported Chemical Fertilizer	4.1	12.6	28.6	35.5	25.2	19.0	13.2	7.1

Source: author.

Unit: 10,000 ton.
Table 2.5 presents compiled data spanning from 2009 to 2016, obtained from the UN Comtrade Database.

Table 2.6 The DPRK's Production of Chuch'e Fertilizer (2009–2016)

Year	2009	2010	2011	2012	2013	2014	2015	2016
Production of Nitrogen Fertilizer	(43.5 – 4.1) = 39.4	(47.5 – 12.6) = 34.9	(73.6 – 28.6) = 45.0	(68.7 – 35.5) = 33.2	(68.6 – 25.2) = 43.4	(72.8 – 19.0) = 53.8	(61.2 – 13.2) = 48.0	(83.7 – 7.1) = 76.6

Source: author.

Unit: 10,000 ton.

resumption of economic reconstruction and the cultivation of technologies and raw materials required for sustained development.

Importantly, the "Arduous March" period represented a unique phase where the DPRK addressed its preexisting weaknesses and fortified its capacity for self-reliance, thereby transcending the challenges it faced. By reintegrating collectivism into the forefront of economic construction and strengthening the foundation of self-reliance, the DPRK successfully navigated the Arduous March and set the stage for future growth.

Appendix to Chapter 2: The Meaning and Implication of the "10·3 Discourse"

The "10·3 Discourse," despite being kept undisclosed to the public, came to light through the efforts of a Japanese NGO organization known as RENK. This organization managed to acquire a copy of the booklet containing the discourse's content and subsequently unveiled it to the world through an article published in the *Mainichi Shimbun* on December 19, 2002.

As a result of RENK's initiative, the previously hidden discourse became widely known. The booklet's title was "Kagyŏkkwa saenghwalbirŭl chŏnbanjŏkŭro kaejŏnghan kukkajŏkchoch'irŭl chal algo kangsŏngdaegukkŏnsŏnŭl himitke tagŭch'ija" (Let Us Be Aware of the National Measures That Have Revised Prices and Living Expenses as a Whole and Move Forward with Constructing a Strong and Prosperous Country), and published in September 2002, offering us a general understanding of its contents.[65]

While the authenticity of this booklet may warrant some scrutiny, it is worth noting that the overall content broadly aligns with Kim Jong Il's documented words and actions, as evidenced in the *SWK* both prior to and following October 3, 2001. Considering this alignment, conducting a reasoned analysis does not stray too far from the realm of scientific inquiry. Therefore, let us scrutinize and interpret the pivotal elements presented within this booklet.

Initially, Kim Jong Il emphasizes that "ensuring practicality in socialist economic construction necessitates the effective utilization of society's human and material resources to bring tangible benefits to the nation's development and the well-being of its people." Furthermore, he asserts that "all issues related to economic management should be resolved with the objective of maximizing practical benefits in production, construction, as well as the management and operation of enterprises, on both a national and sectoral level."

Kim Jong Il continues by highlighting a prevalent concern:

> Year after year, not merely one or two sectors, but various sectors and units, particularly those of strategic significance, consistently fall significantly short of the planned targets. Such a situation not only disrupts economic development but also leads to substantial losses, undermining the advantages of a planned economy.

To tackle this challenge, he asserts that

> in the planning process, it is crucial to address this problem as a top priority, regardless of the costs involved. This necessitates accurately assessing realistic conditions and possibilities and formulating plans based on such assessments. Additionally, we must never disregard reality or manipulate figures and documents, even when faced with numerous tasks and demands.[66]

The crux of Kim Jong Il's remarks lies in the notion that effective economic management should hinge upon maximizing the efficiency of utilizing production factors; failure to do so will result in the failure to achieve planned objectives and a squandering of resources. In Chapter 1, a more comprehensive exploration of this topic is provided, highlighting how Kim Il Sung frequently criticized poorly executed planned projects that invited wastefulness. For instance, during his concluding remarks at the 19th Plenary Session of the 5th Central Committee of the Workers' Party of Korea on December 12, 1979, Kim Il Sung voiced his dissatisfaction with the state planning agencies in the following manner.

> The State Planning Commission and other planning agencies should carefully calculate the demand and supply sources of materials in detail and match them with the plan. When some materials are inevitably less than demand due to limited production capacity, they should not force the numbers to match, but rather guarantee production according to the plan by saving materials by a few percentage points. This should be clearly stated in the plan and implemented as it is.[67]

As evident from the aforementioned discussion, Kim Jong Il echoes the criticisms expressed by Kim Il Sung. Nevertheless, there exists a notable distinction in Kim Jong Il's assertion that the nation was "grossly under-performing its plans, particularly in crucial sectors and indicators of strategic significance." This statement must be examined in light of the challenging circumstances prevalent during the Arduous March period, characterized by a significant downturn in national budget revenues, amounting to only half of the figures recorded in 1993. Moreover, it is crucial to recognize that Kim Jong Il directed a substantial portion of the country's resources toward the defense industry.

Contrary to Kim Il Sung's era, where comprehensive planning encompassed the entire economy, Kim Jong Il's reference to the country being "grossly under-planned, especially in important sectors and indicators of strategic significance" does not imply a blanket application of planning across all sectors. Instead, it highlights the ineffectiveness of planning within critical areas of strategic importance. Given that national investment primarily targeted sectors crucial to national defense, it is reasonable to interpret that industrialization projects were predominantly executed within these sectors, yet failed to achieve significant outcomes or desired effectiveness.

During this trying period, the DPRK focused its planning efforts exclusively on essential sectors of national strategic significance. However, the problems that plagued Kim Il Sung's Unified Detailed Planning System (UDPS) resurfaced, a situation deemed unacceptable by Kim Jong Il. This was largely due to the fact that nearly all the resources available to the DPRK were channeled into these nationally strategic sectors.

Kim Jong Il found himself unable to follow Kim Il Sung's approach of openly criticizing the State planning agencies and encouraging them to rectify the issues at hand. Hence, he asserted, "In the realm of planning, this predicament must be prioritized and resolved at all costs. To do so, we must adhere to the unwavering principle of accurately assessing realistic conditions and possibilities, formulating plans based on such assessments."

Significantly, he emphasized the necessity of addressing all economic management challenges, both at the national level and within individual sectoral units, with a focus on maximizing practicality in production, construction, and enterprise management operations. In essence, despite the scaled-down nature of the current system, inefficiencies persist, necessitating the implementation of an alternative economic management and operational framework within the planning process.

Moving forward, Kim Jong Il remarked, "The DPRK finds itself in a changed environment, demanding corresponding improvements in the planning system and methods. Primarily, this entails rational division of planning indicators between the central and provincial levels, as well as between higher authorities and lower units." He emphasized that **a planned economy does not imply the need for centralized planning of every aspect of production and management across all sectors and units** (emphasis added). Moreover, he stated,

> As the Party has already outlined its policies, the State Planning Commission should exclusively oversee indicators of strategic significance for economic construction, while other minor indicators and detailed standard indicators should be planned by the relevant institutions and enterprise units. It would be reasonable to delegate the division of annual and quarterly planning responsibilities to the ministries, central institutions, or specific provinces.[68]

Kim Jong Il's instructions provide valuable insights into the economic situation prevailing in the DPRK at that time. Ultimately, he emphasizes the requirement for an economic management system that encompasses the division of planning responsibilities according to size and scope, and such a system is not novel. The United Enterprise System (UES) discussed in Chapter 1 represents such an approach. Therefore, the question arises as to why Kim Jong Il is ordering the reimplementation of the UES. It becomes evident that the system had been temporarily abandoned during the initial phase of the Arduous March, a fact confirmed by Kim Jong Il's subsequent statement.

> The State Planning Commission currently oversees comprehensive planning for the entire country, extending its purview even to the minutest details. Such an approach may be deemed unnecessary. In the recent restructuring of the state organizational system, **United Enterprises were dismantled** (emphasis added), and Management Bureaus were established independently from the Departments.

> In the prior United Enterprises framework, factories and enterprises operated under the unified guidance of the Party organization within the United Enterprises. However, with the transition to the Management Bureau System, these Bureaus have assumed responsibilities previously held by United Enterprises, and there are concerns about their effectiveness in this role. This presents an issue that requires corrective measures.[69]

Considering the circumstances prevalent in the DPRK during the Arduous March period, it is plausible that most of the United Enterprises were unable to function effectively after 1995 when the national budget's total revenue plummeted by more than half. As sectors and enterprises of national strategic significance struggled to operate adequately, it is highly likely that the majority of United Enterprises had to be shut down.

The advent of Military-First Politics ushered in a redefinition of economic operations and management within its framework. The management and functioning of the economy likely reverted to the UDPS, leading to the abolition of the UES, as resources were concentrated on the defense industry. However, as the economy reached its nadir in 1998 and showed signs of recovery, coupled with the need to normalize production across all industrial sectors, not just the military, Kim Jong Il issued the directive to reintroduce the UES. This decision can be discerned as the central point of his aforementioned remarks.

In his "10·3 Discourse," Kim Jong Il made significant revisions to the UDPS, stipulating that the central government should oversee sectors of national strategic significance, such as the defense industry and primary heavy industries like metals and chemicals. Meanwhile, the management of the remaining factories and enterprises would be entrusted to the UES. However, due to the national budget revenue being merely half of its pre-Arduous March levels, most factories and enterprises could not resume operations.

The return to the UES held more practical implications for sectors outside those of national strategic significance. Since the State allocated its entire budgetary resources to the sectors of national strategic significance, it was unable to allocate funds to other sectors. As a result, these sectors had to rely on internal planning, intersectoral collaboration, and independent operations. This predicament served as the primary impetus for the reintroduction of the UES in other sectors. Consequently, this revived UES exhibited significant differences from its previous incarnation.

These disparities can be discerned in Kim Jong Il's subsequent statement:

> I believe it would be advantageous for the State Planning Commission to handle comprehensive indicators such as gross industrial production and primary construction investment at the provincial level, along with other pertinent indicators as required. The Commission should specify the equipment and materials that can be guaranteed by the State, assist provinces and counties in planning the distribution and development of detailed indicators at the city, county, and enterprise levels, and enable provinces, counties, and enterprise to adapt them according to their specific circumstances.

Furthermore, he elaborated on supply-related matters in the following manner:

> Material supply should align with the planned production and distribution. However, it is equally essential to establish and manage a 'socialist commodity exchange market' in addition to the planned framework. This would enable enterprises to address surplus or deficit situations of certain raw materials, materials, and accessories through mutually beneficial exchanges. To guarantee a stable supply, factories and enterprises could be mandated to allocate a specified percentage of their production to material exchange. In such instances, the types and scope of materials available for exchange must be appropriately stipulated, and a system for payment through banks should be implemented.[70]

In the previous system, the State Planning Commission was responsible for formulating macro plans and indicators at the national level, which were then allocated to provinces, cities, counties, and enterprises. However, with the reimplementation of the UES, a new approach emerged. Under this system, the State directs cities, counties, and enterprises to carry out a few critical projects and those for which the government can guarantee the necessary materials.

Cities, counties, and enterprises, on the other hand, are tasked with creating detailed plans based on their unique conditions. They are expected to implement the State-ordered plans while also formulating their own plans for other aspects. In essence, the plans in the UES are divided into national indicators and regional/enterprise indicators. The national indicators refer to the plans received from the government for each region and enterprise, whereas the regional/enterprise indicators are the plans devised by the regions and enterprises themselves for their own operations.

Kim Jong Il's directive holds significant importance as it represents a turning point in the evolution of the UES toward a "Socialist Enterprise Responsibility Management System" (SERMS) While national targets are production goals mandated by the State and possess a command-oriented nature, regional/enterprise targets are set by the regions and enterprises themselves. This is because regions and enterprises cannot independently fulfill all the material and resource requirements for production. These targets operate within the realm of the market and can only be achieved through contracts and negotiations between regions, enterprises, and other entities. In other words, the centralized and directive planning in the DPRK economic system was narrowed down to a select few items of strategic significance at the national level.

The remainder of economic activities operated through contracts and negotiations, thus expanding the market sphere. However, it took considerable time for these changes to become evident, as the DPRK economy, while recovering from its worst state, still faced significant challenges, with the national budget revenue hovering at approximately half of its pre–Arduous March levels, and most factories and enterprises not operating at full capacity.

Kim Jong Il's order regarding the supply of materials emphasized the primacy of planning while allowing for supplementation through the "socialist commodity exchange market." This implies that the implementation of plans provided by the State to each region and enterprise should take precedence, followed by the execution of the regions' and enterprises' own plans through the "socialist commodity exchange market."

It is important to note that the market referred to here does not entail a completely "free market system." Kim Jong Il did not permit unrestricted exchange of materials between enterprises belonging to different United Enterprises via the inter-market. Instead, he mandated central approval and required transactions to be conducted through banks.[71]

The instruction provided by Kim Jong Il offers valuable insights into the economic landscape of the DPRK during that period. Kim Jong Il emphasized the significance of accurately assessing financial aspects in order to determine whether the balance was favorable or unfavorable, whether the country and its people were benefiting or incurring losses, and whether the principles of socialist distribution were being appropriately implemented.

Kim Jong Il stressed the necessity of establishing a system of accounting for money and financial planning to comprehensively evaluate and calculate the outcomes of economic management across various sectors of the People's Economy and the entire country. This would allow for an assessment of the profits obtained in relation to the investment of human resources, materials, and capital.

The most notable aspect of Kim Jong Il's statement is his emphasis on allowing factories and enterprises to operate autonomously while strengthening controls to curtail production and management activities in times of financial constraints. This marked a departure from the previous practice of soft budget constraints, which had been a pervasive issue in socialist economies.

Kim Jong Il recognized the chronic moral hazard problem associated with soft budget constraints and aimed to address it. In line with this directive, the DPRK implemented a new national payment system known as the Pŏnsuipchip'yo (Earned Income Index),[72] which aligned with the socialist principle of receiving compensation based on individual contributions.

Furthermore, Kim Jong Il underscored the importance of production specialization by reorganizing the self-sustaining bases that had emerged during the Arduous March. He criticized the tendency of factories and enterprises to set up self-sustaining bases to fulfill all their requirements, deeming it contrary to the nature of a socialist economy and hindering economic development. He called for United Enterprises to be structured around the principle of specialization, advocating for strengthened links and cooperation among factories, enterprises, and economic sectors. Kim Jong Il emphasized the need to gradually rectify the organization of self-sustaining bases within factories and enterprises, reviewing and correcting the structure of self-sustaining enterprises and the affiliations between factories, enterprises, and cooperative farms.

Kim Jong Il's directive highlighted the discouragement of self-sufficiency at the United Enterprise level, instead promoting reorganization based on product specialization. He emphasized the importance of advancing technology, increasing production efficiency, and improving product quality to ensure profitability. Specialization of production was essential, allowing for commodity exchanges between United Enterprises and provinces. Specialization involved focusing on producing goods more cost-effectively within a region or enterprise based on comparative advantage. This strategy could only succeed through market-based trade of goods produced with such comparative advantage.

Therefore, Kim Jong Il's directive to reorganize each United Enterprise based on production specialization can be interpreted as an endorsement of the market as a mechanism for resource allocation. Although the visible effects of this shift would take more than a decade to materialize, the reorganization of United Enterprises toward production specialization established the market as a prerequisite for economic rebuilding and development. It reinforced the orientation toward the SERMS.

In the concluding segment of the speech, Kim Jong Il echoed Kim Il Sung's critique of prevailing "averageism" or egalitarianism, preceding the launch of the UES. He advocated for the comprehensive eradication of egalitarian practices, specifically the indiscriminate distribution of State subsidies, and stressed the paramount importance of adhering strictly to the socialist distribution principle. This principle involves accurate distribution based on the quantity of work performed and the corresponding earnings, aligned with individual performance outcomes.

Kim Jong Il underscored the need for the introduction of novel methods to assess and allocate labor, in consonance with the evolving landscape of socialist construction, reality's changes, and ongoing developments. Furthermore, he emphasized the continual enhancement and refinement of the socialist labor remuneration system.

Kim Jong Il further emphasized the existence of an excess of complimentary offerings within the economic landscape, prompting the need for a comprehensive reassessment. He highlighted that an overabundance of free provisions weakens the incentives and checks on labor, thereby undermining the effective implementation of the socialist distribution principle. Consequently, he deemed it imperative to conduct a thorough review of all aspects related to gratuitous supplies, State compensations, and benefits. Any elements found to be excessive or unwarranted should be identified and subsequently eliminated. Specifically, he called for the discontinuation of State subsidies for food and shelter, stating that,

> In the future, as we resolve issues related to both food and non-commodities, it is envisioned that **workers will have the autonomy to purchase food at full price using their earnings. Additionally, they should have the option to acquire housing through purchase or opt for full rental payment** (emphasis added) … To facilitate this, the pricing of commodities, fundamental to sustaining daily life, should be promptly determined. Subsequently, the prices of other goods and living expenses should generally align with this foundation …

> Social measures need to be promptly implemented in accordance with realistic conditions. We are committed to fortifying and advancing social measures that underscore the strengths of our socialist system. These include the free compulsory education system, the provision of free medical treatment, the social insurance system, the establishment of a regular vacation system, and the provision of preferential treatment for honorary soldiers. Concurrently, we aim to eliminate any unjust or unreasonable elements within these measures.[73]

When Kim Jong Il mentioned that "workers should purchase food at full price using their earnings," he aimed to end the practice of the State purchasing food from cooperative farms at high prices and selling it to urban workers at subsidized rates.[74] By suggesting that urban workers should purchase food at the price at which the State buys it from cooperative farms, he intended to align food distribution with socialist principles rather than communist practices. In this context, the emphasis on "Shilli" (actual benefits) within Kim Jong Il's discourse further supports the instruction to pay the full price for food. Similarly, his directive to pay the full usage fee for housing, reducing subsidies, aligns with the overall context of the discourse.

However, Kim Jong Il's instruction to "workers should even buy house" appears to contradict his previous statement that "private property can never be allowed in the DPRK."[75] This discrepancy presents a challenge in interpretation. How should we interpret Kim Jong Il's statement urging that "even housing should be bought and used"?

The absence of issues in the transcript-making and copying process leads to a singular conclusion. The speech delivered by Kim Jong Il to the responsible officials of the Party Central Committee on October 3, 2001, remains undisclosed to the public, likely due to its departure from Kim Jong Il's customary doctrine, as evident in the unconventional statement, "even housing should be bought and used."

In the DPRK, it is an ironclad rule that Party members must unquestionably accept and implement the conclusions or instructions issued by the supreme leader.[76] However, if there happens to be a contradiction within the supreme leader's instructions (and it is indeed certain), it becomes impossible to carry them out. Consequently, instructions containing such inconsistencies are not made public. This inference provides a possible explanation for why the "10·3 Discourse" has yet to be disclosed.

Certain elements of Kim Jong Il's "10·3 Discourse" were incorporated into the Kyŏngjegaesŏnjoch'i (New Economic Management Improvement Measures), which were implemented on July 1, 2002. In the Republic of Korea, these measures are commonly referred to as the "7·1 Measure." Many observers analyzing the DPRK's economy viewed this development as opening Pandora's box, anticipating that marketization pressures from below would lead to the expansion of market institutions and eventually transform the DPRK's economic system from socialism to capitalism.[77] However, this perspective was a misjudgment stemming from a lack of understanding of the economic construction process in the DPRK and a failure to differentiate between the market as a mechanism for resource allocation and the capitalist market system.

As we have observed, the DPRK responded to the severe resource shortage problem by implementing the Taean System across the entire industry. It aimed to address this challenge through the establishment of a centralized planning system known as the UDPS. Despite numerous efforts, the effective implementation of the UDPS remained elusive, and the resource shortage issue worsened. As a result, the UES was experimented with in 1973 and eventually introduced to the entire economy in 1985. However, this system faced a temporary suspension after 1994 during a period of economic hardship known as the Arduous March. This challenging period witnessed a significant decline in national income, reducing it to less than half its previous level, while numerous factories and enterprises struggled to operate effectively.

Around the year 2000, when the foundations were laid for the economic revitalization, the UES was reintroduced. However, this reintroduction was more than a mere reinstatement of the previous system; it also involved a reorganization of the United Enterprises to ensure maximum efficiency in production, construction, and overall economic management across all sectors.

To elaborate further, the newly established UES maintained the division of planning into units called United Enterprises, as before. However, it also allowed for the allocation of resources in industries beyond those deemed strategically significant at the national level to occur through market mechanisms. This included expanding the availability of necessary materials through market-based exchanges between United Enterprises and provinces when sufficient budgetary allocations from the State were not forthcoming. This approach aimed to promote the rationalization of planning and specialization of production based on comparative advantage.

Furthermore, the system applied the socialist distribution principle of receiving according to one's contribution to both individual workers and enterprises levels, thereby enhancing the material incentives for workers to increase their productivity. Meanwhile, fundamental social security measures such as free medical care and education were preserved. However, subsidies for food and housing were reduced to enhance the rationality of the national budget.

The "10·3 Discourse" delivered by Kim Jong Il showcases a notable characteristic in the management of the DPRK's economy, one that reflects its transitional nature.[78] This stands in contrast to Kim Jong Il's emphasis on economic management as outlined in his letter to the faculty and students at the University of People's Economy on July 1, 1991. In that letter, Kim Jong Il expounded on the principles of socialist economic management in the following manner.

> In socialist economic management, enterprises, owing to the transitional nature of socialist society, operate with relative independence. They employ material incentives for labor and adhere to the principles of commodity-money relations and value as essential tools for economic management. It is crucial, however, to avoid absolutizing the communist character of a socialist society while neglecting its transitional nature … Modern social democrats have erred in overemphasizing and absolutizing economic laws and categories that underscore the transitional character of a socialist society. Such emphasis has drawn them toward the tenets of the capitalist market economy, risking the abandonment of socialism and the resurgence of capitalism …

> The application of economic laws and categories reflecting the transitional nature of socialist societies should be directed solely toward fostering enhanced relations of unity and cooperation grounded in collectivism. These tools should serve to fortify the socialist planned economy, not to promote individualism or revive the capitalist market economy … Collectivism and individualism are fundamentally at odds, and a socialist planned economy based on collectivism and a capitalist market economy rooted in individualism can never coexist.[79]

Kim Jong Il's socialist economic management system, as outlined in his October 3 speech, does not align with a capitalist market economy rooted in individualism. However, upon careful analysis, the call for rationalizing planning by dividing the scale and category of plans, strict adherence to the socialist distribution principle based on earned contributions, and the use of market mechanisms for resource allocation in non-strategic industries do not amount to "embracing the capitalist market economy by excessively emphasizing and absolutizing the economic laws and categories that reflect the transitional nature of socialist society." Nevertheless, there exists a certain divergence from the socialist economic management system described by Kim Jong Il in his letter.

In this regard, the core essence of Kim Jong Il's "10·3 Discourse" can be interpreted as an acknowledgement of the transitional nature of the DPRK and its temporary setback to a lower stage within the transitional period. It serves as a call to restructure the economic management system to better reflect this transitional nature than before. However, by recognizing the regression of social development in the DPRK, Kim Jong Il confronts a complex challenge.

The primary factor contributing to the DPRK's lagging social development can be attributed to the enduring implementation of Kim Il Sung's unattainable UDPS for over two decades. This has further aggravated the issue of resource scarcity and the enforcement of communist measures that are ill-suited for the current stage of social development. Consequently, the unavailability of Kim Jong Il's "10·3 Discourse" to the public is primarily driven by this significant reason, which surpasses the contradictions encompassed within Kim Jong Il's discourse.

Despite the various reasons that prevent the "10·3 Discourse" from being made public, it presented an opportunity to address the loose and haphazard functioning of the DPRK's economic system by facing reality and resolving pressing real-world issues. Therefore, it is necessary to correct the perspective that the economic improvement measures implemented on July 1, 2002, which drew inspiration from certain aspects of the "10·3 Discourse," will inevitably result in the DPRK transitioning to a capitalist system.

As demonstrated, the DPRK has been experimenting with market-based resource allocation since 1973. Through numerous trials and errors, the economic improvement measures implemented on July 1, 2002, established a foundation for market-driven resource allocation across all industries, excluding those of high national importance and strategic significance.

However, it is crucial to differentiate the market as a mechanism for resource allocation from the capitalist market regime. The capitalist market system involves the introduction of money as a medium of exchange within the entire industrial process based on private property. It dictates that income solely arises from selling something, and any source from which an individual receives income is regarded as the outcome of their act of selling.[80]

Markets, on the other hand, have existed throughout various economic systems, whether capitalist or socialist, ancient or modern, as a mechanism for resource allocation. However, the extent and application of markets vary depending on the specific system and historical era. Moreover, as previously analyzed, the DPRK employed the market to eliminate communist measures, avoid mediocrity, uphold the socialist distribution principle of rewarding according to one's contribution, and foster specialization in production. Therefore, the market should be seen as a means to strengthen and uphold the existing system in the DPRK, rather than the other way around.

Following the "10·3 Discourse," the DPRK redirected its approach to economic construction, focusing on the rationalization of planning and production while preserving the foundational framework of social collectivism. Kim Jong Il himself emphasized this by stating,

> We must steadfastly believe in the superiority of the socialist economy and rigorously uphold socialist principles. This commitment is essential for rectifying and enhancing the socialist economic management system and structure, while continually refining economic management methods in harmony with the collectivist nature of the socialist economy and the demands of real-world development. The utmost benefits arise when socialist principles are accurately implemented to safeguard economic interests and reinforce the advantages of the socialist planned economy.[81]

As evidenced earlier, the DPRK's economic system is fundamentally rooted in social collectivism, forming the foundation and framework for its functioning. Moreover, the DPRK has consistently emphasized the importance of adhering to and preserving this social collectivist framework in its pursuit of economic development. Therefore, it is challenging to perceive the country as undergoing a transition from socialism to capitalism.

However, the new direction of economic construction in the DPRK, which focuses on achieving maximum benefits while safeguarding the interests of society as a whole,[82] represents an unprecedented path that no other nation has embarked upon. It is, in essence, a "road that no one has ever footed before."[83]

In 2014, the DPRK implemented a novel economic management system known as the "Socialist Enterprise Responsibility Management System." Described as "our own economic management method studied and developed in alignment with the demands of real-world development," this system marks a significant evolution from the "United Enterprise System." In the ensuing chapter, we will scrutinize the transition from the "United Enterprise System" to the "Socialist Enterprise Responsibility Management System" and delve into the significance and distinctive features of the latter as a management and operational framework within the DPRK socialist economy.

Notes

1 Kim Jong Il, "Chegukchuŭijadŭrŭi, ch'aektongŭn yongnaptoelsu ŏmnŭn ch'imn-yagwahae ch'aektongida: Chosŏllodongdang chungangwiwŏnhoe ch'aegimilgun-dŭlgwa han tamhwa, (chuch'e 87(1998)nyŏn 5wŏl 7il)" (The Imperialists' 'Reform' and 'Opening' Campaigns are Unacceptable Aggression and Dissolution Campaigns: Discourse with the Responsible Officials of the Central Committee of the WPK (May 7, 1998)), *Kimjŏngilsŏnjip19*-chŭngbop'an (*SWK 19* - enlarged edition) (P'yŏngyang: WPK Publishing House, 2012), p. 367.

2 Please refer to Chapter 5 (Economic Setbacks and the Causes of the Decline in Agricultural Production) in Phillip H. Park's *Self-Reliance or Self-Destruction?* for a fuller discussion of the economic downfall of the DPRK in the mid-1990s.

3 Since the fertilizer that the DPRK would use that year was made from crude oil imported in the previous year, it was not until 1995, the year after 1994, when crude oil imports plummeted, that the DPRK began to experience food shortages in earnest.

4 *CCY 1999*, p. 183.

5 As per the *CCY* reports for the years 2000 and 2001, the total national budget revenue for 1999 and 2000 was reported as 20.90343 billion wŏn and 21.63994 billion wŏn, respectively. Notably, the national budget revenue has shown a consistent upward trend since 1998, with no recorded declines. Consequently, in the year 2000, the overall national budget revenue reached a significant milestone by recovering 50% of the 1993 level, which stood at 40.5712 billion wŏn. The positive trajectory has persisted, indicating a continuous increase in total national budget revenue since that time.

6 Chapter 3 explores the complex issue of the DPRK's GDP. For detailed analysis and estimates, turn to the appendix.

7 Kim Il Sung, "Tangmyŏnhan sahoejuŭigyŏngjegŏnsŏlbanghyange taehayŏ: Chosŏllodongdang chungangwiwŏnhoe che6ki che21ch'ajŏnwŏnhoeŭiesŏ han kyŏllon (1993nyŏn 12wŏl 8il)" (On the Immediate Direction of Socialist Economic Construction: Conclusions at the Sixth Plenary Session of the 21st Central Committee of the WPK (December 8, 1993)), *CWK 94* (P'yŏngyang: WPK Publishing House, 2011), p. 155.

8 Kim Il Sung, "Sahoejuŭigyŏngjegŏnsŏresŏ saeroun hyŏngmyŏngjŏkchŏnhwanŭl irŭk'ilte taehayŏ: kyŏngjebumun ch'aegimilgunhyŏbŭihoeesŏ han kyŏllon (1994nyŏn 7wŏl 6il)" (On Making a New Revolutionary Turn in the Construction of a Socialist Economy: Conclusions of the Workers' Council in Charge of the Economic Sector (July 6, 1994)), *CWK 94*, pp. 418–427.

9 Trade in the DPRK has been permissible at the provincial level since the 1970s. However, following the implementation of the Three Sectors First Policy, it appears that trade has been extended to the county level since 1994. This development is explicitly mentioned in a conversation held by Kim Jong Il in October 1994 with responsible officers of the Party's Central Committee. In that discourse, he emphasized the significance of earning foreign currency at the county level as a means to enhance local economies and elevate the standard of living for residents.

Kim Jong Il noted,

Earning foreign currency in the counties is an enriching way to develop the local economy and raise people's living standards. Good foreign currency earning allows us to buy raw materials and materials that we don't have in counties, to turn around local industrial plants, and to buy goods that are desperately needed for the people's lives.

(Kim Jong Il, "Chosŏllodongdang chungangwiwŏnhoe ch'aegimilgundŭlgwa-han tamhwa, (chuch'e 83(1994)nyŏn 10wŏl 20il)" (Let's Make a Transformation in People's Life by Raising the Role of County (Discourse with the Responsible Officials of the Central Committee of the WPK, October 20, 1994), *SWK 18* (P'yŏngyang: WPK Publishing House, 2012), pp. 48–49)

He emphasized the need to establish foreign currency earning bases in all counties, actively engage in the foreign currency earning struggle, and achieve abundance in meeting foreign currency earning targets.

10 Kim Jong Il, "Tangŭi muyŏkcheilchuŭibangch'imŭl kwanch'ŏrhanŭndesŏ nasŏnŭn myŏtkaji munje: Chosŏllodongdang chungangwiwŏnhoe ch'aegimilgundŭlgwahan tamhwa (chuch'e 84(1995)nyŏn 2wŏl 1il)" (Some Problems in Implementing the Party's Trade First Policy: Talks with the Responsible Officials of the Central Committee of the WPK, February 1, 1995), *SWK 18*, pp. 194–196.

11 As the total national budget revenue plummeted to less than half of its pre-crisis level, the shock reverberated across all sectors of the economy, with the agriculture sector bearing the brunt of the impact. According to a 1996 assessment by a Food and Agriculture Organization (FAO) or the World Food Program (WFP) special mission team, cereal production in that year had declined by 40% compared to 1989. The resulting food shortage, however, was not uniformly distributed.

In remote areas inaccessible to trains and lorries due to energy shortages, acute shortages prevailed. Consequently, the breakdown of the Public Distribution System (PDS) in these remote areas left residents with no alternative but to face starvation. Faced with dire circumstances, people voluntarily gathered, engaging in barter to exchange goods for survival, leading to the formation of "Changmadang.".

In regions where the PDS weakened but remained functional, farmers' markets emerged as substitutes, shouldering the burden left unfulfilled by the PDS. For a more in-depth exploration of this topic, please refer to Phillip H. Park's article, "The Process of Marketisation and Economic Realities in the DPRK," published online on October 2, 2023, in the journal *Asian Studies Review* (https://doi.org/10.1080/10357823.2023.2255374).

12 The quoted statement from Kim Jong Il underscores the widespread nature of a particular phenomenon. He remarked, "**While the people of other provinces went in search of food** (emphasis added), the people of Chagang, men and women alike, carried manure by hand and foot, kept the streets and villages sanitary and clean, and lived in an optimistic manner" (Kim Jong Il, "Kongŏppumundŭrŭl hyŏndaejŏkkisullo kaegŏnhamyŏ naraŭi kyŏngjerŭl ch'uk'yŏseunŭndesŏ nasŏnŭn myŏtkaji munjee taehayŏ: Chosŏllodongdang chungangwiwŏnhoe ch'aegimilgundŭrap'esŏ han yŏnsŏl (chuch'e 89(2000)nyŏn 5wŏl12il)" (On Some Problems in Rebuilding the Heavy Industry Sectors with Modern Technology and Building Up the Country's Economy: Speech Before the Responsible Officials of the Central Committee of the WPK, (May 12, 2000)), *SWK 20* (P'yŏngyang: WPK Publishing House, 2013), p. 197).

13 Kim Jong Il, "Tang, kukka, kyŏngjesaŏbesŏ nasŏnŭn myŏtkaji munje taehayŏ (chosŏllodongdang chungangwiwŏnhoe ch'aegimilgundŭrap'esŏ han yŏnsŏl (chuch'e 81(1992)nyŏn 11wŏl 12il)" (On Some Problems in Party, State, and Economic Work (Speech Before the Responsible Officials of the Central Committee of the WPK, (November 12, 1992)), *SWK 17* (P'yŏngyang: WPK Publishing House, 2012), p. 270.

14 Kim Jong Il, "Sahoejuŭinŭn kwahagida: Chosŏllodongdang chungangwiwŏnhoe kigwanjit'enrodongshinmunt'ene palp'yohan ronmun (chuch'e 83(1994)nyŏn 11wŏl 1il)" (Socialism is a Science, (an article published in *Rodong Sinmun* (November 1, 1994)), *SWK 18*, pp. 93–95.

15 Kim Jong Il's exceptional focus on the military is underscored by his roles as the Supreme Commander of the Korean People's Army and the First Vice Chairman of

the National Defense Commission. His effective leadership within the military drew commendation from Kim Il Sung, evident in the following statement:

> It is entirely due to the correct guidance of Comrade Kim Jong Il that the People's Army has been fortified and evolved into a politically, ideologically, and militarily proficient force. It stands today as a unified and revolutionary entity, fulfilling its honorable mission as the guardian of the Party, the revolution, the country, and the people.
>
> (Kim Il Sung, "Sahoejuŭiwiŏbŭi kyesŭngwansŏngŭl wihayŏ hangirhyŏng-myŏngt'usadŭl, hyŏngmyŏnggayujanyŏdŭlgwa han tamhwa (1992nyŏn 3wŏl 13il, 1993nyŏn 1wŏl 20il, 3wŏl 3il)" (Toward the Completion of the Succession of the Socialist Work: Talks with Anti-Japanese Revolutionary Fighters and Descents (March 13, 1992, January 20, 1993, March 3), *CWK 92* (P'yŏngyang: WPK Publishing House, 2010), p. 135)

16 From 1995 to 2001, Kim Jong Il reportedly fielded 1,300 units, including 841 in the Armed Forces (*CCY 2002*, p. 84).
17 Kim Jong Il characterized it in the following manner:

> Our Party's Military-First revolutionary leadership represents a distinctive political approach that encapsulates the ideology emphasizing the significance of the military. The distinctiveness and unparalleled strength of our Party's 'Military-First Politics' lie in prioritizing the military and fortifying the People's Army into an invincible revolutionary force.
>
> This force is dedicated to defending the Party with arms, safeguarding the fatherland, the revolution, and socialism, and vigorously advancing the cause of revolution and construction. All of this is underpinned by the revolutionary and combative spirit of the People's Army.
>
> (Kim Jong Il, "Ch'ŏngnyŏndongmaengch'ogŭpchojiktŭrŭi yŏk'arŭl tŏung nop'ijar kimilsŏngsahoejuŭich'ŏngnyŏndongmaeng mobŏmch'ogŭbilgundae-hoech'amgajadŭrege ponaen sŏhan (chuch'e 88(1999)nyŏn 9wŏl 29il)" (Increasing the Role of Youth League Beginner Organizations: Letter to the Participants of the Model Beginner's Workers' Conference of the Kim Il Sung Socialist Youth League (September 29, 1999), *SWK 20*, p. 30)

18 Kim Jong Il, "Chosŏllodongdang chungangwiwŏnhoe ch'aegimilgundŭlgwa han tamhwa (chuch'e 86(1997)nyŏn 1wŏl 1il)" (Discourse with the Responsible officials of the Central Committee of the WPK (January 1, 1997)), *SWK 19*, p. 4.
19 Kim Jong Il, "Chosŏllodongdang chungangwiwŏnhoe ch'aegimilgundŭrap'esŏ han yŏnsŏl (chuch'e 86(1997)nyŏn 9wŏl27il)" (Speech Before the Responsible Workers of the Central Committee of the WPK (September 27, 1997)," *SWK 19*, pp. 210–214.
20 In addressing the concept of the "Revolutionary Soldier Spirit," Kim Jong Il critiques those overseeing the Cabinet and the economy who do not wholeheartedly embrace his directives, stating:

> The economic leaders' failure to operate and decisively execute economic projects in alignment with the Party's intentions, despite the Party specifying the direction and methods for implementing the 'Revolutionary Economic Strategy' on multiple occasions, is rooted in their lack of the spirit of absoluteness and unconditional acceptance of the Party's policy. Building the country's economy cannot be accomplished with an attitude of "giving up if things do not work out.".

> The Revolutionary Soldier Spirit of the People's Army encompasses the 'Suryŏnggyŏlsaongwijŏngshin' (spirit of defending the leader to the death), the 'Ch'ongp'okt'anjŏngshin' (spirit of turning into bullets and bombs), and the 'Chap'okchŏngshin' (spirit of self-sacrifice). The soldiers of the People's Army

approach their tasks with the determination that they have no right to fail before executing the orders of the supreme commander.

Consequently, they unconditionally undertake any challenging task assigned by the supreme commander. It is imperative for our economic leaders not only to comprehend the Revolutionary Soldier Spirit but also to implement it in practice. The Party has directed us to concentrate our efforts on grain production and the leading sectors of the People's Economy this year, and we must advance these sectors through any means necessary.

> (Kim Jong Il, "Konanŭi haenggun ch'oehudolgyŏkchŏnŭl tŏung himch'age pŏllija: Chosŏllodongdang chungangwiwŏnhoe ch'aegimilgundŭlgwa han tamhwa (chuch'e 86(1997)nyŏn 6wŏl 21il)" (Let's Make the Last Charge of the Arduous March More Vigorously: A Discourse with the Persons in Charge of the Central Committee of the WPK (June 21, 1997)), *SWK 19*, pp. 154–155).

21 Kim Jong Il, "Widaehan suryŏngnimkkesŏ yŏrŏnoŭshin hyŏngmyŏngŭi kirŭl kkŭtkkaji kaya handa: Chosŏllodongdang chungangwiwŏnhoe chojikchidobu pubujangdŭlgwa han tamhwa (chuch'e 100 (2011)nyŏn 9wŏl12il)" (We Must Follow the Revolutionary Road Opened by the Great Leader to the End: A Discourse with the Deputy Heads of the Organizational Guidance Department of the Central Committee of the WPK (September 12, 2011)), *SWK 25* (P'yŏngyang: WPK Publishing House, 2015), p. 377.

22 The spirit and work attitude of the workers during the Building the Foundation of the Party period, as expressed in the editorial "Let us learn from the Fighting Spirit of the Soldiers and Their Work Style during the Building the Foundation of the Party," published in the October 6, 2012, edition of the *Rodong Sinmun*, closely mirrors a replica of the 'Revolutionary Soldier Spirit' witnessed during the 'Arduous March.' The relevant excerpt from the *Rodong Sinmun* editorial is as follows:

> Absolute loyalty to one's leader, unwavering enthusiasm for wholeheartedly implementing the Party's policies without reservation, a robust entrepreneurial drive, steadfast adherence to Party principles, and an uncompromising fighting spirit– these constitute the foundational attributes of the workers during the Building the Foundation of the Party period ....
>
> The workers of that era demonstrated an unwavering commitment to following the Great General, eschewing any deviation from his path, and refusing any compromises in the monumental task of establishing the Party's monolithic leadership system. Such traits became ingrained in the constitutionalized temperament and revolutionary work characteristics of the workers in the 1970s.

23 The Korean People's Army's 549th Armed Forces Unit serves as a notable example of exceptional achievement. Tasked with constructing the Anbyŏn Youth Power Plant and the Naep'yŏng Power Plant, the unit completed these projects within a remarkable three-year timeframe.

Kim Jong Il expressed great satisfaction with their achievements, saying, "I am very satisfied that you have built these large-scale hydroelectric power stations so well." He also visited the 549th Unit's subsidiary farm. There, he learned in detail about the farm's situation, including the size and tidy arrangement of the 1,000-plus acres of subsidiary fields, the small and well-built houses, and the various modern agricultural machinery.

He also expressed great satisfaction with the fact that the unit had built its own power station and was actively promoting electrification, and that it was using its subsidiary fields to produce a lot of various vegetables and grains, and raising a large number of livestock, including goats, sheep, cows, rabbits, and pigs, to provide abundant and nutritious food for its soldiers. Expressing great satisfaction, Kim Jong Il emphasized the significance of such rear supply projects, underscoring that all military units should prioritize similar endeavors (*CCY 2001*, p. 51).

24 Some of the targeted construction projects undertaken by the Armed Forces units and completed during Kim Jong Il's lifetime include Pyŏngyang-Hyangsan Tourist Road, Anbyŏn Youth Power Plant, Naep'yŏng Power Plant, Nyŏngwŏn Power Plant, North P'yŏngan Province, South P'yŏngan Province, Hwanghae Province, Kangwŏn Province, and P'yŏngyang City Land Clearance Project, December 5 Youth Mine, 4.25 Hotel, Wŏlsan Amusement Park, Chicken Factory No. 112, Hwangju Chicken Factory, Kim Il Sung University Swimming Pool and Electronic Library, P'yŏngyang Southern Bird Science Institute, Taedonggang Fruit and Vegetable Farm, Taedonggang Pig Factory, Taedonggang Net Factory, Taedonggang Fruit and Vegetable Farm, Taedonggang Fruit and Vegetable Processing Factory, Taedonggang Beer Factory, Ongnyŏ Restaurant, Ryongji Duck Factory, Taedonggang Fruit and Vegetable Farm, and many more.

25 Kim Jong Il's speech on May 22, 2009, to the heads of the Central Party Commission and the Ryanggang Provice Commission provides insight into this approach. He stated,

> During the 'Arduous March,' "**I dispatched veterans en masse to crucial sectors of the People's Economy, and they have become the core, leading their own units**" (emphasis added). Among the veterans deployed to Taehongdan, many started as entry-level workers, including workshop leaders, and now play a pivotal role in implementing the Party's policy of revolutionizing potato farming.
>
> **The reason why I am sending veterans to Hyesan Youth Mine and Paegam county is not just to improve production, but to ideologically reform those units** (emphasis added). In the future, when veterans are sent to these locations, the revolutionary soldierly spirit will permeate these units, ushering in a new surge in production and construction. The assignment of veterans to key sectors of the People's Economy should be orchestrated in a way that holds political significance and leaves an enduring imprint in their memories. **The veterans serve as a wellspring of cadres** (emphasis added).
>
> (Kim Jong Il, "Ryanggangdoŭi kyŏngjesaŏpkwa inminsaenghwaresŏ hyŏng-myŏngjŏkchŏnhwanŭl irŭk'ilte taehayŏ: Chosŏllodongdang chungangwiwŏnhoe, ryanggangdo wiwŏnhoe ch'aegimilgundŭlgwa han tamhwa (chuch'e 88(2009) nyŏn 5wŏl22il)" (On Making a Revolutionary Transformation in the Economic Work and People's Life of Ryanggangdo Province (Speech to the Central Committee of the WPK and the Workers in Charge of the Ryanggangdo Province Committee, (May 22, 2009)), *SWK* 24 (P'yŏngyang: WPK Publishing House, 2014), pp. 173–174)

26 Given that Kim Jong Il likely handpicked the most capable soldiers from the People's Army for integration into society upon discharge, we applied Pareto's 80/20 rule. Our assumption is that approximately 20% of the discharged soldiers would have been strategically dispatched to various segments of society.

27 On October 26 and 27, 2007, the DPRK hosted a two-day Congress of Party Secretaries. In response to the proceedings, the *Rodong Sinmun* provided its commentary in an editorial, expressing the following sentiments:

> Over the past decade of arduous struggle, our Party, bolstered by tens of thousands of steadfast Party cells, has achieved a historic feat, staunchly defending the socialist red flag to the last and ushering in a new era of constructing a robust and prosperous nation.
>
> In the diverse arenas dedicated to forging an economic powerhouse, spanning locations such as Kimch'ŏl, Nanam, Sŏnggang, Ryŏngsong, Hŭngnam, and Tanch'ŏn, the flames of productive enthusiasm and modernization burn resolutely.

The hearts of our people are infused with the unwavering belief in victory and optimism. This remarkable progress is intricately tied to the dynamic efforts of Party cells diligently upholding the Party's Sŏn'gun leadership
> (Sasŏl, "T'etangŭi kanghwabalchŏn'gwa kangsŏngdaegukkŏnsŏrŭi chŏnhwan-jŏkkyegiro toel chŏn'guktangsep'obisŏdaehoe (chuch'e 86(2007)nyŏn 10wŏl26il)" (Editorial, "National Party Cell Secretaries' Conference to be a Transformative Event for the Party's Strengthened Development and the Construction of a Great Power,") *Rodong Sinmun* (October 26, 2007)

As evident from the aforementioned editorial, the veterans who were earnestly dispatched to labor sites in 1998 later emerged as Party cell secretaries more than a decade thereafter. They stood as the bedrock of the Party's Military-First Politics, actively supporting and executing the Party's policies in their respective domains.

28 Kim Jong Il, "Orhaerŭl sahoejuŭigyŏngjegŏnsŏresŏ hyŏngmyŏngjŏkchŏnhwanŭi haerodoege haja: Chŏndangdangilgunhoeŭi ch'amgajadŭrege ponaensŏhan (chuch'e 87(1997)nyŏn 1wŏl 24il)" (Let This Year Be the Year of Revolutionary Transformation in the Construction of a Socialist Economy: Letter to the Participants of the All-Party Cadres' Conference (January 24, 1997)), *SWK 19*, pp. 26–27.

29 Kim Jong Il, "Chagangdoŭi mobŏmŭl ttara kyŏngjesaŏpkwa inminsaenghwaresŏ saeroun chŏnhwanŭl irŭk'ijar chagangdoŭi yŏrŏ pumun saŏbŭl hyŏnjijido-hamyŏnsŏ ilgundŭlgwa han tamhwa(chuch'e 87(1998)nyŏn 1wŏl16t'on21il, 6wŏl 1il, 10wŏl 20il, 22il)" (Following Chagang Province's Example, Let's Make a New Transformation in Economic Work and People's Life: Discourse with Workers While Providing Local Guidance to Various Sectors in Chagang Province (chuch'e 87(1998), January 16–21, June 1, October 20, 22), *SWK 19*, pp. 246–247.

30 Kim Jong Il, "Chagangdoŭi mobŏmŭl ttara kyŏngjesaŏpkwa inminsaenghwaresŏ saeroun chŏnhwanŭl irŭk'ijar chagangdoŭi yŏrŏ pumun saŏbŭl hyŏnjijidohamyŏnsŏ ilgundŭlgwa han tamhwa(chuch'e 87(1998)nyŏn 1wŏl16t'on21il, 6wŏl 1il, 10wŏl 20il, 22il)" (Following Chagang Province's Example, Let's Make a New Transformation in Economic Work and People's Life: Discourse with Workers While Providing Local Guidance to Various Sectors in Chagang Province (chuch'e 87(1998), January 16–21, June 1, October 20, 22), *SWK 19*, p. 250.

31 Chagang Province serves as the hub for several crucial munitions factories. In addition, the region boasts other significant players, including the Amnokkangdaia Factory, Kanggye Tractor United Enterprise, and the September Textile Factory, all playing pivotal roles in the construction of the DPRK economy.

32 While the DPRK remains reticent about the specific share of its budget dedicated to defense during this period, logical deductions suggest that during the "Kanghaenggun" (Forced March), the most brutal phase of the Arduous March, defense expenditures likely surpassed even the 30% observed in the early part of the Parallel Route. Since the severe economic hardships of the Arduous March drastically reduced the national budget to less than half its pre-crisis level, maintaining the same defense spending as in the early part of the "Parallel Route" era in this context would have led to a remarkable surge in proportional allocation, reaching a staggering 60%.

33 This is evident in the statements made by Kim Jong Il:

> Despite the challenging food situation in the country, we have diligently provided the soldiers with the complete, prescribed amount of food. Notably, we have gone a step further by ensuring the availability of dry soy sauce to meet the dietary needs of our soldiers.
> (Kim Jong Il, Strengthening the People's Armed Forces to Reliably Guarantee the Feat of Building a Strong Nation: A Talk with the Commanding Officers of the Korean People's Armymy (January 24, 1999), *SWK 19*, p. 461)

34 Kim Jong Il, "Chagangdosaramdŭlch'ŏrŏm towa shi, kunŭi sallimsarirŭl chal kkuryŏnagaja: Chosŏllodongdang chungangwiwŏnhoewa chagangdowiwŏnhoe ch'aegimilgundŭlgwa han tamhwa (chuch'e 89(2000)nyŏn 8wŏl31il)" (Like the People of Chagang Have Done, Let us Organize a Good Living Condition for Provinces, Cities and Counties: A Discourse with the Central Committee of the WPK and the Officials in Charge of the Chagang Province Committee (August 31, 2000)), *SWK 20*, p. 258.

35 By 1999, Chagang province had built 332 small- and medium-sized power plants under its power (*CCY 2000*, p. 43). Following this example, more than 5,000 small- and medium-sized power plants were built nationwide, including 290 small- and medium-sized ones in South Hamgyŏng Province without central assistance (*CCY 2000*, p. 56).

36 Kim Jong Il, "Kanghaenggunŭro sahoejuŭigyŏngjegŏnsŏresŏ saeroun chin'gyŏng-norŭl yŏrŏnagaja: Chosŏllodongdang chungangwiwŏnhoe ch'aegimilgundŭlgwa han tamhwa (chuch'e 87(1998)nyŏn 2wŏl 13il)" (Let Us Open a New Path of Advancement in the Construction of the Socialist Economy by Forward March: A Discourse with the Cadres in Charge of the Central Committee of the WPK (February 13, 1998)), *SWK 19*, p. 270.

37 The Samhwa Iron method, utilizing a combination of anthracite coal, cement, and iron ore for iron extraction, holds the distinct advantage of eliminating the need for coke and scrap metal imports. Furthermore, it proves more energy-efficient when compared to the existing methods (Ch'ikwan Kim, "T'ongilbu, Puk 'chuch'e ch'ŏl 'chuch'e biryo,' 'chuch'e sŏmyu,' ch'yulch'n munjejŏm chijŏk" (Unification Ministry Points Out Problems with North's 'Chuch'e Steel,'Fertilizer, Fiber,' and CNC), *TongilNews* (December 18, 2010). http://www.tongilnews.com/news/articleView.html?idxno=92981.

38 *CCY 2000*, p. 32.

39 Chiyŏng Kim, "Mallimaŭi shida/kyŏngjebuhŭnggwa saenghwarhyangsang 2: kŭp-sok'i kwangbŏmwihage toiptoenŭn t'onghapsaengsanch'egye" (2017nyŏn-10wŏl27il) (The Age of Manrima/Economic Revival and Livelihood Improvement 2: Integrated Production System Rapidly and Widely Introduced, *Chosun Shinbo* (October 27, 2017). http://chosonsinbo.com/2017/10/24suk-7.

40 Kim Jong Il, "Orhaerŭl kangsŏngdaegukkŏnsŏrŭi widaehanjŏnhwanŭi haero pin-naeija: Chosŏllodongdang chungangwiwŏnhoe ch'aegimilgundŭlgwahan tamhwa (chuch'e 88(1999)nyŏn 1wŏl 1il)" (Let This Year Shine as a Year of Great Transformation in the Construction of the 'Strong and Great Nation' (Discourse with the Cadres in charge of the Central Committee of the WPK, (January 1, 1999)), *SWK 20*, p. 444.

41 DPRK economist Chongsŏ Ri elucidates this within the framework of the Kangsŏngdaeguk (Strong and Great Nation) construction as follows:

In the pivotal year of chuch'e 89 (2000), marked by total advancement, we are poised to take a decisive stride in realizing the Strong and Great Nation in accord-ance with the resolute decree of our esteemed Party. Economic practitioners must steadfastly embrace the principle of focusing on ideology, military strength, and scientific and technological prowess, driving forward the establishment of a social-ist economic powerhouse.

These three pillars—Thought, Military Strength, and Science and Technology—constitute the foundation for the construction of the Strong and Great Nation.

(Chongsŏ Ri, "Widaehan kimjŏngiltongjikkesŏ cheshihashin hyŏngmyŏngjŏk-kyŏngjejŏngch'aekŭn sahoejuŭigyŏngjeganggukkŏnsŏrŭi chŏnt'ujŏkkich'I (chuch'e 89(2000)nyŏn" (The Revolutionary Economic Policy Presented by the Great Kim Jong Il is a Combative Banner for Building a Socialist Strong and Great Nation), *ER* (2000), no. 1, pp. 2–3)

42 Kim Jong Il's stance on science and technology is succinctly expressed as follows:

Science and technology play pivotal roles as powerful catalysts in the construction of a Strong and Great Nation. The absence of advanced scientific and technological capabilities renders the realization of this vision unattainable. It is imperative for every scientist and technician to hold the Party's leadership in utmost reverence, directing their intellect and passion towards overcoming the scientific and technological challenges essential for the construction of a Strong and Great Nation.

(Kim Jong Il, "Orhaerŭl kangsŏngdaegukkŏnsŏrŭi widaehanjŏnhwanŭi haero pinnaeijar chosŏllodongdang chungangwiwŏnhoe ch'aegimilgundŭlgwahan tamhwa (chuch'e 88(1999)nyŏn 1wŏl 1il)" (Let This Year Shine as a Year of Great Transformation in the Construction of the Strong and Great Nation: A Discourse with the Cadres in charge of the Central Committee of the WPK (January 1, 1999)), *SWK 19*, p. 252)

43 As Kim Jong Il gained confidence in the defense of the DPRK and brought Military-First Politics to the forefront, the trajectory of economic construction shifted toward upholding socialist principles and prioritizing maximum practicality. On October 3, 2001, he delivered a discourse titled "Kangsŏngdaegung kŏnsŏrŭi yogue matke sahoejuŭigyŏngjegwallirŭl kaesŏn'ganghwahal te taehayŏ" (On Improving and Strengthening Socialist Economic Management to Meet the Needs of Building a Strong and Great Nation, from now on referred to as "10·3 Discourse") to the cadres overseeing the Central Committee of the WPK.

On July 1, 2002, a set of economic improvement measures, encompassing elements from the aforementioned discourse, specifically the Kyŏngjegaesŏnjoch'i (Economic Improvement Measures, from now on referred to as "7·1 Measure"), were introduced. For detailed insights into the DPRK's economic system, the "10·3 Discourse" assumes a critical role. Accordingly, a comprehensive discussion of the "10·3 Discourse" will be presented in the appendix of this chapter.

44 "Given the global depletion of coking coal and its escalating prices, other nations are modernizing their metal plants by embracing non-coke methods of steelmaking to mitigate production costs. We, on the other hand, have successfully expedited the implementation of the non-coke method of steelmaking well in advance ... Coal gasification and the non-coke method of steelmaking stand as the vitallifelines for the economic development of our nation" (Kim Jong Il, "Hwanghaejech'ŏllyŏnhapkiŏpsonŭn Chuch'ech'ŏlsaengsant'odaee ŭigŏhayŏ ch'ŏlgangjaesaengsanŭl nop'ŭn sujuneso chŏngsanghwa hayŏya handa: Hwanghaejech'ŏllyŏnhapkiŏpsorŭl hyŏnjijidohamyŏnsŏ ilgundŭlgwa han tamhwa (chuch'e 89(2010)nyŏn 2wŏl20il)" (The Hwanghae Steel United Enterprise Should Normalize Steel Production at a High Level Based on the Foundation of Chuch'e Steel Production: A Discourse with the Workers While Guiding the Hwanghae Iron and Steel United Enterprise (February 20, 2010)), *SWK 24*, p. 494).

45 Kim Jong Il, "Chunggongŏppumundŭrŭl hyŏndaejŏkkisullo kaegŏnhamyŏ naraŭi kyŏngjerŭl ch'uk'yŏseunŭndesŏ nasŏnŭn myŏtkaji munjee taehayŏ: Chosŏllodongdang chungangwiwŏnhoe ch'aegimilgundŭrap'esŏ han yŏnsŏl (chuch'e 89(2000)nyŏn 5wŏl12il)" (On Some Problems in Rebuilding the Heavy Industry Sectors with Modern Technology and Moving the Country's Economy Forward: Speech Before the Cadres in Charge of the Central Committee of the WPK (May 12, 2000)), *SWK 20*, p. 184.

46 Kim Jong Il encouraged the production of vinylon using methanol instead of carbide, stating,

A new vinylon industry should be established. Instead of producing vinylon from carbide, which uses a lot of electricity, as is the case now, we should go in the direction of producing vinylon from methanol

(Kim Jong Il, "Chunggongŏppumundŭrŭl hyŏndaejŏkkisullo kaegŏnhamyŏ naraŭi kyŏngjerŭl ch'uk'yŏseunŭndesŏ nasŏnŭn myŏtkaji munjee taehayŏ:

> Chosŏllodongdang chungangwiwŏnhoe ch'aegimilgundŭrap'esŏ han yŏnsŏl (chuch'e 89(2000)nyŏn 5wŏl12il)" (On Some Problems in Rebuilding the Heavy Industry Sectors with Modern Technology and Moving the Country's Economy Forward: Speech Before the Cadres in Charge of the Central Committee of the WPK (May 12, 2000)), *SWK 20*, p. 184)

Nine years after directing the production of vinylon from methanol, there was a strategic shift to producing vinylon through the coal gasification process, specifically the anthracite gasification process. Kim Jong Il articulated this transition, stating,

> The construction of the anthracite gasification process is directly linked to the well-being of our people, and we must spare no expense in allocating funds for its realization. Today, I am addressing the financial needs for the construction of the anthracite gasification process, a pivotal initiative in resolving the livelihood challenges of our citizens. The necessary funds have already been allocated to the 2·8 Vinylon United Enterprise.
> (Kim Jong Il, "Namhŭngch'ŏngnyŏnhwahangnyŏnhapkiŏpsonŭn kongjanggwalliesŏ hyŏkshinŭl irŭk'igo rodonggyegŭbŭi saemunhwarŭl ch'angjohan ponbogidanwiida: Namhŭngch'ŏngnyŏnhwahangnyŏnhapkiŏpsorŭl hyŏnjijidohamyŏnsŏ ilgundŭlgwa han tamhwa (chuch'e 88(2009)nyŏn 5wŏl28il)" (The Namhŭng Youth Chemical United Enterprise is an Exemplary Unit That Has Revolutionized Factory Management and Created a New Culture Among the Working Class: A Discourse with the Cadres in Charge While Providing On-the-Spot Guidance to the Namhŭng Youth Chemical United Enterprise (May 28, 2009)), *SWK 24*, p. 208)

47 *CCY 2011*, p. 67.

48 Dr. Ung Cho, the head of the Integrated Production System Research Laboratory at the Department of Automation Engineering, Kim Chek University of Science and Technology, remarked,

> Amidst the economic challenges of the late 1990s, the General's decision effectively allocated significant funds, essentially constituting the nation's entire financial resources, towards the advancement of state-of-the-art CNC technology. This strategic investment in CNC has played a pivotal role in modernizing machine shops.
> (Chiyŏng Kim, "The Age of Manrima/Economic Revival and Livelihood Improvement 2: Integrated Production System Rapidly and Widely Introduced (October 27, 2017)," *Chosun Shinbo.*)

In the DPRK, leaders are distinguished by unique titles: Kim Il Sung is revered as the "Suryŏng" (Great Leader), Kim Jong Il as the "Changgun" (General), and Kim Jong Un is referred to as "Wŏnsu" (Marshal). The genesis of these titles can be traced to Kim Jong Il's successor theory. Acknowledging that "Suryong" exclusively belongs to Kim Il Sung (Kim Jong Il. *SWK 20*-enlarged edition, p. 44), Kim Jong Il, as his successor, abstained from permitting anyone to address him by that honorific, emphasizing the singularity of the Supreme Leader.

In lieu of "Suryŏng," the title "General" was bestowed upon Kim Jong Il, symbolizing his leadership in 'Sŏn'gun' (Military-First Politics) and his guidance of the military. The use of "General" underscores his role as the leader advocating and directing the military under this ideology. Continuing in this tradition, Kim Jong Un, as the successor to Kim Jong Il, similarly refrains from being referred to as "Suryŏng." Instead, people spontaneously address him by the title "Wŏnsu" (Marshal), signifying his succession of the General's 'Military-First Politics.'

49 *CCY 2003*, p. 46.

50 Kim Jong Il, "Ragwŏnŭi rodonggyegŭbŭn charyŏkkaengsaengŭi charangsŭrŏun chŏnt'ongŭl kyesong pinnaeyanagaya handa: ragwŏn'gigyeryŏnhapkiŏpsorŭl hyŏnjijidohamyŏnsŏ ilgundŭlgwa han tamhwa (chuch'e 83(2004)nyŏn 5wŏl16il)" (The Working Class of Ragwŏn Must Continue to Shine with the Proud Tradition of

Self-Reliance: A Discourse with the Workers While Guiding the Ragwŏn Machinery United Enterprise (May 16, 2004)), *SWK 22* (P'yŏngyang: WPK Publishing House, 2013), p. 97.

51 *CCY 2006*, pp. 32–33.

52 Kim Jong Il, "Uri shing ch'yulch'ŭimmolkongikaech'ŏk'an sŏnggwawa kyŏnghŏme t'odaehayŏ modŭn punyaesŏ ch'ŏmdanŭl tolp'ahajar chosŏllodongdang chungangwiwŏnhoe ch'aegimilgundŭlgwa han tamhwa (chuch'e 89(2010)nyŏn 1wŏl1il)" (Let's Break Through the Cutting Edge in All Fields Based on the Achievements and Experience of Pioneering Our Own CNC Technology: A Discourse with the Cadres of the Central Committee of the WPK (January 1, 2010)), *SWK 24*, pp. 447–451.

53 "Chŏlseŭi Aegukcha Kimjŏngilchang-gun 5 Urishik CNCHwaŭi Shirhyŏnŭl Wihayŏ" (Unsurpassed Patriot General Kim Jong Il 5: For the realization of Chosun-style CNCization. https://www.youtube.com/watch?v=r9-wPiaPDQg&t=1591s.

54 While not explicitly documented in the *SWK* and the *CCY*, the consistent pattern of Kim Jong Il's frequent visits to strategically significant factories and enterprises, as indicated in Table 2.2, implies a substantial amount of trial and error along with an intricate process involved in their completion.

55 The following remarks by Kim Jong Il during his on-the-spot guidance vividly illustrate the remarkable achievements:

You have accomplished a commendable feat by finalizing the refining process within the '100-Day Battle Period,' exactly as I tasked when inspecting the new process for producing Chuch'e Steel through a rotary furnace and oxygen equipment back in September. In just a few months, extensive work has been carried out, resulting in the successful completion of the Chuch'e steelmaking process at the Sŏngjin Steel United Enterprise.

This signifies the direct production of high-quality steel from Chuch'e Steel. The steel, made with 100% Chuch'e Steel, represents pure Chuch'e Steel in its entirety. The method of steel production utilizing Chuch'e Steel has been triumphantly implemented at the Sŏngjin Steel ….

The attainment of the Chuch'e Steel production system by the dedicated working class of Sŏngjin, using their own strength and technological prowess, marks a distinctive historical event in the evolution of the metallurgical industry—a significant revolution and a triumph surpassing even the third nuclear test. This signifies the culmination of the Chuch'e Steel industry and the achievement of the Chuch'e Metal industry.

(Kim Jong Il, "Sŏngjinjegangnyŏnhapkiŏpsoesŏŭi chuch'ech'ŏlsaengsanch'egyewansŏngŭn yagŭmgongŏppalchŏnesŏ t'ŭkkihal ryŏksajŏksabyŏnimyŏ iltae hyŏngmyŏngida: Sŏngjinjegangnyŏnhapkiŏpsorŭl hyŏnjijidohamyŏnsŏ ilgundŭlgwa han tamhwa (chuch'e 88(2009)nyŏn 12wŏl18il)" (The Completion of the Chuch'e Steel production system at the Sŏngjin Steel United Enterprise is a Unique Historical Event in the Development of the Metallurgical Industry and a Major Revolution: A Discourse with the Cadres while Providing Local Guidance at the Sŏngjin Steel United Enterprise (December 18, 2009), *SWK 24*, pp. 434–435)

56 The 2011 *CCY* report painted a promising picture of the nation's future, highlighting transformative advancements across various sectors.

The year 2010 marked a pivotal turning point, ushering in a series of remarkable achievements. Perhaps most significantly, the 2.8 Vinylon United Enterprise established a state-of-the-art vinylon plant, introducing the domestically produced Chuch'e Fiber to the nation, a milestone that promised to revolutionize the textile industry.

Equally impressive was the completion of the Chuch'e Steel production system at the Kimch'aek Steel United Enterprise, solidifying the foundation for domestic steel production and ensuring self-sufficiency in this critical material. Furthermore, the Namhŭng Youth Chemical United Enterprise implemented a cutting-edge gasification process, enabling the production of Chuch'e Fertilizer, a crucial development for agricultural advancement.

The Ryongsŏng Mechanical United Enterprise saw its capabilities bolstered with the construction of the Sŏn'gun Cast Iron Plant and the Sŏn'gun Compressor Plant, signifying the nation's commitment to industrial expansion and modernization. This drive for progress extended beyond these major sites, with numerous factories and enterprises undergoing upgrades, including the Tanch'ŏn Mining Machinery Plant, the P'yŏngyang Koksan Plant, the September Textile Plant, the Ryongsŏng Food Plant, and local industrial plants in Kanggye and Hamhŭng.

These initiatives served not only as testaments to the nation's pursuit of cutting-edge technology but also embodied the spirit of the Sŏn'gun (Military-First) Policy. Further solidifying this image were remarkable achievements in other areas, such as the successful realization of nuclear fusion, a groundbreaking scientific feat, and the development of domestically produced 100% shaft guns, showcasing advancements in military technology. The creation of a nine-axis turning center at the Ryŏnha-machine group further underscored the exceptional prowess of the domestic machinery manufacturing industry.

(*CCY 2011*, p. 51)

57 Kim Jong Il did not initially embrace a growth strategy centered on technological innovation for economic development, despite having various options available. Upon assuming leadership, however, it became clear that the DPRK's economy could no longer solely rely on labor and capital for growth. Technological innovation emerged as the only viable path forward. Though not his initial preference, circumstances forced him to adopt this approach. Thus, the ironic shift in the DPRK's economic strategy from extensive to intensive sources was a consequence of necessity, not conscious design.

58 China's Maritime Statistics for 2014 reported no crude oil exports to the DPRK, a finding corroborated by the UN Comtrade Database, which indicated zero crude oil exports to the DPRK from the rest of the world during the same period. However, dismissing the possibility of any crude oil imports into the DPRK in 2014 as unrealistic would be imprudent. Looking beyond the data for that specific year, the average annual crude oil imports by the DPRK from 2010 to 2015 stood at 539 thousand tons.

Contrary to the absence of crude oil exports in 2014, the DPRK did not face an oil crisis, and evidence suggests that travelers to the region encountered no significant inconveniences related to petroleum availability, as hiring a taxi remained easy and trouble-free. In light of these considerations, we posit that the DPRK likely maintained a consistent level of oil reserves comparable to previous years. Therefore, we estimate the DPRK's crude oil imports in 2014 to be around 539 thousand tons.

However, while seemingly improbable, there exists an alternative explanation for the DPRK achieving a significant rice yield without relying on imported oil. The DPRK has asserted possession of substantial crude oil reserves, ranging from 60 billion to 90 billion barrels. Some foreign oil and gas entities, such as Aminex, an Irish-Anglo company, estimated a more conservative 4 billion to 5 billion barrels in reserves for the DPRK (Soo-suk Ko, "Another unfathomable in North is oil reserves," *Korea JoongAng Daily*, last updated March 23, 2015, 20:50 23. https://koreajoongangdaily.joins.com/2015/03/23/politics/Another-unfathomable-in-North-is-oil-reserves/3002247.html.

Dr. Bu-Seop Park, a nuclear physicist educated at MIT and actively involved in offshore exploration in the DPRK since the mid-1990s, provided detailed insights into the country's oil reserves. According to Dr. Park, there are five distinct oil deposit zones in the Western Sea, off Namp'o in the South P'yŏngan province. He approximated the oil reserves in these zones, with the first zone holding 65 million tonnes, and the second to fifth zones containing 50 million tonnes, 30 million tonnes, a smaller quantity, and 10 million tonnes, respectively.

Dr. Park also noted the presence of five offshore rigs in the area, suggesting that the DPRK possesses its own oil drilling infrastructure. He asserted that if this region were developed, the DPRK could attain self-sufficiency in oil production (The People's Korea, "DPRK has 12 Mil. Barrels of Oil Reserves in Western Sea: Expert," *The People's Korea* (December 2, 1998). http://www.hartford-hwp.com/archives/55a/161.html.

Despite actively seeking joint ventures with foreign oil and gas companies for comprehensive offshore oil field development in the Korea Bay and entering contracts with entities like Aminex, all projects were terminated due to the prevailing instability and security crises surrounding the DPRK (Keun Wook Paik (Royal Institute of International Affairs), "NORTH KOREA AND SEABED PETROLEUM," https://www.wilsoncenter.org/sites/default/files/media/documents/publication/Keun_Wook_Paik.pdf.

If Dr. Park's assessments align with reality and considering the reported advancements in DPRK drilling technology paralleling improvements in CNC technology since June 1997—when the DPRK first claimed success in producing 450 barrels of crude oil per day from its "No. 406" well off Nampo—this alternative scenario could offer insights into how the DPRK's rice production remained unaffected by the absence of imported crude oil.

59 This information is unofficial, deriving from estimates made by mission teams from the Food and Agriculture FAO and the WFP, who conducted on-site assessments of cooperative farms in the DPRK. These estimates were then cross-referenced with official data from previous years. However, adopting the notion that rice production experienced a sudden surge of 1 million tons or 153% in 2008 compared to 2007 seems unrealistic.

In 2000, crude oil and fertilizer imports stood at 85,600 tons and 62,000 tons, respectively, figures not markedly distant from the 2007 imports of 103,200 tons of crude oil and 65,000 tons of fertilizer (with crude oil imports in 2007 showing an increase of approximately 20% compared to 2000). Given that rice production in 2000 amounted to 1.69 million tons, a more plausible estimation would place the rice production in 2008 at around 2.11 million tons, reflecting an approximately 25% increase.

60 In 1988, 1989, 1990, and 1991, the average annual amount of crude oil secured by the DPRK was 171.2 million tons (calculated as (184.2 + 201.2 + 147.2 + 152.2) /4) during the period before 1992, when the fall of the Soviet Union significantly reduced crude oil imports → see Table 2.1.

61 The total fertilizer supply to the DPRK in 2009 amounted to 43.5 tons, as indicated in Table 2.4. Conversely, Table 2.5 reports a total fertilizer export of 4.1 tons to the DPRK in 2008 according to UN Comtrade data. To determine the nitrogen fertilizer produced within the DPRK, the 4.1 tons (the reported fertilizer imports in 2008) are subtracted from the total supply of 43.5 tons.

This calculation is based on the assumption that the fertilizer required for 2009 was imported in the preceding year, aligning with the DPRK's practice of importing and supplying the necessary fertilizer for the prior year to meet demand, resulting in the Chuch'e Fertilizer production. This methodology was consistently applied from 2010 through 2016 to ascertain Chuch'e Fertilizer production in these subsequent years.

62 Kim Jong Un, "Kyŏngaehanŭn kimjŏngŭndongjikkesŏ chosŏllodongdang chun-gangwiwŏnhoe 2013nyŏn 3wŏlchŏnwŏnhoeŭiesŏ hashin pogo" (Concluding Speech at the March 2013 Plenary Meeting of the Central Committee of the Worker's Party of Korea), *Rodong Sinmun* March 14, 2013.

63 (766,000/837,171) x 100% = 91.5%.

64 This conclusion hinges on several key assumptions, primarily the absence of readily available, developed alternative fuels capable of substituting for petroleum in transportation and shipping. Furthermore, it presupposes a lack of significant breakthroughs in engine-building technology that could offer major improvements in fuel efficiency.

   Consequently, the analysis suggests that under the Chuch'e Fertilizer system, a large portion of imported crude oil would have been diverted from fertilizer production to support other critical sectors, including military and civilian transportation, shipping, and agricultural machinery like tractors.

65 This discussion draws upon a reprinted booklet found in the appendix of Suho Im's book titled *Shijanggwa kyehoegŭi kongjon: Puk'anŭi kyŏngjegaehyŏkkwa ch'ejebyŏn-hwa chŏnmang (The Coexistence of Markets and Planning: Prospects for Economic Reform and Regime Change in North Korea)* (Seoul: Samsung Economic Research Institute, 2008).

66 Suho Im, *Shijanggwa kyehoegŭi kongjon: Puk'anŭi kyŏngjegaehyŏkkwa ch'ejebyŏnhwa chŏnmang (The Coexistence of Markets and Planning: Prospects for Economic Reform and Regime Change in North Korea)* (Seoul: Samsung Economic Research Institute, 2008), p. 251.

67 Kim Il Sung, "Inmin'gyŏngjeŭi kyehoekkyuryurŭl kanghwahamyŏ sahoejuŭi-gyŏngjegŏnsŏresŏ saeroun angyangŭl irŭk'ilte taehayŏ: Chosŏllodongdang chun-gangwiwŏnhoe che5ki che19ch'ajŏnwŏnhoeŭiesŏ han kyŏllon (1979nyŏn 12wŏl 12il)" (On Strengthening the Planning Discipline of the People's Economy and New Uplifting in the Construction of the Socialist Economy: Conclusions at the Fifth Plenary Session of the 19th Central Committee of the WPK (December 12, 1979)), *CWK 70*, p. 490.

68 Suho Im, *The Coexistence of Markets and Planning: Prospects for Economic Reform and Regime Change in North Korea*, p. 252.

69 Kim Jong Il, On Some Problems in Rebuilding the Heavy Industry Sectors with Modern Technology and Building Up the Country's Economy: Speech Before the Responsible Officials of the Central Committee of the WPK, (May 12, 2000)), *SWK 20*, p. 201.

70 Suho Im, *The Coexistence of Markets and Planning: Prospects for Economic Reform and Regime Change in North Korea*, p. 253.

71 As all financial institutions, including banks, are owned and operated by the State in the DPRK, they possess the authority to monitor, guide, and regulate transactions among United Enterprises. Consequently, no enterprise in the DPRK can function or operate in a manner akin to enterprises in capitalist market economies.

72 The Pŏnsuipchip'yo (Earned Income Index) was instituted on July 1, 2002, concurrent with the implementation of the Economic Improvement Measures. This marked a significant shift, increasing the obligations of enterprises to the State. The "earnings distribution" specified the portion allocated to enterprises after prioritizing State contributions from their earnings. Simultaneously, the Pŏnsuipch'egye (Earned Income Index System) bolstered the material incentives for enterprises and their workers.

   The determination of the share of self-appropriation funds and employees' living expenses was linked to the Pŏnsuipsuhaengnyul (Earnings Plan Implementation Rate). This approach is rooted in the socialist distribution principle, ensuring that individuals receive benefits proportionate to their contributions (Yŏnggŭn Ri, "Kiŏpsogyŏngyŏnghwaltongesŏ pŏnsuibŭl nŭrigi wihan pangdo" (Measures to Increase Earnings in Enterprise Management Activities), *ER* (2003), no. 1, p. 43).

73 Suho Im, *The Coexistence of Markets and Planning: Prospects for Economic Reform and Regime Change in North Korea*, pp. 256–257.

74 This sentiment is encapsulated in the following quote from the *CWK*:

"Today, our people revel in a contented life free from concerns about food, thanks to communist measures. In our nation, the State acquires rice from farmers at 60 chŏn per kilogram and distributes it to workers and clerks at 8 chŏn per kilogram—an embodiment of people's and communist initiatives. Every citizen possesses the inherent right to sustenance from the moment of birth, with the State providing a daily allotment of 300 grams of rice to newborns. Given this provision, a newborn receives 9 kilograms of rice each month, and if acquired at the wholesale price, households would incur a cost of 5 wŏn and 40 chŏn. However, as the State dispenses rice to workers and clerks at 8 chŏn per kilogram, the financial benefit to the newborn surpasses 4 won"

(Kim Il Sung, "Ryŏnhapkiŏpsorŭl chojik'amyŏ chŏngmuwŏnŭi saŏm ch'egyewa pangbŏbŭl kaesŏnhalte taehayŏ chosŏllodongdang chungangwiwŏn-hoe chŏngch'iguk'oeŭiesŏ han yŏnsŏl (1985nyŏn 11wŏl 19il)" (On Organizing the United Enterprise and Improving the Work System and Methods of Workers of Administrative Council: Speech at the Political Bureau Meeting of the Central Committee of the WPK (November 19, 1985)), *CWK 82*, pp. 483–484)

75 The following are some of Kim Jong Il's repeated statements that capitalism based on private property can never be allowed in the DPRK.

In a socialist society any deviation from socialist ownership principles and the resurgence of capitalist ownership poses a threat to the economic and material foundations of socialist ideals. Such actions create fertile ground for the emergence of individualism, rigidity, and bourgeois ideologies.

The linkage between private ownership and the cultivation of individualistic tendencies is inexorable, and capitalist ownership, alongside a capitalist market economy, provides a conducive environment for the proliferation of bourgeois ideas. Therefore, socialism is fundamentally incompatible with both private ownership and a capitalist market economy.

(Kim Jong Il, "Sasangsaŏbŭl ap'esunŭn kŏsŭn sahoejuŭiwiŏpsuhaengŭi p'ilsujŏkyoguida (chuch'e 84(1995)nyŏn 6wŏl 19il)" (Putting Thought Work Before Work is an Essential Requirement for Performing Socialist Tasks (June 19, 1995)), *SWK 18*, p. 254)

The experiences of nations where socialism has faced setbacks, leading to the resurgence of capitalism, underscore the critical lesson that the breakdown of socialist ownership and the revival of private ownership invariably propel society toward the capitalist path. To navigate this, it is imperative that we steadfastly adhere to and actively advance socialist ownership of the means of production.

(Kim Jong Il, "Hyŏngmyŏnggwa kŏnsŏresŏ hyŏngmyŏngjŏgwŏnch'ik, kyegŭpchŏgwŏnch'ikŭl ch'ŏlchŏhi chik'ilte taehayŏ: Chosŏllodongdang chungangwiwŏnhoe ch'aegimilgundŭlgwa han tamhwa (chuch'e 85(2006)nyŏn 10wŏl22il)" (On Thoroughly Adhering to Revolutionary and Class Principles in Revolution and Construction: A Discourse with the Responsible Workers of the Central Committee of the WPK (October 22, 2006), *SWK 22*, p. 201)

76 High-ranking cadre Myŏngŏn Mun emphasizes the absolute authority of the supreme leader's decisions, stating:

Party organizations must accept the Great General's pronouncements as paramount and execute them faithfully, adhering to the principle of complete and unwavering commitment. Any attempt to modify or reinterpret decisions already made by the

Great General, under the pretext of one's unit's "special circumstances," constitutes a disrespectful attitude that blatantly undermines the Party's unified system of spiritual guidance.

Only a worker who strives tenaciously and with unwavering dedication to implement the solutions established by the Great General can be considered a true worker in the 'Military-First' era.

(Myŏngŏn Mun, "T'echŏndange tangŭi yuilchŏngnyŏngdoch'egyerŭl t'ŭnt'ŭnhi seunŭn kŏsŭn Chuch'eŭi tanggŏnsŏrŭi kŭnbonwŏnch'ik" (Establishing the Party's Unique Spiritual Leadership System in the Workers' Party is a Fundamental Principle of Party Construction), *Kŭlloja* (2004), No. 12, p. 41)

77 As of 2023, more than two decades have elapsed since the inception of the "7·1 Measure." Notwithstanding this substantial passage of time, there is scant evidence indicating a shift in the DPRK from a socialist system to a capitalist one. As underscored at the beginning of this book, the DPRK persists as a socialist state. Economically, the means of production continue to be under social ownership, and politically, the proclaimed proletarian dictatorship remains in place, with the WPK standing as the singular political entity in the country.

78 Kim Jong Il defined transitional characters as follows:

A socialist society possesses a communist character, serving as a lower stage of a communist society, and exhibits a transitional character, representing an immaturity in comparison to the higher stage of a communist society.

(Kim Jong Il, "Chuch'eŭi sahoejuŭigyŏngjegwallirironŭro t'ŭnt'ŭnhi mujanghaja: ch'angnim 45tolsŭl mannŭn inmin'gyŏngjedaehang kyojigwŏn, haksaengdŭrege ponaen sŏhan (chuch'e 80(1991)nyŏn 7wŏl 1il)" (Let's Arm Ourselves with the Theory of Socialist Economic Management of Chuch'e: Letter to the Staff and Students of the College of People's Economy on the Occasion of Its 45th Anniversary (July 1, 1991)), *SWK 15* (P'yŏngyang: WPK Publishing House, 2012), p. 49)

79 Kim Jong Il, "Chuch'eŭi sahoejuŭigyŏngjegwallirironŭro t'ŭnt'ŭnhi mujanghaja: ch'angnim 45tolsŭl mannŭn inmin'gyŏngjedaehang kyojigwŏn, haksaengdŭrege ponaen sŏhan (chuch'e 80(1991)nyŏn 7wŏl 1il)" (Let's Arm Ourselves with the Theory of Socialist Economic Management of Chuch'e: Letter to the Staff and Students of the College of People's Economy on the Occasion of Its 45th Anniversary (July 1, 1991)), *SWK 15*, p. 54.

80 Karl Polanyi, *The Great Transformation: Political and Economic Origins of Our Time* (Boston: Beacon Press, 2001), p. 44.

81 Kim Jong Il, "Tangi cheshihan sŏn'gunshidaeŭi kyŏngjegŏnsŏllosŏnŭl ch'ŏlchŏhi kwanch'ŏrhaja: Tang, kukka, kyŏngjegigwan ch'aegimilgundŭlgwa han tamhwa (chuch'e 82(2003)nyŏn 8wŏl28il)" (Let's Thoroughly Adhere to the Party's Proposed Path of Economic Construction in the 'Military-First' Era (Discourse with the Responsible Officials of the Party, State, and Economic Institutions, (August 28, 2003)), *SWK 22*, pp. 16–17.

82 The formalization of this concept in Kim Jong Il's words occurred for the first time on July 26, 2002, during a field tour of the Hŭich'ŏn Machine Tool Factory. During this visit, he underscored that "the fundamental orientation of the Party's fulfillment of socialist economic management is to attain the most practical outcomes while unwaveringly adhering to socialist principles.".

Additionally, he emphasized the imperative of strictly adhering to the principle of self-directed planned economic management, ensuring the steadfast centralized and unified guidance of the State, and fostering high-level creativity at the grassroots (*CCΥ 2003*, p. 46).

83 The economic development trajectories of most former and current socialist countries can be broadly classified into two main approaches. The first category includes

nations such as Russia (formerly the Soviet Union), which shifted from a State-controlled socialist system to a State-oriented capitalist system.

The second category features countries like China, where a clear separation between politics and economics exists. In China, the Communist Party retains political control, while the economy embraces market-oriented principles and acknowledges the significance of private property.

However, the DPRK stands as a unique case, where political objectives take precedence in economic management, and economic construction unfolds within the framework of collectivism. In this context, the DPRK's path to economic development can be characterized as "a road that no one has ever treaded before.".

Unlike other nations, the DPRK prioritizes collective goals and underscores the importance of political projects alongside economic considerations. This distinctive approach sets the DPRK apart, rendering its economic construction strategy truly unprecedented compared to other socialist nations.

Bibliography

The Chosun Central News Agency. *Chosun Central Yearbook (CCY) 1999–2011*, P'yŏngyang: Worker's Party of Korea Publishing House, 2000–2012.

FAO. *FAOSTAT*, accessed October 11, 2016. http://faostat.fao.org/site/567/DesktopDefault.aspx?PageID=567#ancor

FAO. *Global Information and Early Warning System on Food and Agriculture - Special Alert No. 340 (Country: The Democratic People's Republic of Korea)*, last updated July 20, 2017. www.fao.org/3/a-i7544e.pdf

Im, Suho. *Shijanggwa kyehoegŭi kongjon: Puk'anŭi kyŏngjegaehyŏkkwa ch'ejebyŏnhwa chŏnmang (The Coexistence of Markets and Planning: Prospects for Economic Reform and Regime Change in North Korea)*, Seoul: Samsung Economic Research Institute, 2008.

Kim, Ch'ikwan, "T'ongilbu, Puk 'chuch'ech'ŏl 'chuch'e biryo,' chuch'e sŏmyu, ch'yulch'n munjejŏm chijŏk" (Unification Ministry Points Out Problems with North's 'Chuch'e Steel,' Fertilizer, Fiber,' and CNC), *TongilNews*, accessed December 18, 2010a. http://www.tongilnews.com/news/articleView.html?idxno=92981

Kim, Chiyŏng. "Mallimaŭi shidae/kyŏngjebuhŭnggwa saenghwarhyangsang 2: kŭp-sok'i kwangbŏmwihage toiptoenŭn t'onghapsaengsanch'egye (2017nyŏn10wŏl27il)" (The Age of Manrima/Economic Revival and Livelihood Improvement 2:Integrated Production System Rapidly and Widely Introduced (October 27, 2017)), *Chosun Shinbo*, accessed October 27, 2017. http://chosonsinbo.com/2017/10/24suk-7/

Kim, Il Sung. "Inmin'gyŏngjeŭi kyehoekkyuryurŭl kanghwahamyŏ sahoejuŭigyŏng-jegŏnsŏresŏ saeroun angyangŭl irŭk'ilte taehayŏ: Chosŏllodongdang chungangwi-wŏnhoe che5kiche19ch'ajŏnwŏnhoeŭiesŏ han kyŏllon (1979nyŏn 12wŏl 12il)" (On Strengthening the Planning Discipline of the People's Economy and New Uplifting in the Construction of the Socialist Economy: Conclusions at the Fifth Plenary Session of the 19th Central Committee of the WPK (December 12, 1979)), *CWK 70*, n.d.-a

Kim, Il Sung. "Ryŏnhapkiŏpsorŭl chojik'amyŏ chŏngmuwŏnŭi saŏm ch'egyewa pang-bŏbŭl kaesŏnhalte taehayŏ chosŏllodongdang chungangwiwŏnhoe chŏngch'ig-uk'ocŭiesŏ han yŏnsŏl (1985nyŏn 11wŏl 19il)" (On Organizing the United Enterprise and Improving the Work System and Methods of Workers of Administrative Council: Speech at the Political Bureau Meeting of the Central Committee of the WPK (November 19, 1985)), *CWK 82*, n.d.-b

Kim, Il Sung. "Sahoejuŭiwiŏbŭi kyesŭngwansŏngŭl wihayŏ hangirhyŏngmyŏngt'us-adŭl,hyŏngmyŏnggayujanyŏdŭlgwa han tamhwa (1992nyŏn 3wŏl 13il, 1993nyŏn 1wŏl 20il, 3wŏl 3il)" (Toward the Completion of the Succession of the Socialist

Work: Talks with Anti-Japanese Revolutionary Fighters and Descents (March 13, 1992, January 20, 1993, March 3), *CWK 92*, P'yŏngyang: WPK Publishing House, 2010b.

Kim, Il Sung. "Tangmyŏnhan sahoejuŭigyŏngjegŏnsŏlbanghyange taehayŏ: Chosŏllodongdang chungangwiwŏnhoe che6ki che21ch'ajŏnwŏnhoeŭiesŏ han kyŏllon (1993nyŏn 12wŏl 8il)" (On the Immediate Direction of Socialist Economic Construction: Conclusions at the Sixth Plenary Session of the 21st Central Committee of the WPK (December 8, 1993)), *CWK 94*, P'yŏngyang: WPK Publishing House, 2011.

Kim, Il Sung. "Sahoejuŭigyŏngjegŏnsŏresŏ saeroun hyŏngmyŏngjŏkchŏnhwanŭl irŭk'ilte taehayŏ: kyŏngjebumun ch'aegimilgunhyŏbŭihoeesŏ han kyŏllon (1994nyŏn 7wŏl 6il)" (On Making a New Revolutionary Turn in the Construction of a Socialist Economy: Conclusions of the Workers' Council in Charge of the Economic Sector (July 6, 1994)), *CWK 94*, n.d.-c

Kim, Jong Il. "Chuch'eŭi sahoejuŭigyŏngjegwallirironŭro t'ŭnt'ŭnhi mujanghaja: ch'angnim 45tolsŭl mannŭn inmin'gyŏngjedaehang kyojigwŏn, haksaengdŭrege ponaen sŏhan (chuch'e 80(1991)nyŏn 7wŏl 1il)" (Let's Arm Ourselves with the Theory of Socialist Economic Management of the Subject: Letter to the Staff and Students of the College of People's Economy on the Occasion of Its 45th Anniversary (July 1, 1991)), *Kimjŏngilsŏnjip15-chŭngbop'an* (*SWK 15*- enlarged edition), P'yŏngyang: WPK Publishing House, 2012a.

Kim, Jong Il. "Tang, kukka, kyŏngjesaŏbesŏ nasŏnŭn myŏtkaji munje taehayŏ (chosŏllodongdang chungangwiwŏnhoe ch'aegimilgundŭrap'esŏ han yŏnsŏl (chuch'e 81(1992)nyŏn 11wŏl 12il))" (On Some Problems in Party, State, and Economic Work (Speech Before the Responsible Officials of the Central Committee of the WPK (November 12, 1992))), *SWK 17*, P'yŏngyang: WPK Publishing House, 2012b.

Kim, Jong Il. "Chosŏllodongdang chungangwiwŏnhoe ch'aegimilgundŭlgwahan tamhwa, (chuch'e 83(1994)nyŏn 10wŏl 20il)" (Let's Make a Transformation in People's Life by Raising the Role of County (Discourse with the Responsible Officials of the Central Committee of the WPK, October 20, 1994)), *SWK 18*, P'yŏngyang: WPK Publishing House, 2012c.

Kim, Jong Il. "Sahoejuŭinŭn kwahagida: Chosŏllodongdang chungangwiwŏnhoe kigwanjit'enrodongshinmunt'ene palp'yohan ronmun (chuch'e 83(1994)nyŏn 11wŏl 1il)" (Socialism is a Science, an article published in *Rodong Sinmun* (November 1, 1994)), *SWK 18*, n.d.-d

Kim, Jong Il. "Tangŭi muyŏkcheilchuŭibangch'imŭl kwanch'ŏrhanŭndesŏ nasŏnŭn myŏtkaji munje: Chosŏllodongdang chungangwiwŏnhoe ch'aegimilgundŭlgwahan tamhwa (chuch'e 84(1995)nyŏn 2wŏl 1il)" (Some Problems in Implementing the Party's Trade First Policy: Talks with the Responsible Officials of the Central Committee of the WPK, February 1, 1995), *SWK 18*, n.d.-e

Kim, Jong Il. "Tangŭi muyŏkcheilchuŭibangch'imŭl kwanch'ŏrhanŭndesŏ nasŏnŭn myŏtkaji munje: Chosŏllodongdang chungangwiwŏnhoe ch'aegimilgundŭlgwahan tamhwa (chuch'e 84(1995)nyŏn 2wŏl 1il)" (Some Problems in Implementing the Party's Trade First Policy: Talks with the Responsible Officials of the Central Committee of the WPK, "Sasangsaŏbŭl ap'esunŭn kŏsŭn sahoejuŭiwiŏpsuhaengŭi p'ilsujŏkyoguida (chuch'e 84(1995)nyŏn 6wŏl 19il)" (Putting Thought Work Before Work is an Essential Requirement for Performing Socialist Tasks (June 19, 1995)), *SWK 18*, n.d.-f

Kim, Jong Il. "Chosŏllodongdang chungangwiwŏnhoe ch'aegimilgundŭlgwa han tamhwa (chuch'e 86(1997)nyŏn 1wŏl 1il)" (Discourse with the Responsible officials of the Central Committee of the WPK (January 1, 1997)), *SWK 19*, P'yŏngyang: WPK Publishing House, 2012d.

Kim, Jong Il. "Chagangdoŭi mobŏmŭl ttara kyŏngjesaŏpkwa inminsaenghwaresŏ saeroun chŏnhwanŭl irŭk'ijar chagangdoŭi yŏrŏ pumun saŏbŭl hyŏnjijidohamyŏnsŏ ilgundŭlgwa han tamhwa (chuch'e 87(1998)nyŏn 1wŏl16t'on21il, 6wŏl 1il, 10wŏl 20il, 22il)" (Following Chagang Province's Example, Let's Make a New Transformation in Economic Work and People's Life: Discourse with Workers While Providing Local Guidance to Various Sectors in Chagang Province (chuch'e 87(1998), January 16–21, June 1, October 20, 22)), *SWK 19*, n.d.-g

Kim, Jong Il. "Orhaerŭl sahoejuŭigyŏngjegŏnsŏresŏ hyŏngmyŏngjŏkchŏnhwanŭi haerodoege haja: Chŏndangdangilgunhoeŭi ch'amgajadŭrege ponaensŏhan (chuch'e 87(1997)nyŏn 1wŏl 24il)" (Let This Year Be the Year of Revolutionary Transformation in the Construction of a Socialist Economy: Letter to the Participants of the All-Party Cadres' Conference (January 24, 1997)), *SWK 19*, n.d.-h

Kim, Jong Il. "Chegukchuŭijadŭrŭi, ch'aektongŭn yongnaptoelsu ŏmnŭn ch'imnyagwahae ch'aektongida: Chosŏllodongdang chungangwiwŏnhoe ch'aegimilgundŭlgwa han tamhwa (chuch'e 87(1998)nyŏn 5wŏl 7il)" (The Imperialists' 'Reform' and 'Opening' Campaigns are Unacceptable Aggression and Dissolution Campaigns: Discourse with the Responsible Officials of the Central Committee of the WPK (May 7, 1998)), *SWK 19*, n.d.-i

Kim, Jong Il. "Konanŭi haenggun ch'oehudolgyŏkchŏnŭl tŏung himch'age pŏllija: Chosŏllodongdang chungangwiwŏnhoe ch'aegimilgundŭlgwa han tamhwa (chuch'e 86(1997)nyŏn 6wŏl 21il)" (Let's Make the Last Charge of the Arduous March More Vigorously: A Discourse with the Persons in Charge of the Central Committee of the WPK (June 21, 1997)), *SWK 19*, n.d.-j

Kim, Jong Il. "Chosŏllodongdang chungangwiwŏnhoe ch'aegimilgundŭrap'esŏ han yŏnsŏl (chuch'e 86(1997)nyŏn 9wŏl27il)" (Speech Before the Responsible Workers of the Central Committee of the WPK (September 27, 1997)), *SWK 19*, n.d.-k

Kim, Jong Il. "Orhaerŭl kangsŏngdaegukkŏnsŏrŭi widaehanjŏnhwanŭi haero pinnaeijar chosŏllodongdang chungangwiwŏnhoe ch'aegimilgundŭlgwahan tamhwa (chuch'e 88(1999)nyŏn 1wŏl 1il)" (Let This Year Shine as a Year of Great Transformation in the Construction of the Strong and Great Nation: A Discourse with the Cadres in charge of the Central Committee of the WPK (January 1, 1999)), *SWK 19*, n.d.-l

Kim Jong Il. "Inmin'gundaerŭl kanghwahayŏ kangsŏngdaegukkŏnsŏrwiŏbŭl midŭmjik'age tambohae nagalte taehayŏr chosŏninmin'gun chihwisŏngwŏndŭlgwa han tamhwa (chuch'e88(1999)nyŏn 1wŏl 24il)" (Strengthening the People's Armed Forces to Reliably Guarantee the Feat of Building a Strong Nation: A Talk with the Commanding Officers of the Korean People's Armymy (January 24, 1999), *SWK 19.*

Kim, Jong Il. "Ch'ŏngnyŏndongmaengch'ogŭpchojiktŭrŭi yŏk'arŭl tŏung nop'ijar kimilsŏngsahoejuŭich'ŏngnyŏndongmaeng mobŏmch'ogŭbilgundaehoech'amgajadŭrege ponaen sŏhan (chuch'e 88(1999)nyŏn 9wŏl 29il)" (Increasing the Role of Youth League Beginner Organizations: Letter to the Participants of the Model Beginner's Workers' Conference of the Kim Il Sung Socialist Youth League (September 29, 1999)), *SWK 20*, P'yŏngyang: WPK Publishing House, 2013a.

Kim, Jong Il. "Kongŏppumundŭrŭl hyŏndaejŏkkisullo kaegŏnhamyŏ naraŭi kyŏngjerŭl ch'uk'yŏseunŭndesŏ nasŏnŭn myŏtkaji munjee taehayŏ: Chosŏllodongdang chungangwiwŏnhoe ch'aegimilgundŭrap'esŏ han yŏnsŏl (chuch'e 89(2000)nyŏn 5wŏl12il)" (On Some Problems in Rebuilding the Heavy Industry Sectors with Modern Technology and Building Up the Country's Economy: Speech Before the Responsible Officials of the Central Committee of the WPK (May 12, 2000)), *SWK 20*, n.d.-m

Kim, Jong Il. "Chagangdosaramdŭlch'ŏröm towa shi, kunŭi sallimsarirŭl chal kkuryŏnagaja: Chosŏllodongdang chungangwiwŏnhoewa chagangdowiwŏnhoe ch'aegimilgundŭlgwa han tamhwa (chuch'e 89(2000)nyŏn 8wŏl31il)" (Like the People of Chagang Have Done, Let us Organize a Good Living Condition for Provinces, Cities and Counties: A Discourse with the Central Committee of the WPK and the Officials in Charge of the Chagang Province Committee (August 31, 2000)), *SWK 20*, n.d.-n

Kim, Jong Il. "Ragwŏnŭi rodonggyegŭbŭn charyŏkkaengsaengŭi charangsŭrŏun chŏnt'ongŭl kyesong pinnaeyanagaya handa: ragwŏn'gigyeryŏnhapkiŏpsorŭl hyŏnjijidohamyŏnsŏ ilgundŭlgwa han tamhwa (chuch'e 83(2004)nyŏn 5wŏl16il)" (The Working Class of Ragwŏn Must Continue to Shine with the Proud Tradition of Self-Reliance: A Discourse with the Workers While Guiding the Ragwŏn Machinery United Enterprise (May 16, 2004)), *SWK 22*, P'yŏngyang: WPK Publishing House, 2013b.

Kim, Jong Il. "Hyŏngmyŏnggwa kŏnsŏresŏ hyŏngmyŏngjŏgwŏnch'ik, kyegŭpchŏgwŏnch'ikŭl ch'ŏlchŏhi chik'ilte taehayŏ: Chosŏllodongdang chungangwiwŏnhoe ch'aegimilgundŭlgwa han tamhwa (chuch'e 85(2006)nyŏn 10wŏl22il)" (On Thoroughly Adhering to Revolutionary and Class Principles in Revolution and Construction: A Discourse with the Responsible Workers of the Central Committee of the WPK (October 22, 2006)), *SWK 22*, n.d.-o

Kim, Jong Il. "Sŏngjinjegangnyŏnhapkiŏpsoesŏŭi chuch'ech'ŏlsaengsanch'egyewansŏngŭn yagŭmgongŏppalchŏnesŏ t'ŭkkihal ryŏksajŏksabyŏnimyŏ iltae hyŏngmyŏngida: Sŏngjinjegangnyŏnhapkiŏpsorŭl hyŏnjijidohamyŏnsŏ ilgundŭlgwa han tamhwa (chuch'e 88(2009)nyŏn 12wŏl18il)" (The Completion of the Chuch'e Steel production system at the Sŏngjin Steel United Enterprise is a Unique Historical Event in the Development of the Metallurgical Industry and a Major Revolution: A Discourse with the Cadres while Providing Local Guidance at the Sŏngjin Steel United Enterprise (December 18, 2009)), *SWK 24*, P'yŏngyang: WPK Publishing House, 2014.

Kim, Jong Il. "Sŏngjinjegangnyŏnhapkiŏpsoesŏŭi chuch'ech'ŏlsaengsanch'egyewansŏngŭn yagŭmgongŏppalchŏnesŏ t'ŭkkihal ryŏksajŏksabyŏnimyŏ iltae hyŏngmyŏngida: Sŏngjinjegangnyŏnhapkiŏpsorŭl hyŏnjijidohamyŏnsŏ ilgundŭlgwa han tamhwa (chuch'e 88(2009)nyŏn 12wŏl18il)" (The Completion of the Chuch'e Steel production system at the Sŏngjin Steel United Enterprise is a Unique Historical Event in the Development of the Metallurgical Industry. "Ryanggangdoŭi kyŏngjesaŏpkwa inminsaenghwaresŏ hyŏngmyŏngjŏkchŏnhwanŭl irŭk'ilte taehayŏ: Chosŏllodongdang chungangwiwŏnhoe, ryanggangdo wiwŏnhoe ch'aegimilgundŭlgwa han tamhwa (chuch'e 88(2009)nyŏn 5wŏl22il)" (On Making a Revolutionary Transformation in the Economic Work and People's Life of Ryanggangdo Province (Speech to the Central Committee of the WPK and the Workers in Charge of the Ryanggangdo Province Committee (May 22, 2009)), *SWK 24*, n.d.-p

Kim, Jong Il. "Namhŭngch'ŏngnyŏnhwahangnyŏnhapkiŏpsonŭn kongjanggwalliesŏ hyŏkshinŭl irŭk'igo rodonggyegŭbŭi saemunhwarŭl ch'angjohan ponbogidanwiida: Namhŭngch'ŏngnyŏnhwahangnyŏnhapkiŏpsorŭl hyŏnjijidohamyŏnsŏ ilgundŭlgwa han tamhwa (chuch'e 88(2009)nyŏn 5wŏl28il)" (The Namhŭng Youth Chemical United Enterprise is an Exemplary Unit That Has Revolutionized Factory Management and Created a New Culture Among the Working Class: A Discourse with the Cadres in Charge While Providing On-the-Spot Guidance to the Namhŭng Youth Chemical United Enterprise (May 28, 2009)), *SWK 24*, n.d.-q

Kim, Jong Il. "Uri shing ch'yulch'ŭimmolkongikaech'ŏk'an sŏnggwawa kyŏnghŏme t'odaehayŏ modŭn punyaesŏ ch'ŏmdanŭl tolp'ahajar chosŏllodongdang chungangwiwŏnhoe ch'aegimilgundŭlgwa han tamhwa (chuch'e 89(2010)nyŏn 1wŏl1il)" (Let's Break Through the Cutting Edge in All Fields Based on the Achievements and Experience of Pioneering Our Own CNC Technology: A Discourse with the Cadres of the Central Committee of the WPK (January 1, 2010)), *SWK 24*, n.d.-r

Kim, Jong Il. "Hwanghaejech'ŏllyŏnhapkiŏpsonŭn Chuch'ech'ŏlsaengsant'odaee ŭigŏhayŏ ch'ŏlgangjaesaengsanŭl nop'ŭn sujunesŏ chŏngsanghwa hayŏya handa: Hwanghaejech'ŏllyŏnhapkiŏpsorŭl hyŏnjijidohamyŏnsŏ ilgundŭlgwa han tamhwa (chuch'e 89(2010)nyŏn 2wŏl20il)" The Hwanghae Steel United Enterprise Should

Normalize Steel Production at a High Level Based on the Foundation of Chuch'e Steel Production: A Discourse with the Workers While Guiding the Hwanghae Iron and Steel United Enterprise (February 20, 2010)), *SWK 24*, n.d.-s

Kim, Jong Il. "Widaehan suryŏngnimkkesŏ yŏrŏnoŭshin hyŏngmyŏngŭi kirŭl kkŭtkkaji kaya handa: Chosŏllodongdang chungangwiwŏnhoe chojikchidobu pubujangdŭlgwa han tamhwa (chuch'e 100 (2011)nyŏn 9wŏl12il)" (We Must Follow the Revolutionary Road Opened by the Great Leader to the End: A Discourse with the Deputy Heads of the Organizational Guidance Department of the Central Committee of the WPK (September 12, 2011)), *SWK 25*, P'yŏngyang: WPK Publishing House, 2015.

Kim, Jong Un. "Kyŏngaehanŭn kimjŏngŭndongjikkesŏ chosŏllodongdang chungangwiwŏnhoe 2013nyŏn 3wŏlchŏnwŏnhoeŭiesŏ hashin pogo" (Concluding Speech at the March 2013 Plenary Meeting of the Central Committee of the Worker's Party of Korea), *Rodong Sinmun*, March 14, 2013c.

Ko, Soo-suk. "Another Unfathomable in North is Oil Reserves," *Korea JoongAng Daily*, last updated March 23, 2015, 20:50. https://koreajoongangdaily.joins.com/2015/03/23/politics/Another-unfathomable-in-North-is-oil-reserves/3002247.html

Mun, Myŏngŏn. "T'echŏndange tangŭi yuilchŏngnyŏngdoch'egyerŭl t'ŭnt'ŭnhi seunŭn kŏsŭn Chuch'eŭi tanggŏnsŏrŭi kŭnbonwŏnch'ik" (Establishing the Party's Unique Spiritual Leadership System in the Workers' Party is a Fundamental Principle of Party Construction), *Kŭlloja* (2004), no. 12, pp. 40–43.

Paik, Keun Wook (Royal Institute of International Affairs). "North Korea and Seabed Petroleum," accessed May 31, 2022. https://www.wilsoncenter.org/sites/default/files/media/documents/publication/Keun_Wook_Paik.pdf

Polanyi, Karl. *The Great Transformation: Political and Economic Origins of Our Time*, Boston: Beacon Press, 2001.

Ri, Chongsŏ. "Widaehan kimjŏngiltongjikkesŏ cheshihashin hyŏngmyŏngjŏkkyŏngjejŏngch'aekŭn sahoejuŭigyŏngjeganggukkŏnsŏrŭi chŏnt'ujŏkkich'I (chuch'e 89(2000)nyŏn)" (The Revolutionary Economic Policy Presented by the Great Kim Jong Il is a Combative Banner for Building a Socialist Strong and Great Nation), *ER* (2000), no. 1, pp. 1–3.

Ri, Yŏnggŭn. "Kiŏpsogyŏngyŏnghwaltongesŏ pŏnsuibŭl nŭrigi wihan pangdo" (Measures to Increase Earnings in Enterprise Management Activities), *ER* (2003), no. 1, 41–44.

Sasŏl. "T'etangŭi kanghwabalchŏn'gwa kangsŏngdaegukkŏnsŏrŭi chŏnhwanjŏkkyegiro toel chŏn'guktangsep'obisŏdaehoe (chuch'e 86(2007)nyŏn 10wŏl26il)" (Editorial. "National Party Cell Secretaries' Conference to be a Transformative Event for the Party's Strengthened Development and the Construction of a Great Power,") *Rodong Sinmun* (October 26, 2007).

Sasŏl. "Tangŭi kich'och'uksŏngshigi ilgundŭrŭi t'ujaengjŏngshin'gwa ilbonsaerŭl ttarabaeuja!" (Editorial. Let us learn from the 'Fighting Spirit of the Soldiers and Their Work Style during the 'Building the Foundation of the Party), *Rodong Sinmun* (October 6, 2012).

The People's Korea. "DPRK has 12 Mil. Barrels of Oil Reserves in Western Sea: Expert," *The People's Korea*, last updated December 2, 1998. http://www.hartford-hwp.com/archives/55a/161.html

UN Comtrade Database. Accessed October 11, 2016. https://comtradeplus.un.org/TradeFlow?Frequency=A&Flows=M&CommodityCodes=270Partners=408&Reporters=all&period=2016&AggregateBy=none&BreakdownMode=plus

3 Socialist Enterprise Responsibility Management System and CNC-Based Reconstruction

3.1 Normalization of Production and the Socialist Enterprise Responsibility Management System

On October 3, 2001, Kim Jong Il issued a directive during a meeting with Central Party leaders, calling for the resumption of the "United Enterprise System" (UES) with necessary adjustments. However, despite the intention behind this more market-oriented approach, most factories and enterprises in the DPRK were unable to fully resume their normal operations. This was not due to inherent flaws in the UES itself, as we discussed in Chapter 2. By the time of the "10·3 Discourse," the country had already made significant progress in recovering from the severe economic crisis known as the "Arduous March." Nonetheless, the overall situation in the DPRK remained challenging, with total State budget revenues only reaching half of their pre-crisis levels.

Given these circumstances, Kim Jong Il made strategic decisions to allocate the majority of the budget to sectors of national strategic significance, namely, defense, machinery, metal, and chemical industries. The machinery industry, which produces Computerized Numerical Control (CNC) lathes and machines, played a particularly critical role. The revitalization and strengthening of the metal and chemical industries were also essential, as they were instrumental in developing CNC technology and supporting other related sectors. The DPRK has sought to establish a self-contained industrial structure based on self-reliance, aiming to overcome the economic crisis by further reinforcing this self-reliance strategy.[1]

The focus on these strategic sectors reflects the DPRK's commitment to nurturing key industries vital to its national interests. By prioritizing the development of CNC technology and enhancing self-reliance in industrial production, the country endeavors to bolster its industrial capabilities and overcome economic challenges. This approach aligns with the DPRK's overarching goal of maintaining an autonomous economic structure that minimizes reliance on external factors.

In the realm of the metal industry, the production of steel assumes a foundational role as it provides the essential framework for the operation of all other factories. Specifically, the mining and extraction equipment must be

DOI: 10.4324/9781003481737-4

manufactured and ensured to effectively extract coal and other minerals crucial for industrial purposes. The DPRK, having built its economy on coal rather than oil, must prioritize the normalization of equipment production, such as excavators capable of coal mining and extraction. This imperative takes precedence within the metal industry, which serves as the primary producer of steel.

By successfully normalizing the coal industry, subsequent efforts can be directed toward normalizing production in the chemical industry, which relies on coal as its primary raw material. In the DPRK, coal holds paramount importance as the primary raw material for chemical fertilizers, including nitrogen fertilizers, as well as essential chemical components for light industry, such as vinylon and other chemical fibers. Recognizing the pivotal role played by the metal and chemical industries, Kim Jong Il emphasized their status as backbone industries for the country.[2] Consequently, his focus centered on improving CNC technology, particularly within these industries, as a means to rebuild the DPRK's economy.[3]

A noteworthy observation emerges when scrutinizing Kim Jong Il's on-site guidance. During the most challenging period of the Arduous March from 1995 to 1998, a time marked by significant difficulties, the predominant focus of Kim Jong Il's on-site guidance was directed toward the military. Remarkably, even beyond this challenging period, the locations that received the most attention from Kim Jong Il were consistently military units, as well as factories and enterprises affiliated with the military, including the notable 534th Unit.[4]

Beyond the military, Kim Jong Il frequently conducted inspections at power plant construction sites and operational facilities.[5] He underscored the critical role of electricity, affirming its indispensable significance in socialist development.[6] Priority was given to supplying electricity to vital sectors such as metallurgy, chemicals, and the machinery industry, particularly in the production of CNC machine tools, to facilitate normalized production processes.

Kim Jong Il's unwavering commitment to the advancement of CNC technology reflects not a blind gamble, but a well-calculated investment. His strategic focus on enhancing capabilities was notably directed toward key institutions like Hŭich'ŏn Machine Tools and Kusŏng Machine Tools, widely recognized as the cornerstone facilities of the DPRK's industrial sector.

Hŭich'ŏn Machine Tools, situated in Hŭich'ŏn City, Chagang Province, has been successfully meeting its electricity requirements since 1998. On the other hand, Kusŏng Machine Tools, known as the pioneering producer of CNC machine tools in the DPRK, is strategically located in Kusŏng City, North P'yŏngan Province. It benefits immensely from a consistent and uninterrupted supply of electricity, sourced from the Sup'ung Power Plant, the largest hydroelectric power plant in the DPRK, as well as the T'aech'ŏn Power Plant, which ranks as the third largest in the country.

Kim Jong Il's strategic emphasis on these specific sectors reflects a pragmatic approach, capitalizing on favorable conditions for success and tackling the country's economic challenges head-on. The concerted investments made in Hŭich'ŏn Machine Tools and Kusŏng Machine Tools, supported by reliable electricity supply, serve as tangible examples of this deliberate strategy.

As evident from Table 3.1, Kim Jong Il's concentrated on-the-spot guidance was primarily directed toward regions including North Hamgyŏng, North Chagang, and North P'yŏngan Provinces. These areas house factories and enterprises of strategic significance in the metals and chemical industries, such as the Sŏngjin Steel United Enterprise in Kim Ch'aek City, North Hamgyŏng Province, 2.8 Vinylon United Enterprise in Hamhŭng, South Hamgyŏng Province, Hŭngnam Fertilizer United Enterprise in Hamhŭng,

Table 3.1 On-the-Spot Guidance of Kim Jong Il's Power Plant Construction Sites and Power Plants

Year	Date of On-the-Spot Guidance	Location
1998	Numerous small and medium-sized hydropower plants, including Changgang No. 1 and 2, Changjasan, Pukch'ŏn No. 3, Namri, and Oejung (January 16–21); Taehongdan No. 2 and Taehongdan No. 5 (October 1); and Onp'o No. 3 and 4 (November 17).	Kanggye City, Chagang Province; Taehongdan County, Ryanggang Province; Kyŏngsŏng County, North Hamgyŏng Province
1999	Small and medium-sized power plants, including Changgang No. 3 Military Youth Power Plant and Pukch'ŏn No. 2 Power Plant (June 15); Mubong Youth Power Plant (August 11); Sŏngch'ŏn'gang No. 22 Power Plant (September 24).	Sŏnggang County, Chagang Province; Shimjiyŏn County, Yanggang Province; Shinhŭng County, South Hamgyŏng Province
2000	Kimch'ŏl, Kŭmgang 2, Kŭmgang 5 (August 1–2); Sŏngch'ŏn'gang 29, 30, 32 (August 26–28); Hŭngju Youth Power Plant; Anbyŏn Youth Power Plant, Naep'yŏng Power Plant (November 7); Taehongdan 4 Youth Power Plant (November 29); Kŭmjin'gang Power Plant (November 30)	Ch'ŏngjin City, Noth Hamgyŏng Province; Shinhŭng County, South Hamgyŏng Province; Changgang County, Chagang Province; T'ongch'ŏn County, Kangwŏn Province; Sep'o County, Kangwŏn Province; Taehongdan County, Yanggang Province; Hamju County, South Hamgyŏng Province
2001	T'aech'ŏn Power Plant (February 14); Kŭmya No. 2 Power Plant (October 25); Sup'ung Power Plant (December 14); Hŭngju Youth Power Plant (December 23)	T'aech'ŏn County, North P'yŏngan Province; Kŭmya County, South Hamgyŏng Province; Sakchu County, North P'yŏngan Province; Changgang County, Chagang Province

(*Continued*)

Table 3.1 (Continued)

Year	Date of On-the-Spot Guidance	Location
2003	Kŭmyagang Power Plant (April 14); Hŭngju Youth No. 2 Power Plant (July 5)	Kŭmya County, South Hamgyŏng Province, Changgang County, Chagang Province
2005	Wŏnsan Youth Power Plant (May 26)	Wŏnsan City, South Hamgyŏng Province
2006	Samsu Power Plant (March 5); Kŭmjin'ganghŭngbong Youth Power Plant (November 15); Ryesŏnggang Power Plant (December 1); Kŭmyagang Power Plant (September 11)	Samsu County, Yanggang Province; Hamju County, South Hamgyŏng Province; Kŭmch'ŏn County, Hwanghae Province; Kŭmya County, South Hamgyŏng Province
2007	T'aech'ŏn Youth Power Plant No. 4 (January 21); Ŏrangch'ŏn Youth Power Plant No. 1 (February 8); Hŭngju Youth Power Plant No. 2 (June 1)	T'aech'ŏn County, North P'yŏngan Province; Ŏrang Country, North Hamgyŏng Province; Changgang County, Chagang Province
2008	Ryesŏnggang Power Plant (January 6)	Kŭmch'ŏn County, Hwanghae Province
2009	Wŏnsan Youth Power Plant (January 6); Ryesŏnggang Youth Power Plant No. 1 (January 31); Hŭich'ŏn Power Plant (March 25, September 17); Nyŏmwŏn Power Plant (April 18); Pukch'ang Power Plant (August 17); Kŭmjin'gangguch'ang Youth Power Plant (November 7).	Wŏnsan City, South Hamgyŏng Province; Kŭmch'ŏn, North Hwanghae Province; Hŭich'ŏn City, Chagang Province; Nyŏmwŏn County, South P'yŏngan Province; Pukch'ang County, South P'yŏngan Province; Chŏnghyŏng County, South Hamgyŏng Province
2010	Hŭich'ŏn Power Plant (January 4, November 3, December 22); Ryesŏnggang Youth Power Plant No. 1 (January 7); Paektusansŏn'gun Youth Power Plant (May 16); Ŏrangch'ŏn Power Plant No. 1 (May 20); Wŏnsan Kun-Min (Military-People) Power Plant (July 7); Kŭmyagang Kun-Min (Military-People) Power Plant (August 5)	Hŭich'ŏn City, Chagang Province; Kŭmch'ŏn County, Hwanghae Province; Paegam County, Ryanggang Province; Ŏrang County, North Hamgyŏng Province; Pŏbwŏn County, Kangwŏn Province; Kŭmya County, South Hamgyŏng Province
2011	Hŭich'ŏn Power Plant (May 28, August 30)	Hŭich'ŏn City, Chagan Province

Source: author

Table 3.1 is compiled from data spanning the years 1998 to 2011, obtained from the *CCY*.

South Hamgyŏng Province, Ryongsŏng Machinery in Hamhŭng, South Hamgyŏng Province, Kimch'aek Iron and Steel United Enterprise in Ch'ŏngjin, North Hamgyŏng Province, and Ragwŏn Machinery in Shinŭiju, North P'yŏngan Province. Notably, South Hamgyŏng and North P'yŏngan provinces are also home to several of these factories and enterprises.

Given that the normalization of production at these strategically significant establishments relies on a stable supply of electricity, it appears that new power plants were constructed at these locations or existing ones were reorganized and strengthened to ensure the necessary conditions for production normalization. Let us now delve into a more detailed analysis, focusing specifically on the case of North P'yŏngan Province.

North P'yŏngan Province is home to two crucial industrial facilities: the Kusŏng Machine Tools Factory, specializing in CNC machine tool production, and the Ragwŏn Machinery United Enterprise, focused on manufacturing excavators and large oxygen separators. These establishments, situated in Kusŏng and Shinŭiju, respectively, hold strategic importance due to their priority access to electricity from the Sup'ung and T'aech'ŏn power plants. The cooperative relationship between these production units plays a significant role in the broader economic landscape of the DPRK.

The Kusŏng Machine Tools Factory assumes a pivotal role in the production of CNC machine tools, which are then supplied to the Ragwŏn Machinery United Enterprise. In return, Ragwŏn Machinery engages in the manufacture of equipment tailored to the specific needs of the mining and extraction industries. The high-quality products generated by Ragwŏn Machinery find application within these industries, forming a critical link in the production chain. Furthermore, Ragwŏn Machinery takes on the responsibility of producing large oxygen separators, a vital component in the Chuch'e Fertilizer production process.[7]

These essential oxygen separators are subsequently supplied to Namhŭng Youth Chemical United Enterprise and Hŭngnam Fertilizer United Enterprise, where their crucial role in supporting and streamlining production processes becomes evident. Leveraging the capabilities of the large oxygen separators, these enterprises engage in the anthracite gasification process, resulting in the production of various chemical raw materials, including fertilizer. The nitrogen fertilizer produced through this process is then distributed to cooperative farms, effectively boosting agricultural productivity. Simultaneously, the remaining chemical raw materials are supplied to light industrial factories such as the Shinŭiju Cosmetics Factory, playing a vital role in facilitating the normalization of their production activities.

The construction and modernization of the Kusŏng Machine Tools Factory serve as prerequisites for the development and modernization of the Ragwŏn Machine Tools United Enterprise. Both entities, situated within North P'yŏngan Province, enjoy priority access to electricity from the Sup'ung, the country's largest hydroelectric power plant, and the T'aech'ŏn, the third largest. Recognizing this intricate interdependence, measures were taken to rehabilitate and expand the capacity of the Sup'ung and T'aech'ŏn power plants. This ensured a steady and sufficient electricity supply to the Kusŏng Machine Tools Factory, creating favorable conditions for the normalization of production and, subsequently, the rebuilding and modernization of the Ragwŏn Machine Tools United Enterprise.[8]

With the exception of Hŭich'ŏn, Paektusan, Wŏnsan, and Kŭmyagang, the majority of plants that Kim Jong Il directed since 1998 were projected to be completed by 2009. It is intriguing to note that 2009 marked a significant milestone for the DPRK as it reached the forefront of CNC technology.[9] The availability of electricity, coupled with the advancements in CNC technology, fostered an environment conducive to the realization of production normalization. In the DPRK, the term "Kisulgaegŏn" (technological improvement) or "Hyŏndaehwa" (modernization) is used to describe the process of achieving production normalization. By 2016, the factories and enterprises enumerated in the *CCY* had either undergone technological improvements or were newly constructed, showcasing the remarkable progress achieved in this regard.

According to Table 3.2, there was a significant surge in the number of factories and enterprises undergoing technological improvements and modernization, commencing in 2009 and reaching its zenith in 2010 and 2011.[10]

Following the passing of Kim Jong Il, the supreme leader position was assumed by Kim Jong Un, who began his local guidance in 2012.[11] It is worth

Table 3.2 Factories and Enterprises That Underwent Technological Renovation, Modernization, or New Construction by 2016

Year	Factory or Enterprise
2003	Hŭich'ŏn Machine Tool Factory
2004	Kusŏng Machine Tool Factory
2005	Ragwŏn Machinery United Enterprise, Taeanch'insŏn Glass Factory
2006	Hŭich'ŏn Machine and Equipment General Factory, Ch'ŏngnyŏn Electricity United Enterprise, Ch'ŏngjin Basic Food Factory, Sŏngjin Steel United Enterprise, Machinery United Enterprise
2007	Hŭngnam Smelter, Kyŏngsŏng Ceramics Factory, Shinŭiju Cosmetics Factory Soap Workshop
2008	2wŏl (February) Steel United Enterprise
2009	Kimch'aek Steel United Enterprise, Ranam Coal Mine Machinery United Enterprise, Hoeryŏng Basic Food Factory, Manp'o Smelter, Sŭngri Automobile United Enterprise, Kusŏng Machine Tool Factory, Hŭich'ŏn Machine Tool General Factory, Youth Electric United Enterprise, Hŭich'ŏn Precision Machinery Factory, Tanch'ŏn Smelter, Taedonggang Steel Tile Factory, Pukch'ang Power Plant, 2·8 Chiktongch'ŏngnyŏn Coal Mine, 5wŏl11il (May 11) Smelter, Transportation Tool Factory, Ryangch'aek Bearing Factory, Shinŭiju Shoe Factory, Changjagang Machine Tool Factory, Kanggye Knitting Factory, P'yŏngyanggoksan Factory, Kanggye Tractor General Factory

(*Continued*)

Table 3.2 (Continued)

Year	Factory or Enterprise
2010	Chaeryŏng Mine, Kangdong Pharmaceutical Instrument Factory, Ryongsŏng Food Factory, Pukchung Machinery United Enterprise, September Iron and Steel Company, Deokhyon Mine, 2. 8 Vinylon United Enterprise, 7wŏl7il (July 7) United Enterprise and Ch'ŏngjin Chemical Fiber Factory, Ch'ilsŏng Electric Factory, Ch'ŏnma Electric Machinery Factory, Taehŭngsan Machinery Factory, Samjiyŏn Factory, Hyesan Steel Factory, Hyesan Shoe Factory, Kwanmobong Machinery Factory, Namhŭng Youth Chemical United Enterprise, 12wŏl5il (December 5) Youth Mine, Changjagang General Food Factory, Kanggye Basic Food Factory, Hŭich'ŏn Youth Electric United Enterprise, 3wŏl5il (March 5) Youth Mine, Manp'o Unified Factory, Changsung Food Factory, newly built soy sauce workshop at Ryongsŏng Food Factory, Kangjil Glass Factory, Kangsŏ Medicinal Water Factory, Paegunsan General Food Factory, Tanch'ŏn Magnesia Factory, Tanch'ŏn Mining Machinery Factory, Musan Mine and Musan Food Factory, Hoeryŏng Food Processing Factory, Hygiene Products Division Factory, newly built women's socks workshop at P'yŏngyang Hosiery Factory, P'yŏngyang Flour Factory, Sŏnhŭng Food Factory, and Hŭich'ŏllyŏn Machinery United Enterprise
2011	Namp'o Glass Bottle Factory, Amnokkang Instrument General Factory, Amnokkang Daily Necessities Factory, Taegwan Glass Factory, 1wŏl18il (January 18) Machinery Factory, Chŏngbangsan General Food Factory, Shinhŭng Machinery Factory, Unsu Tool Factory, Chagang Steel Smelter, Amnokkang Tire Factory, 2wŏl (February) Steelmaking General Enterprise Center, 2. 8 Machinery General Factory, Susŏngch'ŏn General Food Factory, Hyesan Youth Mine, P'yŏngyang Textile Factory, Ponghwa Soap Factory, P'yŏngyang Resin Pencil Factory, Taedonggang Fruit General Processing Factory, 5wŏl11il (May 11) Factory, P'yŏngyang August Pool Processing Factory, the newly constructed wheat weaving workshop at the Kŭmsŏng Food Factory, and Rangnang Honored Soldiers' Resin Daily Necessities Factory, P'yŏngsŏng Synthetic Leather Factory, Solar Equipment Center, Chungang Wool Factory, Tudan Duck Factory, Taedonggang Pig Factory, Taedonggang Net Factory, Taedonggang Tortoise Factory, Taehŭng Youth Hero Mine and Ryongyang Mine, Taesung Machinery Factory, Stone Processing Factory managed by Myŏngje Ri, and the newly constructed Vegetable Vinyl Greenhouse in Hamhŭng City's Hoesang District
2012	Taewŏn Glass Factory, machine shop (machined products) managed by Ch'ŏlyong Hŏ, P'yŏngyang Hosiery Factory, Taedonggang Tile Factory
2013	Newly constructed machine shop managed by T'aeho Kang, Ryongmun Liquor factory, the newly constructed Sŏngch'ŏn'gang Fishing Net Factory and Resin Tube Factory, Posŏng Mushroom Factory, Ch'angsŏng Food Factory, and Aeguk Stone Factory,

(Continued)

Table 3.2 (Continued)

Year	Factory or Enterprise
2014	11wŏl2il (November 2) Factory of the Korean People's Army, Ryongmun Liqour Factory, Kalma Food Factory, Ch'ŏnji Lubricating Oil Factory, 10wŏl8il (October 8) Factory, Chŏngsŏng Pharmaceutical General Factory, (2wŏl20il) February 20 Factory of the Korean People's Army, and General Food Processing Factory under the authority of the 534th Armed Forces Unit.
2015	Fiberglass Ming Resin Liquid Production Plant at Tanjŏn Smelter, Ferric Pyrite Production Plant at Tanch'ŏn Smelter, Graphite Production Plant at Kwangjŏn Mine, Mica Precipitator at P'yŏngyang Mushroom Factory, newly built P'yŏngyang City Mushroom Factory, renovated Wŏnsan Shoe Factory, and newly built Fish Feed Factory by the People's Army. The machine factory (airplane manufacturing plant) operated by Dongnyŏl Chŏn, the newly constructed sanitary ware factory at the 2wŏl1il (February 11) Factory and the 12wŏ7il (December 7) Factory of the Ryongsŏng Machinery United Enterprise, the newly constructed P'yŏngyang Corn Process Plant, the Man'gyŏngdae Taehŭng Food Factory, the P'yŏngyang Cone Process Factory, Stone Crusher and Mine of the Musan Mine United Enterprise No. 3, and the Long-Distance Bulk-Conveyor Spiral line,
2016	P'yŏngyang Mushroom Factory, Ryongaksan Soap Factory, Pogŏn Oxygen Factory, P'yŏngyang Sports Equipment Factory, Kŭmk'ŏp Athletes' General Food Factory

Source: author

Table 3.2 is compiled from data spanning the years 2003 to 2016, obtained from the *CCY*.

Furthermore, as indicated in Table 3.3, Kim Jong Un's local guidance predominantly revolves around military bases and military-affiliated enterprises, factories and enterprises operating in the light industry sector, recreational amenities like Munsu Water Park and Mashingnyŏng Ski Resort, childcare facilities such as nurseries, kindergartens, and Aeyugwŏn (orphanages house), as well as food-producing enterprises such as pig farms and fisheries. This emphasis on sectors other than heavy industry becomes apparent in the analysis.

Kim Jong Un's extensive on-the-spot guidance, predominantly outside the heavy industry sector, is a result of the initiative to normalize production in sectors of national strategic importance, a process that gained momentum in 2009. The groundwork for production normalization in critical factories and enterprises within the heavy industry sector was laid in 2011, even preceding Kim Jong Il's passing.

Chapter 2 expounds on the fact that advanced plants and enterprises in the metal and chemical sectors, crucial at the national level, underwent reconstruction in 2009 and 2010, respectively. The reconstruction of these facilities goes beyond restoring their ability to produce steel, the cornerstone of the DPRK's industrial development, and essential chemical raw materials pivotal for agriculture and light industry.

Table 3.3 Kim Jung Un's On-the-Spot Guidance (2012–2016)

Year	Kim Jung Un's On-the-Spot Guidance
2012	105th Tank Division, 169th Armed Forces Unit, 3870th Armed Forces Unit, 354th Armed Forces Unit, 671st Rally Combat Team, Machinery Factory managed by Chŏlyong Hŏ, Air Force 378th Unit, Air Force 1017th Unit, Navy 587th Unit, 324th Rally Combat Team, 842nd Armed Forces Unit, Navy 123rd Unit, Ch'odo Defense Corps, Ryŏdo Defense Force, Navy's 155th Unit, 655th Combined Force, Rŭngna Amusement Park Development Project, Taegwan Glass Factory, Machinery Factory managed by Chŏlyong Hŏ, 1591st Armed Forces Unit, Ch'angjŏn Street, People's Outdoor Ice Arena Construction Project, Central Zoo, Ch'angjŏn School, Ch'angjŏn Daycare Center, and Ch'angjŏn Kindergarten, (N)Rŭngna Amusement Park and Mammary Gland Tumor Institute, P'yŏngyang Hosiery Factory and Children's Department Store, P'yŏngyang Air Station Construction Site, (N)Ryongryon Amusement Park, Un'gok District General Ranch, Detachment under the 552nd Armed Forces Unit, 1017th Armed Forces Unit, Changjae Island Defense Team and Mudo Defense Team, Kamnamu Company under the 4302nd Armed Forces Unit, Troops under the command and control of the 313th Combined Armed Forces, the 318th Armed Forces Unit, (N)Haemaji Restaurant, the Taedonggang Tile Factory, the T'ongil Street Movement Center, (R)P'yŏngyang Institute of Vegetable Science and the P'yŏngyang Institute of Floriculture, the Ryugyŏngwŏn and People's Outdoor Ice Staking Rink and the Roller Skating Rink, and the Mounted Troops directly under the 534th Armed Forces Unit.
2013	The 323rd Armed Forces Unit, the Detachment Team under the 526th Combined Corps, the 639th Combined Corps, the Changjaedo Defense Battalion and the Mudo Hero Defense Battalion, the Long Range Artillery Detachment under the 641st Armed Forces Unit, the Ryongjŏng Fish Farm, the 1973rd Armed Forces Unit, the 2nd Battalion under the 1973rd Armed Forces Unit, the 1501st Armed Forces Unit, 2wŏl20il (February 20) Factory of the Korean People's Army, Ryongmun Liquor Factory, the 405th Armed Forces Unit, the 621st Breeding Station, General Food Processing Factory under the 534th Armed Forces Unit of the Korean People's Army, T'onghae Rear Base under the 639th Armed Forces Unit, Mashingnyŏng Ski Resort, 8wŏl25il (August 25) Fishery Factory under the 313th Armed Forces Unit, and Songdowŏn International Youth Camp, Songdowŏn Youth Outdoor Theater, Sŏngch'ŏn'gang Net Factory and Resin Tube Workshop, 507th Armed Forces Unit, 549th Armed Forces Unit Pig Factory, Kosan Fruit Farm, Posŏng Mushroom Factory, P'yŏngyang Basic Food Factory, Taegwan Glass Factory, Machinery Factory managed by Chŏlyong Hŏ, 1017th Armed Forces Unit, 1wŏl18il (January 18) Machinery Factory, Namhŭng Youth Chemical United Enterprise, Kanggye Tractor United Enterprise, Kanggye Precision Machinery United Enterprise, Changjagang Workshop, Ryongsŏng Machinery United Enterprise, 2wŏl11il (February 11) Factory, Shinhŭng Machinery Factory, Kangdong Precision Machinery Factory, (N)mushroom factory built on Farm No. 1116 under the 532nd Armed Forces Unit, newly built children's hospital and oral hospital, scientists' living house construction site, Mirim equestrian resort construction site, 5wŏl11il (May 11) Factory, scientists' living house construction site, Mashingnyŏng ski resort construction site, 3404th Armed Forces Unit, Changjado defense team and Mudo hero defense team, patriotic stone factory, Ryongyŏn Sea Fish Farm, (N)P'yŏngyang Gymnasium, Munsu Water Playground, Munsu Mall Playground, Mirim Equestrian Resort, Oral Hospital, 5wŏl1il (May 1) Stadium, Children's Hospital, (N)Central Mushroom Research Center of the Academy of Sciences, (MA)the daily necessities manufacturing factory managed by Ikch'ŏl Kim, Kim Jong Sook P'yŏngyang Textile Factory, Mirim Equestrian Center, (N)Munsu Water Playground, (N)Mirim Equestrian Center, Navy Unit 790, shipyard managed by Joo Sung Ho, Mashingnyŏng Ski Resort, Korean People's Army November 2 Factory, Korean People's Army No. 354 Food Factory, Kim Jong Il Military Research Institute Construction Site, P'yŏngyang University of Architecture, 99th Armed Forces Unit, Korean People's Army Design Institute, shipyard managed by Sŏngho Chu, Mashingnyŏng Ski Resort Construction Site, Korean People's Army 313th Unit, August 25th Fishery Workshop, 526th Combined Unit, (N)Mashingnyŏng Ski Resort

2014	(N)Fishery Refrigeration Facility, Academy of Sciences, 323rd Armed Forces Unit, (N)Light Gun Ammunition Factory and Echo Firing Range, Korean People's Army 11wŏl20il (November 2) Factory, Korean People's Army 1wŏl8il (January 8) Fishery Construction Site, and Songdowŏn International Youth Camp, P'yŏngyang Pharmaceutical and Electrical Instrument Factory, 2620th Armed Forces Unit, 188th Armed Forces Unit, Machinery Factory managed by T'aeho Kang, Ryugyŏng Hospital and Ongryu Children's Hospital, 188th Armed Forces Unit, (N) Korean People's Army 1wŏl8il (January 8) Fisheries Factory, (N)Kim Jŏngsuk P'yŏngyang Textile Factory Workers' Dormitory, (MA)1wŏl18il (January 18) Machinery Factory, 447th Armed Forces Unit, Taesŏngsan General Hospital, The machine shop managed by Tongryŏl Chŏn, Kim Ch'aek University of Science and Technology Educators' Residence, Ch'ŏnma Electric Machinery Factory, Taegwan Glass Factory, Machinery Factory managed by Ch'ŏryong Hŏ, Ryongmun Liquor Factory, Wormwood Island, Taedonggang Fruit Farm and Taedonggang Fruit Processing Factory, Changch'ŏn Vegetable Specialized Cooperative Farm, Meteorological and Hydrological Bureau, Ryŏdo Defense Corps, 863rd Armed Forces Unit, Navy's 167th Armed Forces Unit, Satellite Scientists' Street Construction Site, 5wŏl1il (May 1) Stadium Construction Site, (N)Kalma Food Factory, Hwado Defense Corps, Songdowŏn International Youth Camp, Ongdo Defense Corps, (MA) P'yŏngyang International Airport Aviation Station Construction Site, 171st Armed Forces Unit, Ch'ŏnap'o Fisheries Research Institute, Songch'ŏn'gang Net Factory and Resin Tube Workshop of the Korean People's Army's 1521st Enterprise, Alpine Fruit Farm, Ch'ŏllima Tile Factory, Ch'ŏnji Lubricating Oil Factory, P'yŏngyang Hosiery Factory, Machinery Factory with Electric Line, Kim Chek University Educators' Living House Construction Site, Kalma Food Factory, Yŏnp'ung Scientists' Recreation Center Construction Site, Breeding Station No. 621 of the Korean People's Army, 11wŏl2il (November 2) Factory of the Korean People's Army, 10wŏl8il (October 8) Factory, Satellite Scientist Housing Area, educators' houses of Kim Chek University of Technology, P'yŏngyang Nursery and Childcare Center, and Military Memorial Hall, (Prefectural) P'yŏngyang International Airfield Construction Site, Kyŏngsŏng Pharmaceutical Company, (N)2wŏl20il (February 20) Factory of the Korean People's Army, (N)General Food Factory under the authority of the 534th Armed Forces Unit of the Korean People's Army, (N)Fishery Workshop No. 18 under the authority of the 567th Armed Forces Unit, 991st Armed Forces Unit, Shinch'ŏn Museum, Chosun 4.26 Cartoon Film Studio, Artillery Company under the 963rd Armed Forces Unit, 1313th Armed Forces Unit, May 9th Catfish Factory, 458th Armed Forces Unit, Navy 189th Armed Forces Unit, P'yŏngyang Children's Food Factory, P'yŏngyang Catfish Factory, Korean People's Army 6wŏl8il (June 8) (N)Vegetable Greenhouse, 851st Armed Forces Unit, Women's Artillery Detachment under the 963rd Armed Forces Unit.

(Continued)

Table 3.3 (Continued)

Year	Kim Jung Un's On-the-Spot Guidance
2015	P'yŏngyang Nursery/Childcare Center, 1st Infantry Division of the Front Line Corps, (N)P'yŏngyang City Mushroom Factory, Aviation and Anti-Aviation Command, Kangdong Precision Machinery Factory, Gold Cup Athletes' General Food Factory, Ryuwŏn Shoe Factory, Western Front Mechanized Strike Group, (R)Wŏnsan Shoe Factory, P'yŏngyang Cosmetics Factory, (MA)10-3 Factory, Wŏnsan City Nursery/Child Care Center, Elementary School/Secondary School Construction Site, Future Scientist Street Construction Site, Science and Technology Center Construction Site, 447th Armed Forces Unit, P'yŏngyang City Nursing Home Construction Site, 1016th Armed Forces Unit, 5wŏl27il (May 27) Fishery Workshop, Fishing Gear Factory, (N)Fish Feed Factory, Kŭmsanp'o Salted Fish Processing Factory/Fishery Workshop, Machinery Factory operated by Electric Line, 164th Armed Forces Unit, P'yŏngyang Pharmaceutical and Electrical Instrument Factory, P'yŏngyang International Airfield 2 Air Station, Paektusan Line Military Youth Power Plant Construction Site, Wŏnsan Nursery and Child Care Center, (N)Kukkaujugaebarwŏn Wisŏnggwanje Chonghapchihwiso (National Satellite Control Command Center, Ryongsŏng Machinery Joint Stock Company 2wŏl11il (February 11) Factory, Sinp'o Ocean Fishery Joint Stock Company, 7wŏl18il (July 18) Cow Ranch under the 580th Armed Forces Unit, and Anbyŏn Fish Farm under the 580th Army Force Unit, Shinch'ang Fish Farm, Taedonggang Terrapin Factory, Sŏngmak Atlantic Salmon Nursery and Raksan Sea Salmon Farm under the 810th Armed Forces Unit, General Nursery, Farm No. 1116 under the 810th Armed Forces Unit, Wŏnsan Nursery and Child Care Center, P'yŏngyang Institute of Biotechnology under the 810th Armed Forces Unit, Fatherland Liberation War Historic Site, P'yŏngyang International Airport Aviation Building, Changch'ŏn Vegetable Specialized Cooperative Farm, Automation Research Institute of Kim Chek University of Technology, P'yŏngyang Taegyŏng Seaweed Processing Factory, Rangnang Sanitary Products Factory, Shinŭiju Museum, P'yŏngyang Nursing Home, Farm No. 1116 under the 810th Armed Forces Unit, Taedonggang Fruit Farm, (N)P'yŏngyang River Refrigeration Plant, Measuring Instrument Factory, Paektusan Heroic Youth Development Center, Rasŏn City Recovery Battle Unit, (N)Ch'anggwang Store, Chŏngsŏng Pharmaceuticals General Factory, (N)Kwahakkisulchŏndang (Science and Technology Center), (R)P'yŏngyang Catfish Factory, (R)P'yŏngyang Children's Food Factory, 8wŏl25il (August 25) Fishery Factory under the 313th Armed Forces Unit, Fishery Factory No. 15 of the 549th Armed Forces Unit, Wŏnsan Shoe Factory, (MA)Tree Nursery of the 122nd Korean People's Army, (R)9wŏl9il (May 9) Catfish Factory, (MA)Samch'ŏn Catfish Factory,

2016   Ch'ŏngnyŏnundongsajŏkkwan (Youth Movement History Museum), (R)Kŭmk'ŏp Athletes' General Food Factory, (MA)T'aesŏng Machinery Factory, 10wŏl3il (October 3) Factory under the control of the Navy's 597th Armed Forces Unit, Ryongsŏng Machinery Factory, 2wŏl11il (February 11), Front Line Combat Team, Future Shop and General Service Base, Shinhŭng Machinery Factory, Tonghongsan Machinery Factory, Ryongsŏng Machinery Factory, the Machinery Factory managed by Ch'ŏrho Ri, Mindŭlle (Dandelion) Learning Center Factory, Paekdusan Hero Youth No. 3 Power Plant, the Korean People's Army's No. 122 Yangmyojang (Tree Nursery), the machine factory managed by Ch'ŏryong Hŏ, Nature Museum and Central Zoo, Ryugyŏng Eye and General Hospital Construction Site, Pogŏnsanso (Health Oxygen) Plant Construction Site, P'yŏngyang Sports Material Factory, Ryongaksan Soap Factory, Man'gyŏngjae Youth Camp, Ryugyŏng Kimchi Factory, National Defense University, < Hwasŏng –10> test launch, P'yŏngyang Secondary School, (R)P'yŏngyang Terrapin Factory, P'yŏngyang Synthetic Leather Factory, Paekdusan Architectural Research Institute, Hwasŏng Artillery Units, Fish Feed Factory under the 810th Armed Forces Unit, Ch'ŏllima Feed Factory, (N)Korean People's Army Fishing Gear Factory, 1wŏl18il (January 18) Machinery Factory, (R) Ak'ŭrilgyech'ilgam (Acrylic Paint) Production Plant at Sunch'ŏn Chemical Complex, Taedonggang Fruit and Vegetable Factory, Taedonggang Pig Factory, Strategic Submarine Ballistic Test Launch, Hwasŏng Artillery Units, (N)Pogŏnsanso (Health Oxygen) Factory, Alpine Watchman General Farm, New Type of Propulsion for Geostationary Satellite Carrier Rocket, Base Eruption Test, Taedonggang Syringe Factory, Ryongaksan Spring Water Factory, Man'gyŏngjae Revolutionary Historic Site Souvenir Factory, (N)Ryugyŏng Eye Hospital, (N)Ryongaksan Soap Factory, Korean People Army's 5wŏl170il (May 17) Fishery Plant and 1wŏl8il (January 8) Fishery Plant, Korean People's Army's 8wŏl25il (August 25) Fishery Plant, Korean People's Army 380th Combined Force Unit, Korean People's Army's 1045th Mountain Infantry Battalion's Ski Training, various projects of the Samjiyŏn County, 12wŏl6il (December 6) Boys' Camp in Kangwŏn Province, 525th Special Operations Battalion, (N)Wŏnsan Civil Power Plant, and Korean People Army's No. 15 Fishery Plant,

Source: author.

Note: (N) = newly constructed, (R) = renovated modernized, (MA) = the task of modernization is assigned.
Table 3.3 is compiled from data spanning the years 2012 to 2016, obtained from the *CCY*.

Enhanced CNC technology has not only reinstated their production capacity but significantly boosted productivity, surpassing the levels observed before the Arduous March. This accomplishment has created a favorable environment for the revitalization and normalization of production in other industries.

Kim Jong Un's on-the-spot guidance, as depicted in Table 3.3, underscores his emphasis on reinforcing defense capabilities, mirroring the approach during Kim Jong Il's era, especially amid an increasingly strained relationship with the United States. Concurrently, Kim Jong Un endeavors to normalize production across all industries, extending beyond heavy industry, by leveraging the rebuilt factories and enterprises of national strategic significance, now equipped with heightened capacity and productivity.

It is paramount to recognize that since around 2011, the DPRK has successfully emerged from the economic crisis of the Arduous March, leveraging its strengthened self-regeneration capabilities to pursue production normalization across all sectors. This achievement represents a significant milestone in the nation's economic resilience and resurgence.

The DPRK's remarkable recovery from the challenging period of the Arduous March is substantiated by the analysis of total national budget revenues. Table 3.4 demonstrates this achievement, highlighting the progress made over the years.[12] In 1993, prior to the onset of the Arduous March, the total national budget revenue stood at 40.5712 billion wŏn. By 2009, the revenue had reached 36.9765 billion wŏn, representing almost 90% of the 1993 level. This indicates a significant rebound in the economy. Moreover, in 2011, the total national budget revenue exceeded the 1993 level, reaching 42.5269 billion wŏn.

These figures underscore the extraordinary resilience and recovery of the DPRK's economy. Not only did it exceed the revenue levels observed before the Arduous March, but it also maintained a consistent growth trajectory, assuming no inflation occurred throughout that period.[13] The ability to generate revenue on par with or surpassing the pre-crisis era indicates the effectiveness of the measures implemented to revitalize and strengthen the economy. This achievement signifies the DPRK's commitment to overcome adversity and restore economic stability, fostering an environment conducive to sustained growth and development.

By 2011, the DPRK had made significant strides in preparing its various industry sectors for the normalization of production. This progress laid the foundation for the implementation of a new economic management method, as directed by Kim Jong Il in his seminal speech on October 3, 2001. The DPRK's commitment to revitalizing its economy and pursuing parallel paths of economic construction and nuclear weapons development was further affirmed at the March 2013 plenary session of the Party central committee, during which Kim Jong Un made the following statement:

> To usher in a transformation towards establishing economic powerhouse, it is imperative that we enhance economic guidance and management. It is crucial to engage in a thorough examination and refinement

Table 3.4 National Budget Revenue of the DPRK (1993–2016)

Year	1993	1994–1996	1997	1998	1999	2000	2001	2002
National Budget Revenue	40.5712[14]	NR[15]	19.7116[16]	19.7908[17]	19.8103[18]	20.4532[19]	21.6399[20]	22.6180[21]
Year	2003	2004	2005	2006	2007	2008	2009	2010
National Budget Revenue	23.7344[22]	25.3958[23]	29.5156[24]	30.8143[25]	32.6940[26]	34.5575[27]	36.9765[28]	39.8237[29]
Year	2011	2012	2013	2014	2015	2016	2017	2018
National Budget Revenue	42.5269[30]	45.6534[31]	48.3926[32]	51.2961[33]	53.8609[34]	57.2541[35]	60.0595[36]	Not Available[37]

Source: author.

Note: NR (Not Reported).
Unit: billion wŏn.

of our approach to economic management, aligning it with the demands of practical development. Our economic management methodology, deeply rooted in the Chuch'e idea, must epitomize a socialist enterprise management approach that steadfastly upholds socialist ownership of the means of production. By doing so, we unleash the full potential of the producer masses, not just as workers, but as active owners in both production and management.[38]

In the previous passage, when Kim Jong Un said, "It is crucial to engage in a thorough examination and refinement of our approach to economic management, aligning it with the demands of practical development," this can be interpreted as saying that new economic management methods are needed to leapfrog to the next stage in the context of overcoming the Arduous March and the beginning of the normalization of production. It underscores the urgency and importance of swiftly completing and institutionalizing this method.

As discussed in Chapter 2, Kim Jong Il's "10·3 Discourse" placed significant emphasis on achieving practical benefits while remaining committed to socialist principles.[39] This emphasis is further reaffirmed in Kim Jong Il's February 2006 speech to the responsible officials of the Central Party. In that speech, Kim Jong Il expressed the following viewpoint:

> Economic work must be carried out immediately to meet the needs of the Military-First era and the construction of a "Strong and Great Nation." Many years ago, I set out the principle of ensuring the greatest practicality while firmly adhering to socialist principles in economic work as the basis for socialist economic management, and, starting from the difficult situation of the country and the demands of our revolutionary development, I presented the line of economic construction in our style and indicated the direction and method for its implementation.[40]

The statement made by Kim Jong Un, asserting that

> the economic management method, based on our Chuch'e ideology, should embody a socialist enterprise management approach that empowers the working masses to act as masters in production and management, carrying out independent and creative business activities under the unified guidance of the State, while steadfastly upholding socialist ownership of the means of production

mirrors the sentiments articulated by Kim Jong Il over a decade ago, as evidenced in the aforementioned speech.

Consequently, it becomes clear that Kim Jong Un's intention was not to introduce a new economic management system but, rather, to follow the path of economic construction delineated by his predecessor. This course had been delayed due to challenges in normalizing production across various industry sectors,[41] but it has now been refined and institutionalized to align with the current circumstances. This adaptation has been made possible as the economy has gradually recovered from the difficulties of the Arduous March period and the nation's capacity for self-reliance has increased.

3.2 Key Features of the Socialist Enterprise Responsibility Management System

On May 30, 2014, Kim Jong Un delivered a noteworthy address to the members of the Party Central Committee, presenting a notable development in economic management known as the "Socialist Enterprise Responsibility Management System" (SERMS). While specific details of Kim Jong Un's speech on May 30 are not widely accessible to the public, insights into the fundamental principles and implications of the SERMS can be derived from scholarly works authored by DPRK scholars.

Yŏnghŭng Kim, a scholar from Kim Il Sung University, argues against characterizing the SERMS as a mere copy of foreign models. In his article "The Important Issues in Immediate Implementation of the SERMS," [42] he emphasizes its distinct DPRK character, meticulously tailored to the nation's unique conditions and needs.

Kim paints SERMS as a scientific approach to economic management. It seamlessly integrates core socialist principles established by Kim Il Sung and Kim Jong Il with enhanced accountability in production and operation. This focus on scientific practices and strengthened accountability aims to meet the DPRK's specific development challenges.

The renaming from "Socialist Enterprise Management Method" to SERMS signifies a significant shift. Kim sees it as an embodiment of Kim Jong Un's leadership, reflecting a vision tailored to the DPRK. While upholding socialist principles, SERMS introduces a robust accountability framework, making it both a continuation of Kim Il Sung and Kim Jong Il's legacy and a testament to their influence on evolving economic challenges. Kim underscores SERMS's continuity with the preexisting system established under Kim Il Sung and Kim Jong Il. He emphasizes that while elements have been adjusted, the fundamental framework remains intact. SERMS does not abandon the past but builds upon it, adapting to the present reality.

Kim delves deeper into SERMS's foundation, highlighting the crucial role of comprehensive socialist principles in enterprise management. This means aligning with the Party's economic construction line and adhering to its policies and directives. Kim emphasizes the establishment of "Enterprise Indicators" within the Party's framework, signifying Party guidance. Continued existence and active roles of factory, enterprise, and cooperative Party Committees further substantiate this Party-centric approach.[43] Operating based on the Taean System, SERMS enterprises solidify their adherence to Party principles. This reaffirms SERMS's roots in socialist principles while showcasing its adaptability.

Importantly, Party Committees continue to play a vital role within enterprises. They guide the implementation of the Party's line and policies, ensuring enterprises prioritize attaining "Central Indicators" reflecting strategic objectives. Additionally, Party Committees oversee rear supply projects for worker welfare, including training centers, recreation facilities, and daycare.

While enterprises enjoy greater autonomy and authority, they remain subject to Party Committee guidance and management. This shift implies a reduction in central material and financial support, granting enterprises increased management autonomy. However, they operate within a collectivist framework and are not driven solely by commercial purposes. Party Committees ensure enterprises remain committed to collective goals and the broader social and economic objectives of the nation.

The SERMS can be objectively described as a unique and indigenous economic management approach specifically tailored to the circumstances of the DPRK. It stands apart from merely imitating foreign practices or relying solely on external experiences. Instead, the system is designed to strike a delicate balance between granting enterprises greater autonomy while upholding the collective nature of socialist principles. In this context, Party Committees play a crucial role in harmonizing these objectives.[44]

The SERMS proposes a framework for balancing the preservation of a socialist economic model with adaptations to contemporary realities. This approach aims to empower factories, enterprises, and cooperatives to play a more active role in national development while adhering to the principle of collective ownership. By potentially granting these entities increased autonomy in resource procurement and foreign economic activity, SERMS seeks to unlock their potential for contributing to economic normalization, expansion, and growth.

One key pillar of SERMS lies in empowering enterprises to craft their own paths. Freed from rigid limitations, they can now secure contracts and orders based on their unique strategies, actively seeking out the necessary raw materials, equipment, and resources for efficient production. This newfound autonomy marks a notable shift toward a market-based resource allocation system within the DPRK, acknowledging the effectiveness of such mechanisms within the broader socialist framework.[45]

The SERMS recognizes the potential benefits of international economic interaction. It encourages enterprises to engage in foreign trade, empowering them to address resource needs through direct engagement with international partners.[46] This expansion of trading rights and access to necessary materials opens doors for greater specialization and efficiency.

The SERMS introduces a degree of operational autonomy for enterprises while maintaining the DPRK's commitment to collective ownership. The system combines centralized guidance from the Party and State, embodied in "Chungangjip'yo" (Central Indicators), with enterprise-specific objectives,

"Kiŏpch'ejiryo" (Enterprise Indicators). This interaction aims to balance the pursuit of broader national economic development goals with the operational flexibility of individual enterprises.

The inclusion of the term "Socialist" in the Socialist Enterprise Responsibility Management System stems from this operational structure. Enterprises are granted a greater degree of autonomy compared to the previous economic management system, enabling them to approach their business activities with increased initiative and creativity. However, this autonomy is conditional upon the fulfillment of Central Indicators that reflect the economic construction strategy outlined by the Party and State. Therefore, the system is unequivocally implemented under the unified guidance of the Party and State. Thus far, the SERMS closely aligns with the economic construction approach of the Military-First era, as elucidated by Kim Jong Il in his October 3, 2001, speech, along with its corresponding implementation guidelines.

One notable difference lies in the organization and operation of the material supply business within the new economic operational system proposed by Kim Jong Il. The system incorporates a "socialist commodity exchange market" as a secondary layer. However, in the SERMS resource allocations, apart from the quantity and supply of materials necessary to fulfill nationally strategic indicators, known as "Chungyojip'yo" (Critical Indicators),[47] are conducted through orders and contracts—effectively through market mechanisms. Consequently, the market assumes a leading role in resource allocation pertaining to material quantity and supply, rather than merely a supporting role.

The determination of whether the "socialist commodity exchange market" plays a supporting or leading role in resource allocation depends on the proportion of Critical Indicators within the total set of indicators. However, obtaining specific records of this proportion from DPRK sources and literature, such as the *CCY*, *Rodong Sinmun*, *ER*, or *KUAB*, is challenging. This lack of information is likely due to the application of different weightings to various enterprises.

Nevertheless, an article authored by Kilhyŏn Cho in *KUAB* sheds light on another facet of the SERMS indicating that, on the whole, Critical Indicators do not constitute a significant portion of the total Indicators. Kilhyŏn Cho emphasized the importance of rational sharing of planning indicators between the central and local governments, as well as between higher and lower institutions, as a means to enhance enterprise responsibility and creativity. Expanding on this notion, he provided the following insights.

> A planned economy does not mean that all sectors and units' production management activities must be centrally planned down to the smallest detail. When planning for indicators that have strategic significance in economic construction and essential indicators that must be framed and solved nationally, the indicators should be distributed so that they can be planned within the scope of facilities and materials that can be guaranteed

nationally so that production and consumption, supply and demand, and realistic planning can be achieved.⁴⁸

As evident from the aforementioned, the term "Critical Indicators" refers to indicators of strategic significance in economic development, which the State must establish and address.⁴⁹ Moreover, if enterprises are mandated to implement these Critical Indicators, the State is responsible for ensuring the provision of necessary facilities and materials.

However, increasing the number of Critical Indicators places a burden on the State, contradicting Kim Jong Un's directive to establish a SERMS that enables all enterprises to independently and creatively engage in management activities, allowing the producer masses to fulfill their roles and responsibilities as owners in production and management. Hence, it can be inferred that Critical Indicator will only represent a small proportion of the overall indicators. Consequently, it can also be deduced that the market assumes a leading role in resource allocation under the SERMS.

In his article published in the *KUAB*, Kwangik Tu emphasizes that the successful execution of business activities by enterprises, in line with the principles of the SERMS relies on effectively harnessing the pricing power bestowed upon them by the State. This "pricing power" pertains to the authority granted to enterprises to establish prices based on the guidelines and methodologies specified by the State, either autonomously or through mutual agreement with consumers. Subsequently, these prices are duly registered and implemented through the appropriate national pricing agency.

However, as mentioned by Tu, enterprises can achieve greater autonomy, proactivity, and creativity in the SERMS by fully utilizing the granted "pricing power."⁵⁰ This empowerment is realized when enterprises engage in business activities through consultations and contracts with other enterprises, rather than solely relying on the prices determined by the State for Critical Indicators. Furthermore, the fact that enterprises have been given the authority to set prices reinforces the notion that Critical Indicators constitute only a minor portion of the overall indicators.

This reasoning finds support in the following article by Gyŏngok Kim, which explores the expanded scope of "planning rights" and "production organization rights" for socialist enterprises.

The effective exercise of expanded planning and production organization rights by enterprises necessitates the seamless integration of the State's Central Indicators planning with the planning of Enterprise Indicators through order contracts. Enterprises must embrace rational production organization methods to systematically enhance the production of goods with high social demand. It is the responsibility of the enterprise to independently conduct the planning of both Enterprise Indicators and Central Indicators received from the State through order contracts.

In situations where there is surplus production capacity, the enterprise should prioritize the production of indicators that can be increased or are in high demand. This production should align with the planning imposed by the State, and the produced items should strictly adhere to the orders and contracts specified by Enterprise Indicators.[51]

Since the Critical Indicators that hold national strategic significance are encompassed within the Central Indicators, the aforementioned article by Gyŏngok Kim should be understood as suggesting that all indicators, except for Critical Indicators, should be carried out through market-based order contracts.

While official DPRK data remains murky on the precise breakdown of Central and Enterprise Indicators, glimmers of insight can be gleaned from the emphasis on enterprise autonomy within the SERMS. Unlike past systems, it appears Enterprise Indicators driven by this newfound independence may not be dwarfed by their centrally planned counterparts. Even if Critical Indicators form the bulk of Central Indicators, their combined weight within the overall tally likely falls short of half. This suggests a remarkable shift: more than half of resource allocation for realizing all planned indicators now flows through the pulsating arteries of market mechanisms.

An interesting aspect of the previous article by Kilhyŏn Cho is its striking similarity to what Kim Jong Il articulated in his 2001 "10·3 Discourse," which was discussed in Chapter 2. In his speech on October 3, 2001, Kim Jong Il precisely stated the following.

The planned economy does not necessitate meticulous central planning of every aspect of production and management across all sectors and units. As directed by the Party, the State Planning Commission should focus solely on indicators crucial for strategic economic development ... Relevant agencies and enterprises should be responsible for planning other minor and newly established standard indicators ...

The State Planning Commission's focus should lie on composite indicators like gross industrial product, provincial basic construction investment, and other essential indicators as deemed necessary, alongside quantifying guaranteed state supplies of equipment and materials ... Planning responsibilities should be delegated across cities, counties, and enterprises, with detailed indicator planning entrusted to cities and counties based on their specific circumstances.[52]

This corroborates the earlier inference that the fundamental framework of the SERMS was already delineated in Kim Jong Il's speech on October 3, 2001 (the "10·3 Discourse"). However, its implementation was postponed due to the incomplete normalization of production across various industries. It was not until 2011 that preparations for achieving production normalization were accomplished in all sectors, not solely limited to those of national strategic significance. This enabled a significant shift in economic operational management to align with the "changed reality and the needs of real development" during Kim Jong Il's era.

Supporting this notion, Sŏngnam Kang's article titled "The Immortal Achievements of the Great Leader Kim Jong Il in Improving Socialist Economic Management" extensively draws from Kim Jong Il's instructions in the "10·3 Discourse," providing further affirmation to this point.

> The State Planning Commission should plan indicators of strategic significance in economic construction. These Critical Indicators must be grasped and solved nationally and let the relevant institutions and enterprise centers plan other minor and detailed indicators. For local economic sectors, including local industry, the State Planning Commission should plan comprehensive indicators such as gross industrial product and essential construction investment for each province, as well as some key indicators as needed. Furthermore, the State should plan facilities and materials that can be guaranteed by the State, while allowing cities, counties, and enterprise units to divide the plan and plan detailed indicators according to each of their conditions.[53]

In the intricate ballet of the DPRK's economic system, where State and enterprise pirouette together, financing plays a crucial role. Imagine two stages: one bathed in the spotlight of Critical Indicators, where the State acts as a benevolent patron, showering resources and materials to ensure a flawless performance. In this realm, enterprises waltz without financial worries, their every need effortlessly met. But step off the brightly lit stage, and the music changes. Here, the spotlight illuminates Central Indicators, minus the chosen few Critical ones, and self-determined Enterprise Indicators. In this domain, enterprises become solo acts, tasked with orchestrating their own budgets.[54] Their financial autonomy becomes a double-edged sword: empowering, yet demanding.

To raise the curtain on this funding feat, enterprises have a repertoire of maneuvers. Imagine surpassing the State's production plan for Central Indicators as a grand jeté, each leap beyond expectations translating to increased net income—their own private treasure chest for self-chosen goals.[55] Similarly, cost-cutting becomes a nimble pirouette, every penny saved twirling into their financial coffers. But the most captivating act might be the 8·3 Movement, a self-choreographed routine where enterprises tap into idle resources and labor for their own projects, generating additional income for their Enterprise Indicators.[56] It is a testament to their resourcefulness, a pirouette on a shoestring budget.

Yet, the question lingers: can these self-funding acrobatics truly sustain the entire production? If, as some whisper, these non-guaranteed indicators outnumber the Critical ones, the solo act might feel like a marathon, not a graceful ballet. Perhaps, like a seasoned dancer, DPRK enterprises will need to discover new steps—unearthing fresh revenue streams, forging strategic partnerships, or even venturing into uncharted financial territory—to keep the economic performance on point.

This intricate financial dance underscores the evolving relationship between State and enterprise in the DPRK's economy. While the State remains the choreographer, guiding the overall direction, enterprises are increasingly taking center stage, mastering the art of self-funded maneuvers. Whether they can gracefully navigate the entire ballet remains to be seen, but one thing is certain: their financial footwork will be a captivating performance to watch.

3.3 Commercial Banking and Socialist Enterprise Responsibility Management System

In addition to the aforementioned methods, literature from the DPRK also suggests the option of borrowing funds from banks.[57] Kŭmhyŏk Ku's analysis elevates these loans from mere financial props to vital lifts, propelling enterprises closer to their targets and fueling the construction of a robust socialist state.[58] But banks aren't simply confetti-throwing patrons; they waltz as watchful partners, guiding fund utilization with a firm yet graceful hand.

To keep pace with the country's dynamic rhythm, Kŭmhyŏk Ku urges commercialization, a fresh beat that unlocks internal reserves and transforms banks into active players, mobilizing resources with strategic leaps and bounds.[59] This metamorphosis hinges on two key concepts: the Financial Institution Liability System and Commercial Banking.

Imagine a financial ecosystem where banks, like ballerinas in sleek leotards, balance on their own pointe shoes. This is the essence of the Liability System: banks offset expenses with income from financial activities like loans and savings, ultimately benefiting the country. But to pirouette gracefully, they need commercialization—applying an Independent Accounting System (IAS) that transforms them from passive conduits to proactive players.

Picture this new IAS as a flowing scarf, empowering banks to generate income through loans and savings, cover expenses with this income, and even share a portion of their profits with the State. It mirrors the SERMS—all institutions and enterprises dance to the same tune.

As commercialized banks shoulder the responsibility of covering their expenses, they meticulously assess enterprises' repayment capacity before granting loans. Only those who demonstrate a proven track record can join this financial waltz.[60] This dynamic ignites an unseen competition, compelling enterprises to sharpen their performance for loan eligibility.

From an institutional perspective, "all monetary transactions flow through banks," granting them a front-row seat to oversee and regulate business activities. Imagine them as watchful conductors, orchestrating the financial flow and exercising comprehensive and regular "control by the wŏn" over production and management across all sectors.[61] This shift toward "control by the wŏn" through bank loans addresses a historical clash: the subjectivism of national planners versus the localism of producers. The Taean System attempted to resolve this, but limitations remained until the market took center stage.

With the SERMS and market emphasis, borrowing a significant portion of production and management funds from banks became the new normal. Gyŏngshik Chang called it "full and normal control by the wŏn." Instead of solely relying on the State treasury, institutions and enterprises now waltz with banks, a shift deemed "rational" and "normal" as it avoids past frictions. Chang further clarifies that under this system, the market, not planning, dictates resource allocation,[62] leading the economic ballet.

But where do banks get the funds to lend? They too twirl to the rhythm of deposits and loans, generating income that covers their expenses and fuels lending to enterprises. Unfortunately, data on the exact proportion of bank loans used by enterprises remains shrouded in secrecy. Similarly, the precise amount of loans and enterprise-generated operating income utilized for production and management are undisclosed.

While the details remain veiled, one thing is clear: DPRK enterprises have embraced a new financial dance, with banks playing a crucial supporting role. Whether they can maintain this graceful performance amid the complex economic choreography remains to be seen, but their evolving partnership adds a captivating twist to the DPRK's economic ballet.

While bank loans play a crucial role in financing enterprises, a key question remains: where do banks get the funds to lend? As we discussed before, banks generate income through deposits and loans, but the exact picture is murky. DPRK data isn't exactly forthcoming on the proportion of bank loans used by enterprises, or the precise amount loaned.

Adding to the puzzle, DPRK scholars point to a substantial amount of "Yuhyuhwap'e (idle currency)," both domestic and foreign, stashed away by individuals.[63] Savings, insurance, and currency exchange businesses are seen as key players in mobilizing this unspent wealth and channeling it into banks.[64] However, precise figures remain elusive, leaving us in the dark about the true magnitude of this hidden treasure.

But why does so much money sit idle? The phrase "money lying around" suggests two possibilities: either people are rational consumers saving a portion of their income, or a lack of goods to buy forces their hands. It's likely the latter. Kim Jong Un himself, in a 2013 speech, lamented the scarcity of consumer goods, urging the light industry to ramp up production and bridge the gap between supply and demand. His words paint a picture of eager wallets with nowhere to go.[65]

Echoing this sentiment, economist Sunhwa Ri underscores the fundamental role of balanced supply and demand for a thriving economy. She even praises Kim Jong Un's grasp of this principle, deeming it the "most accurate path" to prosperity.[66] However, Ri's specific details on Kim Jong Un's words are absent. Thankfully, his own 2013 speech sheds light on the prevailing conditions in the DPRK at that time. He explicitly acknowledges a shortage of consumer goods, blaming it on the underperforming light industry. This stark undersupply, compared to the people's demand, created a severe imbalance, exposing a fundamental challenge for their economic efforts.

In light of the current situation, people are inclined to hold onto a substantial portion of their funds rather than spending it. While determining the exact amount of money held by the populace proves challenging, an intriguing indicator emerges from analyzing the DPRK's Compound Annual Growth Rate (CAGR) of national budget revenue.

In the DPRK, all means of production are state-owned, and individuals are guaranteed the right to work by law. This system ensures that the total income generated by enterprises, including factories and Bureaus, constitutes a national income known as "Pŏnsuip" (Earned Income). Economist Sŏnhŭi O delineates Pŏnsuip as follows:

> Pŏnsuip reflects the newly created portion of value in enterprises. Pŏnsuip is the remainder after deducting material expenditures from sales revenue and consist of the value created by labor for itself and the value created by labor for society. Pŏnsuip is enterprise income within the scope of an enterprise and become **Kungminsodŭk (national income)** (emphasis added) within the scope of the entire society.[67]

Within Pŏnsuip, there are two distinct components: "Kukkagiŏmniikkŭm" (State Enterprise Profit Revenue), allocated to the state, and the remainder retained by the enterprise. Specifically, the enterprise's share encompasses "Rodongbosugŭm" (Workers' Living Expenses) and "Kiŏpsogigŭm" (Enterprise's Self-Provisions).[68] While the specific breakdown of Pŏnsuip and its components remains unknown, determining Rodongbosugŭm significantly impacts Pŏnsuip's overall growth. Here's how:

The computation for Workers' Living Expenses Share is straightforward: multiplying Earnings per Worker by the Earnings Plan Execution Rate.[69] In a hypothetical scenario, an enterprise establishes an earnings target of 1,500 wŏn per worker per month, coupled with a State Enterprise Profit Revenue rate of 10%. When a worker surpasses this target with an execution rate of 120%, their share for living expenses increases to 1,800 wŏn (1,500 wŏn x 1.2). This framework directly links exceeding the earnings plan with elevated living expenses for individual workers, thereby incentivizing heightened productivity.

Suppose a worker's Earned Income for the month amounts to 2,000 wŏn, then 200 wŏn is allocated to the State. Following the distribution protocol, the State receives its share before the remaining 1,800 wŏn is allotted to the worker.

A pivotal insight emerges: the growth of Earned Income is steered by workers, with the expansion of Workers' Living Expenses playing a central role. As workers are motivated to boost productivity, the rise in Workers' Living Expenses becomes a catalyst for the expansion of Earned Income. Since the size of State Enterprise Profit Revenue is contingent upon a fixed percentage of Earned Income, its growth is intricately linked to that of Earned Income and, consequently, to the growth of Workers' Living Expenses.

In essence, the growth rates of State Enterprise Profit Revenue and Earned Income become closely aligned, ultimately reflecting the growth rate of Workers' Living Expenses. This interconnection provides valuable insights into estimating the accumulation of funds in individual hands, even in the absence of explicit data.

Using Table 3.4, we can calculate the compound annual growth rate (CAGR) of total national budget revenue for the 17 years from 2000[70] to 2017 as follows.

CAGR = $(FV/PV)1/n - 1$; FV is the year-ending value, PV is the value of the year beginning, and n is the number of years. Therefore, the CAGR from 2000 to 2017 is (60.0595 billion wŏn/20.4532 billion wŏn) ^ (1/17) – 1 = 0.065 or about 6.5%.

Between 2000 and 2017, the DPRK's national budget grew at a steady 6.5% annual rate. It means that State Enterprise Profit Revenue and labor remuneration also saw at least a 6.5% yearly increase. Workers received their share of enterprise income in cash,[71] meaning their wallets were getting fatter alongside the national coffers. With rising salaries came increased purchasing power, and workers naturally looked to fill their baskets with more goods.[72]

However, this seemingly positive equation hinges on one crucial factor: supply keeping pace with demand. If the shelves remain bare while wallets burgeon, inflation rears its ugly head. Prices climb, chasing cash in a self-defeating cycle.[73] Breaking this cycle without importing more goods is a short-term challenge.

Data on DPRK inflation is as elusive as a desert mirage. But, consider the 2009 currency reform, where 100 old wŏn became a single new one. It is clear inflation was already a guest at the economic table. Even Kim Jong Un himself has lamented the inadequate supply of consumer goods post-reform. This scarcity fuels a hunger for cash, as people turn to markets seeking what State-owned stores lack.

This disconnect creates a curious twist in the cash flow dance. Money sashays out of banks, waltzes through offices and businesses, but instead of gracefully returning to its financial home, it gets stashed away in individual pockets.[74] This phenomenon, known as "idle currency," is a substantial hidden stash in the DPRK's economic chest. While pinpointing the exact amount locked away is tricky, its existence is undeniable, and addressing it is paramount.

Wŏnkyŏng Ri's article provides noteworthy clues regarding the "idle currency" held by residents. Ri asserts that "it is a legitimate phenomenon to extensively acquire currency from residents and utilize it to address the increased demand for currency funds in business activities." He further argues:

> Amidst the swiftly evolving domestic and international landscape, the era of the Military-First, which actively pursued the fundamental tenets of the revolution, has emerged. Notable transformations have unfolded in

economic planning and the execution of the national budget, necessitating innovative approaches to address the economic needs of the populace. In response to these imperatives, the implementation of the People's Economy placed significant emphasis on State financing mobilization while also giving due consideration to the activation of internal reserves and the utilization of temporarily idle funds. **Consequently, a trend is emerging where the percentage of idle currency mobilization methods in meeting the demand for funds for People's Economy is relatively increasing compared to the percentage of State fiscal fund mobilization methods**. (emphasis added)[75]

To fully understand Ri's statement on the utilization of "idle currency," we must rewind to the tumultuous period of the Arduous March. This economic crisis saw the national budget plummet, crippling most sectors and leaving the State scrambling to prioritize resources. National defense and other critical areas took precedence, squeezing out funding for broader economic development.

In this austere landscape, a new strategy emerged: mobilizing the significant "idle currency" held by individual residents. Banks began absorbing these dormant funds and channeling them back into the People's Economy, effectively substituting for dwindling State budgetary allocations. This shift marked a turning point, with reliance on people-held cash steadily surpassing traditional budgetary channels.

It is important to note that Ri's article was written in 2002, reflecting the situation prevalent in the early 2000s. Subsequently, the share of "idle currency" mobilized from residents to meet economic financing needs has continued to surpass the share derived from the amount allocated to the People's Economy.

The national budget revenue of 2011 exceeded that of 1993, suggesting a recovery from the economic crisis that originated in 1994, assuming there was no inflation during that period. As production normalization became tangible, it is likely that individuals held onto less idle currency as the economic situation improved. While the exact reduction in the portion of idle currency held by the people is unknown, it is presumed to be less than the amount allocated to the People's Economy since 2011.

The role of "idle currency" in the People's Economy appears to have endured beyond 2014, marking the earnest commencement of the SERMS. Yŏngŭi Hong's article, featured in the third issue of *ER* in 2014, elucidates this continuity. Hong asserts

In a socialist society, a bank serves not only as a credit and payment intermediary but also as a state institution that maximizes the mobilization of idle currency and provides guarantees to institutions and enterprises lacking funds for their production activities.[76]

This passage affirms that even within the framework of the SERMS, the "idle cash" of residents[77] remains a crucial source for fulfilling the demand for funds in the People's Economy.

While the *CCY* does not provide specific figures for total national expenditures and the amount allocated to the People's Economy, estimations can be made based on the available data. The total national budget revenues from 2000 to 2017 have been roughly estimated, as shown in Table 3.4, and the total national budget expenditures for each year are planned based on the previous year's total national revenues. The proportion of the total state budget expenditures to the total national budget expenditures remains relatively consistent. Utilizing this information, it is possible to estimate the expenditures and the remaining amount of idle currency held by the population for each year within the 2000–2017 period.

Table 3.5 elucidates a substantial mobilization of the public's "idle currency," chiefly through bank savings, to meet their economic requirements, constituting roughly half of the annual total national expenditure before 2011. With the progression of production normalization since 2011 and indications of improvement in the light industry, aligning with the normalization of production in nationally significant industries since 2014, the size of these reserves likely experienced a decline. Nevertheless, as of 2018, a significant amount of unutilized currency persists, though not as substantial as in earlier years.[115]

An essential point to highlight is the transformative impact of the "Kŭmyunggigwanch'aesanje" (Financial Institutions Liability System) implemented in 2013. This shift has redefined banking institutions into commercial

Table 3.5 Total National Budget Expenditures, Amount of People's Economy, and Size of "Idle Currency" in the Hands of the Residents

Year	Total National Revenue	Total National Expenditure	Amount of the People's Economy	Size of "Idle Currency"[78]
2000	20.4532	20.95503[79]	8.40297[80]	$\geq$ 8.40297
2001	21.6399	21.67805[81]	9.16982[82]	$\geq$ 9.16982
2002	22.6180	22.57276[83]	5.1292[84]	$\geq$ 5.1292
2003	23.7344	23.7344[85]	5.5301[86]	$\geq$ 5.5301
2004	25.3958	25.2180[87]	10.4150[88]	$\geq$ 10.4150
2005	29.5156	30.8143[89]	12.7263[90]	$\geq$ 12.7263
2006	30.8143	30.8143[91]	12.5772[92]	$\geq$ 12.5772
2007	32.6940	33.2498[93]	13.6657[94]	$\geq$ 13.6657
2008	34.5575	34.5575[95]	13.8230[96]	$\geq$ 13.823
2009	36.9765	36.9025[97]	14.7610[98]	$\geq$ 14.761
2010	39.8237	39.9285[99]	15.0131[100]	$\geq$ 15.0131
2011	42.5269	42.4418[101]	16.9767[102]	< 16.9767
2012	45.6534	45.4708[103]	18.1883[104]	< 18.1883
2013	48.3926	48.0172[105]	21.7038[106]	< 21.7038
2014	51.2961	51.2961[107]	23.9553[108]	< 23.9553
2015	53.8609	53.8609[109]	25.5839[110]	< 25.5839
2016	57.2541	57.2541[111]	27.6537[112]	< 27.6537
2017	60.0595	60.0595[113]	29.0087[114]	< 29.0087

Source: author.

Unit: billion wŏn.

banks, obliging them to generate income through financial operations like savings and loans to cover their expenses. Additionally, a specific portion of their earnings is now allocated to the State.[116] This structural change suggests a growing trend of financing People's Economy sector through financial mechanisms rather than relying on State finances. As this shift progresses, it is anticipated that the proportion of such financing will correspondingly rise, shaping the landscape of economic dynamics.

Yongnam Cho'e's research underscores a persistent trend: a notable volume of cash still remains within the possession of residents as of 2018. This phenomenon points to the vibrancy of a Consumer-to-Consumer (C2C) market, wherein residents engage in direct trade of goods, circumventing the official cash circulation channels. This prompts two intriguing questions that warrant exploration: firstly, how has this C2C market evolved within the dynamic landscape of the DPRK; and secondly, what strategies have the DPRK authorities employed in response to the existence of this informal economic activity?

3.4 Evolution of Market in the DPRK and the Socialist Enterprise Responsibility Management System

During the challenging period of the Arduous March, the markets in the DPRK, whether spontaneously formed or transformed from farmers' markets, played a pivotal role as people relied on them to engage in trade and autonomously procure their daily necessities. Notably, a significant characteristic of the DPRK market during this time was the prevalence of foreign-made light industrial products.

This phenomenon stemmed from Kim Jong Il's directive to import and utilize light industrial goods that were deemed to lack comparative advantage, prioritizing trade as a strategy.[117] The emphasis on mobilizing internal resources for revitalizing the light industry, as emphasized by Kim Il Sung, lost momentum during the scarcity of the Arduous March. Starting from 1994, when trade was permitted at the county level within limited boundaries, the DPRK market witnessed a surge in imports of light industrial products, including daily necessities.

As the most challenging phase of the Arduous March gradually subsided and sectors of national strategic significance began to rebuild, the DPRK brought the autonomous markets under centralized control through the establishment of Chonghapshijang (General Market).[118] This control framework included regulations for stall setups, compulsory registration of sellers with the market, spot taxes levied on stall usage, and restrictions on the sale of staple foods like rice and corn.

However, the prices of goods in the market continued to be determined by supply and demand, reflecting a *laissez-faire* market system. Instead of taking measures to eliminate the market altogether, the DPRK actively promoted the development of the light industry, aiming to boost the production of light goods and enhance the quality of commercial services to compete with the market. During his final on-the-spot guidance at the Kwangbok District Commerce Center, Kim Jong Il provided instructions that underscored this approach.

> The gradual elimination of the market is imperative. Commercial networks like the Kwangbok District Commercial Center should exert pressure on the market ... The market's decline will be organic with the establishment of commercial centers in each district. If these commercial centers offer goods at prices lower than the market, our people will naturally shift away from using the market.

> The Party advocates addressing the gap left by the State's inability to meet the people's demand for light industrial products through the establishment of a network of commercial services, exemplified by the Kwangbok District Commercial Center. It is incumbent upon us to bridge the void resulting from the inadequacy in ensuring the proper production of light industrial products.[119]

Recognizing the lack of competitiveness in the DPRK's production of light industrial goods, Kim Jong Il devised a strategy to compete with the *laissez-faire* market by significantly increasing the production of such goods. This was achieved through independent efforts as well as joint ventures with foreign countries, allowing the goods to be sold to consumers at prices below those prevailing in the market.[120]

Kim Jong Il also established designated mines, factories, and enterprises in the Tanch'ŏn area of South Hamgyŏng Province to secure foreign currency, enabling the reversal of money obtained from these sales into foreign currency at trade banks. This foreign currency was then utilized to purchase machinery and raw materials necessary for manufacturing light industrial products from abroad, thus ensuring the livelihoods of the people.

Despite Kim Jong Il's attention and efforts, State-owned stores struggled to effectively compete with the market. Addressing this issue, Kim Jong Un highlighted the unfinished task of fulfilling Kim Jong Il's last wish to normalize light industry production and ensure an adequate supply of quality goods for the people. In his directive at the National Light Industry Congress on March 18, 2013, Kim Jong Un emphasized the priority of normalizing production in the light industry sector. He called for the significant production of consumer goods essential for people's lives and the substantial increase in the production of basic food and primary consumer goods.

One of the significant challenges in the light industry sector, as pointed out by Kim Jong Un, is the heavy reliance on imports of raw materials and materials. To address this issue, Kim Jong Un suggested that chemical industry factories and enterprises organize economic projects to ensure smooth production of high-quality fibers, resins, and essential chemical products. He emphasized the development of local industries and the establishment of partnerships between central and local industrial plants to facilitate mutual support.

Kim Jong Un has set his sights on a transformative agenda for DPRK's light industry, prioritizing its modernization and scientificization. This ambitious vision goes beyond mere production increases; it seeks to infuse the sector with advanced technology and cutting-edge practices, propelling it into the realm of contemporary industrial prowess.

The core of this strategy lies in equipping light industry with the tools of the future. High-tech machinery, automation solutions, and advanced production processes will replace outdated methods, paving the way for unprecedented efficiency and productivity. Imagine gleaming assembly lines humming with CNC equipment, robots dexterously wielding tools, and intelligent systems optimizing every step of the production chain.

This is the future Kim Jong Un envisions for the DPRK light industry. But technology is just one piece of the puzzle. Scientific principles and data-driven approaches will become the guiding lights, informing every decision and optimizing every operation. From meticulous quality control measures to rigorous process improvements, the emphasis will be on achieving flawless product quality and consistently exceeding set targets. Kim Jong Un's ambitions extend beyond individual factories. He envisions a holistic transformation of the entire light industry ecosystem, revitalized on a new scientific and technological foundation. This involves fostering strong research and development programs, nurturing skilled workforces adept at operating and maintaining cutting-edge equipment, and establishing robust infrastructure to support this modernized industrial landscape.

His dedication to this vision is evident in his relentless calls for action. He exhorts industry leaders to equip facilities with the latest advancements, specifically mentioning CNC and unmanned production processes. He urges them to draw inspiration from the "receiving guidance units"—pioneering factories that both he and his father, Kim Jong Il, have personally championed as models for the future. In his March 13th report to the Party's Central Committee Plenary Session, Kim Jong Un laid bare the Party's unwavering commitment to advancing both economic construction and nuclear weapons development. He underscored that the most pressing and immediate task was to build an economic powerhouse and tangibly improve living standards.[121]

While Kim Jong Il's economic focus was on solidifying the foundations for normalized production in heavy industries like Chuch'e Steel, Textiles, and Fertilizer, Kim Jong Un's gaze shifted toward modernizing and scientificizing the light industry sector and normalizing production within its domain. This prioritization of light industry is readily apparent in Kim Jong Un's numerous on-site guidance sessions. As Table 3.3 reveals, from 2013 to 2016, he provided a staggering 79 instances of local guidance to light industry facilities, nearly 2.5 times the 31 instances for heavy industry during the same period. Furthermore, the *CCY* paints a picture of extensive upgrades and modernizations across light industry plants since Kim Jong Un's ascension to supreme leadership, further solidifying his commitment to this sector's revitalization.[122]

While detailed documentation regarding the outcomes of these upgrades and modernization efforts in the DPRK literature is limited, reports from *Chosun Sinbo* suggest significant changes in the light industry sector since Kim Jong Un's speech at the National Light Industry Congress on March 18, 2013.

> Upon the doors swinging open at 11:00 a.m., the Kwangbok District Commercial Center stores brimmed with activity, teeming with eager customers … Department stores seamlessly imported goods from abroad, primarily encompassing daily necessities, and citizens procured them using Korean currency. The disparity in costs was absorbed within the current expenses of the general trading company, a strategic move to promptly address the populace's immediate material needs at the State's expense.

> At its inauguration, the distribution between domestic and imported goods stood at 4:6. Subsequently, the commercial center underwent evolutions in both management and service methodologies. Presently, the ratio of domestic to imported goods has shifted to 7:3. This transformation aligns with the broader rejuvenation of the country's economy, manifested in a profusion of diverse products emanating from the reconstructed and modernized light industrial factories.[123]

Significantly, the balance between DPRK-made and foreign-made products available at the Kwangbok District Commercial Center has undergone a noteworthy transformation. Initially, upon the center's inauguration in December 2011, the ratio stood at 4:6, indicating a preference for foreign-made products. However, by January 2018, this ratio had undergone a marked reversal, now at 7:3, with a more substantial share attributed to DPRK-made products. Importantly, these foreign-made products are sourced by the Chosŏndaesŏng Trading Company through foreign currency transactions and subsequently made available to consumers at the Kwangbok District Commercial Center using DPRK currency.

To accommodate the exchange rate differences, the State absorbs the expenses, incorporating them into the current expenses of the general trading company. While a conceivable approach for the State to alleviate this burden could involve reducing the proportion of foreign-made products, it is crucial to recognize the Kwangbok District Commercial Center's role as a flagship shopping destination in the DPRK.

Selling DPRK products, which may be perceived as inferior in quality compared to foreign counterparts, alongside them would not have been practical. Consequently, the current 7:3 ratio of DPRK to foreign products reflects the heightened burden on the State. Simultaneously, it signifies an enhancement in the quality of DPRK products since the Center's inception in December 2011. Hence, it can be affirmed that Kim Jong Un's policy of bolstering localization is exerting a discernible and undeniable impact on the practical realities on the ground.

Interestingly, the DPRK's policy of promoting the localization of consumer goods gains momentum under the SERMS, particularly in the face of escalating U.S. economic sanctions. In an interview with *Chosun Sinbo*, Ch'ŏl Kim, the director of the Institute of Economics at the Chosun Academy of Social Sciences, acknowledged the challenges faced by DPRK enterprises due to the phenomenon known as Suippyŏng or the "disease of blind importing."

> The rationale behind enterprises opting for imported goods has its roots in a different context. Specifically, during the Arduous March, notably the period of "Forced March" in the 1990s, domestic production faced challenges in normalization, compelling enterprises to resort to importing essential raw materials and supplies from other countries. Even beyond that challenging period, companies continued to boost their foreign currency earnings, given the flexibility it provided in purchasing foreign products. This pursuit of convenient access to raw materials led to an increased dependence on imported goods, essentially creating an addiction to imports, "Suippyŏng." The ongoing trend of localization signifies a corrective measure aimed at normalizing this aberration …

> Within the framework of the SERMS, enterprises, beyond fulfilling the People's Economic Plan, are mandated to engage in contractual agreements by placing orders and executing them with other enterprises. This collaborative process not only promotes domestic production but also generates income. In essence, as hostile countries impose sanctions, the interactions between enterprises involved in the production of new domestic products intensify, leading to an increase in the society's net income.[124]

Ch'ŏlso Kim's interview paints a compelling picture of a DPRK actively weaning itself off its long-standing dependence on foreign imports. The reliance, he argues, stems not from a lack of capacity but, rather, from a deeply ingrained habit cultivated during times of economic hardship. Now, with self-reliance capabilities steadily growing, the question arises: how can DPRK enterprises break this habit and reap the benefits of domestic production?

The key lies in the SERMS. This economic system grants enterprises significant autonomy in their operations, including the freedom to buy, sell, and trade with each other—once they fulfill their critical production quotas, of course. This creates a dynamic where, in the face of external trade disruptions like sanctions, enterprises have a natural incentive to turn inward. They can produce domestic substitutes for previously imported goods and then trade these among themselves, bolstering their own incomes while reducing reliance on foreign markets.

Kim's assertions are not mere wishful thinking. They are grounded in the reality of DPRK's demonstrably increased self-reliance compared to the past. The strengthened market facilitated by the full implementation of SERMS, as explored in Chapter 2 and this chapter, further supports this notion.

The DPRK's commitment to localization is not new. The country has been actively promoting the production of domestic light industrial goods since the era of Kim Jong Il. With the SERMS in place for nearly a decade and the COVID-19 border closures effectively cutting off most imports, the conditions for a comprehensive localization push seem ripe. The potential impact of such a shift is significant. The General Market,[125] heavily reliant on imported, primarily Chinese goods, could experience significant contraction. This, however, is not necessarily a negative development. A strong, self-sufficient domestic market can provide a more stable and resilient foundation for the DPRK's economy, less susceptible to external disruptions.

Of course, challenges remain. Successfully transitioning from import-reliance to domestic production requires overcoming logistical and technical hurdles. Infrastructure upgrades, skilled workforce training, and efficient distribution networks are crucial for long-term success. Despite the challenges, the potential rewards of a thriving domestic market are undeniable. Increased self-reliance, greater enterprise autonomy, and a more resilient economy are all within reach. Ch'ŏlso Kim's interview serves as a timely reminder that the DPRK's economic future may not lie in chasing foreign imports but in nurturing the seeds of domestic production and reaping the rewards of self-sufficiency.

Appendix to Chapter 3: The Nature of Inflation in the DPRK and Estimation of Gross Domestic Growth of the DPRK after the Normalization of Production

The DPRK implemented a currency reform, known as the redenomination method, in November 2009, where the old currency was converted to the new currency at a ratio of 100:1. This practice of currency reform to combat inflation is shared among countries facing inflationary pressures. Many so-called experts on the North Korean economy have claimed that runaway inflation did indeed occur in the DPRK economy.[126] If we assume this to be true, it is necessary to adjust our estimation of the DPRK's national budget in Tables 3.4 and 3.5 to account for inflation. Specifically, we should discount the inflation from the annual growth rate of the 2000–2009 period. Consequently, the adjusted annual growth rate from 2000 to 2009 should be significantly lower than 6.8 %.[127]

The annual growth rate of national budget revenues from 2000 to 2009 was 6.8%, while from 2009 to 2017 it was 6.3%.[128] Although the exact level of inflation before the currency reform is unknown, any currency reform aims to control hyperinflation. Hyperinflation is typically defined as rapidly rising inflation, usually measured at more than 50% per month.[129]

To align the growth rate with the alleged inflationary reality, one would need to discount at least 1200% from 6.4%. This would push the growth rate deep into negative territory, which is unlikely to have occurred in the DPRK, considering the country's observed recovery and robust growth since 2001, as analyzed in this chapter. Unless the reports and articles listed in the *CCY*, *CWK*, and *SWK* are fabricated or fictitious, it is challenging to reconcile these implications with the argument against their validity.

As inflation should have been under control since the currency reform, the growth rate of 6.3% should be in real terms rather than nominal terms. Interpreting this growth rate in the context of alleged inflationary pressures suggests that budget revenues abruptly surged from a deeply negative level to a high level immediately after the currency reform. This scenario is highly improbable. Therefore, the argument lacks internal consistency and deviates from the principles of economics. How then can we make sense of the findings that the annual growth rate before and after the currency reform is similar?

The 2009 currency reform in the DPRK primarily targeted inflation within consumer-driven transactions, where cash reigns supreme.[130] While aiming to curb price surges in Business-to-Consumer (B2C) and Consumer-to-Consumer (C2C) spheres, it did not directly address cashless Business-to-Business (B2B) transactions, with payments made virtually through bank accounts without physical money.[131]

Crucially, this reform had limited impact on national budget revenue calculated in constant, inflation-adjusted terms (real terms). This stems from the unique "Pŏnsuipch'egye" (Earned Income System), where enterprises contribute a fixed portion of profits to the State, effectively decoupling national income from market fluctuations. However, the emergence of the SERMS in 2014 presents a new wrinkle. By granting enterprises limited market autonomy after fulfilling state quotas, SERMS introduces cash-based transactions outside the planned economy, creating potential inflationary pressures.

This raises a valid point: the purported 6.3% CAGR reported for national budget revenue from 2009 to 2017 may necessitate refinement to accommodate nominal terms and address the plausible inflation stemming from SERMS-related activities. Assuming the premise of SERMS-induced inflation holds true, we might anticipate an annual growth rate exceeding 6.3% for national budget revenue between 2014 and 2017. However, data reveals a mere 5.4% growth during this interval,[132] failing to meet projected expectations.

This discordance suggests two possibilities: either post-quota B2B transactions remain a relatively miniscule portion of the overall activity, or these transactions primarily utilize virtual accounts, shielding them from inflationary pressures. Considering established knowledge that B2B transactions account for over half of all enterprise activities, the first explanation seems improbable. This deduction leads us to infer that the growth rates listed in Table 3.4 reflect real terms, already accounting for internal price fluctuations.

Having meticulously calculated the DPRK's national budget revenue, expenditure, and its allocation to the People's Economy, we stand equipped to analyze crucial aspects of its economic construction. However, these valuable insights fall short of painting a complete picture, akin to discerning the contours of an object shrouded in shadow. Unveiling the full shape and dynamics of the DPRK's economy necessitates delving deeper, seeking the crucial missing piece: Gross Domestic Product (GDP).

To derive an estimate of the DPRK's GDP through our analysis, we must meticulously scrutinize the accessible data concerning consumption, investment, government expenditure, net exports, and the contribution of individual labor. Integrating these variables while considering the unique context and dynamics of the DPRK's economy enables us to formulate a GDP approximation. Nevertheless, due to the scarcity of comprehensive and transparent economic data from the country, attempting to estimate the DPRK's GDP with the available quantitative or qualitative data appears to be an exceedingly challenging endeavor.

Is there a viable method to compute the DPRK's GDP in the absence of requisite data? It is essential to acknowledge that the DPRK, akin to numerous other (former) socialist nations, does not rely on GDP as a gauge of its economic well-being; instead, it employs Net Material Product (NMP). This prompts the inquiry: can NMP adequately substitute for GDP?

GDP encompasses the aggregate of Consumption (C), Investment (I), Government Expenditure (G), and Net Exports (X-M). On the other hand, NMP comprises two components: V, which represents the value created by working individuals for themselves and M, which represents the value created by working individuals for society. While NMP and GDP differ in their composition, it is important to recognize that both metrics aim to provide a measure of economic activity. GDP captures the overall production and expenditure within an economy, while NMP emphasizes the value generated by individual labor for both personal and societal benefit.[133]

$$C + I + G + (X - M) = GDP, \sum (V + M) = NMP$$

The distinction between NMP and GDP lies in the fact that while GDP represents the sum of all values generated by domestically produced materials, goods, and services within a year, NMP excludes the value created in the service sector.

Given the relatively modest contribution of the service sector to the economy in socialist countries and considering the DPRK's status as a developing nation with a less mature service sector, we can employ the DPRK's NMP as a proxy for its GDP. However, a challenge emerges as the DPRK does not disclose the precise figure for NMP. Nonetheless, as elucidated in this chapter, all enterprise earned income, known as "Pŏnsuip," aligns with NMP.[134]

Moreover, as previously established, the DPRK's NMP can be regarded as tantamount to its GDP. Given that Pŏnsuip, representing the aggregate earned income of all DPRK enterprises, serves as a proxy for NMP, discerning its growth rate enables estimation of the DPRK's GDP growth rate. Regrettably, the opacity surrounding Pŏnsuip, the cumulative earned income of all DPRK enterprises, persists. Nevertheless, by exploring its correlation with other pivotal economic metrics, insights into the DPRK's growth trajectory can be obtained.

In this chapter, we have already analyzed the growth rate alignment among Pŏnsuip (Earned Income), Kukkagiŏmniikkŭm (State Enterprise Profit Revenue → M in the NMP), and Rodongbosugŭm (Workers' Living Expenses → V in the NMP). Given that State Enterprise Profit Revenue constitutes a substantial segment of national budget revenue, the growth rate of national budget revenue is also closely aligned with that of State Enterprise Profit Revenue. Subsequently, this interconnectedness allows us to use the growth rate of national budget revenue as a proxy for the growth rate of Earned Income.[135]

Having established a profound correlation between the growth of the DPRK's national budget revenue and its broader economic expansion, as evidenced by our comprehensive budget analysis, it becomes imperative to delve into the actual scale of the DPRK's GDP. Such knowledge would not only corroborate our findings but also offer a more comprehensive understanding of their economic landscape. Nonetheless, the true extent of its GDP remains veiled in secrecy.

While the precise magnitude of the DPRK's GDP remains elusive, an exploration of its national budget revenue and expenditure can yield valuable insights into its economic dynamics. Like all nations, the DPRK's national budget constitutes a portion of its overall GDP. Although the exact ratio remains obscured by limited data, estimating the GDP through assumptions becomes feasible, albeit with an acknowledgment of the inherent limitations in such assumptions.

Given the DPRK's closed socialist framework with minimal international trade, it's conceivable that its budgetary practices may resemble those of China prior to its economic reforms.[136] However, it's important to recognize that significant time has passed since China's pre-opening period (1970–1979), during which economic structures and spending patterns can undergo substantial transformations. Additionally, while both nations operated within socialist paradigms, disparities in their specific political and economic frameworks may have resulted in divergent budgetary allocations and spending priorities.

Acknowledging the constraints posed by limited data on the DPRK's economy, one tentative approach to estimating its GDP involves applying China's pre-opening budget expenditure ratio (12.2%)[137] to the estimated DPRK budget expenditures for a specific period. Nonetheless, exercising extreme caution is imperative due to the marked differences in the economic structures and contexts of the two countries.

For instance, in 2000, with an estimated budget expenditure of 20.95503 billion wŏn, this approach yields an estimated GDP of 171.7625 billion wŏn (20.95503 billion wŏn/0.122). While further estimations based on this method are presented in Table 3.6, it's crucial to underscore the highly speculative nature of these results. The significant disparities between the DPRK and China's economies, encompassing varying levels of government control, economic openness, and industrial structures, render this a highly simplified and potentially misleading approach.

Referring to Table 3.6, our initial calculation provided an overall growth rate of 6.4%, derived from ((492.2910 billion wŏn ÷ 171.7625 billion wŏn) ^ (1÷17) − 1). However, this singular figure oversimplifies the intricate dynamics across this extended period. Recognizing a pivotal economic shift around 2011, marked by the recovery from the Arduous March and the integration of CNC technology, a more insightful analysis divides this timeframe into three distinct segments.

The first phase spans the period from 2000 to 2008, characterized as the "pre-CNC breakthrough period." During this initial phase, the economy exhibited steady growth at a rate of 6.4%, as calculated by ((282.2582 billion wŏn ÷ 171.7625 billion wŏn) ^ (1÷8)) − 1. These early years laid the foundation for subsequent advancements, showcasing resilience and gradual progress.

The second phase, covering 2009 to 2013, is termed the "recover and innovation period." Following the Arduous March, the DPRK implemented effective recovery measures and witnessed the groundbreaking adoption of CNC technology. This phase witnessed accelerated growth of 6.8%, calculated as ((393.5836 billion wŏn ÷ 302.4795 billion wŏn) ^ (1÷4)) − 1, reflecting the positive impact of these strategic moves.

The final five-year period (2014–2017) introduced the Socialist Enterprise Management System alongside ongoing consolidation efforts. Although growth remained positive at 5.4%, calculated as ((492.2910 billion wŏn ÷ 420.4598 billion wŏn) ^ (1÷3)) − 1, it exhibited stabilization compared to the previous phase.

While these estimations offer a potential starting point, acknowledging their inherent limitations is crucial. Assumptions underlying the methodology might not fully capture the nuances of the DPRK's economy, potentially leading to discrepancies with its actual GDP. However, a fascinating angle emerges when comparing these estimations to economic indicators presented in the "DPRK Voluntary National Report on the Implementation of the 2030 Agenda." This comparative analysis can provide valuable insights into the internal consistency of our estimations and potential areas of convergence or divergence with official reports.

In this Voluntary National Report, the DPRK disclosed, for the first time, its GDP and growth rate as follows: "The GDP per capita in 2015 was US$27,412 million and US$33,504 million in 2019. Annual average growth rate of GDP in 2015–2019 is 5.1%, and annual average growth rate of GDP per capita is 4.6%" (p. 29). It's worth noting that the reported GDP per capita figures of US$27,412 million and US$33,504 million in 2015 and 2019,

Table 3.6 Estimated GDP of the DPRK (2000–2017)

Year	2000	2001	2002	2003	2004	2005	2006	2007	2008
GDP	171.7625	177.6889	185.0023	194.5443	206.7049	252.5762	252.5762	272.5393	282.2582
Year	2009	2010	2011	2012	2013	2014	2015	2016	2017
GDP	302.4795	327.2828	347.8836	372.7115	393.5836	420.4598	441.4829	469.2959	492.2910

Source: author.

Unit: 1 billion wŏn.

respectively, appear to be mistaken, as such figures are unprecedented globally. There is a possibility that the GDP figures were intended instead of GDP per capita.

As the DPRK does not disclose its official exchange rate, converting these figures (US$27,412 million and US$33,504 million) to DPRK wŏn presents a challenge. The ROK Unification Ministry annually releases estimated exchange rates of the DPRK, calculated through a method undisclosed to the public. According to the Ministry, the estimated official exchange rate (DPRK wŏn to US$) in 2015 was 108.8:1, and in 2019, it was also 108.1:1.

Converting our estimated 2015 DPRK GDP of 441.4829 billion wŏn to US dollars using the Ministry's estimated official exchange rate would yield a figure of US$4.0577 billion. This is significantly lower, constituting only 15% of the DPRK's reported figure of US$27.412 billion. The discrepancy raises questions about the accuracy of our estimation, particularly in comparison to the DPRK's Voluntary National Report. It prompts a reassessment of our assumptions and approximations, questioning whether they are grounded in reality or based on speculative grounds.

Yet, it's essential to recognize that the figures presented by the Ministry of Unification are also estimations rooted in its assumptions and data gathered by ad hoc groups, some of which may maintain a critical stance toward the DPRK regime. However, the estimated figures in the Ministry's report reveal an intriguing trend. Until the year 2001, a pivotal year preceding the implementation of the so-called "7·1 Measure"—considered by most experts on the North Korean economy as the turning point from a rigid form of socialism to a capitalist variant akin to China—the official exchange rate consistently hovered around 2.2 (2.20 in 1998, 2.17 in 1999, 2.19 in 2000, and 2.21 in 2001).

However, following this measure, the Ministry assumed that the DPRK printed a significantly larger amount of currency in line with market-augmented measures. Contrary to this assumption, our analysis in this appendix section indicates that inflation was confined to the C2C, non-official sector in the DPRK. Based on this observation, it's possible that the DPRK maintains an official exchange rate much lower than the Ministry's estimations.

While the actual rate remains unknown, if our inflation analysis reflects on-the-ground realities, the official rate might be significantly lower than the Ministry suggests. Further research and data collection are crucial to develop a more definitive understanding of the DPRK's exchange rate and the complexities of its economy.[138]

Nevertheless, a noteworthy piece of information from the DPRK Voluntary National Report suggests that our efforts in estimating the DPRK's GDP and its growth are not without merit. The report indicates a GDP growth rate of 5.1% during 2015–2019, a figure similar to our estimation of 5.4% during a comparable period of 2014–2017. This alignment signifies a clear narrative: the DPRK is progressing with a self-reliant approach, sustaining an annual growth rate of over 5% after the implementation of the SERMS.

Notes

1 Upon reflection, the decision of the DPRK to navigate the crisis by fortifying its autonomous capabilities carries a layer of irony. This strategic choice, while motivated by a commitment to self-reliance, was not solely a matter of preference but was, in fact, propelled by the inability to depend on the Soviet Union—the DPRK's primary benefactor during the Cold War era. Furthermore, despite being a neighboring communist nation, China found itself neither inclined nor adequately positioned to offer substantial assistance to the DPRK during this challenging period.

   However, the crux of the matter in opting for a self-reliant approach to tackle the crisis lies in the harsh reality that no nation was willing to extend support or aid to the DPRK. This reluctance was primarily a consequence of the stringent measures imposed by the United States in the form of sanctions. The geopolitical dynamics and global political landscape constrained the DPRK's options, making self-reliance not just a strategic choice but, in essence, a practical necessity amid the complex web of international relations and geopolitical pressures.

2 Kim Jong Il, "Hyŏnshigi tangsaŏpkwa kyŏngjesaŏbesŏ chungyohage chegidoenŭn myŏtkaji munjee taehayŏ: Chosŏllodongdang chungangwiwŏnhoe, naegakch'aegimilgundŭrap'esŏ han yŏnsŏl (chuch'e 94(2005)nyŏn 1wŏl9il)" (On Some Important Issues in Party Work and Economic Work at the Present Time: Speech Before the Central Committee of the WPK and the Responsible Officials of the Cabinet, (January 9, 2005), *SWK 21*, p. 211.

3 Ch'unsik Kang of Kim Il Sung University writes that, under Kim Jong Il, 'miracle' achievements in steel, fiber, and fertilizer production lifted the entire DPRK. He argues that the metal and chemical industries should continue to be twin pillars of revitalization in the Kim Jong Un era, stating:

   Consolidating past achievements and raising them further holds immense significance for recognizing the Great Marshals' economic contributions and accelerating our party's goal of an economic powerhouse. To revitalize the entire economy and improve lives, we must raise the slogan of self-reliance and modernization in these industries. We must vigorously strive to build production based on our own resources, fuels, and the latest science and technology.

   (Ch'unsik Kang, "Kŭmsokkongŏpkwa hwahakkongŏbŭl ssanggidungŭro hayŏ inmin'gyŏngjejŏnbanŭl hwalsŏnghwahago inminsaenghwarŭl hyangsangshik'inŭndesŏ nasŏnŭn chungyomunje" (The Important Problem of Revitalizing the Entire People's Economy and Improving People's Lives with the Metal and Chemical Industries as the Twins), *KUAB* (2014), vol. 60, no. 4, p. 47)

4 My research suggests that the 534th Unit is a specialized logistics unit tasked with supplying essential foodstuffs and amenities to the Armed Forces. As discussed in the previous chapter, while all Armed Forces units are theoretically responsible for their own food and supplies, this self-sufficiency is not always achievable in practice. The 534th Unit appears to bridge this gap by supplying staple foods and other essential provisions to most Armed Forces units.

5 During the span from 1998 to 2011, the *CCY* documented a total of 60 field visits by Kim Jong Il to power plant construction or operation sites. This extensive engagement reflects a commitment to closely overseeing and directing the developments in the power sector throughout the DPRK. The data suggests that Kim Jong Il, with an average of 4.3 visits per year, was deeply involved in monitoring the progress and addressing challenges in various power projects across the country.

Zooming in on individual enterprises, it becomes evident that certain entities captured Kim Jong Il's attention more frequently. The 2.8 Vinylon United Enterprise and the Ryongsŏng Machinery United Enterprise, in particular, emerged as focal points of Kim Jong Il's interest, each garnering 13 visits during the specified period (refer to Table 2.2). These consistent and repetitive visits underscore the strategic importance and, possibly, the unique challenges associated with these enterprises, offering insights into Kim Jong Il's hands-on approach to economic management and development.

6 *CCY 2000*, p. 211.

7 On February 8, 2009, during an on-site inspection of the Ragwŏn Machinery United Enterprise, Kim Jong Il expressed considerable satisfaction with the proactive preparations underway to swiftly complete the production of large oxygen separators required for the new gasification ammonia process at the Hŭngnam Fertilizer United Enterprise.

He emphasized that "the Ragwŏn Machinery United Enterprise should channel all its efforts into the production of these essential oxygen separators." Additionally, Kim Jong Il stressed "the need to manufacture high-quality mechanical products, including excavators, and distribute them across various sectors of the People's Economy, encompassing capital construction sites and the Hŭich'ŏn Power Plant construction site" (*CCY 2010*, pp. 38-39).

8 Kim Jong Il's on-site guidance visits, documented in *SWK* and *CCY*, reveal the intricate connections between key industrial facilities in North P'yŏngan Province. These visits highlight the strategic interplay between power generation and machine tool production.

On February 14, 2001, Kim Jong Il inspected the Kusŏng Machine Tool Factory and the T'aech'ŏn Power Plant. He praised the factory's production of modern machine tools, including CNC lathes and turning centers, acknowledging their crucial role in national modernization. His subsequent visit to the T'aech'ŏn Power Plant emphasized the importance of reliable energy generation for industrial development (*CCY 2001*, p. 29).

From December 14 to 16, 2001, Kim Jong Il visited the Sup'ung Power Plant's 2Palchŏnjikchang and the Kusŏng Machine Tool Factory. He commended the progress made in both facilities, particularly the factory's development of an automated CNC lathe. He emphasized the factory's success in achieving self-reliance by independently designing and constructing the machine, saving foreign currency and showcasing their ingenuity (Kim Jong Il, "P'yŏnganbuktoŭi kongŏppalchŏnesŏ saeroun chŏnhwanŭl irŭk'ilte taehayŏ: P'yŏnganbukto kongŏppumun saŏbŭl hyŏnjijidohamyŏnsŏ ilgundŭlgwa han tamhwa (chuch'100(2001)nyŏn 12wŏl15-16il)" (On Creating a New Turn in the Industrial Development in North P'yŏngan Province: A Discourse with Responsible Officials While Providing Local Guidance to the Industrial Sector in North P'yŏngan Province, 2001 December 15-16)), *SWK 20*, pp. 335-337).

On October 24, 2003, Kim Jong Il inspected the Ragwŏn Machinery United Enterprise. He expressed satisfaction with their latest hydraulic excavator and crane, attributing their success to meticulous research and dedication. He highlighted the significant contribution of these modern machines to production advancements and praised the enterprise's embrace of new technology (*CCY 2004*, pp. 56-57).

These visits illustrate the sequential and interdependent nature of industrial development in North P'yŏngan Province. Stable power generation from T'aech'ŏn and Sup'ung plants enabled the revitalization and modernization of the Kusŏng Machine Tool Factory. The resulting CNC machine tools provided critical equipment for the Ragwŏn Machinery United Enterprise, facilitating their own modernization efforts.

9 In a meeting held on January 1, 2010, with key members of the Party's Central Committee to usher in the New Year, Kim Jong Il expressed his sentiments, stating,

As we welcome 2010 following the remarkable year of 2009, which stands proudly as a transformative period in the history of the Republic's development. Throughout 2009, a year of profound change, we witnessed numerous historic events, including the successful launch of the Kwangmyŏngsŏng-2 artificial earth satellite, a testament to our power and technological prowess, the successful execution of the second nuclear test, and the culmination of the Chuch'e Steel production system.

Among these milestones, I take particular pride in the world-class CNC technology of the Republic, which has firmly established the prestige of our unique achievement in CNC technology among the many accomplishments of the past year.

(Kim Jong Il, "Uri shing ch'yulch'ŭimmolkongikaech'ŏk'an sŏnggwawa kyŏnghŏme t'odaehayŏ modŭn punyaesŏ ch'ŏmdanŭl tolp'ahaja: Chosŏllodongdong chungangwiwŏnhoe ch'aegimilgundŭlgwa han tamhwa (chuch'e 109(2010)nyŏn 1wŏl1il)" (Let Us Break Through to the Cutting Edge in All Fields Based on the Achievements and Experience of Pioneering Our Own CNC technology: Speech to the Responsible Officials of the Central Committee of the WPK, (January 1, 2010)), *SWK 24*, pp. 447–448)

10 The *CCY* frequently records Kim Jong Il's visits to symbolically significant locations, often resulting in an incomplete portrayal of the true extent of modernized factories and enterprises in the DPRK. Ironically, this assertion is supported by the economic section of the 2006 *CCY* report. While acknowledging achievements in socialist economic construction and agricultural successes, the report highlights the completion of more than 130 projects and over 1,600 factories and enterprises surpassing their annual plans ahead of schedule on the occasion of the Party's 60th anniversary (*CCY 2006*, p. 29).

These statistics alone surpass the limited scope of Kim Jong Il's documented visits, indicating extensive modernization efforts beyond his direct oversight. Thus, while the Ragwŏn Machinery and Glass Factory and the Taejungch'insŏn Glass Factory are examples identified through *CCY* records, they likely represent only a fraction of the broader modernization initiatives underway across the DPRK.

11 Kim Jong Un accompanied Kim Jong Il during his local guidance activities, starting on October 5, 2010, with their joint observation of the 851st Armed Forces Unit's coordination exercise. This collaborative engagement continued until December 15, 2011, when both leaders attended the opening ceremony of the Kwangbok District Commercial Center. Throughout this period, Kim Jong Un was an integral part of Kim Jong Il's presence, actively participating in and contributing to various events and initiatives, showcasing a seamless transition and continuity in their leadership roles.

12 Not all of the DPRK national budget revenues from 1993 to 2016 are meticulously documented in the *CCY* or reported in *Rodong Sinmun*. Specifically, the national budget revenues for 1993, 1998, 1999, 2000, and 2001 are itemized in the *CCY*. However, from 2001 onward, they are presented in a format akin to "The national budget revenue plan was fulfilled at 100.5 percent," without providing the specific target of the plan. This lack of detailed information poses a challenge in accurately determining the exact amount of the national budget revenue.

Due to limited availability of definitive data, assessing the DPRK's national budget revenue relies heavily on qualitative insights from *CCY* and *SWK* sources. Table 3.4 summarizes these findings through a meticulous examination and synthesis. It is important to note that the table's accuracy may benefit from further validation. For a more comprehensive understanding, a review of estimated national budget revenue figures from 2002 to 2017 is recommended.

We are confident that our national budget revenue estimates are within a reasonable range. They align well with the arguments presented throughout this book, particularly regarding the DPRK's recovery from the arduous period known as the Arduous March since 2011.

13 This issue of inflation will be discussed in detail in the appendix section of this chapter.

14 The year 1993 stands as a pivotal year in the DPRK history, a juncture where the shadow of the coming Arduous March loomed large and yet, the guiding hand of Kim Il Sung remained firmly on the tiller. It was the last complete year before the economic crisis that would grip the nation, and a final chapter in the long book of Kim Il Sung's leadership, which would end with his passing in July 1994.

This final year under Kim Il Sung's direct rule was marked by a stark contrast in its economic performance. While the winds of hardship were already gathering on the horizon, the official statistics painted a picture of remarkable resilience. The 1994 *CCY* report (p. 90) proudly declares: "The total national budget revenue amounted to 40.5712 billion wŏn, exceeding the plan by a 100.3% and experiencing a 102.6% increase compared to the previous year.".

These figures, while impressive at face value, must be viewed through the lens of impending adversity. The Arduous March, a period of widespread food shortages and economic hardship, was just around the corner. While the national budget exceeded expectations, questions remain about how this success translated into the lives of ordinary citizens. Did it truly reflect a thriving economy, or was it a final burst of effort before the storm?

The year 1993 thus serves as a fascinating and complex year in the DPRK's history. It was a year of contrasts, with glimmers of economic achievement juxtaposed against the looming shadow of hardship. It was the final year of a long era, marked by the passing of a monumental figure and the uncertain dawn of a new chapter.

15 Regrettably, the *CCY* reports for 1995, 1996, and 1997 lack details on total national budget revenues and expenditures for the respective preceding years. This absence strongly implies that the predetermined targets for total national budget revenues, established at the conclusion of each respective year from 1995 to 1997, were not fully realized.

Notably, the 1999 *CCY* discloses the national budget revenue for 1998, which is less than half of the figure reported for 1994. This revelation suggests that even the officials responsible for national statistics were likely taken aback by the stark and drastic decline in budget revenue since 1994, to the extent that they might have hesitated to report it, perhaps out of a sense of embarrassment.

If we entertain the presumption that this conjecture aligns closely with reality and consider national budget revenue as a reflection of national income, given that all DPRK enterprises were State-owned, an extraordinary scenario emerges. It implies that the DPRK underwent an unparalleled experience, where national income plummeted by more than half within a single year and persisted for three consecutive years. This unprecedented downturn raises questions about the underlying factors and challenges faced by the DPRK during this period, presenting a unique case in economic history.

16 The available records lack explicit details on the 1997 budget revenue. However, insights into the 1998 budget revenue and expenditures can be gleaned from the 1999 *CCY*, which notes, "The total amount of national budget revenues and expenditures in 1998 was 19.79080 billion wŏn, marking a notable increase of

100.4 percent compared to 1997, although still below the levels of the early 1990s" (*CCY 1999*, p. 188). Applying this growth rate of 100.4% to the 1998 budget revenue enables us to estimate the 1997 budget revenue at 19.7116 billion wŏn (calculated as 19.7908 billion wŏn multiplied by 0.996).

This estimation provides a retrospective glimpse into the financial landscape of 1997, hinting at a challenging economic scenario that witnessed a subsequent recovery in 1998. Despite the increase, the 1998 budget revenue remained below the levels of the early 1990s, underscoring the complexity of the economic circumstances during that period.

17 The 1995, 1996, and 1997 *CCY* maintained a conspicuous silence on national budget figures, only to break this information drought in the 1999 *CCY*, where the national budget revenues for 1998 were finally revealed: "The total amount of national budget revenues and expenditures in 1998 was 19.7908 billion wŏn ..." (*CCY 1999*, p. 188). As highlighted earlier, this figure represents a stark reality, standing at merely 48.6% or less than half of the national budget recorded in 1993.

The unveiling of these numbers in 1999 serves as a retrospective revelation, emphasizing the substantial decline in national budget revenues during the late 1990s. This revelation, while shedding light on the economic challenges faced by the DPRK during that period, also underscores the magnitude of the subsequent recovery efforts required to address this notable setback in financial stability.

18 The year 1999, etched within the pages of the 2000 *CCY*, paints a portrait of the DPRK's economy still clinging to the nadir of a protracted downturn. While whispers of recovery may have begun to stir, the national budget figures speak volumes about a nation navigating the aftermath of a profound economic shock.

The statistics themselves hold a bittersweet story. National budget revenues, amounting to 19.8103 billion wŏn, fell short of the planned target by a hair's breadth, achieving a respectable 97.2% (*CCY 2000*, p. 189). This near-miss, while a technical shortfall, carries the weight of missed opportunities and unfulfilled aspirations. Yet, compared to the depths of 1998, it represents a flicker of progress, a fragile step toward rekindling the fires of economic growth.

On the flip side, national budget expenditures, clocking in at 20.1821 billion won, also fell short of their intended mark, though by a narrower margin (98.2%). This discrepancy hints at a cautious approach, a prioritization of essential needs over ambitious projects in the face of continued uncertainty.

The year 1999, then, stands at a crossroads. The scars of 1994's economic trauma are still palpable, yet the faint light of a potential turnaround shimmers on the horizon. The budget, with its imperfect figures and cautious spending, becomes a testament to a nation navigating the treacherous terrain of recovery, balancing hope with pragmatism in the face of an uncertain future.

19 The 2001 *CCY* report holds within its pages a story of the DPRK's economy still navigating the intricate terrain of recovery, six years after the Arduous March's brutal grip. While whispers of progress may have begun to stir, the budget figures dance a nuanced ballet, revealing both strides forward and echoes of past hardship.

On the surface, the narrative is one of cautious optimism. National budget expenditures, exceeding initial projections by a remarkable 102.7%, reached a total of 20.95503 billion wŏn, surpassing the planned 20.4532 billion wŏn (*CCY 2001*, p. 174). This overachievement suggests a newfound momentum, a deliberate push toward rebuilding essential infrastructure and services after years of crippling economic contraction.

But beneath the celebratory surface, a different story emerges. The absence of the crucial figure—national budget revenue—casts a long shadow. In the delicate economic ecosystem, expenditures rarely exist in isolation. To bridge this gap, we turn to the historical whispers of past budgets, where revenue and expenditure typically move in tandem. Applying this logic, we arrive at an estimated 20.4532 billion wŏn for 2001's national budget revenue—a figure that carries a significant weight.

While this estimated revenue represents a potential improvement compared to previous years, it still falls short of the 1993 figure, the year before the crisis. This stark reality paints a picture of an arduous climb out of the economic abyss, a journey still far from completion. Six years after the storm, the DPRK's economy remained halfway home, burdened by the scars of a monumental struggle.

20 The 2002 *CCY* report, unlike its cryptic predecessor, throws back the curtain on the DPRK's 2001 budget, offering a glimpse into the nation's continued journey toward economic recovery. The words themselves resonate with cautious optimism: "The national budget for 2001 has been successfully implemented," the report declares, highlighting a budget revenue figure of 21.6399 billion wŏn, exceeding the planned target of 21.570 billion by a commendable 100.3% (*CCY 2002*, p. 164).

Yet, beneath the triumphant fanfare, a more nuanced narrative emerges. While surpassing projections represents a significant achievement, the actual figure remains starkly lower than pre-crisis levels. Compared to the pre-Arduous March peak of 40.5712 billion wŏn in 1993, this 2001 revenue stands at a mere 53.3%. This figure paints a poignant picture of a nation still clambering up from the economic abyss, a journey that, while showing progress, remains far from complete.

The year 2001, as illuminated by the 2002 *CCY* report, becomes a symbol of this complex reality. It showcases resilience, a nation diligently rebuilding its economic pillars and exceeding internal targets. Yet, it also whispers of the long shadow cast by the crisis, a stark reminder of the immense distance still to be traversed.

21 While the 2003 *CCY* lacks a precise figure for DPRK's 2002 national income, it paints a picture of significant economic progress. It highlights "vigorous pursuit of technological improvement and modernization projects," fueling a "revolutionary upsurge in all areas." This translated into a remarkable 112% increase in gross industrial product compared to 2001.

Despite the missing national income data, other positive indicators suggest gradual production normalization. The *CCY* reports successful implementation of the 2002 national budget, exceeding the revenue target by 0.5%. While the specific 2001–2002 revenue increase remains unclear, the 2001 budget saw a 5.8% growth, reaching 21.6399 billion wŏn. Given the average growth rate of 2.4% for the previous three years, applying the 2001 rate to 2002 wouldn't be accurate. A weighted average approach offers a more realistic estimate. Assigning equal weights to the previous three years' average (2.4%) and the 2001 growth (5.8%), we project a 4% growth rate for 2002.

Moreover, the reported 0.5% surpassing of the 2002 revenue target provides a basis for estimating the actual revenue. By incorporating the anticipated 4% growth and the 1.005% overachievement, we derive an estimated 22.6180 billion wŏn for the 2002 national budget revenue (calculated as the quantity of 21.6399 billion wŏn multiplied by 1.04 and then by 1.005).

22 While the 2004 *CCY* remains tantalizingly silent on the precise total national budget revenues for 2003, it offers tantalizing clues within its pages. It proudly proclaims, "In 2003, the national budget was successfully fulfilled, achieving an income of 100.9%" (*CCY 2004*, p. 187). This seemingly innocuous statement hints at a robust performance, exceeding the planned revenue targets.

Furthermore, the *CCY* paints a vibrant picture of economic successes across the board. The gross industrial product, the engine of the economy, surged by a remarkable 110%, leaving its previous growth in the dust. Key industrial sectors like electric power (121%), kite and zinc (a staggering 176%), iron ore (146%), and cement (127%) all witnessed significant leaps, showcasing the triumph of economic construction efforts (p. 186).

However, while these achievements are undeniable, one must consider the context. The report focuses on sectors of national strategic significance, suggesting that perhaps other areas might not have experienced the same meteoric rise. This, coupled with the planned growth rate of 4% mentioned for previous years, leads us to a conservative estimate for 2003's total national budget revenue.

Assuming a continuation of the previous year's planned growth rate and considering the reported 100.9% fulfillment, we estimate a total national budget revenue of 23.7344 billion wŏn (calculated as (22.6180 billion won multiplied by 1.04) multiplied by 1.009). This figure, derived from conservative assumptions and official data, offers a valuable approximation of the DPRK's economic performance in 2003 based on the available information.

23 While the 2005 *CCY* remains coy on the precise figures for 2004's national budget, it whispers potent clues hidden within its pages. The report explodes with tales of economic triumph, most notably a 1.5-fold surge in electric power production compared to 2002—a feat that resonates profoundly considering the energy struggles of the Arduous March. This 50% leap from 2002 wouldn't just illuminate homes; it would potentially electrify economic growth.

The *CCY* masterfully paints a vibrant picture of burgeoning strategic production. Iron ore surged by a staggering 188%, while magnesite ore and kite and zinc saw equally impressive increases of 186% and 114% respectively. Even machine tools, the lifeblood of industry, roared back to life with a 112% rise compared to the previous year. These aren't mere happenstances; they represent a meticulously orchestrated symphony, driven by a strategically planned 150% increase in production compared to 2003.

Fueling such grand ambitions requires no small sum. The national budget, the very lifeblood of these initiatives, undoubtedly saw a significant increase to accommodate this industrial crescendo. While the previous year's 5% rise lays the groundwork, a 7% target for 2004, a deliberate 2% step-up, seems a reasonable assumption to nourish these burgeoning sectors.

Calculating the estimated total national budget revenue for 2004 becomes a simple yet potent formula: 23.7344 billion wŏn (2003's estimate) multiplied by 1.07 (the projected 7% increase) yields 25.3958 billion wŏn. This figure whispers on the wind, corroborated by the *CCY*'s triumphant declaration of a "smoothly executed 2004 national budget.".

While precise details may remain shrouded in secrecy, the 2005 *CCY* offers a tantalizing glimpse into the booming economy of 2004. By deciphering the language of industrial triumphs and meticulously planned growth, we arrive at a plausible estimate of the national budget revenue—a figure that speaks volumes about the DPRK's economic trajectory in that pivotal year.

24 The 2006 *CCY* triumphantly announces 2005 as a banner year for socialist economic construction in the DPRK. Before diving into the cold digits, it paints a vibrant picture of progress: a symphony of booming production across all sectors. Electricity generation climbed a dizzying 111%, coal production echoed it with a 110% upswing, and across the land, factories hummed with newfound life. Over 130 key construction and modernization projects were proudly delivered, testament to the dedication of the People's Armed Forces in gifting their nation this industrial renaissance.

Yet, when the numbers finally emerge, they sing an even louder ballad. In 2005, national revenue soared by a staggering 116.1%, a meteoric rise far surpassing the initial plan of 15.3% growth in comparison to 2004. This translates to actual national budget revenues of 29.5156 billion wŏn (calculated as (25.3958 billion won multiplied by 1.153) multiplied by 1.008) —a figure far beyond even the revised, optimistic target.

Now, let's rewind to 2004. Here, electricity production had already witnessed a 50% surge compared to 2003, hinting at a revitalized industrial landscape and factories equipped for greater output. This laid the groundwork for the monumental gains of 2005.

So, what does this mean? The ambitious leap over the planned 15.3% growth suggests a DPRK laying the critical foundation for normalized production as early as 2004. It whispers of the economic improvement measure implemented on July 1, 2002, finally bearing fruit in 2005. This isn't just a year of exceptional performance; it's a turning point, a testament to the DPRK's determined march toward economic stability.

25 The 2007 *CCY* paints 2006 as a year of crucial transition in the DPRK's audacious quest for Kangsŏngdaeguk—a Strong and Great Nation. As the "fierce fire of the Chosun revolution" blazed onward (p. 184), national budget execution became a vital tool for forging this grand future. Revenues reached 97.5% of the planned target, marking a 4.4% rise from 2005's impressive showing (p. 184).

To truly grasp this 4.4% growth, we must delve into the interplay between planned and actual figures. While the actual revenue climbed to 30.8143 billion wŏn (multiplying 2005's figure by 1.044), the 97.5% execution rate hints at an initial, more ambitious plan of 30.98117 billion won (dividing 2005's figure by 0.975). This planned 7.1% growth, eclipsing 2005's actual 15.3%, reveals a shift in expectations, a recalibration for the long road ahead.

Unlike the detailed reports of 2006, the 2007 *CCY* offers no comprehensive list of factories targeted for reform and modernization. However, it spotlights a select few, industrial giants like the Ryongsŏng Machinery United Enterprise and the Hŭngnam Pharmaceutical Factory that thrived within the People's Economic Plan. It hints at prioritized reforms within fundamental industries, rather than a broad expansion or deeper remodeling across the entire economic landscape.

This strategic shift, coupled with a possible slowdown in overall reconstruction and modernization efforts, paints a picture of a measured 2006. While achieving 97.5% of the planned target is no small feat, it reflects a recalibration of expectations, a prudent step toward Kangsŏngdaeguk. It speaks of a nation not blinded by immediate growth, but focused on sustainable progress, building a strong foundation brick by strategic brick.

26 While 2007 followed the exceptional economic year of 2006, its national budget performance surprised in a positive way. The 2008 *CCY* report (p. 168) reveals that the budget not only grew but exceeded the initial projections by a remarkable margin. Although aiming for a respectable 5.8% increase over the already impressive figures of 2006, the actual growth soared to a significant 6.1%—surpassing the target by a full 0.3%. Therefore, actual national budget revenues in 2007 were 32.6940 billion wŏn (calculated as 30.8143 billion wŏn multiplied by 1.061).

27 The 2009 edition *CCY* provides valuable insights into the unexpected trajectory of the DPRK's national budget in 2008. Within its pages, specifically on page 192, a pivotal revelation unfolds: "Due to a substantial overachievement in planned revenue from state enterprises and cooperatives—the foundation of national income—the actual budget execution reached 101.6% of the targeted figure." This seemingly straightforward statement resonates with significance, akin to a subdued acknowledgment of a notable accomplishment, heralding a growth that far surpassed even the most optimistic forecasts.

Consider a budget plan initially set to achieve a respectable 4.1% increase over the already impressive figures of 2007. Now envision it defying conventional expectations, surging to an astonishing 105.7% growth, leaving the initial target trailing in the wake. This wasn't merely a modest surpassing of expectations; it was an audacious leap, underpinned by the unforeseen performance of the DPRK's economic core—its State-owned enterprises. These entities, rightly characterized as the 'fundamental pillars of national income' by the *CCY*, exceeded targets by a substantial margin, catapulting the national budget to a record 34.5575 billion wŏn (calculated by multiplying 2007's figure by 1.057).

28 The 2010 *CCY* unveils a surprising story of budgetary triumph in 2009. In stark contrast to the initial plan of a 5.3% increase over 2008, the national budget revenue soared by a remarkable 107%, surpassing expectations by a heady 1.7% (p. 266). This meteoric rise translated to a total of 36.9765 billion wŏn (calculated by multiplying 2008's figure by 1.07).

While the details behind this impressive performance remain somewhat opaque, the *CCY* offers tantalizing clues. Its focus on successful completion of major construction projects and increased production across various industries (p. 254) hints at potential sources of this budgetary windfall. Perhaps strategic investments in resource extraction or key manufacturing sectors yielded unexpected returns, fueling the national coffers. However, amid the celebrations, a note of caution is warranted. The lack of explicit details about the specific sectors driving this growth leaves room for speculation. Further information on the performance of different industries and potential external factors would be crucial for a more comprehensive understanding of this economic surge.

29 The 2011 *CCY* buries a fascinating nugget within its pages, offering a glimpse into the DPRK's budgetary performance in 2010. A seemingly innocuous sentence on page 290 whispers of a remarkable achievement: "In 2010, national budget revenues overflowed by 101.3% and grew by 107.7% compared to 2009." This cryptic statement, when decoded, reveals a story of exceeding expectations and defying initial projections.

Let's unpack the numbers. While the initial plan aimed for a modest 6.4% increase in national budget revenue over 2009, something remarkable happened. The actual revenue collection went rogue, exceeding expectations by a staggering 1.3%. This translated to a total of 39.8237 billion wŏn, a figure that would make any finance minister beam (calculated by multiplying 2009's figure by 1.077).

But how do we interpret this budgetary bonanza? The 'overflowing' metaphor used in the *CCY* suggests a sense of abundance, perhaps hinting at unforeseen economic tailwinds propelling the DPRK forward. However, the cautious phrasing regarding the actual growth (1.3% exceeding the plan) also hints at a degree of fiscal prudence.

Perhaps strategic investments in key sectors yielded unexpected returns, boosting national coffers. Or maybe a combination of factors, including increased industrial production or a surge in resource extraction, fueled the budgetary windfall. While the specific drivers remain shrouded in some secrecy, the outcome is undeniable: 2010 was a banner year for the DPRK's national budget.

30 The 2012 *CCY* throws open a window into the DPRK's national budget performance in 2011, albeit through a slightly opaque lens. Page 274 proudly announces that "the plan for national budget revenue in 2011 was executed at 101.1%," but it leaves the actual growth rate cloaked in a veil of silence. However, with a keen eye and a bit of deduction, we can peel back the layers and reveal the story hidden within the numbers.

While the specific percentage remains unstated, the report hints at a measured approach. '101.1%' translates to exceeding the planned target by a modest 1.1%. This suggests a cautious optimism, possibly reflecting adjustments to accommodate external economic uncertainties or prioritize specific developmental goals.

But to truly understand this performance, we need to consider the broader context. Over the past three years, the planned growth rate for national budget revenue has averaged 5.3% (calculated as (4.1%+5.1%+6.4%)/3). However, the actual growth has steadily climbed, exceeding initial projections: 5.7% in 2008, 7% in 2009, and a remarkable 7.7% in 2010.

Therefore, taking into account both the average planned growth and the recent upswing, it's reasonable to estimate the planned growth rate for 2011 at around 5.8% (calculated as the average of the planned growth rates, 5.3%, plus an additional 0.5%). Adding the 1.1% overachievement, we arrive at a final national budget revenue figure of 42.5969 billion wŏn (calculated by multiplying the 2010 figure by 1.058 and then by 1.011). This figure holds an even deeper significance—it surpasses the 1993 national budget revenue of 40.57120 billion wŏn.

Assuming the absence of significant inflation, surpassing the 1993 budget threshold casts a luminous glow on the DPRK's economic horizon. It whispers a tantalizing tale of potential return, a rekindling of the economic spark extinguished during the Arduous March. After decades of hardship, the nation might be nearing a crucial turning point—a restoration of its economy to pre-Arduous March levels. While the *CCY* offers no explicit declarations, this budgetary feat hums with the melodies of resilience and a renewed promise of prosperity.

However, the specter of inflation lingers. A definitive conclusion requires a deeper dive into comprehensive economic data, a task best suited for the appendix of this chapter. Yet, even with inflation factored in, surpassing the 1993 threshold remains a significant stride toward economic recovery. It marks a pivotal moment, a steppingstone on the path to a potentially brighter future for the DPRK.

This budgetary milestone transcends mere numbers. It signifies a nation defying hardship, a testament to the unwavering spirit of a people determined to rebuild their economic strength. It paints a picture of a nation not just navigating toward recovery, but actively charting a course toward a more prosperous future. This is not the end of the story, but a pivotal chapter, pregnant with the possibilities of a reinvigorated DPRK.

31 The 2013 *CCY* maintains a veil of secrecy around the exact growth of DPRK's national budget in 2012. Unlike previous years, it doesn't declare a triumphant percentage, only offering a cryptic clue on page 366: "the planned national budget revenues in 2012 were executed at 101.3%." This seemingly modest statement, however, whispers a story of continued progress, albeit shrouded in a layer of strategic ambiguity.

To decipher this cryptic message, we can turn to the 2011 budget, where a similar 'overachievement' of 1.1% was revealed. Drawing on this precedent, we can assume a cautious approach in 2012 as well. The 101.3% figure likely signifies exceeding the planned growth rate by 1.3%, mirroring the previous year's trend.

Based on this assumption and using the 2011 planned growth rate, we can estimate 2012's planned growth around 5.8%. Adding the 1.3% overachievement, we arrive at an estimated final national budget revenue of 45.6534 billion wŏn (calculated by multiplying the 2011 figure by 1.058 and then by 1.013).

32 The 2014 *CCY* offers a tantalizing glimpse into the DPRK's 2013 national budget performance, tucked away on page 357. It doesn't trumpet a straightforward percentage, but instead whispers a cryptic clue: "In 2013, the national budget revenue plan was fulfilled at 101.8% and grew to 106% compared to the previous year." Decoding this message unveils a story of cautious progress and strategic recalibration.

Let's dissect the layers of this statement. The '101.8%' signifies that the 2013 budget revenue exceeded the initial plan by 1.8%. This hints at a measured approach, perhaps reflecting adjustments to adapt to unforeseen circumstances or prioritize specific developmental goals. While not a meteoric surge, it suggests a nation diligently navigating economic complexities and ensuring continued upward momentum.

But the true surprise lies in the second part: "grew to 106% compared to the previous year." This seemingly innocuous phrase reveals a shift in expectations. Originally, the plan for 2013 aimed for a modest 4.2% growth over 2012. However, the actual performance surpassed this target by a significant margin, reaching a 6% increase. By applying the 6% growth rate to the 2012 figure, we arrive at a final national budget revenue for 2013 of 48.3926 billion wŏn (calculated by multiplying 45,6534 by 1.06).

33 The 2015 *CCY* offers a cryptic clue to the DPRK's 2014 national budget performance, nestled within its pages on page 308. It doesn't announce a straightforward percentage growth, but instead whispers a two-pronged message: "The national budget revenue plan was fulfilled at 101.6%, which is 106% higher than the previous year.".

The "101.6%" signifies exceeding the planned revenue collection by 1.6%. This suggests a measured approach, perhaps reflecting adjustments to external economic fluctuations or strategic prioritization within the national budget. While not a dramatic surge, it hints at a nation diligently navigating economic complexities and ensuring continued upward momentum.

However, the true surprise lies in the second part: "106% higher than the previous year." This seemingly understated phrase reveals a significant upward revision in expectations. Compared to the initial projection of a 4.2% growth over 2013, the actual performance far surpassed it, achieving a remarkable 6% increase.

So, what does this translate to in terms of actual numbers? Applying the revised 6% growth rate to the 2013 figure, we arrive at a final national budget revenue for 2014 of 51.2961 billion wŏn (calculated by multiplying 48.3926 by 1.06).

34 The 2016 *CCY* offers a glimpse into the DPRK's 2015 national budget performance, veiled in characteristically cryptic language. Tucked away on page 422, a seemingly simple sentence holds the key: "The national budget revenue plan was carried out at 101.3%, and it grew to 105% compared to the previous year." While the statement doesn't explicitly declare a growth rate, it whispers clues about exceeding expectations. The "101.3%" suggests exceeding the planned target by 1.3%. This isn't a meteoric surge, but a steady climb, showcasing a nation focused on meticulous execution and incremental progress.

But as always, the true intrigue lies in the second part: "grew to 105% compared to the previous year." In other words, the initial plan for 2015 might have been more modest, but the actual performance surpassed it by a significant margin. Applying the implied 5% growth rate to the 2014 figure, we arrive at a final national budget revenue for 2015 of 53.8609 billion wŏn (calculated by multiplying 51.2961 by 1.05).

35 The insights gleaned from the 2017 edition of the *CCY* offer a detailed perspective on the DPRK's economic landscape in 2016. The publication unveils a significant clue regarding the national budget revenue for that year, emphasizing the meticulous execution of the revenue plan. According to the *CCY*, the national budgetary revenue plan not only met expectations but surpassed them, achieving an impressive 102.2% implementation rate. Furthermore, the revenue exhibited robust growth, reaching a noteworthy 106.3% when juxtaposed with the figures from the preceding year, 2015 (p. 423).

Consequently, the aggregate national budget revenue for 2016 is calculated at 57.2541 billion wŏn, derived from the initial base figure of 53.8609 billion wŏn and the considerable growth factor of 1.063. This financial expansion not only underscores the nation's economic prowess during the specified period but also suggests a capacity for adaptability and resourcefulness in navigating economic challenges.

36 The veil of opacity surrounding the DPRK's economic workings seems momentarily lifted in the pages of the 2018 *CCY*. Amid the characteristically cryptic pronouncements, nestled on page 422, lies a seemingly innocuous sentence pregnant with meaning:

> The 2017 State budget was successfully executed thanks to the great driving force of self-reliance and the power of science and technology, which the entire army and people upheld, following the Chuch'e revolutionary line put forth by the WPK. The national budget revenue plan was fulfilled at 101.7%, and it increased by 104.9% compared to 2016.

While the statement itself refrains from explicitly declaring a growth rate, it whispers secrets between the lines. The figure of '101.7%' hints at exceeding the planned target, not by a dramatic leap, but with a measured 1.3% climb. This subtle detail paints a picture of a nation prioritizing meticulous execution and incremental progress, shunning sensational bursts for steady, controlled advancement.

Yet, the true intrigue lies in the second part: "increased by 104.9% compared to 2016." This seemingly straightforward statement unveils a deeper truth. It suggests that while the initial plan for 2017 might have been conservative, the actual performance significantly outstripped it. Applying this implied growth rate of 104.9% to the 2016 figure, we arrive at a final national budget revenue for 2017 of 60.0595 billion wŏn (calculated by multiplying 57.2541 billion wŏn by 1.049).

37 Even before the border closure in early 2020, the DPRK had halted the dispatch of *CCY* and other materials beyond its borders since 2019, a practice that continues as of January 2024.

38 Kim Jong Un, "Kyŏngaehanŭn kimjŏngŭndongjikkesŏ chosŏllodongdang chungangwiwŏnhoe 2013nyŏn 3wŏlchŏnwŏnhoeŭiesŏ hashin pogo" (Concluding Speech at the March 2013 Plenary Meeting of the Central Committee of the Worker's Party of Korea), Rodong Sinmun (March 14, 2013).

39 The pertinent lines from Kim Jong Il's "10·3 Discourse" underscore the imperative of steadfastly adhering to socialist principles in economic management are as follows:

> While adhering to socialist principles, it is essential to approach economic management with the fundamental principle of ensuring the greatest material benefit, both at the national and individual sector levels, in production, construction, and business operations. Above all, it is crucial to tackle and resolve all issues in economic management by firmly upholding the principles of planned economic management by the State and implementing them correctly.

(Suho Im, p. 250)

40 Kim Jong Il, "Modŭn saŏbŭl ch'angjojŏkŭro hanŭn'gŏsŭn shidaewa hyŏngmyŏngbalchŏnŭi chŏlshirhan yoguida: Chosŏllodongdang chungangwiwŏnhoe ch'aegimilgundŭlgwa han tamhwa (chuch'e 95(2006)nyŏn 2wŏl17il, 19il)" (Creativity in All Work is an Urgent Demand of the Times and Revolutionary Development: A Discourse with the Responsible Workers of the Central Committee of the WPK (2006 February 17 and 19)), *SWK 22*, p. 394.

41 While Kim Jong Il outlined a grand vision for the DPRK's economic development, bringing it to fruition proved elusive. Normalizing production across various sectors posed formidable challenges, acting as a persistent roadblock on the path toward Kangsŏngdaeguk. This, coupled with the presumed non-public nature of Kim Jong Un's May 30, 2014, speech to Party officials, fuels speculation that significant difficulties were encountered in translating Kim Jong Il's vision into tangible progress.

42 Yŏnghŭng Kim, "Sahoejuŭigiŏpch'aegimgwallijerŭl paro shilshihanŭndesŏ nasŏnŭn chungyohan munje" (2016nyŏn11wŏl4il)" (Important Issues for Immediate Implementation of the SERMS), (November 4, 2016)), http://www.ryongnamsan.edu.kp/univ/success/social/part/814.

43 Yŏngsu Ch'a, another scholar from Kim Il Sung University, emphasizes the importance of continuity and adaptation in establishing the DPRK's unique style of economic management. He argues that this process involves "implementing, inheriting, and developing the principles and methods of economic management revealed by the Great Leader and the General" while adapting them to the present reality.

Ch'a identifies the Taean System, created by Kim Il Sung and further developed by Kim Jong Il, as the foundation for this distinct style. He highlights two key reasons for its superiority:

Collective Guidance of the Party Committee: The Taean System emphasizes "conducting business activities under the collective guidance of the Party Committee." Ch'a views this as the "most effective way to realize Party and Manager guidance in our country today," as evidenced by the presence of Party Committees within enterprises under the SERMS.

Effective Implementation of Socialist Principles: Ch'a argues that the Taean System's collective leadership structure ensures the successful implementation of socialist principles in economic management. This is because the Party Committee, representing the collective will of the Party, guides enterprises toward achieving social and economic goals alongside individual productivity.

In essence, Ch'a's analysis highlights the DPRK's ongoing effort to balance the preservation of its socialist economic principles with the need for adaptation to changing realities. The Taean System, with its emphasis on collective leadership and Party guidance, is seen as a key tool in achieving this "balance" (Yŏngsu Ch'a, "T'etaeanŭi saŏpch'egyenŭn kyŏngjegwalliesŏ sahoejuŭiwŏnch'ikŭl kuhyŏnhalsu itke hanŭn kajang uwŏrhan kyŏngjegwallich'egye" (Taean System is the Most Superior Economic Management System to Implement Socialist Principles in Economic Management), *KUAB* (2014), vol. 60, no. 4, p. 63).

44 Within the SERMS, the presence of a Party Committee represents a unique organizational feature. Historically, such committees have been embedded in the DPRK economic management systems. However, the evolving economic landscape, which increasingly incorporates market mechanisms into resource allocation, raises questions about the Party Committee's role within SERMS.

Beyond simply transmitting directives from the Central Party, the Party Committee within SERMS reportedly operates to embody the spirit of the Taean System and adhere to the principles of the mass line. This translates to aligning Central Party directives with the creation of a supportive environment within each production unit. This environment is aimed at encouraging worker cooperation and innovation.

Notably, the Party Committee's function distinguishes SERMS from other frameworks where market forces heavily influence resource allocation. This distinction suggests a unique approach to fostering collaboration and innovation at the production unit level. While operating under the Central Party's overarching guidance, the Party Committee ultimately strives to ensure unity and harmony within the national economic development process.

45 A 2017 article by Gyŏngok Kim published in the first issue of *ER* explores strategies for leveraging expanded planning and production rights under the SERMS framework. Kim proposes a two-pronged approach emphasizing both alignment with national economic goals and enterprise-level flexibility.

Firstly, Kim advocates for seamless integration between centrally defined production targets (Central Indicators) and firm-specific sub-indicators derived from order contracts. This ensures adherence to broader economic objectives while granting enterprises room to adapt strategies to their specific capabilities and market conditions.

Secondly, Kim highlights the potential benefits of selecting optimal production methods based on supply-demand dynamics. She suggests that enterprises can choose from various models, including cooperative, specialized, combined, and large-scale, based on technical characteristics and the need to maximize output of socially desired products. This flexibility, combined with integrated planning, could empower firms to continuously improve their production systems for optimal efficiency and effectiveness (Gyŏngok Kim, "T'esahoejuŭigiŏpch'edŭrŭi hwaktaedoen kyehoekkwŏn'gwa saengsanjojikkwŏnhaengsaŭi chungyoyogu" (Expanded Planning Rights of Socialist Enterprises and Important Requirements for the Exercise of Production Organization Rights)), *ER* (2017), no. 1, p. 14).

46 The precise scope of these activities is not explicitly defined, but it is assumed that they undergo a review and approval process by the Ministry of Foreign Trade. During the inaugural plenary session of the 13th Supreme People's Assembly in April 2014, the DPRK resolved to merge the Trade Ministry, the Joint Investment Committee, and the National Economic Development Committee of the Cabinet into the Ministry of Foreign Economic Affairs. This consolidation of foreign trade responsibilities and oversight within the Ministry of Foreign Economic Affairs is anticipated to enhance the efficiency and simplicity of enterprise trade approvals and procedures.

47 The Critical Indicators are not independent indicators that follow from the Central Indicators but are annual planned production targets for sectors included in the Central Indicators with strategic significance at the national level.

48 Kilhyŏn Cho, "Kiŏpch'edŭrŭi ch'aegimsŏnggwa ch'angbalsŏngŭl nop'ilsu itke inmin'gyŏngjegyehoeksaŏbŭl kaesŏnhagi wihan pangdo" (Ways to Improve the People's Economic Planning Project to Enhance the Responsibility and Creativity of Enterprises), *KUAB* (2014), vol. 60, no. 2, p. 82).

49 So, which sectors are encompassed in the planning of key indicators? Insights from a paper by Sŏngil Kim, published in *ER*, shed light on this matter. In his paper, Kim states that "in the planning of the People's Economy, the State directly delineates significant sectors and target economic indicators with key significance for national security, economic construction, and people's livelihood.

These include the leading sectors of the People's Economy, backbone industries, high-tech industries, and national defense industries. The State guides the economy in a manner that concentrates investment and addresses the current and future stages, enabling reasonable control over the pace and balance of economic development" (Sŏngil Kim, "Kyŏngjebalchŏnŭi soktowa kyunhyŏngjojongesŏ kyehoekkongganŭi hamnijŏngniyong" (Rational Use of Planning Sphere in Controlling the Speed and Balance of Economic Development)), *ER* (2017), no. 1, p. 34).

50 Kwangik Tu, "Kiŏpch'edŭresŏŭi kagyŏkchejŏngbangbŏp" (Pricing Methods in Enterprise), *KUAB* (2014), vol. 60, no. 4, 63.

51 Gyŏngok Kim, "T'esahoejuŭigiŏpch'edŭrŭi hwaktaedoen kyehoekkwŏn'gwa saengsanjojikkwŏnhaengsaŭi chungyoyogu" (Expanded Planning Rights of Socialist Enterprises and Important Requirements for the Exercise of Production Organization Rights)), *ER* (2017), no. 1, pp. 12–13.

52 Suho Im, Shijanggwa kyehoegŭi kongjon: Puk'anŭi kyŏngjegaehyŏkkwa ch'ejebyŏnhwa chŏnmang (The Coexistence of Markets and Planning: Prospects for Economic Reform and Regime Change in North Korea), Seoul: Samsung Economic Research Institute, 2008 p. 252.

53 Sŏngnam Kang, "Widaehanryŏngdojakimjŏngiltongjikkesŏsahoejuŭigyŏngjegwalliŭi kaesŏnwansŏnge ssaaollishin pulmyŏrŭi ŏpchŏk" (The Immortal Achievements of the Great Leader Kim Jong Il in Perfecting the Improvement of Socialist Economic Management), *KUAB* (2016), vol. 62, no. 1, p. 152.

54 Certainly, exceptions exist to this general principle. Specifically, in the instance of newly established enterprises and significant target enterprises, it becomes the responsibility of the State to furnish the necessary liquid funds. This extends beyond merely supporting the fulfillment of Central Indicators but also encompasses the provision of resources for meeting Enterprise Indicators. This financial assistance is warranted when these enterprises lack the requisite conditions to independently generate and utilize liquid funds (Ch'ŏlsu Kim, "Sahoejuŭigiŏpch'edŭresŏ ryudongjagŭm pojangjojigŭi chungyoyogu (The Critical Need of Organizing Liquidity Fund Guarantee for Socialist Enterprises)," *ER* (2016), no. 3, p. 50).

55 T'aesŏng Rim, "Sahoejuŭigiŏpch'eŭi chejŏnggwalligwŏn" (Legislative Control of Socialist Enterprises), *ER* (2016), no. 1, p. 41.

56 Ch'ŏlsu Kim, "Sahoejuŭigiŏpch'edŭresŏ ryudongjagŭm pojangjojigŭi chungyoyogu (The Critical Need of Organizing Liquidity Fund Guarantee for Socialist Enterprises)," *ER* (2016), no. 3, p. 50.

57 These include the following articles. Ch'ŏlsu Kim, "Sahoejuŭigiŏpch'edŭresŏ ryudongjagŭm pojangjojigŭi chungyoyogu" (The Important Needs of Organizing Liquid Fund Guarantee in Socialist Enterprises), *ER* (2016), no. 3; Nyŏn Chŏng, "Hyŏnshigi sangŏpkiŏpsojaejŏnggwalligaesŏnesŏ nasŏnŭn yogu" (The Needs of Improving the Financial Management of Commercial Enterprises), *ER* (2016), no. 4; Unjŏng Han, "T'ehyŏnshigi sahoejuŭisahoe hwap'eryut'ongŭi konggohwashirhyŏnesŏ chegidoenŭn chungyomunje" (Important Issues Raised by the Realization of the Consolidation of the Socialist Monetary System), *ER* (2016), no. 4; Kŭmhyŏk Ku, "Hyŏnshigi ŭnhaenggigwandŭrŭl sangŏbŭnhaenghwahanŭndesŏ nasŏnŭn chungyohan munje" (Important Issues for Commercializing Banking Institutions), *KUAB* (2016), no. 4; Gyŏngshik Chang, "Wŏne ŭihan t'ongjenŭn sahoejuŭiŭnhaengŭi chungyohan kinŭng" (Control by the Wŏn is an Important Function of Socialist Banks), *KUAB* (2017), vol. 63, no. 2; Jŭngbŏm Hong, "Sahoejuŭisangŏbŭnhaenge kwanhan tokch'angjŏgin sasangniron (An Original Theory of Socialist Commercial Banking), *KAUB* (2018), vol. 64, no. 1; Yŏngch'ŏl Han, "Kŭmyunggigwan ch'aesanjewa kŭ unyŏngesŏ nasŏnŭn chungyomunje" (Important Issues in the Settlement System and Operation of Financial Institutions), *KAUB* (2018), vol. 64, no. 1; Ch'ŏlsu Kim "Hyŏnshigi sahoejuŭigiŏpch'aegimgwallijega shilchi ŭnŭl naedorong hagi wihan.

chaejŏngjŏkpangdo" (Financial Measures to Ensure that the Current Socialist Enterprise Responsibility Management System Actually Pays Off), *ER* (2018), no. 4; Yongnam Ch'oe, chaejŏngŭnhaengsaŏbesŏ chŏnhwanŭl irŭk'inŭn'gŏsŭn sahoejuŭiganggukkŏnsŏrŭi chungyoyogu" (Transforming the Financial Banking Business is an Important Requirement for Building a Socialist Power), *KUAB* (2018), vol. 64, no. 2.

58 Kŭmhyŏk Ku, "Hyŏnshigi ŭnhaenggigwandŭrŭl sangŏbŭnhaenghwahanŭndesŏ nasŏnŭn chungyohan munje" (Important Issues in Commercializing Banking Institutions in the Current Era), *KUAB* (2016), vol. 62, no. 4, p. 130.

59 Kŭmhyŏk Ku, "Hyŏnshigi ŭnhaenggigwandŭrŭl sangŏbŭnhaenghwahanŭndesŏ nasŏnŭn chungyohan munje" (Important Issues in Commercializing Banking Institutions in the Current Era), *KUAB* (2016), vol. 62, no. 4, p. 130.

60 Sangguk Ri (associate professor), "T'echaejŏnggyuryulgwa t'ongjerŭl kanghwaralte taehan uri tangŭi rironŭn chaejŏngŭnhaengsaŏbŭi yŏngwŏnhan chidojŏkchich'im" (Our Party's Ruling on Strengthening Fiscal Discipline and Control is the Eternal Guiding Instruction for Fiscal Banking), *ER* (2017), no. 1, p. 46.

61 Gyŏngshik Chang, "T'esahoejuŭigiŏpch'edŭrŭi hwaktaedoen kyehoekkwŏn'gwa saengsanjojikkwŏnhaengsaŭi chungyoyogu" (Expanded Planning Rights of Socialist Enterprises and Important Requirements for the Exercise of Production Organization Rights)), *ER* (2017), no. 1, p. 62.

62 Gyŏngshik Chang, "T'esahoejuŭigiŏpch'edŭrŭi hwaktaedoen kyehoekkwŏn'gwa saengsanjojikkwŏnhaengsaŭi chungyoyogu" (Expanded Planning Rights of

Socialist Enterprises and Important Requirements for the Exercise of Production Organization Rights)), *ER* (2017), no. 1, p. 63.

63 As an illustration, Gŭmhyŏk Ku articulated this perspective: "In reality, the substantial accumulation of hard currency and foreign cash held by the population constitutes a source that cannot be overlooked in the economic development of the country" (Ku, "Hyŏnshigi ŭnhaenggigwandŭrŭl sangŏbŭnhaenghwahanŭndesŏ nasŏnŭn chungyohan munje" (Important Issues in Commercializing Banking Institutions in the Current Era), *KUAB* (2016), vol. 62, no. 4, p. 132).

64 Jŭngbŏm Hong, "Sahoejuŭisangŏbŭnhaenge kwanhan tokch'angjŏgin sasangniron (An Original Theory of Socialist Commercial Banking), *KAUB* (2018), vol. 64, no. 1, pp. 62–63.

65 "In the light industry sector, our primary objective is to establish and maintain production at an elevated level, generating a diverse range of high-quality consumer goods on a large scale. In the course of his visits to factories, enterprises, and commercial service organizations within the light industry sector, the General emphasized the importance of creating prototypes and samples, showcasing them in shops, and subsequently standardizing production for public distribution. Regrettably, the light industry factories have fallen short in fulfilling the General's final directive to normalize production" (Kim Jong Un, "Kyŏngaehanŭn kimjŏngŭndongjikkesŏ chosŏllodongdang chungangwiwŏnhoe 2013nyŏn 3wŏlchŏnwŏnhoeŭiesŏ hashin pogo" (Concluding Speech at the March 2013 Plenary Meeting of the Central Committee of the Worker's Party of Korea), Rodong Sinmun (March 14, 2013)).

66 Sunhwa Ri, "Kyŏngjegyunhyŏngch'egyeesŏ suyowa konggŭbŭi kyunhyŏngi ch'ajihanŭn wich'iwa ŭiŭi" (The Place and Significance of the Balance of Supply and Demand in the Economic Equilibrium System), *ER* (2013), no. 1, pp. 17–18.

67 Sŏnhŭi O, "Shillirŭl nat'anaenŭn chip'yoŭi hamnijŏngniyong (The Rational Use of Actual Profit Indicators)," *ER* (2003), no. 3, pp. 27–28.

68 It is around 3–4% of Workers' Living Expenses according to economist Gwangyŏng Chŏng:

It is deemed prudent to establish the enterprise reserve fund at 3% of the workers' living expenses plan for entities operating under the general Independent Accounting System and 4% of the workers' living expenses plan for those affiliated with the United Enterprise under the double Independent Accounting System.
(Gwangyŏng Chŏng, "Kiŏpsogigŭmgwa kŭ chŏngnimniyongesŏ nasŏnŭn chungyomunje" (Important Issues Arising from the Accumulation and Use of Enterprise Reserve Funds), *ER* (2005), no. 3, p. 32)

69 Sŏngŭn Chang, "Kongjang, kiŏpsoesŏ pŏnsuibŭi ponjilgwa kŭ punbaeesŏ nasŏnŭn wŏnch'ikchŏkyogu" (The Essence of Earned Income in Factories and Enterprises and the Principled Demand in Its Distribution), *ER* (2002), no. 4, p. 40.

70 As is discussed previously, the DPRK's national budget revenue experienced a precipitous drop, plummeting by over 50% since 1994. It remained stagnant for a grueling six years, unable to claw its way back even halfway. But amid this period of economic hardship, a flicker of hope emerged in 2000. The nation witnessed a significant rebound, bouncing back to reach half its pre-decline level. This pivotal turnaround year serves as the launch pad for our analysis, offering a glimpse into the DPRK's economic trajectory in the years that followed.

71 Workers are remunerated in cash, as affirmed by Ryŏna Kim in the following article:

Considering that the primary source of workers' income is in cash, effectively managing the interplay between income and expenditure becomes crucial in determining residents' satisfaction of needs and maintaining equilibrium in the balance of payments. This dynamic directly influences everyday life and contributes to overall economic stability.

> (Ryŏna Kim, "Chiyŏkpyŏl, kyech'ŭngbyŏl chuminŭi hwap'esujigyunhyŏngp'yo-jaksŏngnŭl wihan chip'yogyesanesŏ nasŏnŭn munje (Problems in Calculating Indicators for Calculating the Balance of Payments of Residents by Region and Category), *ER* (2013), no. 3, p. 26)

72 Hyangmi Pong, "Saenghwalbiwa kagyŏgŭi kyunhyŏngŭl pojanghanŭn'gŏsŭn rodongja, samuwŏndŭrŭi saenghwarŭl anjŏnghyangsangshik'igi wihan chungyod-ambo" (Ensuring the Balance of Cost of Living and Prices is an Important Collateral for Improving the Livelihood Security of Laborers and Office Workers), *ER* (2017), no. 1, p. 35.

73 The issue at hand appears to have escalated significantly after the implementation of the economic improvement measures on July 1, 2002. Ch'unghan Kim, characterizing these measures as "a major effort to adjust commodity prices and enhance workers' living standards to address the shifting environmental dynamics," expressed apprehension about potential inflation in the following manner:

> In order to rectify the altered environmental biases, economic workers must operate factories and enterprises at full capacity, ensure timely provision of living expenses for workers, and organize work processes to guarantee an ample supply of goods as living costs rise. Despite facing challenging conditions, workers must strive to maximize production so that the national initiatives aimed at adjusting commodity prices and living expenses yield positive outcomes.

> This, in turn, will bolster the purchasing power of the currency, enhance the quality of people's lives, and maintain a seamless flow of currency in circulation. Failure to keep up with the revised prices and living expenses through adequate commodity production could result in an excess of circulating currency, rendering it difficult to effectively utilize fiscal and financial resources for the reproduction and enhancement of people's lives

> (Ch'unghan Kim, "Kagyŏkkwa saenghwalbirŭl kaejŏnghan kukkajŏkchoch'iga tŏ k'ŭn ŭnŭl naege haja" (Let Us Redouble Our Efforts to Ensure the National Measures Aimed at Revising Prices and Cost of Living Have a Tangible Impact On our Daily Lives), *Kŭlloja* (2003), no. 3, p. 54)

74 Many economists and experts in the DPRK have acknowledged the presence of a substantial amount of cash in the hands of residents but have provided limited elaboration. However, Sunhak Kim offers a more detailed explanation.

Kim suggests that the central bank should establish new indicators to regulate the size of cash reserves within individual institutions, enterprises, and among residents. Additionally, he proposes the incorporation of specific indicators such as ticketing plans and cash income and expenditure plans to precisely assess the country's currency status and conduct scientific analysis. A key aspect of this proposal involves reformulating and reusing indicators for individual residents' hard currency income to align with the evolving reality.

Kim emphasizes that while banking institutions may have a good understanding of enterprise liquidity, the situation is different for residents. Using outdated indicators based on the cost-of-living level for analyzing residents' currency income can hinder the ability to take scientifically informed measures. He underscores the importance of carefully selecting indicators that accurately capture the shift in cash flow from Bureaus and enterprises to individual residents, now primarily circulating within the individual resident community.

This shift in reality implies that **the predominant cash flow, once primarily between Bureaus and enterprises, now predominantly occurs among individual residents** (emphasis added). Consequently, the buying and selling of consumer goods among individual residents have become the primary driver of cash flow. (Sunhak Kim, "Hwap'eǔi anjǒngsǒngǔl pojanghanǔndesǒ nasǒnǔn chungyohan munje" (An Important Issue in Ensuring the Stability of the Currency), *KUAB* (2018), vol. 64, no. 2, p. 95).

75 Wǒn'gyǒng Ri, "Inmigyǒngjejǒkchagǔmsuyohaegyǒrǔi wǒnch'ikchǒkpangdo" (A Principled Approach to Solving the Demand for Funds in the People's Economy), *ER* (2002), no. 3, p. 28.

76 Yǒngǔi Hong, "Ǔnhaengǔi yǒk'arǔl nop'inǔn kǒsǔn kyǒngjeganggukkǒnsǒresǒ nasǒnǔn chungyohan yogu (It is an Important Demand Arising from Economic Development to Enhance the Role of Banks," *ER* (2014), no. 3, p. 39.

77 However, an intriguing question lingers concerning the magnitude of "idle currency" held by residents. Has it diminished as urged by DPRK scholars, who propose that these funds should be absorbed by banks? The noticeable decline in articles addressing this topic in academic journals since 2016 hints at a shift in focus.

While alternative sources of funding may explain this shift, a more compelling possibility arises: the stockpile of idle currency may have indeed decreased. The economic upswing since 2011 plays a significant role in this hypothesis. Empowered by newfound prosperity, citizens might have begun tapping into their concealed reserves, directing their spending toward goods and leaving less currency to accumulate unused. This shift from hoarding to spending aligns with the observed decrease in discussions about "idle currency.".

The diminishing discourse around "idle currency" goes beyond being a mere financial indicator; it could serve as a marker of societal change. The DPRK appears to be tentatively moving away from a culture of scarcity and embracing the promise of a brighter future. It reflects a cautious optimism—a hesitant stride toward normalcy, where desperation is gradually replaced by newfound hope.

78 Building on Wǒn'gyǒng Ri's observation that "A trend is emerging where the percentage of idle currency mobilization methods in meeting the demand for people's economic funds is relatively increasing compared to the percentage of State fiscal fund mobilization methods," it was deduced that the aggregate "idle currency" retained by individuals has equaled or exceeded the funds allocated to the People's Economy from 2000 to 2010.

Nevertheless, considering the potential scenario of banks actively participating in saving initiatives to attract individuals' "idle currency," we have postulated that since 2011, the amount of "idle currency" held by individuals would be less than the funds allocated to the People's Economy.

79 "The national budget expenditure exceeded expectations by 102.7%, reaching an actual amount of 20.95503 billion wǒn compared to the planned 20.40532 billion wǒn" (*CCY 2001*, p. 174).

80 "The State allocated funds amounting to 40.1% of the total budget expenditure to the People's Economy sector to facilitate a decisive breakthrough in socialist economic construction" (*CCY 2001*, page 174). Consequently, the total expenditure on the People's Economy in 2000 was 8.40297 billion wǒn (calculated as 20.95503 million wǒn x 0.401).

81 "The national budget expenditure exceeded expectations by 100.5%, totaling an actual amount of 21.67805 billion wǒn compared to the planned 21.5702 billion wǒn" (*CCY 2002*, p. 164).

82 "Allocating 42.3% of the total national budget to the economic construction sector, the Republic aimed to enhance production in vital sectors of the People's Economy and actively advance the construction, renovation, and modernization of factories and enterprises essential for people's lives (*CCY 2002*, p. 164). Consequently, the total expenditure on the People's Economy in 2001 amounted to 9.16982 billion wǒn (calculated as 21.67805 billion wǒn x 0.423).

83 The official 2003 *CCY* document does not explicitly list the total national expenditure for 2002. However, several indicators suggest adherence to the original plan. Firstly, the document states that "the 2002 national budget was executed successfully" (p. 182), implying that expenditures aligned with the intended course. Secondly, with a planned national revenue of 22.6180 billion wŏn and an achieved execution rate of 99.9%, a strong argument can be made that the total national expenditure in 2002 also reached 22.5954 billion wŏn.

84 "To propel a new advancement in economic power, the State dedicated funds representing 22.7% of the total national budgetary expenditure to diverse sectors of the People's Economy. A substantial amount was also invested in science and technology, leading to significant advancements in these fields" (*CCY 2003*, p. 183). Consequently, the total expenditure on the People's Economy in 2002 was 5.1292 billion wŏn (calculated as 22.5954 billion wŏn multiplied by 0.227).

85 While the 2004 *CCY* does not provide the total national expenditure for 2003, it's possible to make an estimate based on assumptions regarding the DPRK's budgetary practices during the Arduous March period. Assuming the DPRK prioritized fiscal prudence and austerity during this challenging period, it's reasonable to expect that planned expenditures wouldn't exceed planned revenue. Considering the remarkable 99.9% execution rate achieved in 2002, we can estimate the total national expenditure in 2003 to be approximately 23.7344 billion wŏn, treating the execution rate as virtually 100%.

86 "As a consequence of allocating 23.3% of the total national budget to the projects on People's Economy, pivotal sectors within the People's Economy, such as the electric power industry, gained a robust material and technological foundation, and active efforts were undertaken to modernize the light industry" (*CCY 2004*, p. 187). Therefore, the corresponding figure is 5.5301 billion wŏn (calculated as 23.7344 billion wŏn multiplied by 0.233).

87 "The national budget was executed at a rate of 99.3%" (*CCY 2005*, p. 185). Therefore, the total amount of the 2004 national budget is 25.2180 billion wŏn (calculated as 25.3958 billion wŏn multiplied by 0.993).

88 "This year, 41.3% of the total expenditures were allocated to the People's Economy, and 40.8% to social and cultural affairs, thus ensuring the success of projects aimed at developing the country's economy and fostering a socialist culture" (*CCY* 2005, p. 185). Therefore, the total amount of expenditures on the People's Economy in 2004 was 10.4150 billion wŏn (calculated as 24.74678 billion wŏn multiplied by 0.413).

89 "This year's national budget expenditures exceeded the plan by 104.4%" (*CCY 2006*, p. 211). Therefore, the total amount of national budget expenditures in 2005 was 30.8143 billion wŏn (calculated as 29.5156 billion wŏn multiplied by 1.044).

90 "The national budget actively promoted the construction of a socialist economy by allocating 41.3% of the total expenditures to the People's Economy sector" (*CCY 2006*, p. 211). Therefore, the total expenditure on the People's Economy in 2005 was 12.7263 billion wŏn (calculated as 30.8143 billion wŏn multiplied by 0.413).

91 "This year's national budget was executed at 99.9% of the plan" (*CCY 2007*, p. 184). Treating 99.9% as 100%, the total expenditure on the People's Economy in 2006 was 30.8143 billion wŏn.

92 "The national budget invested 40.8% of the total expenditure in various sectors of the People's Economy to propel a new leap forward in the construction of economic power" (*CCY 2007*, p. 184). Therefore, the total expenditure on the People's Economy in 2006 was 12.5772 billion wŏn (calculated as 30.8143 billion wŏn multiplied by 0.408).

93   "The national budget was over-executed by 101.7% against the plan due to unexpectedly large amounts of funds, including funds for disaster recovery, being added
during the execution process" (*CCY 2008*, p. 168). Therefore, the total national
expenditure in 2007 was 33.2498 billion wŏn (calculated as 32.6940 billion wŏn
multiplied by 1.017).

94   In 2008, the *CCY* report subtly sidesteps revealing the exact total expenditure on
the People's Economy for 2007, but discernible highlights allude to a sustained
and substantial financial commitment. The document proudly showcases significant increments in investment across pivotal sectors, including a remarkable 108.5%
surge in agriculture, enhancements in light industry, pivotal developments in crucial infrastructure such as electricity and railways, and notable advancements in
scientific research projects. These strategic investments are in line with the Party's
strategic focus on fortifying the economic bedrock (p. 168).

While the passage refrains from directly comparing these increments to planned
growth rates or the overall budget allocation, a critical clue surfaces in relation to
the total budget spending for 2007. The report notes, "In 2007, the State budget
expenditure surpassed the plan by 1.7%, buoyed by unexpected large amounts of
funds, including flood damage recovery" (*CCY 2008*, p. 168).

Given the DPRK's propensity to omit minor figures (those less than 98%
compared to the previous year), it becomes apparent that two key assertions are
likely: Firstly, the DPRK intended to allocate more funds to the People's Economy
in 2007 compared to 2006. Secondly, the 1.7% divergence from the planned
budget for the People's Economy can be attributed to resources redirected toward
repairing flood damage.

In light of these observations, it is reasonable to infer the following: The
additional 2% expenditure was premeditated for the People's Economy, aligning
with the Party's commitments. Unexpected flood damage induced a 1.7%
reduction in the realized budget expenditure. This adjustment results in the
realized expenditure amounting to 41.1% of the total budget, corresponding to a
96% execution rate.

Consequently, within the 2007 budget expenditures, the portion earmarked for
the People's Economy is estimated at 13.6657 billion wŏn (calculated as 33.2498
wŏn multiplied by 0.411).

95   "This year's national budget was executed at a rate of 99.9 percent" (*CCY 2009*, p.
192).

96   The 2008 *CCY* does not explicitly reveal the percentage of the total national budget allocated to the People's Economy. However, it is indicated as follows:

In the national budget expenditures, while upholding the Party's line of a vigorous
'Military-First' revolution and exerting great efforts to strengthen the country's
defense power, we directed our focus on investing funds in the leading sectors of
the People's Economy, essential industries, and improving people's lives

(*CCY 2009*, p. 192)

Given that Defense expenditures in 2008 constituted 15.8% of the total budgeted
expenditures, nearly identical to the preceding year's 15.7%, it is reasonable to
assume that the proportion of People's Economy expenditures in 2008 to the
total budgeted expenditures was 40%, as in the prior year. Consequently, the total
amount of Defense expenditure in 2008 was 13.823 billion wŏn (calculated as
34.5575 billion wŏn multiplied by 0.4).

97   "This year, 99.8% of the national budget was executed." Therefore, the total actual
national budget for 2009 is 36.9025 billion wŏn (calculated as 36.9765 wŏn multiplied by 0.998).

98 While the 2010 *CCY* provides limited details on the precise percentage allocated to the People's Economy in 2009, it paints a picture of continued development and investment in key sectors. The text highlights significant budget increases for metal industry, energy, infrastructure, and R&D, resulting in a 6% overall industrial production growth. Agriculture and light industry also received boosts, aimed at promoting rural development and technological modernization (*CCY 2010*, p. 266).

However, the *CCY* typically avoids disclosing unfulfilled targets, making it difficult to assess the full picture. Nevertheless, the consistency of the 15.8% Defense budget since 2007 suggests a potential 40% allocation for the People's Economy in 2009, similar to previous years. This estimation yields a figure of 14.761 billion wŏn for the 2009 People's Economy budget (calculated using the reported national budget of 36.9025 billion wŏn multiplied by 0.4).

99 "This year, 99.9% of the national budget was executed, an increase of 108.2% from the previous year" (*CCY 2011*, p. 290). Hence, the budget expenditure in 2010 is 39.9285 billion wŏn (calculated as 36.9025 billion wŏn multiplied by 1.082).

100 While the 2011 *CCY* remains tight-lipped about the exact percentage of the 2010 national budget allocated to the People's Economy, it offers clues through budgetary shifts. Notably, spending on defense held steady at 15.8%, but expenditures on the People's Economy, encompassing critical elements like free education, healthcare, and social services, dipped by 6% compared to 2009.

Given the typical 40% share of the People's Economy in the national budget, this drop might seem puzzling. However, a closer look reveals that the decrease only represents 2.4% of the total budget allocation (calculated as 6% decrease of 40% share). With defense unchanged, the remaining 2.4% shift appears to have been redistributed elsewhere in the national budget, resulting in a slightly smaller share for the Peoples Economy in 2010. Therefore, we can estimate that the 2010 People's Economy budget stood at 15.0131 billion wŏn, calculated as 37.6% (40% – 2.4%) of the reported national budget expenditure of 39.9285 billion wŏn.

101 "The national budget was executed at a rate of 99.8%" (*CCY 2012*, p. 274). Therefore, the total amount of the national budget expenditure for 2011 is 41.67345 billion wŏn (calculated as 41.75696 billion wŏn multiplied by 0.998).

102 The 2012 *CCY* offers no specific details on the 2011 People's Economy budget. However, a clue emerges from the unwavering 15.8% allocated to Defense expenditures. This consistency, coupled with the lack of mention of any changes in People's Economy spending, suggests a continuation of the 40% allocation observed in 2010. Applying this assumption to the reported total national budget expenditure of 41.67344 billion wŏn yields an estimated 16.9767 billion wŏn (calculated as 42.4418 billion wŏn multiplied by 0.4) for the 2011 People's Economy budget.

103 "The national budget expenditure was executed at 99.6%" (*CCY 2013*, p. 366). Therefore, the total amount of national budget expenditure in 2012 was 45.4708 billion wŏn (as calculated as 45.6534 billion wŏn multiplied by 0.996).

104 In the 2013 *CCY*, the specific expenditure on the People's Economy was not detailed. Nevertheless, given that 38.9% of the national budget was allocated to people-oriented policies and social and cultural policies, and 15.9% was allocated to defense (*CCY 2013*, p. 366), which returned to normal levels, it can be inferred that the share of the People's Economy in the total budget was approximately 40%, a standard level. Therefore, the total amount of expenditure on the People's Economy in 2012 was estimated to be 18.1883 billion wŏn (calculated as 45.4708 billion wŏn multiplied by 0.4).

105 "The national budgetary expenditure plan was executed at 99.7% and increased to 105.6% compared to the previous year" (*CCY 2014*, p. 357). Therefore, the

total amount of national budget expenditures in 2013 was 48.0172 billion wŏn (calculated as 45.4708 billion wŏn multiplied by 1.056).

106 "The national budget spent 45.2% of the total expenditure on the economic construction sector to financially guarantee the investment to build a self-reliant economy, generate productive upsurge in various sectors of the People's Economy, including the agricultural sector, and usher in the peak period of construction" (*CCY 2014*, p. 357). Therefore, the expenditure on the People's Economy in 2013 was 21.7038 billion wŏn (calculated as 48.0172 billion wŏn multiplied by 0.452).

107 "The national budget expenditure plan was executed at 99.9%" (*CCY 2015*, p. 308).

108 "The national budget earmarks 46.7% of the total expenditure for the development of the People's Economy, supporting efforts to boost agricultural production, fortify the economic foundation for becoming a knowledge economy powerhouse, and usher in a prosperous period of construction" (*CCY 2015*, p. 308). Therefore, the expenditure on the People's Economy in 2014 was 23.9553 billion wŏn (calculated as 51.2961 billion wŏn multiplied by 0.467).

109 "The national budgetary expenditure plan was executed at 99.9%" (*CCY 2016*, p. 422).

110 "The national budget allocates 47.5% of the total expenditure to building an economic power and improving people's lives" (*CCY 2016*, p. 422). Therefore, the expenditure on People's Economy in 2015 was 25.5839 billion wŏn (calculated as 53.8609 billion wŏn multiplied by 0.475).

111 "The national budgetary expenditure plan was executed at a rate of 99.9%" (*CCY 2017*, p. 423).

112 "Using the 'Five-Year Strategy for National Economic Development' as a guide, 48.3% of the total expenditure was allocated to the People's Economy sector, including the electric power, coal, metal, chemical industry, and railroad transportation sectors, which contributed to demonstrating the power of the self-reliant economy and building a socialist economic powerhouse" (*CCY 2017*, p. 423). Therefore, the expenditure on the People's Economy in 2016 was 27.6537 billion wŏn (calculated as 57.2541 billion won multiplied by 0.483).

113 "The national budget expenditure plan was executed at 99.9%" (*CCY 2018*, p. 244).

114 "Guided by the 'Five-Year Strategy for National Economic Development,' 48.3% of the total expenditure was directed towards the People's Economy sector. This encompassed vital areas such as electric power, coal, metal, chemical industry, and railroad transportation, aiming to showcase the strength of the self-reliant economy and foster the establishment of a socialist economic powerhouse" (*CCY 2018*, p. 244). Therefore, the expenditure on the People's Economy in 2018 was 29.0087 billion wŏn (calculated as 60.0595 billion wŏn multiplied by 0.483).

115 Addressing the issue of "idle domestic and foreign currency," economist Yongnam Ch'oe proposed a strategy to leverage this untapped resource. He suggested a system that would incentivize individuals to entrust their savings to the State, offering both security and profit potential. This, he argued, would concentrate funds, and enable the state to effectively utilize them for strengthening the socialist system (Yongnam Ch'oe, op. citi., p. 83).

116 The following passage from Yŏngch'ŏl Han affirms that, following the adoption of the "Financial Institution Liability System," the majority of banks in the DPRK operated as "commercial banks":

The more actively commercial banks engage in financial activities for self-financing channels, the greater their business income will be, ensuring the balance of payments for the banks and generating more benefits for the country. Consequently, the Financial Institution Liability System utilizes various self-financing avenues to centralize the currency funds of all institutions and enterprises in banks.

This system ensures that currency transactions exclusively occur through banks, and it maximizes the mobilization and utilization of individuals' "idle currency," facilitating smooth currency transactions across all banking operations.

> (Yŏngch'ŏl Han, "Kŭmyunggigwan ch'aesanjewa kŭ unyŏngesŏ nasŏnŭn chungyomunje" (Important Issues in the Financial Institution Liability System and Its Operation), *KUAB* (2018) vol. 64, no. 1, p. 72)

117 In a January 2000 address to the responsible officials of the Party's Central Committee, Kim Jong Il articulated,

All nations are advancing their light industries in accordance with their unique circumstances, addressing their light industrial product requirements through the principle of interdependence. No country fulfills its entire demand for light industrial products by domestically manufacturing 100 percent of them ....

To address the essential requirement for light industrial products in the lives of our people, it is imperative to significantly diminish the prevailing light industrial production index, producing only what is essential and procuring additional goods for public consumption from other nations to satisfy the demand.

> (Kim Jong Il, "Inminsaenghwarŭl nop'inŭndesŏ nasŏnŭn myŏtkaji kwaŏbe tachayŏ chosŏllodongdang chungangwiwŏnhoe ch'aegimilgundŭlgwa han tamhwa (chuch'e 89(2000)nyŏn 1wŏl23il)" (On Some Tasks in Raising People's Life: A Discourse with the Responsible Officials of the Central Committee of the WPK (January 23, 2000)), *SWK 20*, pp. 88–89)

118 As per information from a Korean Chinese acquaintance with relatives residing in the DPRK who frequently visit the country, informal or unofficial markets persist alongside the officially recognized General Market. However, the significance of these informal markets has markedly declined since 2005, coinciding with the introduction of the pilot General Market in P'yŏngyang, Nasŏnjigu (Nasŏn District), and Shinŭiju, eventually extending nationwide. These General Markets absorbed and consolidated spontaneously established markets initiated by residents.

Similar to street vendors near or at the entrance of traditional markets in the Republic of Korea, vendors in these markets offer daily necessities at or near the entrance or exit of the General Market, often at prices lower than those within the market itself. Their ability to provide goods at reduced prices is believed to stem from their exemption from sales tax. Nevertheless, a combination of increased crackdowns by authorities and the expansion of the General Market has led to a decline in their numbers, making them increasingly rare sights since 2016.

119 Kim Jong Il, "Gwangbokchigusangŏpchungshimŭn inminsaenghwarhyangsange ibajihanŭn hyŏndaejŏgin sangŏppongsagijiida: Gwangbokchigusangŏpchungshimŭl hyŏnjijidohamyŏnsŏ ilgundŭlgwa han tamhwa (chuch'e 100(2011)nyŏn 12wŏl15il)" (The Kwangbok District Commercial Center is a Modern Commercial Service Base Contributing to the Improvement of People's Lives: A Discourse with the Workers During the Local Guidance of the Light Welfare Commercial Center (December 15, 2011)), *SWK 25*, p. 521.

120 Kim Jong Il, "Che2ch'a p'yŏngyangje1paek'wajŏmsangp'umjŏnshihoejangŭl torabomyŏnsŏ ilgundŭlgwa han tamhwa(chuch'e 100(2011)nyŏn 7wŏl10il)" (A Discourse with the Officials While Visiting the Exhibition Hall of the Second P'yŏngyang First Department Store (July 10, 2011)), *SWK 25*, p. 345.

121 Kim Jong Un, "Kyŏngaehanŭn kimjŏngŭndongjikkesŏ chosŏllodongdang chungangwiwŏnhoe 2013nyŏn 3wŏlchŏnwŏnhoeŭiesŏ hashin pogo" (Concluding Speech at the March 2013 Plenary Meeting of the Central Committee of the Worker's Party of Korea), *Rodong Sinmun* (March 14, 2013).

122 According to the *CCY*, the following light-industrial plants have been rehabilitated and modernized under Kim Jong Un's local guidance: Taedonggangt'ailgongjang (Taedonggang Tile Factory) (*CCY 2013*, p. 177), 534Kunbudaegwanha chonghapshingnyogagonggongjang (General Food Processing Factory under the 534th Armed Force Unit) (*CCY 2014*, p. 115), P'yŏngyanggich'oshikp'umgongjang (P'yŏngyan Basic Food Factory) (*CCY 2014*, p. 132), Kimikch'ŏri saŏp'anŭn iryongp'umgongjang (Daily Necessities Manufacturing Factory managed by Ikch'ŏl Kim (*CCY 2014*, p. 187), Chosŏninmin'gun che354hoshingnyogongjang (Food Factory No. 354 of the Korean People's Army) (*CCY 2014*, p. 200), Chosŏninmin'gun 11wŏl2ilgongjang (Korean People Army November 2 Factory) (*CCY 2015*, p. 80), Kalmashingnyop'umgongjang (Kalma Food Factory (*CCY 2015*, p. 142), 10wŏl8ilgongjang (October 8 Factory) (*CCY 2015*, p. 147), 2wŏl20ilgongjang (February 20 Factory) (*CCY 2015*, p. 162), Che534kunbudaegwanha chonghapshingnyogagonggongjang (General Food Processing Plant under the authority of the 534th Armed Force) (*CCY 2015*, p. 163), P'yŏngyangshibŏsŏtkongjang (P'yŏngyang City Mushroom Factory) (*CCY 2016*, p. 109), Wŏnsan'gudugongjang (Wŏnsan Shoe Factory) (*CCY 2016*, p. 119), P'yŏngyanggangnaengigagonggongjang (P'yŏngyang Corn Factory) (*CCY 2016*, p. 200).

Chŏngsŏngjeyakchonghapkongjang (Chŏngsŏng Pharmaceutical Company) (*CCY 2016*, 2016, p. 211), P'yŏngyangmegigongjang (P'yŏngyang Catfish Factory) (*CCY 2016*, p. 222), P'yŏngyangŏrinishingnyop'umgongjang (P'yŏngyang Children's Food Factory) (*CCY 2016*, p. 226), August 25 Chosŏninmingun Che313kunbudaegwanha (Fishery Factory under the 313th Armed Force Unit of the Korean People's Army) (*CCY 2016*, p. 229), 8Wŏl25ilsusansaŏpso (May 9 Catfish Factory) (*CCY 2016*, p. 240).

123 Jiyŏng Kim, "Mallimaŭi shidaet'kyŏngjebuhŭnggwa saenghwarhyangsang 7 poda sujunnop'ŭn pongsarŭl wihan paek'wajŏmdŭrŭi kyŏngjaeng" (Department Stores Compete for Higher Level of Service in '*Manima*'s Era/Economic Revival and Livelihood Improvement – part 7), *Chosun Sinbo* (January 17, 2018). http://chosonsinbo.com/2018/01/17suk-10/.

124 Jiyŏng Kim, "<Int'ŏbyu> Sahoegwahagwŏn kyŏngjeyŏn'guso kimch'ŏlsojangr chosŏni soet'oega anin sangsŭngŭi kirŭl kŏnnŭn riyu (Interview with Ch'ŏlso Kim, Director of the Institute of Economics at the DPRK Academy of Social Sciences: The Reason for the DPRK's Path to Rise, Not Decline," *Chosun Sinbo* (January 5, 2018). http://chosonsinbo.com/2018/01/27suk-8/.

125 In the DPRK's unique economic landscape, markets play a crucial role in facilitating both business-to-business (B2B) and business-to-consumer (B2C) transactions. These markets, operating within a collectivist framework, allow for a degree of profit but prioritize collective goals over individual gain. Within this framework, B2B transactions ensure the smooth flow of goods and services between enterprises, while B2C interactions connect producers directly with consumers.

Distinct from these collectivist markets stands the General Market. This market operates outside the collectivist framework, primarily driven by profit motives. Here, consumers engage in peer-to-peer (C2C) transactions, buying and selling goods and services for personal gain.

126 Despite the considerable attention drawn to this issue, there are only a few academic works available that delve into the topic. One notable example is the research conducted by Seung-Ho Jung, Ohik Kwon, and Sung Min Mun, titled "Dollarization, Seigniorage, and Prices: The Case of North Korea," published in *Emerging Markets Finance and Trade* in 2017 (vol. 53, issue 11, pp. 2463–2475).

However, there are numerous reports and essays discussing the DPRK's 2009 currency reform and hyperinflation. Regrettably, the authenticity of these accounts is often assumed without undergoing rigorous scientific inquiry. To provide a glimpse into some of the prominent reports and essays on the matter, the following are worth mentioning:

Steve H. Hanke, "North Korea: From Hyperinflation to Dollarization?" *Center for Financial Stability* (July 13, 2013). https://centerforfinancialstability. org/oped/NorthKoreaJuly13.pdf; Nicholas Eberstadt, "North Korean Money Troubles - Kim Jong Il's currency revaluation is on the verge of sparking a hyperinflation," *Wall Street Journal* (January 11, 2010). https://www.wsj.com/ articles/SB10001424052748704500104574651090133811018; Bill Powell, "Economic Reform in North Korea: Nuking the Won," *Time* (Thursday, Dec. 03, 2009). https://content.time.com/time/world/article/0,8599,1945251,00. html; Jiro Ishimaru, "Hyperinflation and Worsening Food Supplies to The Troops," *Rimjin-gang Periodic Report* (Feb. 09, 2011). https://www.asiapress. org/rimjin-gang/2012/06/military/hyperinflation-food-supplies/.

127 Derived from Table 3.4, the 2000 national budget revenue is 20.4533 billion wŏn and that of 2009 amounts to 36.9765 billion wŏn. Applying these figures to the CAGR formula $[(FV/PV) \wedge (1/n) - 1]$, the result is 0.0680 or 6.8%, calculated as $((36.9765 \text{ billion} /20.4533 \text{ billion wŏn}) \wedge (1/9) - 1)$.

128 Based on national budget revenues in Table 3.4 (36.9765 billion wŏn in 2009 and 60.0595 billion wŏn in 2010), the calculated CAGR $[(FV/PV) \wedge (1/n) - 1]$ is 6.3%.

129 Jared Bonebright, "Is the US Heading for Hyperinflation?" *Michigan Journal of Economics* (November 22, 2021). https://sites.lsa.umich.edu/mje/2021/ 11/22/is-the-us-heading-for-hyperinflation/.

130 In this realm, inflation indeed occurred, likely stemming from a monetary policy conceived by Namki Pak, who served as the Director of the Planning and Financing Bureau within the WPK until 2009. This is evident in Wŏnkyŏng Ri's discourse in *ER*:

> The pivotal concern here lies in ensuring that we do not succumb to even the slightest inclination to overly prioritize the monetary sphere as the fundamental mechanism for enhancing economic management. It is imperative that we guard against any tendency to view the monetary sphere as the primary tool for navigating through challenging economic circumstances.
>
> This inclination to prioritize the monetary sphere as the primary instrument for addressing challenging economic conditions stems from a misguided bias that overestimates the significance and role of the monetary domain within socialist society. It is crucial to recognize that the notion equating money and monetary circulation as the "bedrock of social reproduction," and **the belief that the socialist state can "actively regulate and control the reproduction process" through the manipulation of monetary circulation, represents a distinctly right-wing perspective** (emphasis added).

> Should such a perspective gain traction and influence monetary circulation practices, it could result in the adoption of capitalist monetary regulatory methodologies and an exaggerated emphasis on the role of the monetary sphere across all economic activities. This, in turn, could distort the implementation of the economic management ideology advocated by our Party and impede the proper realization of the Party's intent to prioritize production enhancement.
>
> (Wŏnkyŏng Ri, "Hwap'ye, hwap'yeryut'ongŭn kyehoekchŏkkyŏngjegwalliŭi pojojŏksudan (Currency and Currency Circulation are Auxiliary Means of Planned Economic Management.), *ER* (2009), no. 3, p. 40)

> Ri articulated the aforementioned sentiments upon observing a policy aimed at increasing the money supply, a policy that manifested in reality. Considering the Bureau of Planning and Financing of the WPK held the highest authority in DPRK's monetary policy, it is evident that Ri's criticism was directed at the Bureau.

While Namki Pak's reported execution in 2010 has been attributed to the failed currency reform, his tenure as Director of the Planning and Financing Bureau until 2009 suggests an alternative explanation. It's possible that his execution, if indeed it occurred, was not a direct consequence of the reform's failure but, rather, a result of his controversial policy of expanding the money supply.

131 Ch'anghyŏk Ri explains the unique payment system of the DPRK in the following terms:

> In our country, the use of cash and cashless transactions is strictly divided based on various factors such as the purpose of the money, the goods being circulated, and the ownership of the entities involved. Cash is primarily used for individual or private transactions involving personal goods. Cashless transactions are reserved for situations where goods fulfill societal needs and the exchange occurs between state-owned entities
>
> (Ch'anghyŏk Ri, "Hwap'yeryut'ongbŏpch'igŭi chakyongnyŏngyŏge taehan yŏn'gu" (Study on Application Realm of the Law of Currency Circulation), *ER* (2005), no. 3, p. 26)

132 Based on Table 3.4, the CAGR between the 2014 national budget revenue (51.2961 billion wŏn) and the 2017 figure (60.0595 billion wŏn) is 5.4% $[((60.0595/51.2961)\wedge(1/3)-1)]$.

133 Péter Földávri, Bas van Leeuwen, and Dmitry Didenko, "Capital Formation and Economic Growth Under Central Planning and Transition: A Theoretical and Empirical Analysis," CA 1920–2008, *Acta Oeconomica* (2005) vol. 65, no. 1, p. 28.

134 Sŏngŭn Chang's elucidation of Pŏnsuip affirms the equivalence of these two metrics:

> When we subtract the cost of production from the enterprise's total sales revenue, we arrive at the Pŏnsuip, denoted as $(V + M)$. This income is subsequently allocated into two distinct segments: the State's portion (M) and the enterprise's portion (V).
>
> The State's share encompasses the State Enterprise Profit Revenue and the local maintenance fund, which play pivotal roles in bolstering both the national budget and local infrastructure upkeep. Conversely, the enterprise's share serves dual purposes: it caters to the living expenses of workers and contributes to the self-accumulation fund, fostering future investments and operational endeavors.
>
> (Sŏngŭn Chang, "Kongjang, kiŏpsoesŏ pŏnsuibŭi ponjilgwa kŭ punbaeesŏ nasŏnŭn wŏnch'ikchŏkyogu" (The Essence of Earned Income in Factories and Enterprises and the Principled Demand in Its Distribution), *ER* (2002), no. 4, p. 40)

135 This approach acknowledges the limitations in data availability and utilizes reasonable assumptions to provide an indirect estimate of the DPRK's GDP growth rate. However, it's important to recognize that these estimations might not be perfect due to potential variations in the relationships between the indicators and the influence of external factors.

136 In 1981, China embarked on a transformative journey of economic opening, reshaping its trajectory profoundly. As noted by an expert in China's economic development, that year marked a significant shift in the trading sector, with the country cautiously opening its doors to the world. Guided by the "adjust, reform, rectify, and improve" principle outlined in the Sixth Five-Year Plan (1981–1985), China actively pursued twin goals: bolstering exports in international markets and attracting foreign investment.

A key strategy to achieve these objectives was the establishment of Special Economic Zones. These zones, designated as hubs for experimentation and market-oriented reforms, played a pivotal role in China's economic opening (O. Drobotiuk, "Evolution of China's Economic Development Model," *Kitaêznavcì doslìdžennâ* (2019), no. 1, p. 83. https://doi.org/10.15407/chinesest2019.01.076).

As we have analyzed, in 2014, the DPRK implemented a new economic management system known as the SERM, which bears resemblance to China's economic reform measures during its early stages. Despite this initiative, the DPRK continues to be regarded as a closed economy due to stringent sanctions imposed by the United States and the United Nations. Consequently, it is pertinent to draw comparisons using the average of China's national budget expenditure in its GDP during its pre-opening period.

137 The provided table displays data from the World Bank on China's National Budget Expenditure (NBE) as a share of GDP (NBE/G) from 1970 to 1979.

Year	1970	1971	1972	1973	1974	1975	1976	1977	1978	1979
NBE/ GDP	11%	11.8	12%	11.5%	12%	11.7%	12.7%	12.5%	12.9%	13.8%

Source: Compiled by the author using data from the World Bank, "General Government Consumption Expenditure (% of GDP) – China." https://data.worldbank.org/indicator/NE.CON.GOVT.ZS?locations=CN.

As evident from the table, the NBE/G ratio fluctuated between 11% and 13.8% during this period, resulting in an average of 12.2%.

138 We can provide a speculative analysis to estimate the official exchange rate of the DPRK. Our preceding analysis illuminated the persistent existence of a substantial volume of "idle currency" within the DPRK's economy as of 2018. This raises apprehensions regarding the potential devaluation of the wŏn, even following the 2009 currency reform aimed at curbing inflation. While inflation did manifest in the peer-to-peer (C2C) goods transaction domain, it is imperative to discern how this inflation interrelates with the overarching inflationary trend in the DPRK, given its direct implications for the value of the wŏn. Access to official data, if attainable, could fortify this correlation.

The significant presence of "idle currency" intimates that inflation may not be entirely reined in, which could potentially impact the overall value of the wŏn vis-à-vis the US dollar. Nevertheless, quantifying this impact remains arduous owing to the absence of a publicly accessible official exchange rate. Although precise figures evade us, we can entertain some informed approximations.

Considering that the People's Economy traditionally encompasses roughly half of the national budget expenditure, an estimated 6% of the DPRK's GDP (derived from 0.122 multiplied by 0.5) may be susceptible to C2C inflation. The 2009 redenomination, at a ratio of 100:1, hints at a conceivable 100-fold surge in the money supply prior to the reform. Consequently, this suggests that 6% of the 2010 GDP, ballooned by 100 folds, translates to approximately 1,814.877 billion wŏn (calculated as 302.4795 billion wŏn multiplied by 0.06 and then multiplied by 100).

This figure roughly equates to a sixfold increase in money supply compared to the 2010 GDP of 327.2828 billion wŏn. If this sixfold increase is accurate, it could imply a commensurate sixfold devaluation of the wŏn. Given the pre-reform exchange rate of 2.2 wŏn per US dollar, this simplified scenario could signify a potential post-reform rate of 13.2 wŏn per US dollar.

While this calculation operates under the hypothetical assumption that trade dynamics do not impact the devaluation of the wŏn, this premise could hold validity, especially given the DPRK's historical tendency to maintain minimal trade activity and the imposition of severe economic sanctions during the specified period. However, it's important to acknowledge that additional economic and political variables, not addressed here, could potentially influence the real exchange rate. For the sake of simplicity in explanation, we choose not to delve into these factors.

Moving forward, the alignment of the money supply with the growth of Workers' Living Expenses (previously referred to as "V" from the Net National Material formula) becomes crucial. We have analyzed that Workers' Living Expenses serve as a significant driver behind GDP growth. With the CAGR of GDP during 2010–2017 calculated at 6% (derived as $((492.2010/327.2828)$ ^ $(1/7) -1))$, the growth rate of Workers' Living Expenses during the same period is determined to be at least 6%. This implies that the money supply also increased by at least 6% per annum during this timeframe.

Taking into account this annual growth of the money supply, the final exchange rate ratio could potentially be 19.8 wŏn (calculated as $13.2 \times (1 + 0.06)^7$) per US dollar. Extrapolating this rate to the 2015 GDP, which stood at 441.4829 billion wŏn, would yield a value of US$22.994 billion, closer to the US$27.412 billion reported in the Voluntary National Report.

Bibliography

Chang, Gyŏngshik. "Wŏne ŭihan t'ongjenŭn sahoejuŭiŭnhaengŭi chungyohan kinŭng" (Control by the Wŏn is an Important Function of the Socialist Bank), *KUAB* (2017), vol. 63, no. 2, pp. 61–63.

Chang, Sŏngŭn. "Kongjang, kiŏpsoesŏ pŏnsuibŭi ponjilgwa kŭ punbaeesŏ nasŏnŭn wŏnch'ikch'ŏkyogu" (The Essence of Earned Income in Factories and Enterprises and the Principled Demand in Its Distribution), *ER* (2002), no. 4, pp. 39–42.

Ch'a, Yŏngsu. "T'etaeanŭi saŏpch'egyenŭn kyŏngjegwalliesŏ sahoejuŭiwŏnch'ikŭl kuhyŏnhalsu itke hanŭn kajang uwŏrhan kyŏngjegwallich'egye" (Taean System is the Most Superior Economic Management System to Implement Socialist Principles in Economic Management), *KUAB* (2014), vol. 60, no. 4, p. 63–65.

Cho, Kilhyŏn. "Kiŏpch'edŭrŭi ch'aegimsŏnggwa ch'angbalsŏngŭl nop'ilsu itke inmin'gyŏngjegyehoeksaŏbŭl kaesŏnhagi wihan pangdo" (Ways to Improve the People's Economic Planning Project to Enhance the Responsibility and Creativity of Enterprises), *KUAB* (2014), vol. 60, no. 2, pp. 82–84.

Ch'oe, Yongnam. "Chaejŏngŭnhaengsaŏbesŏ chŏnhwanŭl irŭk'inŭn'gŏsŭn sahoejuŭiganggukkŏnsŏrŭi chungyoyogu" (Transforming the Financial Banking Business is an Important Requirement for Building a Socialist Power), *KUAB* (2018), vol. 64, no. 2, pp. 82–84.

Chŏng, Gwangyŏng. "Kiŏpsogigŭmgwa kŭ chŏngnimniyongesŏ nasŏnŭn chungyomunje" (Important Issues Arising from the Accumulation and Use of Enterprise Reserve Funds), *ER* (2005), no. 3, pp. 31–34.

Chŏng, Nyŏn. "Hyŏnshigi sangŏpkiŏpsojaejŏnggwalligaesŏnesŏ nasŏnŭn yogu" (The Needs of Improving the Financial Management of Commercial Enterprises), *ER* (2016), no. 4, pp. 38–39.

The Chosun Central News Agency. *Chosun Central Yearbook (CCY) 1998–2017*, P'yŏngyang: Worker's Party of Korea Publishing House, 1999–2018.

Drobotiuk, O. "Evolution of China's Economic Development Model," *Kitaêznavčì doslìdžennà* (2019), no. 1, pp. 76–93, accessed November 19, 2023. doi: https:// doi.org/10.15407/chinesest2019.01.076

Eberstadt, Nicholas. "North Korean Money Troubles - Kim Jong Il's currency revaluation is on the verge of sparking a hyperinflation." *Wall Street Journal*, last updated January 11, 2010. https://www.wsj.com/articles/SB10001424052748704500104574651090133811018

Földávri, Péter Bas van Leeuwen, and Dmitry Didenko. "Capital Formation and Economic Growth Under Central Planning and Transition: A Theoretical and Empirical Analysis, CA 1920–2008," *Acta Oeconomica* (2005), vol. 65 no. 1, pp. 27–50.

Government of the DPRK. *DPRK's Voluntary National Report on Implementation of the 2030 Agenda - Prepared in Consultation with National Partners in the DPRK (June 2021)*, accessed August 21, 2021. https://sustainabledevelopment.un.org/content/documents/282482021_VNR_Report_DPRK.pdf

Han, Unjŏng. "T'ehyŏnshigi sahoejuŭisahoe hwap'eryut'ongŭi konggohwashirhyŏnesŏ chegidoenŭn Chungyomunje" (Important Issues Raised by the Realization of the Consolidation of the Socialist Monetary System), *ER* (2016), no. 4, pp. 40–41.

Han, Yŏngch'ŏl. "Kŭmyunggigwan ch'aesanjewa kŭ unyŏngesŏ nasŏnŭn chungyomunje" (The Basic Direction of Financial Management and Method of Solving the Financial Problem revealed by Kimilsung-Kimjongilism), *KUAB* (2014), vol. 60, no. 2, pp. 61–63.

Han, Yŏngch'ŏl."Kŭmyunggigwan ch'aesanjewa kŭ unyŏngesŏ nasŏnŭn chungyomunje" (Important Issues in the Financial Institution Liability System and Its Operation), *KUAB* (2018), vol. 64, no. 1, pp. 70–72.

Hanke, Steve H. "North Korea: From Hyperinflation to Dollarization?" *Center for Financial Stability*, accessed June 3, 2019. https://centerforfinancialstability.org/oped/NorthKoreaJuly13.pdf

Hong, Jŭngbŏm. "Sahoejuŭisangŏbŭnhaenge kwanhan tokch'angjŏgin sasangniron" (An Original Theory of Socialist Commercial Banking), *KAUB* (2018), vol. 64, no. 1, pp. 61–63.

Hong, Yŏngŭi. "Ŭnhaengŭi yŏk'arŭl nop'inŭn kŏsŭn kyŏngjeganggukkŏnsŏresŏ nasŏnŭn chungyohan yogu" (It is an Important Demand Arising from Economic Development to Enhance the Role of Banks), *ER* (2014), no. 3, 74–76.

Ishimaru, Jiro. "Hyperinflation and Worsening Food Supplies to The Troops," *Periodic Report (Feb. 09, 2011) Rimjin-gang*, accessed April 9, 2019. https://www.asiapress.org/rimjin-gang/2012/06/military/hyperinflation-food-supplies/

Jung, Seung-Ho, Ohik Kwon, and Sung Min Mun. "Dollarization, Seigniorage, and Prices: The Case of North Korea," *Emerging Markets Finance and Trade* (2017), vol. 53, no. 11, pp. 2463–2475.

Kang, Ch'unsik. "Kŭmsokkongŏpkwa hwahakkongŏbŭl ssanggidungŭro hayŏ inmin'gyŏngjejŏnbanŭl hwalsŏnghwahago inminsaenghwarŭl hyangsangshik'inŭndesŏ nasŏnŭn chungyomunje" (The Important Problem of Revitalizing the Entire People's Economy and Improving People's Lives with the Metal and Chemical Industries as the Twins), *KUAB* (2014), vol. 60, no. 4, pp. 47–49.

Kang, Sŏngnam. "Widaehan ryŏngdoja kimjŏngiltongjikkesŏ sahoejuŭigyŏngjegwalliŭi kaesŏnwansŏnge ssaaollishin pulmyŏrŭi ŏpchŏk" (The Immortal Achievements of the Great Leader Kim Jong Il in Perfecting the Improvement of Socialist Economic Management), *KUAB* (2016), vol. 62, no. 1, pp. 151–153.

Kim, Chiyŏng. "Mallimaŭi shidaet'kyŏngjebuhŭnggwa saenghwarhyangsang 7 poda sujunnop'ŭn pongsarŭl wihan paek'wajŏmdŭrŭi kyŏngjaeng" (Department Stores Compete for Higher Level of Service in 'Manima's Era/Economic Revival and Livelihood Improvement – part 7), *Chosun Sinbo*, accessed on January 17, 2018a. http://chosonsinbo.com/2018/01/17suk-10/.

Kim, Chiyŏng. "<Int'ŏbyu> Sahoegwahagwŏn kyŏngjeyŏn'guso kimch'ŏlsojangr chosŏni soet'oega anin sangsŭngŭi kirŭl kŏnnŭn riyu" (Interview with Ch'ŏlso Kim, Director of the Institute of Economics at the DPRK Academy of Social Sciences: The Reason for the DPRK's Path to Rise, Not Decline), *Chosun Sinbo* (January 5, 2018b), accessed on January 17, 2018, http://chosonsinbo.com/2018/01/17suk-10/

Kim, Ch'ŏlsu. "Sahoejuŭigiŏpch'edŭresŏ ryudongjagŭm pojangjojigŭi chungyoyogu" (The Critical Need of Organizing Liquidity Fund Guarantee for Socialist Enterprises), *ER* (2016a), no. 3, pp. 50–51.

Kim, Ch'ŏlsu. "Hyŏnshigi sahoejuŭigiŏpch'aegimgwallijega shilchi ŭnŭl naedorong hagi wihan chaejŏngjŏkpangdo" (Financial Measures to Ensure that the Current Socialist Enterprise Responsibility Management System Actually Pays Off), *ER* (2018c), no. 4. pp. 56–57.

Kim, Ch'unghan. "Kagyŏkkwa saenghwalbirŭl kaejŏnghan kukkajŏkchoch'iga tŏ k'ŭn ŭnŭl naege haja" (Let Us Redouble Our Efforts to Ensure the National Measures Aimed at Revising Prices and Cost of Living Have a Tangible Impact on Our Daily Lives), *Kŭlloja* (2003), no. 3, pp. 53–55.

Kim, Gyŏngok. "T'esahoejuŭigiŏpch'edŭrŭi hwaktaedoen kyehoekkwŏn'gwa saengsanjojikkwŏnhaengsaŭi chungyoyogu" (Expanded Planning Rights of Socialist Enterprises and Important Requirements for the Exercise of Production Organization Rights), *ER* (2017a), no. 1, pp. 12–13.

Kim, Jong Il. "Inminsaenghhwarŭl nop'inŭndesŏ nasŏnŭn myŏtkaji kwaŏbe taehayŏ chosŏllodongdang chungangwiwŏnhoe ch'aegimilgundŭlgwa han tamhwa (chuch'e 89(2000)nyŏn 1wŏl23il)" (On Some Tasks in Raising People's Life: A Discourse with the Responsible Officials of the Central Committee of the WPK (January 23, 2000)), *SWK 20*, n.d.-a.

Kim, Jong Il. "P'yŏnganbuktoŭi kongŏppalchŏnesŏ saeroun chŏnhwanŭl irŭk'ilte taehayŏ: P'yŏnganbukto kongŏppumun saŏbŭl hyŏnjijidohamyŏnsŏ ilgundŭlgwa han tamhwa (chuch'100(2001)nyŏn 12wŏl15-16il)" (On Creating a New Turn in the Industrial Development in North P'yŏngan Province: A Discourse with Responsible Officials While Providing Local Guidance to the Industrial Sector in North P'yŏngan Province, (December 15–16, 2001)), *SWK 20*, n.d.-b.

Kim, Jong Il. "Hyŏnshigi tangsaŏpkwa kyŏngjesaŏbesŏ chungyohage chegidoenŭn myŏtkaji munjee taehayŏ: Chosŏllodongdang chungangwiwŏnhoe, naegakch'aegimilgundŭrap'esŏ han yŏnsŏl (chuch'e 94(2005)nyŏn 1wŏl9il)" (On Some Important Issues in Party Work and Economic Work at the Present Time: Speech Before the Central Committee of the WPK and the Responsible Officials of the Cabinet (January 9, 2005)), *SWK 21*, n.d.-c.

Kim, Jong Il. "Modŭn saŏbŭl ch'angjojŏkŭro hanŭn'gŏsŭn shidaewa hyŏngmyŏngbalchŏnŭi ch'ŏlshirhan yoguida: Chosŏllodongdang chungangwiwŏnhoe ch'aegimilgundŭlgwa han tamhwa (chuch'e 95(2006)nyŏn 2wŏl17il, 19il)" (Creativity in All Work is an Urgent Demand of the Times and Revolutionary Development: A Discourse with the Responsible Workers of the Central Committee of the WPK (2006 February 17 and 19)), *SWK 22*, n.d.-d.

Kim, Jong Il. "Uri shing ch'yulch'ŭimmolkongikaech'ŏk'an sŏnggwawa kyŏnghŏme t'odaehayŏ modŭn punyaesŏ ch'ŏmdanŭl tolp'ahaja: Chosŏllodongdong chungangwiwŏnhoe ch'aegimilgundŭlgwa han tamhwa (chuch'e 109(2010)nyŏn 1wŏl1il)" (Let Us Break Through to the Cutting Edge in All Fields Based on the Achievements and Experience of Pioneering Our Own CNC technology: Speech to the Responsible Officials of the Central Committee of the WPK, (January 1, 2010)), *SWK 24*, n.d.-e.

Kim, Jong Il. "Che2ch'a p'yŏngyangje1paek'wajŏmsangp'umjŏnshihoejangŭl torabomyŏnsŏ ilgundŭlgwa han tamhwa(chuch'e 100(2011)nyŏn 7wŏl10il)" (A Discourse with the Officials While Visiting the Exhibition Hall of the Second P'yŏngyang First Department Store (July 10, 2011)), *SWK 25*, n.d.-f.

Kim, Jong Il. "Gwangbokchigusangŏpchungshimŭn inminsaenghwarhyangsange ibajihanŭn hyŏndaejŏgin sangŏppongsagijiida: Gwangbokchigusangŏpchungshimŭl hyŏnjijidohamyŏnsŏ ilgundŭlgwa han tamhwa (chuch'e 100(2011)nyŏn 12wŏl15il)" (The Kwangbok District Commercial Center is a Modern Commercial Service Base Contributing to the Improvement of People's Lives: A Discourse with the Workers During the Local Guidance of the Light Welfare Commercial Center (December 15, 2011)), *SWK 25*, n.d.-g.

Kim, Ryŏna. "Chiyŏkpyŏl, kyech'ŭngbyŏl chuminŭi hwap'esujigyunhyŏngp'yojaksŏng nŭl wihan chip'yogyesanesŏ nasŏnŭn munje" (Problems in Calculating Indicators for Calculating the Balance of Payments of Residents by Region and Category), *ER* (2013), no. 3, p. 25–26.

Kim, Sŏngil. "Kyŏngjebalchŏnŭi soktowa kyunhyŏngjojongesŏ kyehoekkongganŭi hamnijŏngniyong" (Rational Use of Planning Sphere in Controlling the Speed and Balance of Economic Development), *ER* (2017b), no. 1, pp. 33–34.

Kim, Sunhak. "Hwap'eŭi anjŏngsŏngŭl pojanghanŭndesŏ nasŏnŭn chungyohan munje" (An Important Issue in Ensuring the Stability of the Currency), *KUAB* (2018d), vol. 64, no. 2, pp. 94–96.

Kim, Yŏnghŭng. "Sahoejuŭigiŏpch'aegimgwallijerŭl paro shilshihanŭndesŏ nasŏnŭn chungyohan munje (2016nyŏn11wŏl4il)" (Important Issues for Immediate Implementation of the SERMS), accessed November 4, 2016b, http://www.ryongnamsan.edu.kp/univ/success/social/part/814

Ku, Kŭmhyŏk. "Hyŏnshigi ŭnhaenggigwandŭrŭl sangŏbŭnhaenghwahanŭndesŏ nasŏnŭn chungyohan munje" (Important Issues in Commercializing Banking Institutions in the Current Era), *KUAB* (2016), vol. 62, no. 4, pp. 129–131.

Sŏnhŭi, O. "Shillirŭl nat'anaenŭn chip'yoŭi hamnijŏngniyong" (The Rational Use of Actual Profit Indicators), *ER* (2003), no. 3, pp. 26–29.

Powell, Bill. "Economic Reform in North Korea: Nuking the Won," *Time*, last updated December 03, 2009. https://content.time.com/time/world/article/0,8599,1945251,00.html

Pong, Hyangmi. "Saenghwalbiwa kagyŏgŭi kyunhyŏngŭl pojanghanŭn'gŏsŭn rodongja, samuwŏndŭrŭi saenghwarŭl anjŏnghyangsangshik'igi wihan chungyodambo" (Ensuring the Balance of Cost of Living and Prices is an Important Collateral for Improving the Livelihood Security of Laborers and Office Workers), *ER* (2017), no. 1, pp. 34–35.

Ri, Ch'anghyŏk. "Hwap'yeryut'ongbŏpch'igŭi chakyongnyŏngyŏge taehan yŏn'gu" (Study on Application Realm of the Law of Currency Circulation), *ER* (2005), no. 3, pp. 25–28.

Ri, Sunhwa. "Kyŏngjegyunhyŏngch'egyeesŏ suyowa konggŭbŭi kyunhyŏngi ch'ajihanŭn wich'iwa ŭiŭi" (The Place and Significance of the Balance of Supply and Demand in the Economic Equilibrium System), *ER* (2013), no. 1, pp. 17–18.

Ri, Wŏn'gyŏng. "Inmigyŏngjejŏkchagŭmsuyohaegyŏrŭi wŏnch'ikchŏkpangdo" (A Principled Approach to Solving the Demand for Funds in the People's Economy), *ER* (2002), no. 3, pp. 17–18.

Ri, Wŏn'gyŏng. "Hwap'ye, hwap'yeryut'ongŭn kyehoekchŏkkyŏngjegwalliŭi pojojŏksudan" (Currency and Currency Circulation are Auxiliary Means of Planned Economic Management), *ER* (2009), no. 3, pp. 39–42.

Rim, T'aesŏng. "Sahoejuŭigiŏpch'eŭi chejŏnggwalligwŏn" (Legislative Control of Socialist Enterprises), *ER* (2016), no. 1, pp. 40–41.

Tu, Kwangik. "Kiŏpch'edŭresŏŭi kagyŏkchejŏngbangbŏp" (Pricing Methods in Enterprise), *KUAB* (2014), vol. 60, no. 4, pp. 62–64.

World Bank. "General Government Consumption Expenditure (% of GDP) – China," accessed October 9, 2023. https://data.worldbank.org/indicator/NE.CON.GOVT.ZS?locations=CN

4 General Summary and Evaluation of the DPRK's Socialist Economic Construction and Economic Management System

4.1 The Kim Il Sung Era (1949–1994): Building Socialist Economic Construction and Management Based on Taean System

The economic endeavors undertaken by the DPRK serve as a litmus test for the feasibility of constructing a self-reliant economy within a nation grappling with arduous conditions for self-sufficiency. Moreover, they shed light on the extent to which such a feat can be accomplished. At the momentous Sixth Plenum of the Central Committee of the Workers' Party of Korea on August 5, 1953, which took place shortly after the armistice was signed, the DPRK's leadership unmistakably delineated its course toward self-reliant economic development by embracing the "strategy of prioritizing heavy industry while concurrently fostering the growth of light industry and agriculture" (also known as Heavy Industry Prioritization Strategy).

However, this strategy, which vested heavy industry as the principal recipient of State investments, was met with disdain by the so-called "Yŏnan Group" and the "Soviet Group," political factions that posed as rivals to the staunch supporters of Kim Il Sung within the DPRK. Particularly displeased by this approach was the Soviet Union, which had rendered substantial aid to the country throughout its liberation struggle and had lent support to its economic reconstruction. Between the months of June and July in 1956, leveraging Kim Il Sung's absence from the nation, the "Yŏnan Group" and the "Soviet Group," wielding a certain degree of influence within the Party and the Cabinet, initiated what would come to be known as the "August Sectarian Incident."

Politically, they demanded that the DPRK relinquish its system of singular leadership in favor of adopting a collective leadership model akin to that of the Soviet Union. Economically, they implored the nation to discard the "Heavy Industry Priority Strategy" and adopt an economic development trajectory that championed light industry. However, their efforts were met with resistance by Kim Il Sung's unwavering adherents, who possessed a more entrenched presence within the Party and the Cabinet. Consequently, the proponents of the "Heavy Industry Prioritization Strategy" managed to expel their opponents from the Party and the Cabinet, leading some of them to seek political

DOI: 10.4324/9781003481737-5

refuge in China and the Soviet Union. The strategy of prioritizing heavy industry thus became more firmly entrenched as the chosen path for the Party and the nation's economic construction.

Nonetheless, the Soviet Union's unaccommodating stance presented a significant hurdle for the DPRK's commitment to the Heavy Industry Prioritization Strategy. At that time, the Soviet Union was actively promoting the Council for Mutual Economic Assistance (COMECON), an economic integration organization within the socialist bloc, and had made its opposition to the Heavy Industry Prioritization Strategy abundantly clear. This strategy, which aimed to forge a self-reliant economy, ran counter to the Soviet Union's expectations, and as such, the Soviet Union demanded the DPRK's inclusion within COMECON.

When Kim Il Sung refused to acquiesce to their demands and proceeded to purge the "Yŏnan Group" and the "Soviet Group," who championed joining COMECON and opposed the "Heavy Industry Prioritization Strategy," the Soviet Union exerted pressure on the DPRK. Their response was to drastically reduce aid to the DPRK by over 50% during the three-year period of postwar recovery. This blow proved devastating to a nation that had placed heavy industry at the forefront of its economic development endeavors. To successfully pursue this trajectory, the nation required concentrated investment in heavy industry and access to substantial investment funds. At that time, nearly half of these crucial investment funds were sourced from the Soviet Union.

Kim Il Sung, faced with the inability to secure foreign investment, whether in the form of loans or otherwise, for the development of heavy industry in the DPRK, sought an alternative source of investment within the nation itself. He chose to directly address the working masses, sharing with them the country's challenges and encouraging increased production. In a remarkable display of responsiveness, the workers at the Kangsŏn Steel Mill, inspired by Kim Il Sung's appeal, achieved a near-miraculous production of 120,000 tons of steel from a capacity of 60,000 tons.

This resounding success prompted Kim Il Sung to initiate a nationwide series of localized campaigns aimed at rallying the working masses to bolster production. This movement, known as the Ch'ŏllima Movement, quickly became synonymous with the economic construction of the DPRK. Under its banner, the nation achieved an average annual growth rate of 36.6% during the Five-Year Plan period spanning from 1957 to 1961.

While the Ch'ŏllima Movement undeniably targeted production increases, it transcended mere economic goals. At its core, it embodied Kim Il Sung's vision of collectivism, emphasizing overcoming challenges through collaboration and unity. This ideology aimed to build an ideal communist society where individual contributions were seamlessly woven into a collective tapestry. Initially, the movement encouraged individual efforts to boost output, fostering a sense of shared purpose without necessarily mandating cooperation. However, it later evolved into the Ch'ŏllimajagŏppanundong (Ch'ŏllima Work Group Movement), which explicitly championed collaboration and teamwork as the key drivers of production.

This transformation was imperative because the products generated in factories, farms, and mines throughout the DPRK were the result of division of labor and collaboration among workers at a collective level, rather than the outcome of individual craftsmanship. It is important to note that the transition to collective production did not automatically instill a collectivist mindset in every worker, with their interests subservient to the group. Kim Il Sung, however, believed in the potential to cultivate and educate individuals into becoming such collectivist beings. The task and responsibility of Party cadres, therefore, was to nurture and guide members of each work group, enabling them to prioritize the interests of the collective over their own and wholeheartedly dedicate themselves to its advancement.

Consequently, the Ch'ŏllima Work Group Movement transcended mere expansionism aimed at increasing production; it served as a transformative process, a political endeavor that aimed to convert individual workers into collectivist (communist) human beings.[1] This aspect holds utmost significance when analyzing the distinctive characteristics of the DPRK's economic construction. Kim Il Sung's objectives extended beyond mere efficiency-driven economic growth, which sought to augment consumption by enhancing production efficiency.

Kim Il Sung firmly believed that as production was the result of collective labor, its maximization necessitated the highest degree of cooperation and coordination among workers. He firmly maintained that when cooperation and coordination were maximized, as demonstrated by the Kangsŏn Steel Mill's astonishing achievement in which the workers miraculously produced 120,000 tons of steel from a 60,000-ton capacity mill, in response to his appeal.[2] Consequently, in Kim Il Sung's perspective, transforming individuals into collectivist human beings, a task encompassing political work, took precedence over efficiently organizing production. This approach ensured the optimization and synergistic alignment of the collective's interests.

The Party Committees established within factories and enterprises played a crucial role in supervising the political affairs within their respective units, operating under the guidance of higher Party organizations. Larger factories or enterprises, such as those at the first or second level, fell under the jurisdiction of provincial Party Committees, while county Party Committees oversaw other factories or enterprises. It was the responsibility of Party cadres in each production unit to avoid two undesirable tendencies: "following the tail of the administrative officers" and "taking over the administrative and economic work."

The phrase "following the tail of the administrative officers" refers to the risk of Party cadres neglecting their political duties by overly prioritizing the administrative and economic tasks handled by administrative officers. This inclination toward economism can undermine the essential role of the Party in guiding the overall direction and objectives of the unit.[3] Conversely, "taking over the administrative and economic work" denotes the potential issue of Party cadres assuming the responsibilities traditionally assigned to managers in the workplace. This behavior can lead to bureaucratic tendencies, where Party cadres exert their influence with the backing of the Party, possibly hindering the efficient functioning of the unit.[4]

Ultimately, both scenarios pose challenges to the establishment of a truly socialist and communist society, as they hinder the unity and collaboration of workers, who should strive not solely for personal gain but for the collective welfare of all. It is essential to strike a balance where Party cadres fulfill their political responsibilities while recognizing the expertise and contributions of administrative officers and managers within the workplace. This harmony will facilitate the achievement of broader socialist objectives while ensuring the effective functioning of the economic system.

Kim Il Sung's pursuit of increased production was not driven solely by the goal of quantitative growth or increased consumption. It was crucial to establish the material foundation for a communist society through economic construction, but even more vital was the transformation of people's mindset toward communism (collectivism). By prioritizing the collective's interests over individual ones, production could be maximized, a proper socialist society could be established, and the transition to a communist society could become a reality.[5]

Unraveling the intricate tapestry of Kim Il Sung's instructions, the unique bond between Party cadres and workers cultivated during political work, and the visionary aspirations embedded within it presents a formidable challenge. While familiar frameworks like socialist and communist economic theory may fall short, James M. Burns' "Transformation Leadership Theory" offers a compelling lens through which we might glimpse its essence.

Burns posits two fundamental leadership styles: transactional and transformational. Transactional leadership incentivizes followers with tangible rewards like salary raises or bonuses for specific actions. This purely instrumental relationship fades once the transaction is complete. In contrast, transformational leadership elevates the relationship to a higher level of mutual motivation and ideological alignment. Morally grounded, it fosters ethical awareness and transforms both parties, merging them into a "unified whole."[6]

In the context of the DPRK, particularly within the framework of the Taean System, Burns' transformational leadership principles manifest in a distinctive manner. Rather than relying solely on hierarchical authority and traditional methods of command, Party cadres actively engage with workers on a personal level, integrating themselves within the workforce. This direct engagement involves the explanation and promotion of the Party's policies and collectivist ideology within the production areas, with the aim of fostering a deep-seated commitment to the collective cause over individual self-interest.

In addition to disseminating Party directives, it is imperative for cadres to attentively listen to the concerns and challenges voiced by the working masses. Collaboration with workers on the ground is essential, soliciting their input and involving them in decision-making processes. By immersing themselves in the working environment and engaging directly with workers, rather than solely issuing directives from administrative offices, cadres demonstrate a genuine commitment to understanding the realities faced by the workforce.

The effectiveness of this approach is exemplified by Kim Il Sung's experience at the Kangsŏn Steel Mill, where the principles of collectivism yielded remarkable results in terms of productivity. Kim Il Sung's personal visit to the mill deeply moved and inspired the workers, who recognized the significance of their contributions to addressing national issues, as emphasized in Kim's speech. Motivated by a shared sense of purpose, the workers pooled their efforts and worked synergistically, exceeding expectations. Despite Kim's modest request for a slight increase in steel production, the workforce produced twelve tons of steel from a six-ton smelting furnace.

By applying this approach consistently across all sectors and units of socialist construction, Kim Il Sung hoped that the DPRK can make significant strides toward its goal of becoming a communist society, representing a higher stage of social and historical development. As meticulously analyzed in Chapter 1, it became evident that Kim Il Sung had to confront the realities on the ground and make adjustments to his initial aspirations. While he did not officially abandon the "Unified and Detailed Planning System" (UDPS), he recognized the necessity of adapting it to a more feasible and practical approach. This realization led to the introduction of the "United Enterprise System" (UES), serving as a precursor to the "Socialist Enterprise Responsibility System" in its embryonic form.

Despite facing challenges and exhibiting some stubbornness in sticking to the UDPS, Kim remained committed to the pursuit of an economic management system that would prove practical and effective. Through a process of trial and error, he demonstrated his determination to find solutions that would align with the realities on the ground, even if it meant revising his original approach. Throughout these changes, one element of the economic management system remained consistent: the presence of the Party Committee within each production unit. This underscored the ongoing importance of the Party's presence and guidance in driving economic activities and upholding the principles of the Taean System.

Kim Il Sung's unwavering conviction regarding the indispensable role of the Party in economic construction was evident even before the establishment of the DPRK. This steadfast belief can be considered his unalterable principle and fundamental thesis on the subject. At the Fifth Session of the Central Committee of the WPK on February 13, 1949, he articulated his perspective in the following manner:

Our Party must not only dedicate itself to the arduous task of constructing a robust and independent nation but must also take charge of organizing and directing economic development while enhancing the quality of life for our people. The success of economic construction projects hinges on the strengthened guidance provided by the Party, aligning them with the Party's vision. This is crucial for the revitalization and growth of the national economy, the establishment of a solid material foundation for an independent country, and the systematic enhancement of the people's material and cultural well-being.

The Party's guidance of economic construction work is not merely an administrative or economic responsibility; it is, fundamentally, a political and organizational endeavor. However, it is observed that some Party organizations are currently conflating Party guidance with the State's administrative and economic guidance. It is imperative to recognize that the Party's role extends beyond mere administration, emphasizing the political and organizational dimensions that are integral to the successful execution of economic construction projects in alignment with the Party's overarching objectives.[7]

Kim Il Sung's theories on economic construction formed a cornerstone of his vision for the DPRK's development. He aimed to apply these theories comprehensively across all sectors of the economy, seeking to harness the collective efforts of the populace to propel economic growth. This ambition catalyzed the transformation of the Ch'ŏllima Movement from its origins as an individualistic endeavor into the Ch'ŏllima Work Group Movement, a broader initiative aimed at mobilizing collective labor to transform natural resources and elevate human consciousness.[8]

Central to Kim Il Sung's approach was the recognition of workers' consciousness and thinking as crucial drivers of progress in productive forces, particularly in the aftermath of socialist transformations in production relations. He believed that by cultivating a deep-seated communist awareness among workers, it would be possible to unlock their full potential and drive forward the country's economic development.

In pursuing economic construction, Kim Il Sung adopted a distinctive strategy that combined political and moral incentives with material stimuli. This multifaceted approach aimed to address both the ideological and practical aspects of economic growth. Political and moral incentives were employed to foster a sense of collective purpose and commitment to socialist ideals, while material stimuli provided tangible rewards for labor and productivity.

This methodology of economic construction set the DPRK apart from other socialist nations, such as the Soviet Union and China, as well as capitalist countries, which often relied on different economic models such as neoclassical or Keynesian approaches. By prioritizing consciousness and thought alongside material incentives, Kim Il Sung sought to create a uniquely DPRK-centric path to economic development, one that reflected the country's specific historical, cultural, and ideological context.

Building upon his ideas and theories on economic construction, Kim Il Sung established a unique economic management system known as the Taean System. This system embodies the Ch'ŏngsan-ri Spirit and Ch'ŏngsan-ri Method within the industrial sector. At its core, the Taean System emphasizes the comprehensive implementation of the "Revolutionary Mass Line" in production guidance.[9] Central to this system is the notion that cadres and workers should merge as a cohesive unit, with cadres actively engaging in production activities rather than confining themselves to their desks, merely issuing instructions and commands.

Contrasting with the prevailing "Manager Monolithic Management System,"[10] where the manager assumes sole responsibility for and oversees the management of each factory and enterprise, the Taean System called for managers and those people in the leadership position to immerse themselves in the production sites, working alongside the laborers to both produce and manage.[11] This approach fostered a sense of collective responsibility and collaboration, redefining the dynamics of economic management within the DPRK.

The significance of the Taean System as a novel framework for economic management and operation, incorporating and epitomizing Kim Il Sung's ideas and theories on economic construction, becomes evident through his own description of this system.

> The Taean System, the Ch'ŏngsan-ri Spirit, and the Ch'ŏngsan-ri Method are cornerstones of our Party's revolutionary line, guiding both economic management and leadership practices. These systems and methods demand that leading workers actively eliminate bureaucracy, engage directly with the workers they serve, prioritize political work that motivates and empowers the masses, and guide production while relying on the collective strengths of the Party organization and the people, not on individual limitations.[12]

Kim Il Sung unequivocally expressed that the Taean System represented a revolutionary approach to managing and operating the DPRK's economy, as he stated, "the Taean System is the most advanced communist economic guidance system that should be embraced by all sectors and enterprises."[13]

It becomes apparent that this system of economic management and operation embodied Kim Il Sung's ideas and theories on economic construction, emphasizing the primacy of political work and the mobilization of the masses to accomplish economic tasks.[14] The implementation of the Taean System across all units and sectors of the DPRK economy signaled a shift toward Party leadership and the prioritization of political work in economic construction.

Recognizing the Taean System as the embodiment of his economic principles, Kim Il Sung harbored the belief that this system could effectively address all the challenges faced in economic management within the DPRK. He went so far as to proclaim that "nothing would be impossible under the Taean System."[15] Fueled by his convictions and perceptions, the DPRK embraced a comprehensive economic management system known as the UDPS. Operating within the framework of the Taean System, this new approach aimed to eliminate uncertainties within the economy, enabling seamless integration of plans and ensuring detailed planning for every sector and unit. Such measures were essential for the realization of Kim Il Sung's vision for the DPRK's economic development.

The implementation of a comprehensive the UDPS proved to be an unattainable goal. Nevertheless, Kim Il Sung persisted in advocating for a centralized planning approach, while simultaneously criticizing the National Planning Commission and Party cadres for their perceived lack of quality and effort.

However, this centralized planning approach faced inherent limitations when it came to resolving the persistent issue of the "accumulation and consumption" imbalance.

As previously analyzed, the DPRK's pursuit of a self-reliant economic foundation, with a focus on heavy industry, placed consumption in a subordinate position to accumulation. This created an ongoing challenge as the country strived to build its economic strength without external assistance. The imbalance between "accumulation and consumption" was further intensified during the implementation of the First Seven-Year Plan (1961–1970) under the Parallel Route, which sought to simultaneously develop the economy and defense capabilities. The plan heavily concentrated investments in heavy industry, resulting in an unsustainable pattern of economic construction.

Originally intended to conclude in 1967, the First Seven-Year Plan faced significant disruptions due to the severe imbalance between heavy and light industries, as well as adverse effects on the material motivation of the working masses. Consequently, the plan was extended for an additional three years, ultimately concluding in 1970.

To rectify the imbalance between heavy and light industry, the DPRK opted for a six-year plan instead of the customary seven-year plan. Spanning from 1971 to 1976, this period witnessed the DPRK's concerted effort to catalyze a widespread activation of light industry across all units, employing the "Branch Factory System," as well as regions, through initiatives like the local industry program.

Furthermore, the "Local Budget System" was introduced down to the county level. This aimed to ease the financial burden on the central government by empowering local authorities to manage their own finances and livelihoods. This system operated outside the centralized planning sphere, prioritizing the development of local industries to meet the needs of regional consumers and foster self-sufficiency.

The focus on local industries continued throughout the Second Seven-Year Plan (1977–1984) under the "Light Industry Revolution" initiative. This involved establishing small- and medium-sized light industry factories across various regions, utilizing local resources and idle labor. This not only revived the earlier "8·3 Movement for Increasing Production of Consumer Goods" but also expanded its influence nationwide, further promoting the growth of light industry outside the central planning system.

Despite the challenges faced in balancing the "accumulation and consumption" dichotomy, the DPRK persisted in implementing various strategies and initiatives to address these concerns and propel its economic development forward.

Under the framework of the Taean System, the light industry revitalization movement and the corresponding development policy empowered factories and enterprises to take responsibility for the well-being and essential needs of their workers at the unit level. As this policy progressed, factories and enterprises gained greater autonomy. However, the effectiveness of the UDPS grew increasingly detached from reality. The intermittent mass mobilization campaigns further contributed to the system's notoriety for inefficiency. Nevertheless, Kim Il Sung placed a higher priority on preserving the framework of the Taean System, which entailed prioritizing political work and mobilizing the masses in economic endeavors, rather than strictly centralizing the national economic plan and meticulously detailing supply and demand.

In 1986, recognizing the impracticalities of the UDPS, Kim Il Sung spearheaded a transition from central planning to the UES. This strategic shift addressed the challenge of cumbersome planning by introducing "United Enterprises" and bolstering the "Independent Accounting System" (IAS) within factories and enterprises. This restructuring facilitated the emergence of internal markets within each United Enterprise, thereby underscoring the market's role through the reinforced IAS.

Kim Il Sung envisioned and aimed for this adaptation to prevent the market from evolving into a market-driven system, instead confining its function to that of a resource allocation mechanism. With his endorsement, the UES was fully enacted in 1986 with the objective to "strictly adhere to the principles and methods of socialist economic management, deepen and refine the State enterprise IAS based on the Taean System, and harmonize with the evolving realities and socialist economic laws of the DPRK." It represented a pioneering economic framework and operational model within the DPRK.

4.2 The Kim Jong Il Era (1995–2011): Two Means of Overcoming Arduous March: Military-First Politics and Advancement in Science and Technology

The DPRK embarked on the implementation of the Third Seven-Year Plan (1987–1993) under the banner of UES. Nevertheless, the unforeseen disintegration of the Soviet Union ushered in an unparalleled economic crisis that would be remembered as the "Arduous March." This crisis reverberated throughout the DPRK's economic landscape, leaving an indelible mark on its system.

The onset of the Arduous March brought about a cascade of profound transformations within the economic fabric of the DPRK. National income was mercilessly slashed by more than half, causing a cataclysmic halt to production activities in a multitude of factories, enterprises, and farms. Compounded by the inability of the country's rationing system to function effectively, the workforce found itself adrift, forsaking their workplaces in a desperate quest for sustenance. In this harrowing state of affairs, a unique phenomenon emerged organically: the birth of markets. As individuals sought to exchange goods and services based on their relative abundance, these markets gradually became an indispensable lifeline for the people.

Following the passing of Kim Il Sung in 1994, Kim Jong Il faced a critical and daunting challenge. The ideological foundation of the Party cadres had been visibly shaken, as there was a noticeable departure from the unwavering commitment to the Taean System. This system revolved around a strict Party-guided approach to economic construction. Instead, a growing inclination toward "economism" emerged, which placed greater emphasis on economic priorities over ideological considerations.[16] Recognizing the potential risks associated with this shift, Kim Jong Il steadfastly reaffirmed his unwavering dedication to the Taean System in economic construction, emphasizing the following:

> Championing ideological reform and political work is a fundamental principle and natural requirement of a socialist society ... In socialist construction, we must actively prioritize these efforts to educate the masses, ignite their revolutionary fervor and creativity, and unleash the full potential of socialism ... Relying on the capitalist method of using money to move people, the hallmark of capitalism, not only fail to foster such enthusiasm and dynamism but also corrupt and threaten the very fabric of our socialist system. By relentlessly prioritizing ideological and political work, our Party has harnessed the masses' revolutionary fervor and creativity to dramatically propel the revolution and construction, showcasing the undeniable superiority of socialism.[17]

However, Kim Jong Il encountered a formidable challenge as he sought to rebuild the economy while maintaining the principles of the Taean System. The stark reality was that a significant number of factories and enterprises were inactive, suspended due to a severe economic crisis that had caused national income to decline by over half.

The Party, which had traditionally played a central role in political mobilization and engagement with the working class, faced difficulties and limitations. In response to these critical circumstances, Kim Jong Il adopted an alternative approach, shifting his focus toward economic construction and reconstruction in collaboration with the military rather than relying solely on the Party apparatus.[18]

It is important to discern that this paradigm shift was not intended to transform the nation into a militarized entity, where military considerations reign supreme in the implementation of all national policies. Rather, the underlying principle was to utilize the military as a vehicle for revolutionary work, particularly in the realm of economic construction.

This approach emphasized the ideal of the "Revolutionary Soldier Spirit," embodying the ethos of warriors who wholeheartedly adhere to and execute the commands of the supreme commander, even if it entails sacrificing their lives. By placing the military at the forefront of economic construction and rallying them to toil for the greater good of the supreme commander and the people, regardless of material rewards, the ideology of the Revolutionary Soldier Spirit assumed paramount importance.

In essence, the "Military-First Politics" should be comprehended as an extension of Kim Il Sung's distinctive approach to economic construction. By elevating the ideology of the Revolutionary Soldier Spirit to a central position in economic reconstruction efforts, Kim Jong Il sought to perpetuate and expand upon the foundations laid by his predecessor, thereby forging a path forward amid the immense challenges that beset the nation.

As detailed in Chapter 2, following the passing of Kim Il Sung, certain individuals within the Party and Cabinet advocated for "Reform" and "Opening-up" in a manner reminiscent of the Soviet Union and China. However, Kim Jong Il firmly rejected these calls and resolutely affirming his commitment to upholding the quintessential tenets of Kim Il Sung's economic blueprint.[19] Central to this approach was the precedence accorded to ideology, surpassing all other considerations, and the prioritization of political endeavors over economic pursuits. In line with the specific circumstances of the DPRK at that time, this commitment materialized in what came to be known as the Military-First Politics. Kim Jong Il's ability to successfully implement and promote the Military-First Politics stemmed from the valuable experience gained in city of Kangge in Chagang Province. Notably, it had effectively addressed its energy challenges through the spirit of self-reliance, serving as a tangible demonstration of his commitment to upholding the principles of self-reliance.

The experience of Chagang Province stood as living proof that the ideology of self-reliance could yield practical solutions, further reinforcing Kim Jong Il's resolve to prioritize the nation's independent capabilities. By leveraging this example, Kim Jong Il effectively advanced the Military-First Politics agenda, underscoring the significance of self-reliance as a guiding principle in the pursuit of the nation's economic and political goals.

Kim Jong Il christened this epoch-defining feat of self-sustenance, primarily centered in the city of Kanggye within Chagang Province, as the "Spirit of Kanggye." The actualization of self-regeneration during such arduous circumstances constituted an empirical validation of the efficacy of Kim Il Sung's methodology for economic construction, which places unwavering emphasis on ideology and accords precedence to political endeavors over economic initiatives. As such, the experiential manifestation of self-regeneration centered around Chagang Province's Kanggye instilled the essence of the Kanggye Spirit, which was subsequently accentuated as a cardinal pillar of ideological tenets.

The Kanggye Spirit emerged as a veritable exemplar of self-renewal that all regions within the DPRK were urged to emulate during the trying period known as the Arduous March. This paradigm enabled Kim Jong Il to pursue pragmatic economic reconstruction not only for military purposes but also to enhance the welfare of the working class. Consequently, the profound experience of self-renewal, rooted in the environs of Kanggye, served a dual purpose: it legitimized the adherence of Kim Jong Il to the Kim Il Sung-style economic construction method, while simultaneously affording him the opportunity to allocate a substantial portion of State investment toward scientific and technological innovation.

The recognition of the imperative to foster economic growth by augmenting productivity through scientific and technological innovation was already apparent in Kim Il Sung's Third Seven-Year Plan. Nevertheless, it was the remarkable feat achieved at the Kangsŏn Steel Mill in 1957 that cemented Kim

Il Sung's conviction that any obstacles could be surmounted through political mobilization and the consolidation of the collective consciousness among the laboring masses. Emboldened by the success at the Kangsŏn Steel Mill, Kim Il Sung persisted in his endeavors. However, when subsequent efforts failed to yield substantial results, Kim Il Sung discerned that the most crucial task of the Third Seven-Year Plan (1987–1993) lay in "developing science and technology, fortifying the technological innovation movement, and advocating for the technological transformation of the People's Economy."

Essentially, Kim Il Sung came to recognize the limitations of relying solely on extensive sources of growth, such as increasing labor and capital, to drive the economic expansion of the DPRK over a span of three decades. He realized that sustainable economic progress could be achieved only by embracing intensive sources of growth, facilitated by technological innovation. However, he passed away before he could translate this realization into tangible policies.

It was Kim Jong Il, his successor, who incorporated this recognition at the core of the economic recovery strategy and subsequent development efforts. Kim Jong Il's adoption of this approach was not merely due to his role as a dutiful son and successor but also because he had no alternative. Kim Il Sung had already exhausted the potential of extensive sources, such as capital and labor, for driving growth in the country.

After successfully enduring the most challenging phase of the Arduous March, Kim Jong Il steered the nation's entire investments toward the advancement of science and technology. Concurrently, he revitalized and bolstered the role of the Party committee within the UES. In doing so, he continued the legacy of Kim Il Sung's economic construction methods, which prioritized the prominent role of ideology and political endeavors in driving economic development forward.

Kim Jong Il's strategy can be defined by a deliberate and strategic allocation of resources to a specific sector, which would serve as the foundation and catalyst for economic recovery and subsequent development. He identified Computerized Numerical Control (CNC) technology, which automates machine tools, as the linchpin for revitalizing the DPRK's economy.

Through meticulous planning, he directed a significant portion of the available resources toward the development and innovation of CNC technology. Kim Jong Il acknowledged the paramount importance of leveraging CNC technology as a transformative force to reshape and rejuvenate the economy, propelling it toward a new era of growth while enhancing self-reliance. For Kim Jong Il, economic reconstruction surpassed the mere restoration of the economy's size and growth rate to its pre-Arduous March state.[20]

The most profound economic crisis experienced by the DPRK, precipitated by the dissolution of the Soviet Union, stemmed from its incapacity to import coke and crude oil—essential resources for steel production and chemical fertilizer manufacturing, respectively. For a considerable period, the DPRK had been engaged in research and experimentation to produce steel without coke and fertilizer without crude oil. Ultimately, the breakthrough arrived in the form of "high-temperature air combustion technology," enabling the gasification of anthracite coal, an inexhaustible resource within the DPRK, as an alternative. Crucially, CNC technology played a pivotal role in facilitating the viability of this "high-temperature air combustion technology."

For Kim Jong Il, the conclusion of the Arduous March signaled that the economic reconstruction of the DPRK would rest upon amplifying the nation's capacity for self-renewal, colloquially referred to as "gaining hegemony over CNC technology." Beyond its significance in economic revitalization, CNC technology assumed indispensable importance in the production of nuclear and long-range missiles. Consequently, the advancement and refinement of CNC technology became the quintessential achievement upon which Kim Jong Il's aspiration of building a "Strong and Great Nation" since 1999 hinged.

In 2009, Kim Jong Il asserted that the DPRK had surpassed the most advanced CNC technology in the world. This claim, however, must be considered in light of the realities on the ground. The Chuch'e Steel production system, a method for steel production that circumvents the use of coke, along with the Chuch'e Fertilizer production system, which produces chemical fertilizers without relying on crude oil, and the Chuch'e Textile production system utilizing vinylon, a synthetic fiber derived from polyvinyl alcohol using abundant domestic resources like anthracite and limestone, were all being developed at advanced factories from 2010 onward. Notably, the vinylon production system required significantly less electricity compared to previous methods.

By 2011, the total national budget revenue, a proxy for the total national income of the DPRK, had surpassed pre–Arduous March levels, validating Kim Jong Il's strategy of prioritizing CNC technology as the primary driver of national economic reconstruction and concentrating investments in this area. This achievement not only bolstered the nation's economic recovery but also attested to the successful execution of Kim Jong Il's intended objectives.

Equally significant was the DPRK's pursuit of a delicate balance between "accumulation and consumption," a crucial goal that had been diligently pursued. Through intensive growth rooted in technological innovation, with the development of CNC technology serving as a central pillar, the DPRK had set its sights on achieving this equilibrium. By 2011, major factories and enterprises of national significance had completed their technological overhauls, prompting Kim Jong Il to shift his focus toward bolstering local guidance in the light industry sector. The Kwangbok District Commercial Center in P'yŏngyang bore witness to his final endeavors in providing local guidance.

It is essential to recognize that the extensive growth strategy pursued under Kim Il Sung had long contended with the challenge of resource scarcity. The reliance on limited domestic labor and capital for growth inevitably confronted the law of diminishing returns. As labor and capital inputs increase, the corresponding output diminishes. Hence, the DPRK's economy found itself trapped in a perpetual cycle, succumbing to the limitations imposed by the law of diminishing returns since the conclusion of the First Seven-Year Plan, as expounded upon in Chapter 1.

In essence, while acknowledging the accomplishments and progress made in the realm of technological innovation and economic reconstruction under Kim Jong Il's leadership, it is imperative to maintain a nuanced understanding of the underlying complexities and constraints that shaped the course of the DPRK's economic development.

Ironically, amid the most profound economic tribulations ever witnessed in its history, the DPRK directed its unwavering focus toward CNC technology innovation, an endeavor that demanded an overwhelming majority of the nation's available resources. This singular pursuit laid the groundwork for intensive growth, an approach that fosters economic expansion through technological innovation.

As the intensive growth system matured, projects for technological improvement proliferated within factories and enterprises in the light industry sector, resulting in substantial leaps in productivity and output. Under the leadership of Kim Jong Il, the DPRK's economy began constructing a framework for the intensive growth system, predicated on technological advancement, thereby establishing the foundation for achieving a delicate equilibrium between "accumulation and consumption," an elusive goal throughout Kim Il Sung's tenure.

Kim Jong Il, in the meanwhile, inherited Kim Il Sung's distinctive approach to economic construction, which placed paramount importance on the supremacy of ideas and the prioritization of political endeavors within the realm of economic development. However, faced with the unparalleled economic hardship endured during the Arduous March, wherein national income plummeted by more than half and numerous factories and enterprises grappled with the inability to conduct regular production activities, certain adjustments to the content and procedures of Kim Il Sung's economic construction methodology became inevitable to suit the prevailing circumstances.

While Kim Jong Il remained steadfast in his commitment to a collectivist framework that prioritized ideology and upheld the primacy of political work in economic construction, he recognized the need to address the shortcomings of communist measures prevalent during the Kim Il Sung era. With utmost discretion, so as not to openly contradict his predecessor's directives, he initiated changes in the management of the economy, aiming to minimize communist practices and maximize production efficiency.

This adjustment was executed within a system firmly rooted in the principles of socialist distribution, guided by an Independent Accounting System. Kim Jong Il referred to this approach as the "Basic Direction of Completion of Socialist Economic Management" (Basic Direction of Economic Management), which encapsulated the essence of his slogan: "Staunchly upholding socialist principles while achieving the greatest practical benefits (Shilli)." Faced with a severe economic crisis, the implementation of the Basic Direction of Economic Management marked a momentous transformation within the economy, commencing with the introduction of the "Economic Improvement Measures" on July 1, 2002.

On October 3, 2001, a significant and historic event unfolded when Kim Jong Il delivered a lecture known as the "10·3 Discourse" to the members of the Central Party Committee. This address elaborated on the Basic Direction of Economic Management. It marked a profound turning point in the direction of economic construction and the management system in the DPRK, as the insights shared during the "10·3 Discourse" reverberated throughout the nation, shaping its economic landscape in the years that followed. However, due to the ongoing challenges in the general economic situation, it took more than a decade for the specific contents of the discourse to materialize and firmly establish themselves within the nation's economic framework.

In 2014, precisely 13 years after the groundbreaking "10·3 Discourse," the principles articulated by Kim Jong Il found tangible expression and were institutionalized through the implementation of the 'Socialist Enterprise Responsibility Management System.' This system served as a significant milestone in the pursuit of completing socialist economic management, embodying the core tenets and guidelines outlined by Kim Jong Il. Its establishment held paramount importance as it aimed to pave the way for the conclusion of the Arduous March and the subsequent restoration of production normalcy in the DPRK.

As discussed earlier, it was not until 2011 that the DPRK emerged from the challenging era of the Arduous March. Interestingly, this same year, 2011, marked the passing of Kim Jong Il, signifying a significant leadership transition. Consequently, it took an additional three years from 2011 for the principles expounded in the "10·3 Discourse" to be effectively implemented and consolidated as a comprehensive system.

4.3 The Kim Jong Un Era (2012–): The Era of the Socialist Enterprise Responsibility Management System, the Embodiment of DPRK's Unique Economic Management System Based on the Legacies of Kim Il Sung and Kim Jong Il

On the night of December 17, 2011, following the passing of Kim Jong Il, Kim Jong Un convened a meeting at the Kŭmsusan Memorial Palace with members of the Political Bureau of the Party Central Committee. During this gathering, Kim Jong Un informed them of Kim Jong Il's demise, delivered a discourse highlighting his father's life and achievements, and provided details regarding the funeral arrangements. Notably, the conclusion of the speech featured significant remarks made by Kim Jong Un, as follows:

> We face a monumental challenge and sacred duty: carrying the revolutionary torch of General Kim Jong Il through unforeseen trials and tribulations … We must march united, forging an unbreakable bond, to build a strong socialist country on the Korean Peninsula, just as the

General envisioned. There can be no concessions, no dithering, on this path to actualizing his noble vision. As his unwavering disciple, I will carry his great work to the end, with unwavering commitment in every step … Though the General has passed, his words and policies remain the guiding light for our work and actions. Let us move forward vigorously, armed with his wisdom, dealing decisively with every challenge that arises.[21]

Essentially, in the aforementioned speech, Kim Jong Un affirmed his unwavering dedication to continuing the path paved by his late father, Kim Jong Il. He emphasized his commitment to closely follow in his father's footsteps and diligently work toward achieving the goals that were set. It is crucial to recognize that Kim Jong Il's path was firmly rooted in the principles established by Kim Il Sung. Thus, when Kim Jong Un expresses his intention to inherit Kim Jong Il's path, it inherently signifies his intention to carry forward the legacy of Kim Il Sung as well.

In the context of economic construction, Kim Jong Il had adopted and adapted the Kim Il Sung style of economic development, which emphasized prioritizing ideological principles and political projects. This approach aimed to achieve maximum practical benefits while upholding socialist ideals. The specifics of this system of socialist economic management were outlined in the "10·3 Discourse" by Kim Jong Il. However, the full implementation of this management system was not visible during his lifetime due to the need for the normalization of production.

Starting in 2010, the normalization of production gradually took place in sectors of national significance and later expanded to other heavy industries. As a result, the necessity for an economic management system that corresponded to this reality became evident. It was in 2012, soon after the passing of Kim Jong Il, that the need for such a system became more pronounced.

During much of 2012, Kim Jong Un focused his efforts on conducting field visits to various military units, emphasizing his commitment to continuing Kim Jong Il's Military-First Politics. In the "Report of the Central Committee of the Workers' Party of Korea to the March 2013 Plenum," Kim Jong Un highlighted the importance of institutionalizing the approach to achieving the completion of socialist economic management, which aimed to "obtain maximum practical benefits while upholding socialist principles." In his report, Kim Jong Un dedicated significant attention to the simultaneous development of nuclear armament capabilities and economic progress.

However, in the concluding remarks of the report, Kim Jong Un emphasized the importance of developing an effective economic management method that meets the requirements of genuine development. He stated, "We must study and refine our own economic management method to meet the demands of genuine development."

Kim Jong Un outlined the characteristics that this method should possess, emphasizing the need for a socialist enterprise management approach that upholds the principles of socialist ownership of the means of production, while granting enterprises the autonomy and creative freedom necessary for independent operations. The State plays a unifying role in ensuring that all enterprises fulfill their responsibilities and fulfill their roles as owners in the realms of production and management.[22] Kim Jong Un's explanation of the fundamental principles and guiding framework for this future economic management method echoed the path laid out by Kim Jong Il in the "10·3 Discourse" 13 years earlier.

Approximately one year later, the economic management method was officially named the "Socialist Enterprise Responsibility Management System" (SERMS). This system represented the realization of the instructions outlined by Kim Jong Il in his "10·3 Discourse." As discussed in Chapter 3, under the SERMS, DPRK enterprises display motivations and management strategies that share some similarities with capitalist counterparts. However, each enterprise is overseen by a Party Committee, meticulously organized, providing steadfast guidance. It is important to note that the underlying principle of this institutionalized guidance prioritizes the interests of the State, distinguishing these enterprises from *laissez-faire* capitalist counterparts that primarily focus on individual profit. Therefore, one could argue that these enterprises continue to operate within a collectivist framework firmly grounded in socialist principles.

In examining the categorization of the economic system in the DPRK within the context of comparative economic systems, one encounters a complex task. As detailed in Chapter 3, the SERMS defies easy classification as either a centralized planning system or a capitalist market system. Its distinctive characteristics set it apart from the capitalist market system, which operates on the principles of private property and the use of money as a medium of exchange, with income predominantly derived from sales transactions.

When it comes to economic indicators, the "Critical Indicators" display characteristics reminiscent of a centralized planning system. The State assumes the responsibility of planning and supplying the necessary raw materials and resources required by enterprises to execute their plans. The achievement of these Critical Indicators takes precedence over all other considerations. On the other hand, the "Central Indicators," excluding the Critical Indicators, are determined based on the capacities and needs of individual enterprises, allowing for the utilization of market mechanisms. However, it is important to note that this does not resemble a *laissez-faire* or free market.

While the market in the DPRK incorporates elements of collaboration and a controlled division of labor, it operates within a framework where the State exerts influence and control. Instead of imposing a detailed and unified plan, the State provides a direction and framework for economic development known as the "Economic Development Strategy."[23] This controlled approach ensures that enterprises fulfill the Central Indicators assigned to them.

A notable distinction between the SERMS and the UDPS lies in the active role assumed by enterprises within the former. Unlike the latter, where enterprises passively adhere to tightly interwoven plans controlled by the State, the SERMS empowers enterprises to actively implement Central Indicators in accordance with their own capacities. While prioritizing the fulfillment of these State-mandated indicators, enterprises operating within this system are also required to generate the majority of funds necessary for their operations, management, and maintenance through their own means. Consequently, the achievement of production targets and operating profits, as stipulated by self-imposed "Enterprise Indicators," assumes heightened importance.

It is crucial to recognize that although these Enterprise Indicators are implemented through a market mechanism, this market is distinct from the *laissez-faire* and free competitive markets typically associated with capitalist systems. In the DPRK, enterprises primarily secure funds for production and management through loans facilitated by State-controlled banks. This arrangement engenders a State-mediated form of market interaction known as "control by wŏn" (as extensively analyzed in Chapter 3), wherein the business strategies of enterprises are subject to constant monitoring and indirect state control.

What truly sets the SERMS apart from other economic management systems is the presence and integral role of Party Committees within enterprises. Across the entirety of the DPRK, Party Committees are established within all enterprises, assuming primary responsibility for safeguarding the State's interests and ensuring the steadfast implementation and achievement of Critical Indicators within Central Indicators, and the rest of Central Indicators.

While it is true that China also possesses Party committees in significant State-owned enterprises, such committees are not a universal presence and are limited in scope. Moreover, it is important to note that in China, individuals can indirectly possess ownership of enterprises and land through long-term leases, facilitating a degree of privatization of the means of production. This stark contrast makes direct comparisons with the DPRK challenging, as any form of privatization of the means of production remains strictly prohibited.

The fundamental duties and roles of Party Committees within DPRK enterprises have remained consistent throughout the eras of Kim Il Sung and Kim Jong Il. Their primary responsibility is to ensure the implementation of the Party's directives in the production and management activities of the enterprise, with a clear emphasis on political work. This distinctive focus underscores the uniqueness of the SERMS, which is exclusive to the DPRK.

As long as the DPRK continues to pursue its path of self-reliance without significant deviations and maintains its capacity for self-reliance, it is highly likely that the country will persist in adhering to and preserving its distinct socialist economic system, epitomized by the SERMS. This system, with its integration of political considerations into economic management, reflects the enduring commitment of the DPRK to its socialist principles.

Notes

1 In this context, Kim Il Sung underscored the paramount importance of preceding all endeavors in socialist construction with political work. He asserted,

> The true proprietors of production are the masses of producers, who possess an unparalleled understanding of production. Consequently, the most crucial assurance for advancing production and attaining success in productive activities lies in the execution of political work among Party members and workers. This involves elevating their levels of ideological consciousness and kindling their self-conscious enthusiasm. It represents the decisive superiority of socialism over capitalism and arises from the very essence of the socialist economic system.

> Kim Il Sung emphasized that the revolutionary imperative could not be realized solely through the strength of a few individuals but necessitated the united struggle of the entire populace. He stressed the obligation not to leave any Party members and workers lagging behind but to transform them into true revolutionaries through a communist approach.
>   He articulated,

> Our revolutionary task can only be achieved through the collective effort of all people. Therefore, it is imperative to ensure that every Party member and worker becomes a genuine revolutionary through communist reforms. If we can instill in everyone the heightened consciousness of a revolutionary, production will thrive, and any deficiencies in enterprise management can be rectified promptly.
>   (Kim Il Sung, "Sae hwan'gyŏnge matke kongŏbe taehan chidowa kwallirŭl kaesŏnhalte taehayŏ: Taeanjŏn'gigongjangjangwiwŏnhoe hwaktaehoeŭiesŏ han kyŏllon (1961nyen 12wel16il)" (On Improving the Guidance and Management of Industry to Meet the New Conditions: Conclusions at an Enlarged Meeting of the Committee of Factory Directors of the Taean (December 16, 1961)), *CWK 28*, pp. 278–280

2 Kim Il Sung, "Charyŏkkaengsaengŭi hyŏngmyŏngjŏngshinŭl nop'i parhwihayŏ sahoejuŭigyŏngjegŏnsŏrŭl tagŭch'ija kyŏngjebumun: Ch'aegimilgundŭlgwa han tamhwa (1987nyŏn 1wŏl 3il)" (Let's Build a Socialist Economy by Exerting the Revolutionary Spirit of Self-Renewal Highly: A Discourse with the Workers in Charge of the Economic Sector (January 3, 1987)), *CWK 85* (P'yŏngyang: WPK Publishing House, 2009), p. 10.

3 Kim Il Sung, "Tangŭl chilchŏkŭro konggohi hamyŏ kongŏpsaengsane taehan tangjŏkchidorŭl kaesŏnhalte taehayŏ: Chosŏllodongdang chungangwiwŏnhoe chŏngch'iwiwŏnhoesŏ han kyŏllon (1953nyŏn 6wŏl 4il)" (On Qualitatively Consolidating the Party and Improving Party Guidance of Industrial Production: Conclusions of the Political Commission of the Central Committee of the WPK (June 4, 1953), *CWK 15* (P'yŏngyang: WPK Publishing House, 1996), p. 408.

4 Kim Il Sung, "Tangsaŏbŭl kanghwahamyŏ naraŭi sallimsarirŭl alttŭrhage kkurilte taehayŏ: Chosŏllodongdang chungangwiwŏnhoe che4ki che12ch'ajŏnwŏnhoeŭiesŏ han kyŏllon (1965nyŏn 11wŏl 15–17il)" (On Strengthening the Party Work and Making the Country's Living Affordable: Conclusions at the Fourth Plenary Session of the Twelfth Central Committee of the WPK (November 15–17, 1965)), *CWK 36*, p. 35.

5 Kim Il Sung, "Ch'ŏllima shidaee mannŭn munhagyesurŭl ch'angjohaja (1960nyŏn 11wŏl 27il)" (Let's Create Literature and Art for the Age of Ch'ŏllima (November 27, 1960)), *CWK 26* (P'yŏngyang: WPK Publishing House, 2001), p. 290.

6 James McGregor Burns, *Leadership* (New York: Harpers, 1978), pp. 19–20.

7 Kim Il Sung, "Tangdanch'edŭrŭi saŏbŭl kaesŏn'ganghwahalte taehayŏ: Pukchosŏllodongdang chungangwiwŏnhoe che5ch'ahoeŭiesŏ han kyŏllon (1949nyŏn 2wŏl 13il)" (On Improving and Strengthening the Work of Party Organizations:

Conclusions at the Fifth Meeting of the Central Committee of the WPK (February 13, 1949)), *CWK 9* (P'yŏngyang: WPK Publishing House, 1994), p. 120.

8 Jongsu Ri, "Sahoejuŭi kŏnsŏrŭi sae immuwa chingmaeng tanch'eŭi kyoyangjŏng yŏk'al" (The New Task of Socialist Construction and the Educating Role of Labor Organizations), *Kŭlloja* (1962), no. 1, p. 38.

9 Kim Il Sung, "Taeanch'egyeŭi yogudaero sŏngŭi chidorŭl kaesŏnhaja kigyegongŏppumunilgunhyŏbŭihoeesŏ han yŏnsŏl (1962nyŏn 9wŏl 19il)" (Improve the Guidance of Provinces as Required by the Taean System: Speech to the All-Union Council of the Mechanical Industry Sector (September 19, 1962)) *CWK 29* (P'yŏngyang: WPK Publishing House, 2000), p. 404.

10 To borrow a phrase from Kim Il Sung, this is how he put it:

The Taean System is, in a word, a work system that embodies the revolutionary crowd line of our Party in economic management. It is a system in which the upper helps the lower and the known helps the unknown. **Thus, instead of the system of manager monolithic management, in which the manager alone is in charge of all the business** (emphasis is added), we demand that the collective guidance of the Party committee solve important problems in the management of enterprises, and that the technical preparatory work, including inspection and maintenance of facilities, drawing up designs, and preparing accessories, and the foresting of raw materials and materials, be carried out to normalize production.

(Kim Il Sung, "Chungshimgundangwiwŏnhoeŭi kwaŏbe taehayŏ: Chungshimgundangwiwŏnjangdŭrap'esŏ han yŏnsŏl (1963nyŏn 4wŏl 27il)" (On the Tasks of the Central Military Commission: Speech Before the Chairmen of the Core County Party Committees (April 27, 1963)), *CWK 31* (P'yŏngyang: WPK Publishing House, 2000), p. 91)

11 Kim Il Sung, "Chidoilgundŭrŭi tangsŏng, kyegŭpsŏng, inminsŏngŭl nop'imyŏ inmin'gyŏngjeŭi kwalliunyŏngsaŏbŭl kaesŏnhalte taehayŏ: Chosŏllodongdang chungangwiwŏnhoe che4ki che10ch'ajŏnwŏnhoeŭiesŏ han kyŏllon (1964nyŏn 12wŏl 19il)" (On Raising the Party, Class and People's Character of the Leading Workers and Improving the Work of Managing the People's Economy: Conclusions at the Tenth Plenum of the Fourth Central Committee of the WPK (December 19, 1964)), *CWK 33*, p. 464.

12 Kim Il Sung, "Yŏsŏtkaegoji chŏmnyŏngŭl wihan t'ujaengesŏ iruk'an sŏnggwarŭl tŏung konggo palchŏnshik'ija: Chosŏllodongdang chungangwiwŏnhoe che4ki che5ch'ajŏnwŏnhoeŭiesŏ han kyŏllon (1962nyŏn 12wŏl 14il)" (Let Us Further Consolidate and Develop the Achievements Made in the Struggle for the Occupation of the Six Highlands: Conclusions at the Fourth Plenary Session of the Fifth Central Committee of the WPK (December 14, 1962)), *CWK 30*, p. 88.

13 Kim Il Sung, "Sae hwan'gyŏnge matke kŏnsŏre taehan chidowa kwallirŭl kaesŏnhalte taehayŏ: kukkagŏnsŏrwiwŏnhoedangch'onghoeesŏ han yŏnsŏl (1965nyŏn 3wŏl 26il)" (On Improving the Guidance and Management of Construction to Fit the New Environment: Speech at the Party Congress of the National Construction Commission (March 26, 1965)), *CWK 28*, p. 93.

14 In a pivotal speech, Kim Il Sung laid bare the core principle of his Party's economic guidance: empowering the lower levels, mobilizing the masses through political work, and building economic strength upon their wisdom. He proclaimed the Taean System the "brilliant embodiment" of this principle, stating, "If all Party officials and economic managers work in accordance with its requirements, the economic guidance work will flourish" (Kim Il Sung, "Sae hwan'gyŏnge matke kŏnsŏre taehan chidowa kwallirŭl kaesŏnhalte taehayŏ: Kukkagŏnsŏrwiwŏnhoedangch'onghoeesŏ han yŏnsŏl (1965nyŏn 3wŏl 26il)" (On Improving the Guidance and Management of Construction to Fit the New Environment: Speech at the Party Congress of the National Construction Commission (March 26, 1965)), *CWK 35*, p. 92.

15 Kim Il Sung, "Kunŭi yŏk'arŭl kanghwahamyŏ chibanggongŏpkwa nongch'on'gyŏng-nirŭl tŏung palchŏnshik'yŏ inminsaenghwarŭl hwŏlssin nop'ija: Chibangdang min kyŏngjeilgunch'angsŏngyŏnsŏk'oeŭiesŏ han kyŏllon (1962nyŏn 8wŏl 8il)" (Strengthening the Role of the County and Further Developing Local Industry and Rural Economy to Make People's Living Standard Much Higher: Conclusions at the Conference of the Local Party and Economic Workers' Party (August 8, 1962)), *CWK 29*, p. 246.

16 "The Forced March within the Arduous March stands as the gravest test our revolution has faced," declared Kim Jong Il.

Following the Great Leader's passing, hostile forces converged, eager to extinguish our socialist beacon. They prophesied our demise within three years. Imperialist pressure, both political and military, intensified alongside economic strangulation. The fall of the global socialist market, coupled with relentless natural disasters, plunged us into food, raw material, and power shortages.

Substitute meals became commonplace, factories fell silent, and economic development faltered. Adding to this crucible, internal traitors and impure elements sought to exploit these hardships, sowing discord among the people and threatening the unity of party and masses.

> (Kim Jong Il, "Kanggyejŏngshinŭn konanŭi haenggunshigie ch'angjodoen sahoejuŭisuhojŏngshin, pulgurŭi t'ujaengjŏngshinida: Chosŏllodongdang chungangwiwŏnhoe ch'aegimilgundŭlgwa han tamhwa (chuch'e 97(2008)nyŏn 1wŏl30il)" (The Kanggye Spirit is the Spirit of Defending Socialism and the Indomitable Spirit of Struggle Created During the Arduous March: A Discourse with the Responsible Workers of the Central Committee of the WPK (January 30, 2008)), *SWK 23* (P'yŏngyang: WPK Publishing House, 2014), pp. 305–306

17 Kim Jong Il, "Sahoejuŭinŭn kwahagida: Chosŏllodongdang chungangwiwŏn-hoe kigwanjit'enrodongshinmunt'ene palp'yohan ronmun (chuch'e 83(1994) nyŏn 11wŏl 1il)" (Socialism is a Science: Thesis published in *Rodong Sinmun*, the organ of the Central Committee of the WPK (November 1, 1994), *SWK 18*, pp. 90–91.

18 Under "Military-First Politics," State investment prioritizes the military and related heavy industries, mirroring the earlier focus on heavy industry. However, this policy goes beyond mere investment prioritization. It is a system that elevates Kim Jong Il's ideology and imbues economic construction with a distinct revolutionary character, shaping the way reconstruction is carried out.

19 On this, Kim Jong Il said precisely the following.

Building a strong nation under the banner of self-renewal is the essence of constructing the DPRK. This ambitious project, fueled by our own strength, technology, and resources, may face challenges and setbacks, but we must not succumb to external calls for "Reform" and "Opening-up.".

The path to ruin lies in dependence on others. Ours is a self-renewing strong country ... We must make a new turn in Party work to build a strong country, with Party organizations and field forces leading the charge. Through effective organizational and political work, we must mobilize all party members and workers in the nationwide effort to build a strong nation.

> (Kim Jong Il, "Orhaerŭl kangsŏngdaegukkŏnsŏrŭi widaehanjŏnhwanŭi haero pinnaeija: Chosŏllodongdang chungangwiwŏnhoe ch'aegimilgundŭlgwa-han tamhwa (chuch'e 88(1999)nyŏn 1wŏl 1il)" (Let This Year Shine as a Year of Great Transformation in Building a Strong Country": A Discourse with the Responsible Workers of the Central Committee of the WPK (January 1, 1999)), *SWK 19*, pp. 449–450)

20 In this regard, Kim Jong Il said the following.

> Now some people think that when we say we are revitalizing the economy, we are simply restoring the economy to the same level as in the past, but that is a wrong view. Revitalizing the economy means, in essence, building an economy fit for the 21st century.
>
> (Kim Jong Il, "Kimilsŏnggunsajonghaptaehakkwa kimilsŏngjŏngch'idaehakŭl chungshihayŏya handa: Chosŏninmin'gun chihwisŏngwŏndŭlgwa han tamhwa (chuch'e 89(2000)nyŏn 2wŏl5il)" (Attention Should Be Given to the Kim Il Sung Military University and the Kim Il Sung Political University: A Discourse with Members of the Command Staff of the Korean People's Army (February 5, 2000)), *SWK 20*, p. 121)

21 Kim Jong Un, "Widaehan kimjŏngiltongjiŭi kogwihan saengaewa hyŏngmyŏngŏpch'ŏkŭn ch'ŏnch'umandaee kiri pinnal kŏshida: Chosŏllodongdang chungangwiwŏnhoe chŏngch'igung sŏngwŏndŭlgwa han tamhwa (chuch'e100(2011)nyŏn 12wŏl 17il)" (The Noble Life and Revolutionary Work of the Great Comrade Kim Jong Il will Shine for a Thousand and Ten Thousand Generations: A Discourse with Members of the Political Bureau of the Central Committee of the WPK (December 17, 2011)). http://www.dprktoday.com/index.php?type=98&no=627.

22 Kim Jong Un, "Kyŏngaehanŭn kimjŏngŭndongjikkesŏ chosŏllodongdang chungangwiwŏnhoe 2013nyŏn 3wŏlchŏnwŏnhoeŭiesŏ hashin pogo" (Concluding Speech at the March 2013 Plenary Meeting of the Central Committee of the Worker's Party of Korea), *Rodong Sinmun* (March 14, 2013).

23 Under Kim Jong Il, economic challenges, particularly during the Arduous March, made formulating detailed economic plans impractical. Even with some production normalization under Kim Jong Un, no such plan has been implemented. Following the introduction of the SERMS, the Cabinet outlined the DPRK's Five-Year Strategy for National Economic Development (2016–2020).

Unlike Kim Il Sung's detailed quantitative plans, this strategy charts a course for economic construction by focusing on broader objectives. As Kim Jong Un himself stated,

> the Five-Year Strategy aims to revitalize the entire economy, ensure balance among sectors, and lay the foundation for sustainable development. Key goals include revitalizing leading sectors and basic industries, increasing agricultural and light industrial production, and improving people's livelihoods through the 'Party's new path' and addressing the energy problem.
>
> (Kim Jong Un, "Chosŏllodongdang che7ch'adaehoeesŏ han tangjungangwiwŏnhoe saŏpch'onghwabogo" (Report on the Work of the Central Committee of the WPK at the 7th Congress of the WPK). http://www.dprktoday.com/index.php?type=98&no=323)

Bibliography

Burns, James McGregor. *Leadership*, New York: Harpers, 1978.

Kim, Il Sung. "Tangdanch'edŭrŭi saŏbŭl kaesŏn'ganghwahalte taehayŏ: Pukchosŏllodongdang chungangwiwŏnhoe che5ch'ahoeŭiesŏ han kyŏllon (1949nyŏn 2wŏl 13il)" (On Improving and Strengthening the Work of Party Organizations: Conclusions at the Fifth Meeting of the Central Committee of the WPK (February 13, 1949)), *CWK 9*, P'yŏngyang: WPK Publishing House, 1994.

Kim, Il Sung. "Tangŭl chilchŏkŭro konggohi hamyŏ kongŏpsaengsane taehan tangjŏkchidorŭl kaesŏnhalte taehayŏ: Chosŏllodongdang chungangwiwŏnhoe chŏngch'iwiwŏnhoeesŏ han kyŏllon (1953nyŏn 6wŏl 4il)" (On Qualitatively Consolidating the Party and Improving Party Guidance of Industrial Production: Conclusions of the

Political Commission of the Central Committee of the WPK (June 4, 1953)), *CWK 15*, P'yŏngyang: WPK Publishing House, 1996.

Kim, Il Sung. "Ch'ŏllima shidaee mannŭn munhagyesurŭl ch'angjohaja (1960nyŏn 11wŏl 27il)" (Let's Create Literature and Art for the Age of Ch'ŏllima (November 27, 1960)), *CWK 26*, P'yŏngyang: WPK Publishing House, 2001.

Kim, Il Sung. "Sae hwan'gyŏnge matke kŏnsŏre taehan chidowa kwallirŭl kaesŏnhalte taehayŏ: kukkagŏnsŏrwiwŏnhoedangch'onghoeesŏ han yŏnsŏl (1965nyŏn 3wŏl 26il)" (On Improving the Guidance and Management of Construction to Fit the New Environment: Speech at the Party Congress of the National Construction Commission (March 26, 1965)), *CWK 28*, n.d.-a

Kim, Il Sung. "Sae hwan'gyŏnge matke kongŏbe taehan chidowa kwallirŭl kaesŏnhalte taehayŏ: Taeanjŏn'gigongjangjangwiwŏnhoe hwaktaehoeŭiesŏ han kyŏllon (1961nyen 12wel16il)" (On Improving the Guidance and Management of Industry to Meet the New Conditions: Conclusions at an Enlarged Meeting of the Committee of Factory Directors of the Taean (December 16, 1961)), *CWK 28*, n.d.-b

Kim, Il Sung. "Kunŭi yŏk'arŭl kanghwahamyŏ chibanggongŏpkwa nongch'on'gyŏngnirŭl tŏung palchŏnshik'yŏ inminsaenghwarŭl hwŏlssin nop'ija: Chibangdang min kyŏngjeil-gunch'angsŏngyŏnsŏk'oeŭiesŏ han kyŏllon (1962nyŏn 8wŏl 8il)" (Strengthening the Role of the County and Further Developing Local Industry and Rural Economy to Make People's Living Standard Much Higher: Conclusions at the Conference of the Local Party and Economic Workers' Party (August 8, 1962)), *CWK 29*, n.d.-c

Kim, Il Sung. "Taeanch'egyeŭi yogudaero sŏngui chidorŭl kaesŏnhaja kigyegongŏppu-munilgunhyŏbŭihoeesŏ han yŏnsŏl (1962nyŏn 9wŏl 19il)" (Improve the Guidance of Provinces as Required by the Taean System: Speech to the All-Union Council of the Mechanical Industry Sector (September 19, 1962)), *CWK 29*, P'yŏngyang: WPK Publishing House, 2000a.

Kim, Il Sung. "Yŏsŏtkaegoji chŏmnyŏngŭl wihan t'ujaengesŏ iruk'an sŏnggwarŭl tŏung konggo palchŏnshik'ija: Chosŏllodongdang chungangwiwŏnhoe che4ki che5ch'ajŏnwŏnhoeŭiesŏ han kyŏllon (1962nyŏn 12wŏl 14il)" (Let Us Further Consolidate and Develop the Achievements Made in the Struggle for the Occupation of the Six Highlands: Conclusions at the Fourth Plenary Session of the Fifth Central Committee of the WPK (December 14, 1962)), *CWK 30*, n.d.-d

Kim, Il Sung. "Chungshimgundangwiwŏnhoeŭi kwaŏbe taehayŏ: Chungshim-gundangwiwŏnjangdŭrap'esŏ han yŏnsŏl (1963nyŏn 4wŏl 27il)" (On the Tasks of the Central Military Commission: Speech Before the Chairmen of the Core County Party Committees (April 27, 1963)), *CWK 31*, P'yŏngyang: WPK Publishing House, 2000b.

Kim, Il Sung. "Chidoilgundŭrŭi tangsŏng, kyegŭpsŏng, inminsŏngŭl nop'imyŏ inmin'gyŏngjeŭi kwalliunyŏngsaŏbŭl kaesŏnhalte taehayŏ: Chosŏllodongdang chun-gangwiwŏnhoe che4ki che10ch'ajŏnwŏnhoeŭiesŏ han kyŏllon (1964nyŏn 12wŏl 19il)" (On Raising the Party, Class and People's Character of the Leading Workers and Improving the Work of Managing the People's Economy: Conclusions at the Tenth Plenum of the Fourth Central Committee of the WPK (December 19, 1964)), *CWK 33*, n.d.-e

Kim, Il Sung. "Sae hwan'gyŏnge matke kŏnsŏre taehan chidowa kwallirŭl kaesŏnhalte taehayŏ: Kukkagŏnsŏrwiwŏnhoedangch'onghoeesŏ han yŏnsŏl (1965nyŏn 3wŏl 26il)" (On Improving the Guidance and Management of Construction to Fit the New Environment: Speech at the Party Congress of the National Construction Commission (March 26, 1965)), *CWK 35*, n.d.-f

Kim, Il Sung. "Tangsaŏbŭl kanghwahamyŏ naraŭi sallimsarirŭl alttŭrhage kkurilte taehayŏ: Chosŏllodongdang chungangwiwŏnhoe che4ki che12ch'ajŏnwŏn-hoeŭiesŏ han kyŏllon (1965nyŏn 11wŏl 15–17il)" (On Strengthening the Party Work and Making the Country's Living Affordable: Conclusions at the Fourth

Plenary Session of the Twelfth Central Committee of the WPK (November 15–17, 1965)), *CWK 36*, n.d.-g

Kim, Il Sung. "Charyŏkkaengsaengŭi hyŏngmyŏngjŏngshinŭl nop'i parhwihayŏ sahoe-juŭigyŏngjegŏnsŏrŭl tagŭch'ija kyŏngjebumun: Ch'aegimilgundŭlgwa han tamhwa (1987nyŏn 1wŏl 3il)" (Let's Build a Socialist Economy by Exerting the Revolutionary Spirit of Self-Renewal Highly: A Discourse with the Workers in Charge of the Economic Sector (January 3, 1987)), *CWK 85*, P'yŏngyang: WPK Publishing House, 2009.

Kim, Jong Il. "Sahoejuŭinŭn kwahagida: Chosŏllodongdang chungangwiwŏnhoe kig-wanjit'enrodongshinmunt'ene palp'yohan ronmun (chuch'e 83(1994)nyŏn 11wŏl 1il)" (Socialism is a Science: Thesis published in *Rodong Sinmun*, the organ of the Central Committee of the WPK (November 1, 1994)), *SWK 18*, n.d.-a

Kim, Jong Il. "Orhaerŭl kangsŏngdaegukkŏnsŏrŭi widaehanjŏnhwanŭi haero pin-naeija: Chosŏllodongdang chungangwiwŏnhoe ch'aegimilgundŭlgwahan tamhwa (chuch'e 88(1999)nyŏn 1wŏl 1il)" (Let This Year Shine as a Year of Great Transformation in Building a Strong Country: A Discourse with the Responsible Workers of the Central Committee of the WPK (January 1, 1999)), *SWK 19*, n.d.-b

Kim, Jong Il. "Kimilsŏnggunsajonghaptaehakkwa kimilsŏngjŏngch'idaehakŭl chungshi-hayŏya handa: Chosŏninmin'gun chihwisŏngwŏndŭlgwa han tamhwa (chuch'e 89(2000)nyŏn 2wŏl5il)" (Attention Should Be Given to the Kim Il Sung Military University and the Kim Il Sung Political University: A Discourse with Members of the Command Staff of the Korean People's Army (February 5, 2000)), *SWK 20*, n.d.-c

Kim, Jong Il. "Kanggyejŏngshinŭn konanŭi haenggunshigie ch'angjodoen sahoe-juŭisuhojŏngshin, pulgurŭi t'ujaengjŏngshinida: Chosŏllodongdang chungangwi-wŏnhoe ch'aegimilgundŭlgwa han tamhwa (chuch'e 97(2008)nyŏn 1wŏl30il)" (The Kanggye Spirit is the Spirit of Defending Socialism and the Indomitable Spirit of Struggle Created During the Arduous March: A Discourse with the Responsible Workers of the Central Committee of the WPK (January 30, 2008)), *SWK 23*, P'yŏngyang: WPK Publishing House, 2014.

Kim, Jong Un. "Widaehan kimjŏngil tongjŭi kogwihan saengaewa hyŏngmyŏngŏp-chŏkŭn ch'ŏnmandaee kiri pinnal kŏshimnida: Chosŏllodongdang chungangwiwŏn-hoe chŏngch'igung wiwŏndŭrege han tamhwa" (The Noble Life and Revolutionary Work of the Great Comrade Kim Jong Il will Shine for a Thousand and Ten Thousand Generations: A Discourse with Members of the Political Bureau of the Central Committee of the Workers' Party of Korea (December 17, 2011)), accessed May 17, 2021a, http://www.dprktoday.com/index.php?type=98&no=627.

Kim, Jong Un "Kyŏngaehanŭn kimjŏngŭndongjikkesŏ chosŏllodongdang chungang-wiwŏnhoe 2013nyŏn 3wŏlchŏnwŏnhoeŭiesŏ hashin pogo" (Concluding Speech at the March 2013 Plenary Meeting of the Central Committee of the Worker's Party of Korea), *Rodong Sinmun* (March 14, 2013).

Kim, Jong Un. "Chosŏllodongdang che7ch'adaehoesŏ han tangjungangwiwŏnhoe saŏpch'onghwabogo" (Report on the Work of the Central Committee of the WPK at the 7th Congress of the WPK), accessed December 3, 2021b, http://www.dprktoday.com/index.php?type=98&no=323.

Ri, Jongsu. "Sahoejuŭi kŏnsŏrŭi sae immuwa chingmaeng tanch'eŭi kyoyangjŏng yŏk'al" (The New Task of Socialist Construction and the Educating Role of Labor Organizations), *Kŭlloja* (1962), no. 1.

Epilogue

To what extent can the DPRK's economy thrive and progress under the guidance of socialist enterprise responsibility management? As expounded upon in Chapter 3, the DPRK's national budget revenue has surpassed the pre–Arduous March levels of 2011. In 2017, the national budget revenue amounted to 60.0595 billion wŏn, nearly 1.5 times the figure recorded in 1993, which stood at 40.5712 billion wŏn. From 2000 to 2017, the national budget revenue showed a steady annual growth rate of 6.5%. Additionally, as detailed in the appendix of Chapter 3, it is estimated that the DPRK's gross domestic product experienced an annual growth of 6.4% during the period from 2000 to 2017.

Considering the intricate interdependence of the DPRK's economic structure and its reliance on domestic factors, it is remarkable for the GDP to sustain an average annual growth rate of 6.4% over nearly two decades. Sustaining positive economic growth for close to 20 years in a self-sustaining manner presents a formidable challenge for a country the size of the DPRK, which, by no means, is a large nation.

In the 1990s, the DPRK encountered formidable economic challenges. The sturdy pillars of self-sustaining economic construction, namely, the metal and chemical industries, faced considerable hurdles. Operational difficulties besieged these vital sectors, as the DPRK grappled with the impediments of importing crucial resources like coke and crude oil. These precious commodities were indispensable for the production of steel and chemical fertilizers, and their scarcity induced disruptions across various industries and factories. As if this predicament were not dire enough, insufficiencies in agricultural output compounded the distress, leading to a widespread scarcity of food. The combined impact of these tribulations cast the entire economic construction into a relentless downward spiral of negative growth.

Through a persistent process of trial and error, the DPRK demonstrated resilience and managed to liberate itself from the grip of the devastating cycle it faced. Emerging victorious over the challenges of the Arduous March, the country achieved a remarkable feat. This notable accomplishment was realized by embracing a groundbreaking technology called the "hot air combustion process" or "anthracite gasification process." However, the success of this

DOI: 10.4324/9781003481737-6

technology hinged on the crucial role of Computerized Numerical Control (CNC). CNC machining enabled the precise and efficient creation of the complex components required for the gasification process. By implementing this revolutionary innovation, the DPRK achieved what appeared insurmountable at the time: the production of steel and chemical fertilizers without relying on the conventional dependencies of coke and crude oil.

This remarkable breakthrough not only liberated the DPRK from its reliance on scarce resources but also engendered significant advantages. By harnessing the power of the "anthracite gasification process" technology, the nation could substantially curtail electricity consumption during vinylon production. The commercialization of this technology not only marked the end of the grueling era of the Arduous March but also heralded a transformative shift in the DPRK's economic landscape. It signaled the country's capacity to build an economy rooted in the abundant reserves of coal (anthracite) instead of relying solely on oil. This achievement lays a robust groundwork for self-reliance, effectively harnessing the country's own resources to fuel economic development.[1] This reality is underscored by the following events:

In pivotal months, namely, September and December 2017, the United Nations Security Council, guided by the United States, passed resolutions 2375 and 2376, respectively. These resolutions were strategically crafted to primarily disrupt fuel supplies to the DPRK in response to its sixth nuclear test and long-range missile launch. This concerted international effort aimed to exert significant pressure on the DPRK regime, pushing for the abandonment of its nuclear ambitions and adherence to global disarmament norms.

Expanding on this initiative, President Trump took unprecedented action in February 2018 by unveiling a comprehensive set of sanctions against the DPRK. These measures targeted 27 organizations, 28 vessels, and 1 individual implicated in aiding the DPRK's evasion of sanctions and channeling funds toward nuclear and missile development. Such stringent measures were deemed necessary to impede the DPRK's nuclear advancements. The international community, led by the United States, not only aimed to deter direct actors but also extended punitive actions to those facilitating the DPRK's noncompliance with global sanctions.

China, a major exporter of crude oil and refined petroleum to the DPRK, played a crucial role in enforcing these sanctions. Fearing potential secondary boycotts by the United States, China actively supported and enforced the sanctions. The impact was palpable, resulting in a significant reduction in refined petroleum entering the DPRK throughout 2018.[2] However, despite concerted efforts to curtail the DPRK's economic resources, as of December 2023, the dire economic hardships reminiscent of the Arduous March, a period of acute food crisis and economic difficulties in the 1990s, have not resurfaced in the DPRK.[3]

Some argue that the DPRK's economy remains mired in a state reminiscent of the Arduous March, posing a significant threat to the regime. Consequently, they view the lifting of economic sanctions, coupled with external economic support, as the paramount objective of the DPRK's nuclear negotiations with the United States. However, in his "April 13, 2019, Administrative Policy Speech," Kim Jong Un made a decisive declaration.

He asserted that even if nuclear talks with the United States were to linger and economic sanctions were to persist, the DPRK would steadfastly pursue self-reliance, as it has done in the past. This unequivocal statement underscores the DPRK's commitment to economic construction firmly grounded in the principles of self-reliance. In the words of Kim Jong Un:

> As the U.S. imposes conditions that contradict the DPRK's fundamental interests for the lifting of any sanctions, we anticipate a prolonged confrontation with the U.S., and hostile powers will likely continue to enforce sanctions. Despite the enduring imposition of sanctions by hostile powers, we must ensure that this does not become a chronic obstacle to the advancement of our revolution …

> We must overcome these sanctions through self-reliance and self-motivation, just as we neutralized the prolonged nuclear threat with nuclear weapons. We possess the capacity and foundation for swift self-reliant development, which will invigorate our nation's economy and elevate it to a prominent position globally. Our invaluable strategic resources encompass the self-reliant economic foundation we have diligently built over decades, our robust scientific and technological capabilities, and the creative power of our patriotic people who are unwaveringly dedicated to self-reliance and revitalization.[4]

Kim Jong Un's speech vividly demonstrates that the DPRK's economic development strategy strives to achieve rapid growth and elevate the economy to new heights through self-reliant scientific and technological innovation. The strategic objective for innovation in science and technology within the DPRK revolves around the automation and intellectualization of all production processes and the establishment of unmanned factories and enterprises, referred to as the "Inmin'gyŏngjeŭi hyŏndaehwawa chŏngbohwa" (Modernization and Digitization of the People's Economy).

The realization of the "Modernization and Digitization of the People's Economy" is specifically attained through the modernization and digitization of individual factories and enterprises. This modernization and digitization materialize through the implementation of integrated production systems and unmanned labor systems. However, these systems necessitate the management and operation of all production and management activities through modern scientific and technological means, including information technology.

This is accomplished through a flexible production system and a business management information system equipped with information facilities, including CNC machine tools.[5] Consequently, the achievement of modernization and digitization in the People's Economy demands the development of state-of-the-art CNC technology and the establishment of the CNC industry based on it. These advancements will enhance the production capacity of each sector, factory, and enterprise, propelling the economy to grow at an accelerated pace and reach unprecedented levels.

As expounded earlier, in meticulous detail across Chapters 2 and 3, the DPRK has already laid the groundwork for a self-reliant economic foundation bolstered by cutting-edge CNC technology to embark on a path of self-renewal. The sweeping wave of the "Modernization and Digitization of the People's Economy" is permeating through the heavy industry sector, seeping into the light industry sector, and permeating every facet of the economy.

The establishment of the CNC industry and the realization of the "Modernization and Digitization of the People's Economy" hold the promise of multiplying productive capacity and propelling economic growth and development at an accelerated pace. However, attempting to cultivate and expand the DPRK's economy solely through the domestic market will encounter insurmountable obstacles. This predicament arises from the inherent limitations of the DPRK's domestic market in scale.

To address this challenge, the DPRK has established 20 economic development zones across each province as of 2019.[6] These zones are designed to attract foreign investment and promote joint corporations and ventures, reflecting the DPRK's commitment to utilizing economic development zones as catalysts for expansion and progress in its foreign economic relations. This strategic initiative builds upon the knowledge gained and successes and failures achieved in the establishment and advancement of special economic zones, including the Rasŏn Economic and Trade Zone, Hwanggŭmp'yŏng, and Wihwa Island Economic Zone.

According to a DPRK scholar, each economic development zone is meticulously planned and executed, taking into account the unique environment and distinctive characteristics of its respective province.[7] The other DPRK scholar elaborates on these zones:

> A defining trait shared by these zones is their strategic placement in highly advantageous regions conducive to fostering foreign economic relations. Geography, location, and the level of productive capacity development are all thoughtfully considered. Unlike other regions within the DPRK, these zones are specially designed and constructed to flourish in an export-oriented direction.[8]

If these zones fulfill their designated roles as envisioned, they will contribute to hastening the pace of economic growth and propelling the DPRK's development to even loftier heights. The DPRK's geographical proximity, nestled alongside China, which burgeons as the world's largest market, and the Russian Far East, harboring unparalleled underground resources, offers a fortuitous position.

The DPRK finds itself better positioned than any other nation to export to China and partake in and reap the rewards of the forthcoming development of the Russian Far East. Moreover, the DPRK's strategic geopolitical position affords it the opportunity to bridge maritime powers, spearheaded by the

United States and Japan, with continental powers, led by China and Russia. This facilitates economic cooperation, propelling the DPRK's economic growth and fostering its development.

Looking beyond the economic landscape of the Korean Peninsula, the cooperation between the DPRK and ROK brings forth mutual benefits, exemplified by the success of the Kaesŏng Industrial Complex.[9] If hostilities between the two Koreas were to be ultimately resolved, allowing entrepreneurs from both sides to freely invest in economic development zones and jointly manage and operate them, the entire Korean Peninsula would become a hub, igniting the convergence of maritime and continental forces. The immense positive economic outcomes that would arise from this collaboration would be shared and enjoyed by both the DPRK and the ROK.

From this perspective, esteemed global investor Jim Rogers, who recognizes the DPRK's economic growth and development potential, expressed his willingness to invest his entire wealth in the country.[10] Even Donald Trump, the 45th President of the United States and a renowned real estate developer, voiced his belief in the DPRK's remarkable potential, envisioning it as an economic and financial powerhouse in the near future.[11] However, the realization of this potential hinges on improved relations between the DPRK and the United States and the establishment of a peace system on the Korean Peninsula.

Yet, one must ponder the future of the DPRK's economy should the relations between the United States and the DPRK remain in a state of stagnation, failing to yield a much-anticipated peace regime. How would the nation navigate such circumstances? In response to the unprecedented economic crisis, the DPRK embarked on a distinctive path known as "Military-First Politics." This approach to economic construction placed ideology and political work at the forefront, constituting a framework of self-renewal.

Guided by this methodology, the DPRK confronted the daunting challenges of the Arduous March and emerged with enhanced rationality and efficiency in its economic endeavors. Key components, including the Financial Liability System, the Local Budget System, and the Market, played instrumental roles in the nation's perseverance. Furthermore, scientific and technological innovations were infused into the fabric of production, bolstering productivity.

These elements proved transformative, empowering the DPRK to surmount its most formidable economic crisis and ultimately bring an end to the era of the Arduous March. Over time, they were incorporated and institutionalized within the fabric of the Socialist Enterprise Responsibility Management System. By continually integrating more advanced and sophisticated scientific and technological innovations into economic construction, the DPRK's economy could experience accelerated growth and ascend to higher levels of development.

It is crucial to recognize the inherent limitations of the DPRK's domestic market in terms of its size. Without leveraging foreign trade and economic cooperation to drive development, the nation's economic growth and progress will be constrained, making it challenging for the DPRK to achieve President Trump's ambitious vision of becoming a formidable "Economic and Financial Powerhouse."

Nonetheless, the ultimate goal of the DPRK's economic construction is the realization of a "Sahoejuǔigyŏngjeganggukkŏnsŏl" (Socialist Economic Powerhouse), rooted in the principles of strong self-reliance, self-determination, and scientific and technological advancement. This vision aims to ensure domestic production of the material resources necessary for national defense, economic prosperity, and the well-being of its people. The envisioned power would embody a self-sustaining and knowledge-based economy, where science and technology seamlessly integrate with production, with high-tech industries leading the way in driving economic growth.[12]

As elucidated earlier, the attainment of this goal does not hinge solely on trade reliance or its utilization. Instead, the DPRK's ability to uphold and enhance its capacity for self-regeneration under the Socialist Enterprise Responsibility Management System, coupled with its unwavering commitment to continuous pursuit of scientific and technological innovations, as well as the swift integration of these innovations into economic construction, will determine the pace and success in realizing the goal of establishing a "Socialist Economic Powerhouse."

Notes

1 While oil (petroleum) remains essential for transportation, its usage is relatively limited in this sector. Railroads, which boast electrification of approximately 80%, play a dominant role, accounting for over 60% of passenger transportation and more than 90% of cargo transportation.

2 H. J. Kim's report offers valuable insights into China's refined oil exports to the DPRK from January to May 2018. As reported to the U.N. Security Council's 1718 Committee, the data reveals a fluctuating pattern of monthly exports: 201 tons in January, followed by 1,392 tons in February, 2,438 tons in March, 437 tons in April, and 1,451 tons in May, totaling approximately 47,400 barrels over five months.

While exceeding the U.N.'s one-month allowance, it's crucial to consider the annual limit of 500,000 barrels. This translates to a monthly average of about 41,000 barrels, significantly below the actual exports. This comparison highlights China's compliance with international sanctions. Furthermore, the 500,000-barrel annual limit represents a 75% reduction from the previous resolution's 2 million barrels, reflecting intensified efforts to curb the DPRK's access to refined oil (Hyun Jin Kim, "China Supplied 5,921 Tons of Refined Oil to North Korea in January-May, Far Below U.N. Sanctions Cap," *Voice of America* (July 6, 2018). https://www.voakorea.com/a/4469490.html.

3 In early 2020, amid the global COVID-19 pandemic, the DPRK took strict measures, including sealing its borders and suspending trade with other nations, including China. While this limited information flow from within the country, raising concerns about potential food shortages, there have been no reported deaths attributed to starvation as of December 2023. However, assessing the true situation remains challenging due to the isolation. The absence of international organizations like the FAO and WFP, who could conduct on-the-ground assessments, further hinders clear understanding.

It is important to note that during the devastating food shortages of the mid-1990s, the DPRK actively sought international aid. They welcomed WFP and FAO missions, granting them access to conduct field studies (Phillip H. Park, *Self-Reliance or Self-Destruction?: Success and Failure of the Democratic People's Republic of Korea's Development Strategy of Self-reliance 'Juche,'* (New York:

Routledge, 2001), p. 90). Comparing this historical context with the recent border closure, even affecting trade with China, suggests a potential belief in their ability to manage the food situation internally. Therefore, while conclusive evidence is limited, the absence of reported starvation deaths and historical aid-seeking behavior suggest that the DPRK hasn't experienced an "Arduous March"-level economic crisis as of December 2023.

4 Kim Jong Un, "Hyŏn tan'gyeesŏŭi sahoejuŭigŏnsŏlgwa konghwagukchŏngbuŭi taenaeoejŏngch'aege taehayŏ: Chosŏnminjujuŭiinmin'gonghwagung ch'oegoinminhoeŭi che1t'oekki chet'oech'ahoeŭiesŏ han shijŏngyŏnsŏl (chuch'e108(2019) nyŏn 4wŏl12il)" (On Socialist Construction at the Present Stage and the Internal and External Policies of the Government of the DPRK: Administrative Policy Speech Delivered at the First Session of the Fourth Supreme People's Assembly of the DPRK on April 12, 2019, *Rodong Sinmun* (April 13, 2019).

5 Ch'unkil Yang, "Chishikkyŏngjerŭl seunŭn kŏsŭn tangŭi saeroun chŏllyakchŏngnosŏnŭi chungyot'ujaengmokp'yo" (Building a Knowledge Economy is an Important Struggle Goal of the Party's New Strategic Line), *ER* (2018), no. 4, pp. 11–12.

6 Within the DPRK, an "Economic Development Zone" (EDZ) signifies a specially designated area within the country offering distinct economic advantages. These advantages are outlined in special State-enacted laws and regulations designed to attract domestic and foreign investment, technology, and resources.

Effectively, these zones function as isolated pockets with a more welcoming economic and legal climate for investors and businesses compared to the rest of the nation. Such areas offer various incentives and conveniences to encourage economic activity within their boundaries. (Myŏngsuk Ri, "Taeoegyŏngjegwan'gyeŭi hwaktaebalchŏnesŏ kyŏngjegaebalguga nonŭn yŏk'algwa kaebalgwajegyŏngjegaebalgugaebalsaŏbŭl chŏkkŭng milgonaganŭn'gŏsŭn hyŏnshigi uriap'e nasŏnŭn chungyohan kwaŏp" (The Role of Economic Development Zones in the Expansion of Foreign Economic Relations and the Development Task of Economic Development Zones is an Important Task in Front of Us at the Present Time), *KUAB* (2017), vol. 63, no. 3, p. 120).

7 The article authored by Myŏngjin Ri offers a comprehensive overview of the economic development zones established across various provinces in the DPRK:

In alignment with the forward-thinking initiative spearheaded by the supreme leader, Kim Jong Un. Remarkably, more than 20 specialized and comprehensive economic development zones have been declared in each province, exemplifying a concerted effort to foster multifaceted growth in foreign economic relations.

One exemplar is the Hŭngnam Industrial Development Zone, strategically focused on bonded processing, chemical production, catalyst manufacturing, machinery and equipment production, building materials, and pharmaceuticals. Its proximity to Hŭngnam Port, coupled with its historical legacy as a chemical and large-scale machinery manufacturing hub, positions it favorably for overseas exports.

Similarly, the Wado Export Processing Zone, situated centrally in P'yŏngyang and Namp'o City, stands as a pivotal nexus with direct access to neighboring countries and Southeast Asia. Its strategic location lends itself to advantageous domestic and foreign water transportation, facilitating the seamless flow of people, goods, and funds.

Presently, our nation possesses substantial potential to actively drive the development of regional economic zones. Endowed with favorable natural and geographical conditions, as well as abundant human and material resources, we are poised to engage in economic cooperation and exchanges with nations across the globe.

Drawing from over two decades of experience in establishing and operating economic zones such as the Rasŏn Economic and Trade Zone, and developing the Hwanggŭmp'yŏng and Wiwado Economic Zones, the DPRK has successfully established several key zones, including the Yalu River Economic Development Zone,

Ch'ŏngsu Tourism Development Zone, Manp'o Economic Development Zone, Wiwŏn Industrial Development Zone, Shinp'yŏng Tourism Development Zone, Songnim Export Processing Zone, Hyeondong Industrial Development Zone, Hŭngnam Industrial Development Zone, Pukch'ŏng Agricultural Development Zone, Ch'ŏngjin Economic Development Zone, Ŏrang Agricultural Development Zone, Onsŏng Island Tourism Development Zone, Hyesan Economic Development Zone, Ŭnjŏng High-tech Development Zone, Kangnyŏng International Green City Demonstration Zone, Waudo Export Processing Zone, Chindo Export Processing Zone, Ch'ŏngnam Industrial Development Zone, Sukch'ŏn Agricultural Development Zone, and the ongoing emphasis on developing the Wŏnsan-Kŭmgangsan International Tourism Zone. This robust framework underscores our commitment to fostering economic growth and international cooperation

(Myŏngjin Ri, "T'ekyŏngjegaebalgugaebalsaŏbŭl chŏkkŭng milgona-ganŭn'gŏsŭn hyŏnshigi uriap'e nasŏnŭn chungyohan kwaŏp" (Actively Pushing Forward with the Development of Economic Development Zones is an Important Task Before Us), *KUAB* (2015), vol. 61, no. 4, pp. 76–77)

8 Myŏngsuk Ri, "Taeoegyŏngjegwan'gyeŭi hwaktaebalchŏnesŏ kyŏngjegaebalguga nonŭn yŏk'algwa kaebalgwajegyŏngjegaebalgugaebalsaŏbŭl chŏkkŭng milgona-ganŭn'gŏsŭn hyŏnshigi uriap'e nasŏnŭn chungyohan kwaŏp" (The Role of Economic Development Zones in the Expansion of Foreign Economic Relations and the Development Task of Economic Development Zones is an Important Task in Front of Us at the Present Time), *KUAB* (2017), vol. 63, no. 3, p. 121.

9 The following table highlights the significant growth achieved by enterprises within the complex. Output revenue saw a remarkable increase of 43.8% annually between 2005 and 2015. This impressive growth reflects the success of the complex in fostering a productive economic environment.

Unit: 10,000 US$

Year	2005	2006	2007	2008	2009	2010	2011	2012	2013	2014	2015
Output Revenue	1,491	7,373	18,478	25,142	25,648	32,332	40,185	46,950	22,378	46,997	56,330

Source: Ministry of Unification, ROK (https://www.unikorea.go.kr/unikorea/business/statistics/).

10 "If I could, I would invest all of my money in North Korea," Rogers said in an interview with <CNN Money> on May 5, when asked if he would invest in the country. (Chiwŏn Ch'oe, "Segyejŏng t'ujaga chim rojŏsŭ t'epuk'ane chŏnjaesan t'ujahago shiptat'e" (Global Investor Jim Rogers Wants to Invest All His Money in North Korea), *Hankyoreh Newspaper* (Internet edition, May, 6 2015, 19:46). http://www.hani.co.kr/arti/international/globaleconomy/690045. html#csidx03357821d6b9206818f0c71e46bd02d.

11 "Our United States team has arrived in North Korea to make arrangements for the Summit between Kim Jong Un and myself. **I truly believe North Korea has brilliant potential and will be a great economic and financial Nation one day** (emphasis added). Kim Jong Un agrees with me on this. It will happen!" (Donald J. Trump@realDonaldTrump 5:09 AM – May 28, 2018. https://twitter.com/realdonaldtrump).

12 Kim Jong Un, "Hyŏn tan'gyeesŏŭi sahoejuŭigŏnsŏlgwa konghwagukchŏngbuŭi taenaeoejŏngch'aege taehayŏ: Chosŏnminjujuŭiinmin'gonghwagung ch'oegoin-minhoeŭi che1t'oekki chet'oech'ahoeŭiesŏ han shijŏngyŏnsŏl (chuch'e108(2019) nyŏn 4wŏl12il)" (On Socialist Construction at the Present Stage and the Internal and External Policies of the Government of the DPRK: Administrative Policy Speech Delivered at the First Session of the Fourth Supreme People's Assembly of the DPRK on April 12, 2019, *Rodong Sinmun* (April 13, 2019).

Postscript

As we finalize this book, recent updates from the DPRK offer insight into its GDP performance and economic condition spanning from 2020 to 2023. Let's integrate this fresh information into our analysis. On December 31, 2023, Kim Jong Un, in his "Report on the Ninth Enlarged Plenum of the 8th WPK Central Committee," presented crucial figures regarding GDP growth during this timeframe. He indicated,

> Compared with the total growth of the economic sector in 2020, the year preceding the 8th Party Congress, significant indices saw substantial increases in 2023. Production figures for critical sectors rose significantly, including a 3.5-fold increase in Samhwa iron, a 2.7-fold increase in pig iron, a 1.9-fold increase in rolled steel, a 5.1-fold increase in machine tools, a 1.4-fold increase in cement, a 1.3-fold increase in nitrogen fertilizer, and **a GDP growth of 1.4 times** (emphasis added).[1]

In essence, the DPRK's GDP surged by 140% during the 2020–2023 period. However, specific GDP figures for 2020, 2021, or 2023 were not provided in the report.

We have previously discussed in the appendix to Chapter 3 that the growth rate of national budget revenue aligns with the GDP growth rate in the DPRK. According to the January 12, 2021, edition of *Chosun Shinbo*, national budget revenues for the previous year were realized at a rate of 100.1%, marking a year-on-year growth of 104.3%.[2]

Furthermore, the DPRK Voluntary Report indicates that the DPRK's 2019 GDP stood at US$33,504 million. Utilizing this information, we estimate the DPRK's 2020 GDP at US$34,945 million (calculated as US$33,504 million multiplied by 1.043). Consequently, the DPRK's 2023 GDP is estimated at US$48,923 million (calculated as US$34,945 million multiplied by 1.4).

As we have discussed previously, inflation is not an issue in the DPRK's official transaction as these occur without cash; on the other hand, however, non-official transactions are not recorded and evaded the purview of State.[3] Accordingly, we may take the aforementioned GDP figures for 2020 and 2023 as real rather than

DOI: 10.4324/9781003481737-7

nominal. With these figures, we could calculate the CAGR of the DPRK's GDP during 2020–2023 period as 0.119 or 12% (calculated as ((US$48,923 ÷ US$34,945 million) ^ (1÷3) – 1).

Achieving a CAGR of 12% in GDP over three years is undoubtedly a remarkable feat. What makes it even more remarkable is the context: the DPRK implemented a complete border closure during this period to combat the spread of COVID–19, leading to the cessation of all international trade, notably with China. In essence, this substantial CAGR of 12% in GDP over three years was solely driven by internal efforts within the DPRK.

This exponential growth rate from 2020 to 2023, which is nearly two and a half times higher than the GDP growth rate of 5.1% recorded from 2015 to 2019, prompts profound interpretation. As extensively discussed in Chapters 2 and 3, the DPRK successfully surmounted the challenges akin to the "Arduous March" by fortifying its self-reliant capabilities through advancements in science and technology. Transitioning from an extensive growth strategy to an intensive one, anchored in harnessing advanced technology for economic development, enabled the DPRK to emerge from a protracted economic crisis.

This technological advancement, permeating across all sectors from heavy industry to light industry, facilitated exponential economic growth. This revitalized self-reliance not only shielded the country from the hardships of the Arduous March but also engendered a virtuous cycle of economic enhancement across all sectors. Each sector's interdependence effectively reinforced economic growth, evident in the remarkable two and a half times higher growth rate experienced from 2021 to 2023 compared to the preceding period from 2015 to 2019.

However, Kim Jong Un voiced concern over significant disparities in living conditions between the capital and the provinces, as well as between urban and rural areas. He urged corrective measures for this imbalance in an administrative policy speech titled "On the Tasks for the Reconstruction and Development of the Republic and the Welfare of the People," delivered at the Tenth Session of the 14th Supreme People's Assembly on January 15, 2024. Specifically, he stated:

> There is not a single factory in the provinces that is up to the demands of the times. This should no longer be ignored, but should be recognized … It is the immediate task before our government, and the desire of our Party, to shake off the century-old backwardness, reduce the gap between the capital and the provinces … We will directly control the policy task of building 20 modern local industrial factories every year, and we will execute it without fail to the level of Kimhwa County, so that within 10 years, all cities and counties in the country, in other words, the basic material and cultural living standards of all the people in the country, will be raised by one level.

We will name this policy of our Party, which aims to vigorously promote the development of local industry in order to raise the basic material and cultural living standards of the local people nationwide in the shortest possible time, as the "Local Development 20x10 Policy" and vigorously promote it. This is a gigantic transformation, different from what we have only talked about before, to shake off the centuries-old backwardness of the local area, to fulfill the long-cherished desire of the local people, and to bring about a change in the cognitive domain of our people. It is a great revolution![4]

Despite the observed phenomenon of GDP growth, a pressing issue persists in the DPRK economy: urban-rural disparity. Specifically, as highlighted by Kim Jong Un, living standards in rural areas starkly lag behind those in urban areas due to the absence of modern factories catering to the needs of rural inhabitants. This urban–rural disparity mirrors a classic challenge in development economics, for which numerous solutions have been proposed by economists. However, most of these solutions are grounded in capitalist market economics, leveraging market mechanisms and price signals.

As a socialist country, the DPRK offers a distinct solution. As elucidated in Kim Jong Un's address, the DPRK's approach centers on socialist principles, with the Party assuming responsibility and augmenting State investment in rural regions. Kim Jong Un emphasized the necessity of rectifying this issue within a ten-year timeframe. Notably, our analysis reveals that it took approximately 15 years for the DPRK to overcome its most significant economic crisis, the "Arduous March." Consequently, the decision to address the urban–rural disparity within a decade underscores the formidable nature of this challenge.

Nevertheless, the commitment to narrow the gap in living standards between urban and rural areas holds profound implications for the DPRK economy. As of 2024, the DPRK demonstrates the capacity to reallocate its resources and focus toward enhancing the living standards of the entire populace, including rural communities, underpinned by a self-reliant economic structure.

Notes

1 KCNA, "Report on 9th Enlarged Plenum of 8th WPK Central Committee," *Korean Central News Agency* (December 31, 2023). http://kcna.kp/en/article/q/5a9ffe6c4d6704ac1838b14785365295.kcmsf.
2 Chosun Shinbo, "Ch'oegoinminhoeŭi che14ki che4ch'ahoeŭie chegihan kuk-kayesanbogot'chosŏnminjujuŭiinmin'gonghwagung chuche109(2020)nyŏn kuk-kayesanjip'aengŭi kyŏlsan'gwa chuch'e 110(2021)nyŏn kukkayesane taehayŏ" (State Budget Report to the Fourth Session of the Fourteenth Term of the Supreme People's Assembly:On the conclusion of the execution of the State Budget of the Democratic People's Republic of Korea for the year 2020 and the State Budget for the year 2021), *Chosun Shinbo* (January 18, 2021 06:25). https://chosonsinbo.com/2021/01/18-19/.

3 This perspective is echoed in the writings of former Premier Sŏngnam Hong, as evidenced by his article published in *ER*. In the article, Hong emphasizes the significance of the light industry, stating:

The light industry, primarily focused on consumer goods production, underscores its progress through quantity and quality enhancement. The growth of consumer goods directly contributes to the expansion of gross social product and national income. Furthermore, it plays a pivotal role in bolstering fiscal revenues derived from transaction fees. State Transaction Revenue constitutes a substantial portion of the national budget income, making the development of light industry crucial for generating the necessary funds to enhance people's living standards.

In alignment with the trajectory of cutting-edge science and technology, modernizing light industry facilities and integrating CNC technology are imperative for scaling up production and enhancing product quality. It is imperative to elevate the nation's entire light industry onto a new scientific and technological pedestal to effectively meet the evolving material and cultural needs of the populace while fortifying the nation's fiscal position.

(Sŏngnam Hong, "Hyŏnshigi kyŏnggongŏbŭl palchŏnshik'inŭndesŏ nasŏnŭn chungyomunje" (Important Issues in Developing Light Industry at the Present Time), *KUAB* (2014), vol. 60, no. 2, pp. 75–76)

Hong identifies shortcomings in light industry, such as low production volume and quality, leading to decreased government revenue from state stores. He proposes adopting CNC technology to improve both quantity and quality of goods. Implicitly, Hong suggests that increased consumer purchases from state stores, with their associated transaction fees, would strengthen the national budget.

This perspective connects directly to the concept of "idle currency" discussed in Chapter 3. Consumers, with money to spend, seek out variety and higher-quality imported goods in unofficial markets like "Chonghap Shijang." These markets evade transaction fees by operating outside state control.

Since unofficial transactions are excluded from official metrics like GDP and national budget revenue, these figures can be considered more representative of real value rather than inflated numbers. This distinction is important because inflation primarily affects unrecorded cash transactions outside the official economy. As a result, the DPRK's official statistics, including GDP and budget revenue, appear less susceptible to inflationary pressures.

4 Chosun Shinbo, "Kimjŏngŭnwŏnsunimkkesŏ ch'oegoinminhoeŭi che14ki che10ch'ahoeŭiesŏ kangnyŏngjŏgin shijŏngyŏnsŏrŭl hashiyŏtta" (Marshal Kim Jong Un delivered a Commanding Administrative Policy Speech at the 10th Session of the 14th Supreme People's Assembly) *Chosun Shinbo* (January 16, 2024, 06:10). https://chosonsinbo.com/2024/01/16-148/.

Index

Pages in **bold** refer to tables and pages followed by "n" refer to notes.